The Nurse Manager
The Law

Carmelle Pellerin Cournoyer, R.N., M.A., J.D.

Nurse, Attorney, Health Law Educator
Manchester, New Hampshire

AN ASPEN PUBLICATION®
Aspen Publishers, Inc.

1989

Rockville, Maryland
Royal Tunbridge Wells

This publication is designed to provide accurate and authoratative information in regard to the subject matter covered. It is sold with the understanding that the publisher is not engaged in rendering legal, accounting, or other professional service. If legal advice or other expert assistance is required, the service of a competent professional person should be sought. *(From a Declaration of Principles jointly adopted by a Committee of the American Bar Association and a Committee of Publishers and Associations.)*

Library of Congress Cataloging-in-Publication Data

Cournoyer, Carmelle Pellerin.
The nurse manager & the law/Carmelle Pellerin Cournoyer.
p. cm.
"An Aspen publication."
Includes bibliographies and index.
ISBN: 0-8342-0049-X
1. Nursing--Law and legislation--United States. 2. Medical laws and legislation--United States. 3. Nurse administrators--Legal status, laws, etc.--United States. I. Title. II. Title: Nurse manager and the law.
[DNLM: 1. Legislation--nurses' instruction. 2. Nursing, Supervisory. JF 423 C861n]
KF2915.N8C66   1989   344.73'0414--dc19   [347.304414]
DNLM/DLC
for Library of Congress   88-38840
CIP

Editorial Services: Ruth Bloom

Library of Congress Catalog Card Number: 88-38840
ISBN: 0-8342-0049-X

Printed in the United States of America

1 2 3 4 5

**With profound gratitude for their patience and encouragement,
I dedicate this book to**

My husband
> *Roland*

My children
> *Eric Paul, Ann Elizabeth, Karen Leslie, Dawn-Ellen*

My family
> *Valeda Pellerin*
> *Alphege and Lillian Cournoyer*

and
To the memory of
> *Claire Cournoyer*

A Reminder

The purpose of this book is purely educational—it offers a starting point for nurse managers who need to understand the law and the legal process. Laws, legal principles, and judicial opinions are examined and discussed so that nurse managers will become more aware of, and more comfortable with, the law and the legal process.

Every reasonable effort has been made to ensure that the legal information presented in the text is current and accurate. The reader is reminded, however, that the law, especially health law, changes faster than books can be published and that cases and laws that were relevant at the time of publication may be altered or overruled by new laws or court decisions.

The statements, guidelines, nursing management implications, and legal skills should not be construed as legal advice or opinion or as a substitute for legal advice or opinion. The reader is advised to seek the services of an attorney if legal advice or other expert assistance is required.

Table of Contents

Preface   xi

Acknowledgments   xv

PART I—THE NURSE MANAGER AND THE LAW   1

Chapter   1—The Nurse Manager   3
        What Is a Nurse Manager   4
        Who Is a Nurse Manager   5
        Nurse Manager Environment   6
        Nurse Manager Information Needs   6
        Nursing Management Decision Process   8
        Legal Foundation for Nursing Management Decisions   9

Chapter   2—The Law   12
        Origin of Law   12
        Definition of Law   14
        Sources of Law   15
        Organization of Government   19
        Purpose of Law   21
        United States Court Systems   23
        Language of Law   30

Appendix I—Implications for Nurse Managers   32

PART II—CONSTITUTIONAL LAW: EXPANDING RIGHTS AND REMEDIES **35**

Chapter 3—Constitutional Law 37
Patient's Rights 38
Concept of Rights 38
Constitutional Rights 39
Sources of Constitutional Rights 39

Chapter 4—Constitutional Rights: The Fourteenth Amendment 43
Person 43
State 43
Liberty 44
Property 45
Due Process 45
What Process Is Due 46
Equal Protection 47
Judicial Review 48

Chapter 5—Civil Rights Legislation: Constitutional Remedies 53
Civil Rights Act of 1871 53
Freedom of Religion 56
Religious Discrimination in Employment 58
Freedom of Speech 60
Freedom from Unreasonable Searches 62

Chapter 6—Privacy: Expanding Constitutional Rights 68
Marital Privacy 68
Privacy of Individuals 69
Abortion 69
Removal of Life-Support Systems 70
Self-Determination 70
Minor's Right of Privacy 70
Limitation of Privacy Right 71

Chapter 7—Freedom from Discrimination 73
Constitutional Protection 73
Public Accommodation 74
Race, Color, National Origin 74
Handicap 74
Age 75
Equal Pay 76
Employment Discrimination 76

Sexual Harassment 78
Patient Advocacy 78

Appendix II—Implications for Nurse Managers **80**

**PART III—ADMINISTRATIVE LAW: REGULATING
         HEALTH CARE** **85**

Chapter   8—Administrative Law **87**
Source 87
Types of Agencies 87
Commissions and Departments 88
Federal and State Law 88
Administrative Procedure Act 89
Rule-Making Power 89
Rule-Making Procedure 90
Investigations 91
Hearings 91
Judicial Review 93

Chapter   9—Administrative Agencies **96**
Federal Agencies 96
State Agencies 96
Private Agencies 97
Licensure and Accreditation 97
Professional Organizations 98
Certification 98
Agency: Purpose, Power, Process 99
Equal Employment Opportunity Commission 101
National Labor Relations Act 102
1974 Health Care Amendments 103
Rights of Employees 103
Unfair Labor Practices 104
Board Composition 104
Election Process 104
Filing an Unfair Labor Practice Charge 105
Unfair Labor Practice Hearing 105

Chapter 10—Nursing Practice Regulation **108**
Nursing Practice Acts 108
Definition of Nursing Practice 108
Advanced Practice 109
Board of Nursing 110
Licensing Power 111

Rule-Making Power 112
Adjudicatory Power 113
Judicial Review 114
Challenges to Board Power 115

Appendix III—Implications for Nurse Managers **120**

PART IV—CIVIL LAW: ASSIGNING LEGAL LIABILITY **125**

Chapter 11—Civil Law and Liability **127**
Hospital Governance 127
Corporate Liability 130
Vicarious Liability 132
Joint Liability 133
Tort Liability 135
Nurse Manager Liability 136

Chapter 12—Maintaining the Standard of Care **140**
Negligence and Malpractice 140
Duty 141
Standard of Care 142
Causation 145
Res Ipsa Loquitur 146
Injury 146
Defenses and Counterclaims 147
Admission 152
Discharge 155
Diagnostic Related Groups 155

Chapter 13—Nursing Practice Litigation **159**
Nursing Practice Management 159
Nursing Malpractice Litigation 160
Assessments and Interventions 161
Technical Skills 166
Nurse and Physician Relationship 170
Nursing Documentation 176
Nurses' Notes in Litigation 179
Hospital Documents in Litigation 182

Chapter 14—Consent **187**
Consent and Informed Consent 187
Valid Consent Requirements 188
Proof of Consent 190

Responsibility for Obtaining Consent 193
Exceptions to Consent Requirement 195
Withdrawal and Refusal of Consent 196
Tort Liability: Battery and False Imprisonment 201

Chapter 15—Confidentiality **208**
Informational Privacy 208
Patients' Right of Privacy 209
Employees' Right of Privacy 210
Invasion of Privacy 211
Defamation 213
Medical Record 219
Nurse Manager's Responsibility 231

Chapter 16—Contract Law and Liability **235**
Elements of a Contract 236
Express and Implied Contracts 238
Oral and Written Contracts 238
Statute of Frauds 238
Parol Evidence Rule 239
Termination of a Contract 239
Collective Bargaining Agreements 240
Collective Bargaining Subjects 244
Employee At Will Doctrine 248
Nurses' Refusal To Provide Nursing Care 254
Express Contracts 258
Negotiating an Express Contract 258
Antitrust Law 260
Insurance Contracts 264

Appendix IV—Implications for Nurse Managers **273**

PART V—CRIMINAL LAW: INDIVIDUAL VS. STATE **277**

Chapter 17—Criminal Law: Individual vs. State **279**
Criminal Process 280
Pretrial Procedures 284
Trial 292
Appeal 294
Criminal Liability 295
Controlled Substance Diversion in Hospitals 304
Reporting and Recording Statutes 308
Obtaining and Preserving Evidence 313

Appendix V—Implications for Nurse Managers 324

PART VI—LEGAL SKILLS: PARTICIPATING IN THE
            LEGAL PROCESS 329

Chapter 18—Legal Skills: Participating in the Legal Process 331
            Skill 1: Finding and Interpreting a Statute 331
            Skill 2: Finding and Interpreting a Case 333
            Skill 3: Understanding the Civil Trial Process 337
            Skill 4: Participating in Discovery 343
            Skill 5: Testifying As a Witness 348
            Skill 6: Retaining an Attorney 352
            Skill 7: Understanding the Legislative Process 356
            Skill 8: Lobbying 361

Index of Cases 365

Index 367

About the Author 383

Preface

This book has been written for all nurses who function in the corporate hospital environment. It is specifically addressed to nurse managers, who spend their professional lives walking the middle ground between that of clinical specialists and business managers, a position that offers maximum visibility and maximum exposure to the needs and problems of both disciplines. The overlapping environment imposes a dual obligation on nurse managers: (1) there is the expectation by staff nurses and the nursing profession that nurse managers will safeguard and promote the ethics and standards of professional nursing practice, and (2) there is the expectation of hospital management that they will do so within the philosophy and objectives of the institution.

Nurses are intelligent, compassionate, and talented people who possess a sophisticated level of knowledge and skill in the biological and social sciences on which nursing practice is founded. Their knowledge of law, however, is likely to be fragmented, partially because of the integrated approach to the study of law that is common in many nursing education programs. Nursing texts and nursing seminars also tend to isolate and segregate the legal issues from the foundation in which they arise. This approach makes it more difficult for nurse managers to identify the extent of the law's influence on nursing practice; it is like trying to visualize a picture puzzle by examining each piece separately. Nurses and nurse managers who work in the cost-conscious, collaborative, and competitive environment of today's hospitals must be familiar with all of the areas of law and potential legal liability so that they can better predict, prevent, confront and resolve the medical-legal problems.

The Nurse Manager and the Law is a legal primer for nurse managers. It is organized in a manner that explains and illustrates the law and its consequences. The pattern is the same throughout the book. In each section (1) the area of law is explained in a simple and orderly manner; (2) the health care issues are identified and examined; (3) the federal and state laws and cases that explain and/or determine the issues are examined; (4) the nursing management implications are identified and the appropriate behaviors discussed; and (5) the people, places, and publications that nurses should be aware of in order to make informed management decisions and contributions are listed.

Each part and chapter of this book has been selected and written to assist nurse managers to expand their knowledge of the law and their understanding of how it can be effectively applied in their professional lives. As a woman who spends much of her time trying to explain the nursing profession to attorneys and the law to nurses, I would hope that the information in this book engenders in nurses a new respect for the law and the system of government under which we live and practice our chosen professions. I also hope that attorneys who may read it will obtain a better understanding of the legal issues surrounding the nursing profession.

All of the major areas of law are examined. Part I, The Nurse Manager and The Law, introduces the nurse manager, whom I define as a professional nurse who has assumed some level of management responsibility and whose decision-making process must now consider the needs of the patient, the nurses, the staff, and the hospital management. The law is first examined from its source so that nurses will see it as a universal concept adapted by various groups of people according to their particular philosophy of social order. The historical perspective reveals the movement and momentum of the law, exposing its ability to expand and contract as the public need and the public conscience may require. Part II, Constitutional Law, examines the Constitution, civil rights laws, and court decisions that define the nurses' and the patients' rights to life, liberty, property, privacy, and employment. Part III, Administrative Law, explains the laws and agencies that license and regulate health care professionals and hospitals. The state regulation of nursing practice is examined and discussed. Part IV, Civil Law, reviews the more familiar areas of nursing negligence and nursing tort liability. The nurses' contractual relationships with the hospital are also examined, as is the issue of patient advocacy and job security. Part V, Criminal Law, introduces a fairly new area of law, the nurse as defendant, and examines the traditional areas of police–hospital relationships. Part VI, Legal Skills, explores the areas in which nurses need to develop some basic legal skills, such as how to find a case, interpret a statute, or testify as a witness. These legal skills are analogous to nurses teaching patients how to take their blood pressure or how to communicate effectively with their physician.

The major objective of this book is to provide nurse managers with the legal information that they need to

- Use appropriate legal terminology when expressing their views
- Adopt, support, and defend their management programs and decisions
- Identify the benefits and risks inherent in their status as employees
- Participate in the development and implementation of policies that are based on current legal expectations
- Maintain their legally separate professional identities when cooperating and collaborating with other health care professionals
- Provide a reasonable standard of nursing care for all patients
- Promote, preserve, and protect their legal rights and those of their patients
- Participate in the legislative process in making and changing the laws that regulate and influence the delivery of health care services

This book is for nurses and nurse managers who want and need to know about the law. The law permeates the practice of nursing like the veins that run through a leaf—the law gives nursing its definition, strength, and integrity. This book has been written so that nurses will come to know and understand that the nursing profession continues to expand and develop not in spite of the law but because of it.

Carmelle Pellerin Cournoyer
March 1989

Acknowledgments

Writing is a horrible, exhausting struggle, like a long bout with some painful illness. One would never undertake such a thing if one were not driven by some demon whom one can neither resist nor understand.

George Orwell

For making it possible to exorcise the demon and achieve my goal of writing a comprehensive legal text for nurse managers, I acknowledge and express my profound appreciation to

The nurses whom I have worked with for the past 25 years.

A special thank you to Lorraine Pelkey, RN, BSN, a "nurse's nurse," whose lifelong commitment to nursing education and nursing practice has taught me what being a nurse is all about.

The nurses throughout New England who have attended my classes and seminars and candidly shared their experiences with nursing and the law. I am impressed with their eagerness to learn the law and share their absolute conviction that knowing the law will help them make the hospital a safer and fairer place for patients and for nurses.

A special thank you to H. Irene Peters, RN, MEd, former vice-president for education and research, New Hampshire Hospital Association, a competent and gracious administrator who fostered collaboration and cooperation between health care professionals and always helped me to understand the hospital's perspective.

The Faculty of the Franklin Pierce Law Center, who patiently introduced me to the law, reminding me that K meant contracts as well as potassium, as they skillfully helped a nurse become an attorney.

A special thank you to Cynthia Landau, Esq., a classmate and a law librarian at the Franklin Pierce Law Center who, from the very beginning, provided encouragement for the project and assistance in finding the legal resources that I needed.

In addition, I wish to thank Peter Steckowych for his help in creating the art work for this book.

Part **I**

The Nurse Manager
and the Law

THE NURSE MANAGER

We have noted how powerful forces and movement in political, economic, and social life have acted and reacted on the development of nursing, helping to direct its course and modify its character.

Lavinia L. Dock, RN
A Short History of Nursing (1931)

THE LAW

The life of the law has not been logic; it has been experience. The felt necessities of the time, the prevalent moral and political theories, intuitions of public policy, avowed or unconscious, even the prejudices which judges share with their fellow-men, have had a good deal more to do than the syllogism in determining the rules by which men should be governed.

Supreme Court Justice Oliver Wendell Holmes, Jr.
The Common Law (lecture 1, 1881)

Chapter 1

The Nurse Manager

In the United States the delivery of health care services has undergone three stages of growth and development. The basic system that developed from 1875 to 1930 was followed by the era of third party payment that extended from 1930 to 1965 and gradually evolved into the present era of management and control.[1] Hospitals have survived the era of management and control by reorganizing their management structure and revising their services. These actions have resulted in their adopting the language and practices of business and industry. In the 1980s, hospitals refer to patients as clients and the community is considered a market whose members are courted as potential consumers of a product line of health care services.[2] Some hospitals have added the objectives of competition and profit to their traditional purpose of providing safe and competent patient care.

The evolution of the delivery of hospital services into the corporate world of health care has resulted in a significant change in the environment in which nurses practice their profession. Many nurses can remember a time when most of a hospital's professional personnel were clinical specialists directly involved in patient care. Today, however, professionals of diverse disciplines are employed by hospitals. It is not unusual to hear graduates of diploma nursing programs describe the shock they suffered when, on a nostalgic visit to their nursing school, they discovered that the nursing school had been demolished to make way for a new hospital and that the old hospital had been converted into corporate offices where the business professionals plan, implement, evaluate, and market the hospital's services to the community. These changes have accompanied the gradual transition of hospitals from institutions built to accommodate the needs of physicians to the multifaceted health care facilities that are today recognized by the public and the courts as responsible for the provision of safe and competent care.

Nurses, who traditionally have comprised the largest group of clinical practitioners, have had to adapt to the expansion of their professional environment in a manner that would ensure that the responsibility and accountability for the quality and quantity of nursing services to the public remained with the nursing profession. The corporate world of health care has created a need for nurses who can merge the requirements of comprehensive and competent nursing practice with the administrative and economic realities of the business of health care. The nursing profession's response to this need has been the emergence of the nurse manager. The concept of the nurse manager is just developing and time is needed to discover the direction it will take, the responsibilities it will assume, and, ultimately, the influence it will have on the quality, quantity, and cost of professional nursing services available to the community.

WHAT IS A NURSE MANAGER

Nurses are, and always have been, managers. Nurses practice professional nursing by implementing the nursing process, a clinical management system that provides nursing services according to individual patient needs. What has changed in the developing concept of a nurse manager is that the emphasis has been placed on business management as well as on nursing practice. Professional nurses are being asked to acquire the skills and expertise of the business professional, in effect to merge the beliefs, attitudes, and objectives of two distinct professions into one person. Nurse managers are taking one step away from the patient and one step closer to management. It is a move that may require a philosophical reorientation as they attempt to integrate the emerging concept of health care as a business with the nursing profession's traditional view of health care as a public service.[3]

Attempts at categorizing and explaining the role of the nurse manager have taken a variety of approaches. The American Nurses' Association (ANA) identifies the three levels of nursing administration as the executive level, the middle level, and the first-line level.[4] A statement published by the Commission on Nursing Services describes the characteristics and responsibilities of each level. Executive level nursing administrators are responsible for the nursing department and manage from the perspective of the organization as a whole. They are responsible for the integration of nursing with other functional areas of the health care agency in the mutual achievement of organizational goals. Nurse executives ensure that the standards of nursing practice are established and implemented. Middle level nursing administrator positions are characterized by their coordinative functions between executive and first-line administration. There may be a number of middle level administrative positions with varying roles and responsibilities. The first-line level nursing administrators are accountable to the middle level manager for the implementation of the philosophy, goals, and objectives of the nursing department. Their primary responsibility is the direction of staff members in the delivery of nursing care. First-line administrators are responsible for delivery of care that is therapeutically effective and safe as well as cost effective.[5]

Research into the nurse manager role suggests that there is still a need to clearly identify expected behaviors, especially those for first-line managers.[6] One response to this need has been the *Development of the New Nurse Manager* model.[7] This approach defines the role of the nurse manager in the acute care setting as directing the staff to provide good patient care systematically within the hospital's organizational framework. Planning, organizing, directing, and controlling are the four functions that constitute the core of the model. In order to activate the core, the new nurse manager must first possess the ability to make a role transition, the ability to communicate effectively, and the ability to lead.[8] Another approach suggests that managing people is the primary purpose of health care managers. In *Managing the Health Care Professional*, McConnell states, "the fundamental task of management—the business of getting things done through people—is reflected in practices such as proper delegation, clear and open two-way communication, budgeting and cost control, scheduling, handling employee problems and applying disciplinary actions."[9]

Given the variety of opinions and the diversity of tasks deemed suitable for nurse managers, perhaps the most appropriate definition is the simplest and the most obvious one. A nurse manager is a professional nurse who has assumed some level of management responsibility and whose decision-making process must now consider the needs of the patients, the nurses, the staff, and the hospital management.

WHO IS A NURSE MANAGER

Nurses arrive at management positions from various routes: some actively seek the management position, others reluctantly yield to their supervisors' requests that they assume a management role, and still others inherit the responsibility because they have seniority in a clinical position. Traditionally, the director of nursing service has been recognized as a nurse manager; however, the scope of this person's responsibility was often not clearly delineated, as was also the case with the house supervisors and head nurses who assisted the director in providing nursing services within the institution. Today, directors of nursing service are being renamed vice-presidents for nursing and are expected to assume total administrative responsibility for the delivery of nursing services within the institution. Top level nurse managers are charged with providing nursing services in accordance with the institution's policies for quality care and cost containment. This can only be accomplished if the executive level nurse managers are able to create and maintain effective lines of communication with nurses at all levels of management and clinical practice. Clinical supervision and evaluation, the traditional role and major responsibility of nursing supervisors and head nurses, does not provide a scope of function or authority that is able to absorb the broader, management-oriented objectives of today's nursing service departments. This has created a need for hospitals to review the roles and responsibilities of supervisors and head nurses and to encourage the development of hospital management knowledge and skills in the professional nursing staff.

Nurses who assume a management position are being asked to add to the knowledge and skill they possess as licensed professionals. When nurses accept hospital management functions, they are assuming responsibilities that they were not prepared for in their basic nursing program. Some are acquiring the information in a formal academic setting and earning advanced degrees in nursing management or business management, others are pursuing continuing education in the area of business management, and still others are learning by trial and error on the job. Nurses who assume management positions without adequate preparation are courting disillusionment and failure. Common errors attributed to first-time managers include not obtaining enough training or appropriate orientation to management, believing their profession is considerably more important than other occupations, and favoring the side they are most comfortable with.[10] Feelings of uncertainty are characterized as "not knowing enough" or "not knowing what I don't know."[11] It is essential that the knowledge and skills required by nurse managers continue to be identified so that nurses who select the management role can obtain the education that they will need in order to function effectively in this new and complex environment.

NURSE MANAGER ENVIRONMENT

Nurse managers spend their professional lives walking the middle ground between that of clinical specialists and business managers. It is a position of maximum visibility and maximum exposure to the needs and problems of both disciplines. Nurse managers must identify and respond to these diverse needs and problems, knowing that their decisions are being evaluated by both sides. Nurse managers function in two separate but overlapping environments (Figure 1-1). In the clinical environment, they work with nurses, physicians, and other clinical specialists whose purpose and goals are to provide their professional services to individual patients and families; whereas in the business environment, they work with administrators and business specialists whose purpose and goals are to provide current, competent, cost-effective hospital services to patients and families.[12] The groups officially communicate with each other through the language of policy and procedure arrived at in a multiple committee structure. It is an environment that generates a need for professionals who can understand the aspirations, problems, and concerns of both sides and can translate that understanding into effective policies, procedures, and practices. The nurse manager environment imposes a dual obligation on nurse managers: there is the expectation by nurses and the nursing profession that they will safeguard and promote the ethics and standards of professional nursing practice and the expectation from hospital management that they will do so within the philosophy and objectives of the institution. Nurse managers who have a solid foundation in nursing, management, and law will be better prepared to meet the requirements of this complex yet challenging environment.

NURSE MANAGER INFORMATION NEEDS

The ANA Commission on Nursing Service has stated that "knowledge of administrative concepts, organizational behavior, management processes and legal matters as they pertain to health care organizations and to the profession is essential."[13] Many of the responsibilities assumed by nurse managers require an understanding of all three areas. For example, in situations in which nurse managers have to dismiss employees for incompetence, their nursing expertise allows them to recognize nursing incompetence and the manner in which it can be corrected, their management expertise tells them when the employee should be dismissed and how the subject should be approached, and their legal expertise advises them of the need to follow hospital policy, to respect the employees' rights, and to avoid actions that may involve them in the areas of libel or slander. The ability to integrate their nursing, management, and legal expertise helps

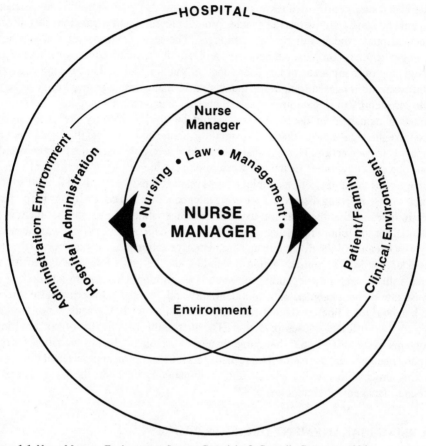

Figure 1-1 Nurse Manager Environment. *Source:* Copyright © Carmelle Cournoyer 1986.

them make the right decision, in the right manner, at the right time and ensures that they will have all the clinical, managerial, and legal information that is needed to support their action.

Nurse managers function at different levels and have diverse and varied nursing and management responsibilities; therefore, it is difficult to determine the exact amount of nursing, management, and legal knowledge that is required. Of the three areas, the law is the one most often neglected by nurse managers because many of them believe that legal concepts are elusive, ambiguous, and confusing. The persistence of these attitudes demonstrates a need for nurse managers to obtain a more thorough understanding of the law and the legal process.

Nurse Managers' Needs for Legal Information

Hospitals comprise a major part of a highly regulated industry whose business and health care practices are closely scrutinized by Congress and the state legislatures.

Federal and state courts often review and decide cases that involve health care practices. Federal and state administrative agencies promulgate rules and regulations that directly affect hospitals and health care practitioners. The legal environment that surrounds nursing practice is complex and pervasive and requires that nurse managers have an understanding of many areas of law. Seminars on "nursing law" that concentrate on tort liability are no longer sufficient for today's nurse managers, who need to develop the ability to identify the legal implications of nursing management situations. In arriving at a nursing management decision, they should be able to identify the areas of law, recognize the legal actions that arise from these areas, and correlate the legal principles that apply to each action. Nurse managers should also be able to transfer their knowledge from one area to another so that they can anticipate the full legal potential of nursing management situations. For example, a nurse manager may be involved in a situation in which a nurse is facing dismissal for having allegedly diverted control drugs for personal use. In investigating the situation the nurse manager should be aware that there is the potential for the following: a negligence suit from a patient if the patient was harmed in any way because of the diversion; an administrative action requiring a report to the state board of nursing; a contract action depending on the procedure established for the nurse's dismissal; and, depending on state law, criminal charges. In addition, if the investigation is not handled with confidentiality and the suspicions prove false, there is the potential for a libel or slander suit by the nurse involved. The same set of facts can lead to five different causes of action. The increasing complexity of potential legal problems makes it essential that nurse managers establish a legal foundation for their nursing management decisions. Nurse managers must adopt an approach to the decision-making process that will logically and systematically examine the legal aspects of nursing management situations.

NURSING MANAGEMENT DECISION PROCESS

Changes are taking place in the decision-making process and nurse managers are particularly affected. Levenstein states that the slow yet adequate deliberation processes of past times are inadequate for today's changing environment and suggests that the pace of decision making be stepped up:

> What is called for is something that managers refer to as QRC—Quick Reaction Capability. The voice of authority must make itself heard as soon as conflict develops. To delay decisions can only intensify animosities. In short, the higher levels of the organization must be prepared to engage in frequent consultation with subordinates, must be responsive to communications from below, and must encourage joint problem solving.[14]

Nurse managers are expected to act quickly and appropriately in confronting the many and varied nursing management situations. They cannot do so if they lack the knowledge and skill that is required to identify and act on the legal implications of these situations. Failure to recognize and appropriately respond to the legal aspects of a situation may involve the hospital in costly and time-consuming meetings and negotiations and may even result in unnecessary litigation. It is therefore essential that nurse managers be able to integrate quickly and accurately the legal aspects of a nursing management situation into their decision-making process.

LEGAL FOUNDATION FOR NURSING MANAGEMENT DECISIONS

Nurse managers may need help in identifying how the legal information should be considered. The guide shown in Exhibit 1-1 proposes a series of behaviors that will provide a legal foundation for nursing management decisions. The term *guide* was deliberately selected for this group of behaviors because it best expresses their purpose of showing a way of integrating legal information so that the legal aspects are fairly and fully considered in arriving at a final decision.

Nurse Managers' Guide for Integrating Legal Information

The following is a general description of each behavior. The general areas of law, the legal process, causes of action, and principles of law are identified and discussed throughout the text.

1. *Investigate the situation and obtain the facts.* Two principles that law students are exposed to early in their legal education are, first, that every situation has an "on the other hand" and, second, that "the best prepared usually wins." Starting with an open mind and investigating all the possibilities serves both principles well. For nurse managers, that means get all the facts, get all the versions of the facts, and always begin with an unbiased, comprehensive understanding of the situation. Nurse managers should obtain the information themselves or, if that is

---

Exhibit 1-1 Integrating Legal Information Guide

Nurse Manager's Guide for Integrating Legal Information

1. Investigate the situation and obtain the facts.
2. Assess the hospital's legal obligation.
3. Identify the areas of law involved in the situation.
4. Identify the specific legal claims relevant to the situation.
5. Identify the legal principles applicable to each claim.
6. Compare the facts of the situation to the legal principles.
7. Make a decision and immediately evaluate the nature of the evidence that will support your decision.
8. Implement your decision.
9. Evaluate the reaction of nursing and management to your decision.
10. Evaluate the long-term effect of your decision.

Source: Copyright © Carmelle Cournoyer 1986.

not possible, assign people who will adopt an unbiased, comprehensive approach.

2. *Assess the hospital's potential legal obligation.* Major legal obligation of hospitals includes the following:

  • Fulfilling the legal duties of all businesses, including strict adherence to the articles of incorporation and the bylaws

  • Employing and supervising competent staff

  • Providing patients with a reasonable standard of care

  • Preserving and promoting the rights of patients and staff

3. *Identify the areas of law involved in the situation.* Major areas of law relevant to health care include constitutional law, civil law (commercial law, contractual law, intentional and unintentional torts), administrative law, and criminal law.

4. *Identify the specific legal claims relevant to the situation.* Examples of legal claims or "causes of action" are breach of contract, negligence, invasion of privacy, and civil rights violations. Counterclaims that the hospital may want to consider, such as comparative negligence and privilege, should be included.

5. *Identify the legal principles applicable to each legal claim.* Every cause of action has elements or requirements that must be fulfilled. For example, in negligence actions all four elements—duty, breach of duty, causation, and damages—must be proven for a plaintiff to succeed. Or, for a signature to be considered valid it must be proven that the person has the capacity to sign the document and did so freely without undue influence.

6. *Compare the facts of the situation to the legal principles.* For example, a patient has signed a consent form and is scheduled for surgery. On the morning of the surgery he changes his mind and informs the nurse. The nurse manager, who knows that a cause of action for battery could result from the unconsented touching of a person, will take the appropriate measures to stop or at least delay the surgery and notify the physician, who can discuss the situation with the patient.

7. *Make a decision and immediately evaluate the nature of the evidence that will support your decision.* Nurse managers have to support and defend their decisions. The type of information that would demonstrate the basis for their judgments includes witnesses, documents, medical records, nursing notes, hospital policies and procedures, staffing schedules, patient and family comments, and any type of supporting evidence, including the nurse manager's nursing or management expertise.

8. *Implement the decision.* Nurse managers should assimilate their nursing and management knowledge and skill in implementing the decision and in obtaining the approval and cooperation of the nursing staff and/or management.

9. *Evaluate the reaction of nursing and management to your decision.* Questions to ask include the following: Did you receive the support of your colleagues? Was your decision appropriate and timely? Are the people involved satisfied with the

way the situation has been resolved? Is top level management satisfied that your decision was appropriate? Was your decision sustained or overturned?

10. *Evaluate the long-term effect of your decision.* Questions to ask include the following: Has the situation been successfully resolved? What part did your decision play in the resolution of the problem? Was new hospital policy enacted or existing policy enforced or amended? Were the legal considerations an essential part of the final decision?

The guide was prepared to encourage nurse managers to acquire the habit of incorporating the legal aspects of nursing management situations into their decision-making process. It can be adapted to accommodate the individual needs of nurse managers with diverse and varied responsibilities.

Nurse managers who develop a legal foundation for their nursing management decisions by integrating the legal information with the nursing and management considerations will be prepared to make management decisions that are timely, accurate, consistent, and defensible. In order for nurse managers to successfully adopt this approach, they must understand the law and the legal system and they must also develop an ability to recognize how the nursing management information will be interpreted and used in the legal process.

NOTES

1. Odin W. Anderson, *Health Services in the United States, A Growth Enterprise since 1875* (Ann Arbor, Mich.: Health Administration Press, 1985), 3.

2. Robin Scott MacStravic, "Product-Line Administration in Hospitals," *Health Care Management Review* 11, no. 2 (Spring 1986):35–43; see also, John K. Ruffner, "Product-Line Management," *Healthcare Forum* (September-October 1986):11–14.

3. Rufus C. Rorem, U.S. Department of Health and Human Services, Office of Health Maintenance Organization, *Focus* 3 (October 1980):4.

4. American Nurses' Association, Commission on Nursing Services, *Roles, Responsibilities and Qualifications for Nurse Administrators* (Kansas City, Mo.: American Nurses' Association, 1978), 4.

5. Ibid., 4–7.

6. Anita Beaman, "What Do First Line Managers Do?" *Journal of Nursing Administration* 16, no. 5 (May 1986):6.

7. Donna Richards Sheridan et al., *The New Nurse Manager* (Rockville, Md.: Aspen Publishers, Inc., 1984), 2.

8. Ibid., 11.

9. Charles R. McConnell, *Managing the Health Care Professional* (Rockville, Md.: Aspen Publishers, Inc., 1984), 160.

10. Ibid., 151–159.

11. J. Lanigan and J. Miller, "Developing Nurse Managers," *Nursing Administration Quarterly* 5, no. 2 (1981):21–24.

12. Stuart J. Marylander, "Management Professionals vs. Medical Professionals," and James O. Hepner, "Conflict Rationality in Hospital Management," in *Hospital Administrator–Physician Relationships*, ed. James O. Hepner (St. Louis: C.V. Mosby Co., 1980), 3–17.

13. American Nurses' Association, Commission on Nursing Services, *Roles, Responsibilities and Qualifications for Nurse Administrators*, 3.

14. Aaron Levenstein, "Caught in the Middle," *Nursing Management* 16, no. 2 (February 1985):56.

Chapter 2

The Law

A deliberate and purposeful journey into the legal environment should begin with an examination of law and the American legal system.

ORIGIN OF LAW

Much of the world today is governed by laws derived from either the Roman civil law or the English common law. The laws of the Roman Empire and the Ancient World formed the basis of law for modern continental Europe and South America, while the English common law followed the development of the English race to England, Ireland, and the United States.[1]

The fundamental principles of American Law were initially identified and developed as the law of England. After the American Revolution, they were restored, expanded, and ratified as the law of the United States of America. The history of Anglo-American law is a chronicle of events, crises, and compromises revolving around the appropriate allocation of power between the people and their sovereign. Legal historians generally identify the following events as significant in the development of Anglo-American law.

The Norman Conquest

The Norman Conquest of England by William II in 1066 resulted in an administrative unification of the country. The king wanted to know what he had won, specifically who and what he had to rule, and, of paramount importance, what there was to tax. The Domesday Survey was conducted in order to determine the answer to questions such as who owned the land, what was built on it, how much was it worth, how many peasants belonged to a manor, how many burghers lived in a town, what were the local customs and privileges, and, finally, could better use be made of the land. The king's ministers obtained this information by means of an inquest, which consisted of going into the towns and asking some of the people to answer these questions under oath. The results of the Survey listed in the *Domesday Book* gave William II, and future historians, a clear picture of England in 1086. The presence of the king's ministers in the town for the purpose of gathering information gradually evolved into their being used to settle disputes. As they assumed an adjudicatory role, they continued the practice of asking the people of the neighborhood to report the facts relevant to the dispute. The Norman administrative inquest and the subsequent involvement of the community in the local adjudicatory process constituted the beginning of the Anglo-American practice of trial by jury.[2]

The Triumph of the Common Law

William II placed the shires under central control by replacing the Saxon earls with his own lieutenants. The sheriffs were direct agents of the king: they ran the shire and collected the money that the courts brought in; however, the law that they enforced was the local customary law.[3]

During the reign of Henry II and after his death, the royal courts expanded, depriving the feudal courts of power. Gradually, the council that heard matters of land title evolved into the King's Court of Common Pleas, the council that heard criminal matters evolved into the Court of King's Bench, and the council that handled rents and tax collection became the Court of the Exchequer. The three great courts of common law were well established by 1300, but they remained fingers of the royal fist.[4] The king's judges continued to apply the custom of the local courts; however, in order to rule consistently in the king's name they began to adopt some customs and reject others. Gradually the customs that the royal courts adopted and attempted to apply uniformly became the customs "common" to all the king's land. By following, combining, or rejecting these customs the courts eventually developed a law common throughout England—"a common law."[5]

In the sixteenth century the judges were no longer counselors of the king, and by the seventeenth century the courts had become an independent branch of government, looking only to the law, no longer to the crown. The supremacy of the common law became a supremacy over everyone, including the monarch himself. As Rembar observed, "The triumph of the common law was at first a royal triumph, and then a royal defeat. The kings had made a monster that devoured them."[6]

Magna Carta

The Great Charter of 1215 was the first of a series of documents collectively known as the Magna Carta. This constitutional enactment granted by King John to the barons at Runnymede is considered the foundation of English constitutional liberty. Among its 38 chapters are provisions that regulate the administration of justice, guarantee a right to a trial by a jury of one's peers, secure the rights to liberty and personal property, and set limits to taxation. Rembar states, "The nature of the Charter, and the fact of the Charter, gave added strength to the idea of law, the thought that there should be rule by rule rather than by ruler. Once this idea was firmly founded, democracy could build; the people were unintended beneficiaries."[7] The Charter proclaimed specific rights of the people and placed restraints on the exercise of government, legitimizing the two powerful ideals that would later inspire the creation of a new nation.

The Declaration of Independence

Believing that the law was corrupted and that King George III had abandoned the (British) Constitution, the American colonists sought to create a new nation. On July 4, 1776, the Declaration of Independence, a public act of the Second Continental Congress, declared the colonies to be free and independent from Great Britain. The first sentence of the document creates the ''one people,'' who now find it necessary ''to dissolve the political bands which have connected them with one another and to assume among the powers of the earth, the separate and equal station which the Laws of Nature and of Nature's God entitles them.'' The document is directed at Great Britain, but its message presumes a universal audience as it speaks in a unanimous voice for the ''thirteen United States'' and their ''people.''[8]

The ''people'' proclaim ''self-evident'' truths of equality and ''unalienable rights'' that they believe the government is obligated to secure. The age-old problem of the sovereign versus the people is resolved in favor of the people with the statement ''that to secure these rights, Governments are instituted among Men, deriving their just powers from the consent of the governed.'' The ''people'' go one step further and proclaim their right to ''alter'' or ''abolish'' ''any Form of Government that becomes destructive of these ends'' and claim the right ''to institute a new Government, laying its foundation on such principles and organizing its powers in such form, as to them shall seem most likely to effect their Safety and Happiness.'' There is no doubt that this voice is recalling the old principles of the Magna Carta, but at the same time it is creating something new, exciting, and dangerous. Rembar describes the event by stating, ''With a steadfast backward gaze, the American rebels take up arms. In the name of precedent, they effect a revolution and create a set of political rights the world has not seen before.''[9] With this document the people created a new nation, a new language, and, when the revolution was over, they created a new law.

DEFINITION OF LAW

Our law is a combination of divine or moral law, natural law, and human experience. It is an invention of the human intellect subject to all the inspiration and perversion of the human mind and spirit. Law is a social contract designed to assist people to order their society, organize their affairs, and settle their problems; it sets standards for human conduct and provides an alternative to confusion and force.

There are many definitions of law, all of them right. Attempting to define law is something like attempting to describe the image that is seen through a kaleidoscope. It is not difficult to describe the first image that appears, but if the cylinder is rotated, another image emerges requiring another description, both of them accurate. Principles, customs, statutes, regulations, holdings, orders, decisions, processes, and procedures are some of the pieces of colored glass that make up the rich and varied images of law.

What people think of the law, what it does for them or to them, and what they demand or expect of it depends to a great extent on what they are looking at, on their particular point of view.

Efforts to understand the whole of the law by examining its parts have produced a number of categories of law, the most basic of which are substantive law and procedural law. Substantive law determines the subject matter of a legal proceeding. It creates and defines the rights and duties that may give rise to a cause of action. Procedural law is the form, the machinery of a legal proceeding. It includes the pleadings, practice, and process in the trial courts, the appellate courts, and the administrative tribunals. Procedural law not only determines the rules for the parties and the subject matter before the courts but also regulates the conduct of the court itself. Legal substance and legal process constitute the double helix of our legal system. Together they create, support, and advance each area of law.

SOURCES OF LAW

The two basic sources of law in the United States are written law and common law.

Written Law

Written law is the fundamental source of power. It defines the specific powers of the President, Congress, governors, and state legislatures; it also creates the courts and authorizes them to function. The executive and legislative branches of the government create and promulgate the written law in the form of

- Federal and state constitutions
- Treaties made by the President with a foreign country
- Federal and state statutes
- Interstate compacts
- Executive orders of the President and governors
- Regulations and decisions of administrative agencies
- Laws and ordinances of city and county governmental units

The hierarchy of written law is determined by Article VI of the Constitution, which is also known as the Supremacy Clause because it states that the Constitution, federal law, and treaties made under the authority of the United States are the supreme law of the land and take precedence over the constitutions and laws of the states.[10] It is this clause that creates one federal state by incorporating the national government and the states into one governmental organization.

There are four major sources of written law: treaties, constitutions, statutes, and administrative regulations and decisions. Treaties are formal written agreements between the United States and one or more foreign nations. Treaties are made by the President with the advice and consent of the Senate.

Constitutions

The Constitution of the United States and the 50 state constitutions set out in formal written terms the structure and powers of government. They also define political relationships, enumerate the rights and liberties of citizens, and place limits on the way those who govern can use their power.

The Constitution is published in the *United States Code* (U.S.C.), the official codification of federal statutes, and in the *United States Code Annotated* (U.S.C.A.). Annotated versions of statutes have information as to the legislative history and references to court decisions that have interpreted the statute. State constitutions are published in the annotated statutes of each individual state.

Statutes

Statutes are formal written enactments of federal, state, and local legislative bodies. Statutes translate ideas into law; they articulate and communicate the policies of government. The power to write statutes must be based on the constitution. If laws are not made pursuant to a constitutional power, they are invalid. There is a hierarchy in law by which federal law supersedes state law and state law supersedes local law.

State and federal statutes are published in three primary forms: (1) as individual slip opinions when they are first officially published, (2) as a periodic compilation of new laws, sometimes called "session laws," and (3) as unified codes. The unified codes arrange the law by subject matter and contain all public law currently in force in a particular area. The *United States Code* (U.S.C.) is the official codification of federal statutes that is printed and distributed by the U.S. Government Printing Office. In addition, there are two unofficial codes, the *United States Code Annotated* (U.S.C.A.), published by the West Publishing Company, and the *United States Code Service* (U.S.C.S.), published by the Lawyers' Co-operative Publishing Company.

States also publish their laws in separate publications according to subject matter. The names of the codified statutes vary from state to state. For example, in New Hampshire they are called the *New Hampshire Revised Statutes Annotated* (N.H. REV. STAT. ANN.), whereas in Massachusetts they are entitled the *Massachusetts General Laws Annotated* (MASS. GEN. LAWS ANN.) and in Montana they are known as the *Revised Codes of Montana Annotated* (MONT. REV. CODES ANN.).

Administrative Rules and Decisions

Administrative agencies are created by statute to assist the legislatures and the courts in certain fields that require nonlegal expertise. The statute that creates the agency determines the extent of its authority and power. If an agency acts outside or beyond the statutory limit, its actions are invalid.

Administrative agencies are endowed with both legislative and judicial power; their rules and regulations are similar in format to statutes, and their decisions closely resemble court opinions. In general, courts can modify or overturn agency rules. They also possess the power to review agency decisions on questions of law and on the reasonableness of their fact determinations.

The Federal Register Act of 1935 set up a federal system of rules publication and created the *Federal Register*. The 1937 amendment to the act created the *Code of Federal Regulations* (C.F.R.). In accordance with the Administrative Procedure Act (5 U.S.C. § 553), rules proposed or adopted by federal agencies are published chronologically in the *Federal Register*, a daily publication. This requirement is strictly enforced so that unpublished rules are given no legal effect by the courts unless the government can prove a party had actual knowledge. Rules and regulations currently in force are published in the *Code of Federal Regulations* that consists of 50 titles arranged alphabetically. Some states publish state agency rules and regulations in administrative codes. If there is no code, then state agencies usually publish their rules and regulations in pamphlets that are distributed to individuals and companies directly affected by their activities and are available to the public on request.

Common Law

Common law, also called "judge made" law, refers to the law that results from court decisions when there is no written law that applies to the particular fact situation. When judges are asked to resolve legal disputes that are not adequately covered by constitutions, legislation, or administrative rule or decision, they will look to the decisions of other judges in similar circumstances. English common law had been applied uniformly throughout the colonies, but after the American Revolution, each state adopted all or part of the common law and expanded it according to their individual needs, thus precluding the development of a national common law. American common law developed and continues to develop on a state-by-state basis, with one exception. The state of Louisiana followed the Roman, French civil law tradition and adopted the Napoleonic Code as a basis for its civil code. Although the common law on specific subjects may differ from state to state there is some uniformity in the manner in which the courts reach their decisions.

Precedent and Stare Decisis

Initially, judges arrive at their decisions by taking into account the local customs and common beliefs of the community and by attempting to determine what most people would think of as right in the particular situation. They write an opinion that exposes the reasoning and explains the choices that resulted in their decision, which is called a finding or a holding. If other judges follow the decision it becomes precedent, and if the precedent is followed by a large number of judges, it becomes common law.[11]

The doctrines or principles of precedent and *stare decisis* provide the framework for the courts' decisions. Precedent, the broader principle, means that if a court within a similar legal system has previously considered and resolved a particular issue, its decision is worthy of consideration in resolving a future case. *Stare decisis* translates as "to stand by things decided" and means that a court will generally follow its own prior decision and also that a court is expected to follow the decisions of courts to which it is subordinate. These doctrines create two types of authority in the judicial systems. There is a mandatory authority, that which the courts generally consider themselves bound to follow, and a persuasive authority, that which the courts should consider and may be inclined to follow. Mandatory authority is often determined by whether federal or state law applies. For example, state courts are bound by the U.S. Supreme Court decisions on federal questions whereas the federal courts are bound by the state court decisions on nonfederal matters. The supreme courts of the states and the nation have considerable discretion to reject the precedents that they themselves generate, but the intermediate appellate courts and the trial courts below them cannot, in their reasoning, select precedents from any jurisdiction—they are bound by the precedent of their jurisdiction.

Revising and Expanding the Common Law

Despite the seemingly restrictive environment created by precedent, the courts do expand and revise the common law. They may find slight differences in a situation that allows them to distinguish between a current case and a precedent. Occasionally, they will find that a common law rule is no longer beneficial to public needs and decide to depart from or overturn a precedent. Llewellyn, in *The Common Law Tradition*, provides a list of 64 techniques for handling precedent illustrated by reference to American cases. He describes 8 ways to constrict a precedent, 8 ways to stand by it, 32 ways to expand it, 12 ways to avoid it, and 4 ways to kill it.[12]

Values Supporting Precedent

All courts adjust the law to fit new situations, but only rarely do they abandon a precedent. These principles make judges accountable for their actions. As Rembar observes, "*Stare decisis* is an anti-corruption device. If courts are not bound by external rules, if they are not called upon to explain their decisions in terms of precedent, corruption is made easier."[13] *Stare decisis* makes it complicated and awkward for judges to be dishonest because their decisions must appear consistent with what they have done in the past and more than an appearance of consistency is needed to avoid reversal on appeal.[14]

The principles of precedent and *stare decisis* dictate the form of legal argument and judicial reasoning, but it is the values that support these principles that ultimately determine how the legal conflict will be resolved. Requiring continuity and cohesion in the judicial application of rules promotes stability in the court systems. Allowing judges to seek the guidance of other judges instead of deciding every case as an original proposition saves time and encourages efficiency in a chronically overburdened court system. The system encourages reliance and confidence in the law by protecting those persons who have relied on the announced law in planning their affairs. The fundamental principle of equality is upheld by the equal treatment of persons equally situated and when similar cases receive similar treatment and results. Finally, adherence to precedence promotes the equal administration of justice and projects to the public that the courts do administer justice. It has been said that it is not enough that the courts administer justice, they must also appear to be doing so.[15]

Equity

Equity refers to the spirit and habit of fairness, justice, and fair dealing. It can signify justice as ascertained by reason or ethical insight independent of the formulated body of law. Equity developed because the civil law courts of England had become extremely rigid, adhering strictly to specific writs and forms of action and restricting their relief to money damages regardless of the injury. People seeking other types of relief petitioned the king through his chancellor. They appealed to the king's innate sense of justice and right and requested that he provide a remedy by using his arbitrary power to do good and dispense justice. In time, the king established the Court of Chancery for the purpose of doing justice between parties in those cases where the common law was inadequate. The Court of Chancery developed its own rules and precedents that could prevail over the rules and precedents of the civil law courts if the two were in conflict.

In general, separate courts of equity were not established in the United States. Instead, courts of law were vested with the power to hear cases in equity. Equity gives judges the power to issue injunctions, order specific performance, or take any preventive or remedial action to redress the wrong that the party is complaining of. Plaintiffs continue to petition the courts to use their power of equity when money damages, the remedy at law, are inadequate. There is no jury in an equity case, and the rules are not as rigid as in an action in law. The judge alone decides whether to grant the relief that the plaintiff is requesting. It has often been stated that equity acts in accordance with the spirit, not the letter, of the law.

ORGANIZATION OF GOVERNMENT

The Revolution gave the American people their freedom and the opportunity to create a new system of government. First, a democracy was created by placing the supreme power in the hands of the people. Then a republican form of government was adopted in which the people would exert their power through their elected representatives. Profoundly aware of the need to reconcile personal freedom with the power of the state, the Founding Fathers, guided by the philosophy of Locke and Montesquieu, invented the idea that the law should govern both the citizens and the government.[16] To realize their goal of an effective but limited state, they enacted the U.S. Constitution as the "organic law" that defines and establishes the organization of government.

The Constitution divides the power to make law between the national government and the state under a system of government known as Federalism. The Constitution creates a federal government that governs the people of all the states and has only limited powers granted to it by the states. The rest of the power is retained by the states and the people in them. The Tenth Amendment of the U.S. Constitution specifically states, "The powers not delegated to the United States by the Constitution, nor prohibited by it to the States, are reserved to the States respectively, or to the people." The United States of America is a democracy with a constitutional system of law and a republican form of government.

Separation of Powers

The principle of separation of powers seeks to prevent the undue concentration of power in any one governmental unit. In accordance with this principle, Articles I, II, and III of the Constitution divide the major functions of government into three distinct branches with clearly defined powers. The legislative branch creates, amends, and repeals laws; the executive branch administers and enforces the law; and the judicial branch applies and interprets the law. Each branch is designed to make law, and each branch checks and balances the others so that none can abuse their power. For example, the primary power to make law belongs to Congress, but the President can veto legislation and the Presidential veto can be overridden by a two-thirds vote of each house of Congress. The judiciary is empowered to review legislation and declare all or part of it invalid if it finds it violates the Constitution, and Congress can amend the legislation to meet the constitutional standard. Congress can investigate the President and control the jurisdiction of the federal courts. Presidential nominees to the Supreme Court and the federal courts must be approved by the Senate. The Constitution also addresses the individual abuse of power by offering procedures for the removal of the President, senators, representatives, judges, and all others in a position of governmental authority. The constitutions of the 50 states also divide the power between the legislative, executive, and administrative branches of government.

Legislative Branch

Congress and the legislatures possess the primary authority to make law. When the legislature enacts law to address a public problem, that law (if it is constitutional) controls or supersedes the policies of chief executives or judges. Individual legislators can advocate policy decisions, but they cannot create law. The legislature must consider and vote on a written proposal. Only a duly enacted statute has the force of law. The process of enacting a statute begins when one or more legislators sponsor and introduces a bill. The bill is assigned to the appropriate legislative committee, which conducts investigations and holds public hearings to obtain information concerning the proposed legislation. The committee members study the bill and then send it to the legislature with recommendations. They may recommend that it needs more study or that it is inexpedient to legislate, or they may present the bill to the full legislative body for debate and consideration. In Congress, and in every state legislature, except Nebraska which has only one legislative house, all bills must be considered by both bodies of the legislature. Joint Committees of Conference are sometimes required to assist the legislators to settle their differences so that both houses can pass an identical bill. Once an identical bill has been passed by both houses it is sent to the chief executive.

Executive Branch

The executive branch administers and enforces the law. The law-making powers of the President and governors lie in their power to approve or veto the legislation proposed by Congress and the legislatures. An executive veto will prevent a bill from becoming law unless the legislature votes to override the veto. Executive orders of the President can also be a significant source of law. For example, Executive Order No. 11478 established equal opportunity in federal employment. Executive orders are initially published in the *Federal Register*, then compiled annually and reprinted in numerical order in Title 3 of the *Code of Federal Regulations*. The executive branch has a departmental structure, and each department is responsible for administering and enforcing the law in its area. Both the federal and state departments of health and human services play a major role in the delivery of health care services.

Judicial Branch

The judicial branch of government has the authority to interpret and apply statutory law and to create, amend, and overturn the common law. Courts are structured to give close, careful, and continuous attention to the meaning of the U.S. Constitution and state constitutions. It is by enforcing these constitutions that they preserve individual freedom and limit the power of the government.[17] Judicial opinions give meaning to all types of legal rules. Judges use federal and state statutes, agency rules and decisions, and the common law in resolving conflicts; they interpret and apply the rules that define and shape and ultimately resolve the legal controversy. At the center of the judicial process is the need to encourage cooperation, to recognize that the people in conflict cannot resolve the disagreement without cooperating with each other on a deeper level by jointly agreeing to argue within the limits of disagreement that the rules provide.[18] The judicial branch of government provides the forum for the peaceful resolution of legal conflicts that can arise between two or more people or between the people and their government.

PURPOSE OF LAW

Among the legitimate purposes of law enumerated by the U.S. Constitution are the responsibility to establish and maintain order, protect the individual, settle disputes, and promote the general welfare.[19] In order to accomplish these objectives the law must be concerned with preserving and protecting the legal relationships between individuals and between individuals and the government. The manner in which this is accomplished is easier to understand if the law is categorized as public law and private law.

Public Law

Public law is concerned with the state in its political capacity. It defines, regulates, and enforces the relationships between individuals and the government. Public law consists of constitutional law, administrative law, and criminal law. Constitutional law considers a person's rights under the state and federal constitutions. A person's right to life, right to die, and rights to privacy and self-determination are founded in constitutional law. Administrative law concerns the executive departments and administrative agencies, boards, and commissions that are legislated by Congress and the state legislatures. For nurse managers, the most important administrative agency is the state board of nursing that is created by each state's nursing practice act. Criminal law concerns conduct that has been found offensive to society as a whole and involves the public right and authority to punish unlawful conduct. Criminal acts are defined in the federal and state criminal codes. Crimes that are relevant to health care providers include manslaughter, criminal negligence, illegal possession of controlled drugs, and aiding and abetting an unlicensed person to practice nursing or medicine. Although nurses do commit crimes, it is more likely that their involvement in the area of criminal law would be as a witness testifying to some information obtained as a result of having provided nursing care to the victim or the perpetrator of a crime.

Private Law

Private law, also known as civil law, is concerned with the rights and duties of private persons. It defines, regulates, and enforces legal relationships of individuals and organizations. Private law consists of contract law and tort law. Contract law involves agreements between one or more persons to do something for some type of remuneration. It is essentially a "bargained for exchange." Contracts, whether oral or written, have the power to create, modify, or destroy legal relationships. The effective and efficient delivery of health care services requires a network of contractual agreements that involve hospitals, nurses, physicians, and many other health care providers. Tort law is concerned with the recognition of noncontractual rights and obligations and with the reparation of wrongs or injuries inflicted by one person on another. The tort of negligence, the failure to meet a reasonable standard of care, is the most common type of litigation for hospitals, nurses, and physicians.

Burden of Proof

In a court or in an agency hearing, the moving party normally has the burden of proof. In other words, the person or agency bringing the action before the court has the responsibility of proving the facts that support their case. The burden of proof, which is the standard by which the evidence will be weighed or evaluated, varies according to the area of law that is involved. Criminal law requires that the prosecution prove its case "beyond a reasonable doubt," a phrase that is usually explained to the jury as the degree of doubt that causes reasonable persons to refrain from acting. Failure of the prosecution to meet the burden of proof will result in the acquittal of the defendant. In civil actions, the plaintiff needs to prove his or her case by a "preponderance of the evidence," which is usually understood to mean the evidence that has greater weight and is most convincing in the minds of the jurors. If the plaintiff does not meet the burden of proof, the judge may dismiss the case or the jury may find for the defendant. Administrative hearings often follow the civil standard; however, the legislation that creates the agency or the legislation that determines the agency's procedures may indicate what the standard will be for their particular type of proceeding. Agency standards sometimes refer to the documentation that is being presented to the tribunal, such as a standard that requires "sufficient evidence on the record" or "substantial evidence on the record."

The judge explains the law to the jury by citing the law applicable to the case before them. The judge also instructs the jury as to what the law requires by way of factual elements. The jury then determines what they believe the facts to be, applies the law to those facts, and renders a verdict for the plaintiff or for the defendant.

UNITED STATES COURT SYSTEMS

There are two court systems in the United States: the federal system, which is maintained by the federal government, and the state or local system in each state and in the District of Columbia, Puerto Rico, and the territories. The state court system is of colonial origin, having developed from the courts that existed and continued to function after the American Revolution. State constitutions and state statutes determine the state's court system. The federal court system is created by Article III, Section 1 of the Constitution, which states, "the judicial power of the United States shall be vested in one Supreme Court, and in such inferior courts as the Congress may from time to time ordain and establish." The two types of courts found in both the federal and state court systems are trial courts and appellate courts.

Trial Courts

It is in the trial courts that legal controversies are first considered and resolved. During a trial, witnesses are heard, evidence is introduced, and arguments are presented by opposing attorneys. First the plaintiff attempts to prove what he or she believes are the facts and then the defendant attempts to disprove them. The judge acts as a referee to keep the parties within the rules when asked to do so by a party who objects to what the other side is doing. A trial court consists of a single judge who decides all of the issues of law that arise during the trial. For example, the judge decides whether a person qualifies as an expert witness, if certain evidence is admissible, and whether an attorney's line of questioning is relevant. The jury decides the facts, such as which witness is telling the truth, what the reasonable standard of care is in a particular situation, and how important the records and documents are to the case. It is the jury's responsibility to listen and observe and eventually to make a decision based on the testimony of the witnesses and the evidence that was introduced in the courtroom during the trial. Prior to deliberations the judge will provide jury instructions as to the law applicable to the case. If the plaintiff has waived the right to a jury trial, then the judge determines both the issues of fact and the issues of law. The jury renders its verdict, and if the judge and both parties are satisfied with the verdict, the case ends. If the losing party (the appellant) believes that errors have been made in the way the trial was conducted, he or she can file an appeal, which is a request that an appellate court review the case. Throughout the trial, the lawyers for both sides are expected to voice their objections to the judge's rulings if they believe the rulings are erroneous. These objections become part of the record and preserve these issues for the appeal.

Judges have significant control over the trial. If they find that insufficient evidence has been presented for the jury to resolve the issue, they can dismiss the case or they can direct the jury to decide the case in a specific way. Occasionally, a judge may find that the jury's verdict has no reasonable support in fact or is contrary to the law and will issue a judgment notwithstanding the verdict (judgment N.O.V.), which reverses the decision of the jury. All of the decisions of trial judges are subject to review by an appellate court.

Trials do not, as a rule, produce precedents because trial judges usually keep their legal opinions at the relatively informal oral level. Also, a trial judge's decisions are available as part of the trial record but they are not published separately, as are appellate court decisions.

Appellate Courts

Appellate courts are reviewing courts. They receive requests for review of lower trial court decisions. The appellant tries to convince the court of appeals that the trial court decided the case incorrectly. There are no witnesses and no juries in appellate courts. To prevent a tie vote, appellate courts always have an odd number of judges: the federal appeals courts have three judges; the Supreme Court, nine. The judges review the trial transcript and the written briefs filed by the attorneys. In some cases they hear oral arguments from the opposing attorneys, which provides them the opportunity to question the attorneys on the issues. Because the jury and the trial judge actually saw and heard the witnesses, they will usually accept their determination of the facts and base their review on whether proper procedure was followed and whether the trial judge interpreted the law correctly. Appellate courts decide whether the lower trial court decision should be affirmed, remanded to the trial court with specific instructions, or reversed and a new trial ordered. In cases in which the appellate court finds that an error has been made by the trial court but that it is not an error that significantly affected the case, they will label it as "harmless error" and let the lower court decision stand. The controlling decision is based on a majority vote of the participating judges; however, individual judges can file concurring or dissenting opinions. Precedents are established by appellate courts through their written opinions. Appellate court decisions are published in a reporter system and preserved in law libraries, where they are available to lawyers who seek precedents for future cases.

Federal Court System

The U.S. Supreme Court, the appellate courts, and the district courts make up the federal court system (Figure 2-1). The federal system has two areas of jurisdiction or power. The first area involves cases in which there is a federal question. This refers to controversies that concern the U.S. Constitution, a federal treaty entered into by the President or a federal statute passed by Congress. The second area of power involves cases in which a citizen of one state is being sued by a citizen of another state. This is known as diversity of citizenship jurisdiction and is designed to prevent claims of state court prejudice against a citizen of another state.

United States District Courts

The country is divided into 94 districts. Each state has its own district, with larger states having several districts within their borders. There are also district courts in the District of Columbia, Puerto Rico, the Canal Zone, and Guam. The district courts are the basic trial courts of the federal system. Federal district courts have jurisdiction over

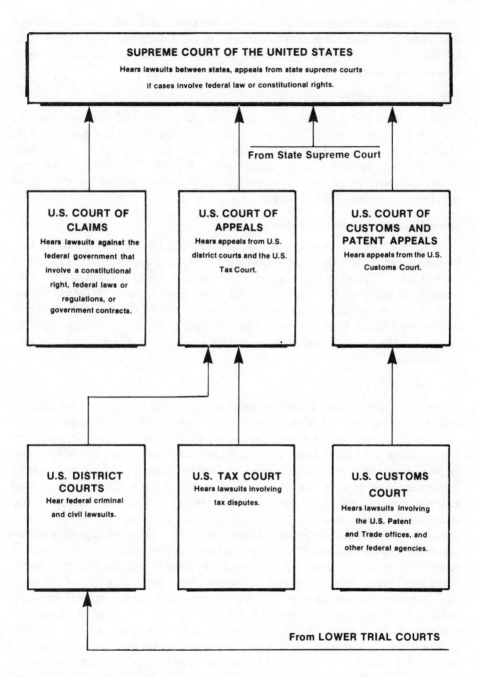

SUPREME COURT OF THE UNITED STATES

Hears lawsuits between states, appeals from state supreme courts
if cases involve federal law or constitutional rights.

From State Supreme Court

**U.S. COURT OF
CLAIMS**

Hears lawsuits against the
federal government that
involve a constitutional
right, federal laws or
regulations, or
government contracts.

**U.S. COURT OF
APPEALS**

Hears appeals from U.S.
district courts and the U.S.
Tax Court.

**U.S. COURT OF
CUSTOMS AND
PATENT APPEALS**

Hears appeals from the U.S.
Customs Court.

**U.S. DISTRICT
COURTS**

Hear federal criminal
and civil lawsuits.

U.S. TAX COURT

Hears lawsuits involving
tax disputes.

**U.S. CUSTOMS
COURT**

Hears lawsuits involving
the U.S. Patent
and Trade offices, and
other federal agencies.

From LOWER TRIAL COURTS

Figure 2-1 Federal Court System

admiralty and bankruptcy cases, federal crime violations, civil cases over $10,000 that arise under the Constitution, laws or treaties of the United States, civil cases over $10,000 in which the parties are citizens of different states, and certain actions of administrative agencies.

United States Appellate Courts

The U.S. Courts of Appeals, also known as the circuit courts, are the basic appellate courts in the federal system. There are 13 federal judicial circuits that cover all of the 94 districts as well as the District of Columbia (Figure 2-2). The appellate courts have jurisdiction over appeals from the district courts, the U.S. Tax Court, the territorial courts, and independent regulatory agencies, such as the National Labor Relations Board and the Federal Trade Commission.

Federal Courts of Limited Jurisdiction

The federal system also has specialized courts with very limited jurisdiction. The U.S. Customs Court deals with matters involving customs, and appeals from this court are taken to the U.S. Court of Customs and Patent Appeals. The U.S. Court of Claims is a special court that hears only cases involving money claims against the federal government. Although the government cannot be sued without its consent, federal statutes such as the Federal Torts Claims Act allows citizens to sue the United States for money damages for torts committed by federal employees during the course of their employment.

U.S. Supreme Court

The U.S. Supreme Court is the final appellate body (court of last resort) for the entire federal judicial system as well as for the state court systems when the state courts have a question of federal law. The Constitution gives the Court original jurisdiction to hear cases between the United States and a state; between two or more states; by a state against a citizen of another state, an alien, or a foreign country; and involving a foreign ambassador, ministers, or consuls. Original jurisdiction means that the Court has the authority to act as a trial court; however, in most instances it prefers to have the district courts handle these cases.

Appeals are brought to the Supreme Court from the U.S. Courts of Appeals, the Court of Customs and Patent Appeals, the Court of Claims, and the highest court of the various states by filing a *writ of certiorari*. This writ is a petition that asks the Supreme Court to hear a case because there is a federal question involved; however, given the volume of cases urged on the court each year, it is more than likely that the writ will be denied unless it involves a case of substantial federal importance or a conflict between the decisions of two or more U.S. Appeals (Circuit) Courts. The Supreme Court must hear an appeal from the highest court of a state if that state court has ruled that a federal statute or treaty is unconstitutional. Denial of an appeal should not be interpreted as meaning that the Supreme Court approves of the lower appellate court's decision; it only means that it declines to review the decision and that the lower court decision will remain in effect. The Supreme Court comprises nine judges who hear and decide the case. Usually

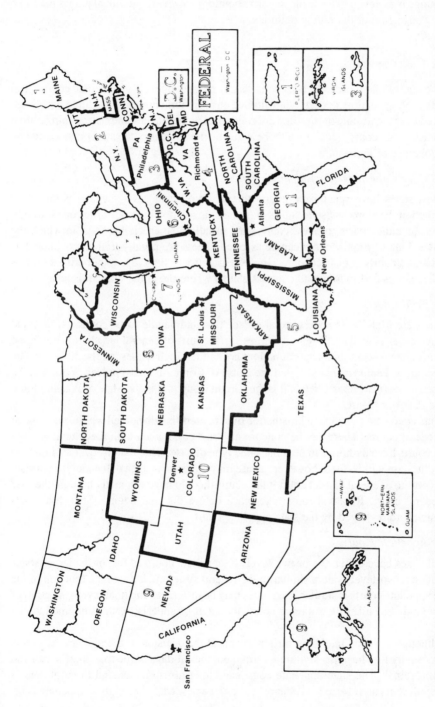

Figure 2-2 The Thirteen Federal Judicial Circuits. *Source:* Reprinted from *West's Law Finder: A Research Manual for Lawyers*, p.4, with permission of West Publishing Company, © 1985.

one judge is assigned to write the majority opinion; however, individual judges may also write concurring or dissenting opinions.

State Court Systems

The court system in most states consists of one or two levels of appellate courts, trial courts, and specialized courts with limited jurisdiction (Figure 2-3). State courts are created by the state constitution and are concerned with state law and state administrative agencies. State court judges are either elected by the citizens of the state or appointed by the governor or legislature.

State Courts of Limited Jurisdiction

Most states have specialized courts that can only hear cases that fall within their jurisdiction. Examples of state courts of limited jurisdiction include traffic courts, family courts, juvenile courts, probate courts, and usually a small claims court in which the smallest kind of money claim can be asserted. There are usually trial courts known as magistrates courts or district courts whose jurisdiction is limited to minor crimes such as misdemeanors and to torts and contract claims where the dollar amount is small.

State Trial Courts

The state trial courts have general jurisdiction and handle torts, contracts, tax, and divorce cases as well as all serious crimes. Trial courts of general jurisdiction are found in every state, and although their functions are similar, their names may be different. The trial court in Pennsylvania is called the Court of Common Pleas; in New York it is the Supreme Court; while in Oregon it is the Circuit Court and in the State of Washington it is the Superior Court.

State courts have exclusive jurisdiction over matters that do not fall within the scope of the federal courts. There can be concurrent jurisdiction when both the federal and the state courts have authority to hear the same type of case. The plaintiff decides in which court the case will be filed; however, a case may be removed by a defendant from a state trial court to a federal district court if the plaintiff could have originally brought the case in federal court. Removal must take place before the trial begins. State trial court decisions are reviewed by the state appellate courts.

State Appellate Courts

All states have either one or two levels of appellate courts. Most of the larger states maintain a two-level system similar to the federal system. Although the function of the state appellate courts is similar, the names may be different. The final reviewing court of a state may be called the supreme court, the court of appeals, or the supreme judicial court.

Although a person may have a right to appeal the decision of a trial court, he or she must usually file the appeal within a certain number of days or the trial court's decision becomes final. The state appellate court can either affirm or remand the trial court's decision, or it can reverse the decision and order a new trial. The highest appellate court

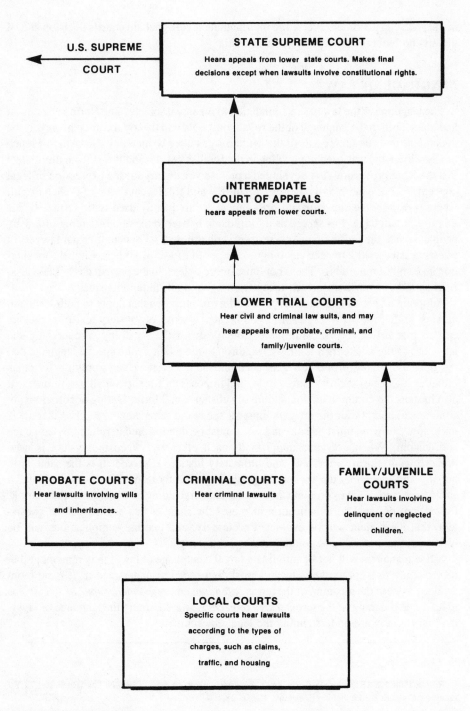

Figure 2-3 State Court System

in the state can affirm or reverse the intermediate level appellate court's decision and, if there is no federal issue, its decision is final.

LANGUAGE OF LAW

The language of the law has its foundation in medieval society. The Norman Conquest had made French the language of the royal household and the royal courts; however, the documents and formal records of the Middle Ages were written in Latin. Anglo-French or "law French" was used in pleading in the English courts, and it was from this dialect that the legal profession first developed a precise vocabulary for the expression of legal concepts.[20] For example, the words "plaintiff" and "defendant" are of French origin, whereas *respondeat superior* and *prima facie* are frequently used Latin terms.[21] This mixture of languages has served as a formidable barrier to the understanding of law by people outside the profession. As one observer has noted, "For centuries our lawyers, a priestly caste, used a mysterious tongue composed of Latin, French, English, incantation and a bit of mumbling. These continue, more or less, to the present day—Latin less, English more, French absorbed, incantation down a bit, mumbling steady."[22]

Adopting a special language serves a variety of purposes that apply to both legal and nursing professions. Professional jargon creates a sense of mystery and promotes an elitism that effectively separates the "them" from the "us" by discouraging the advances of the amateur. It is, however, through the medium of a special language that the business of the profession gets accomplished. Learning and applying formulas provides a sense of security, saves time, and imposes an equality on all practitioners. It also hastens the common understanding of substance and form. During negotiations, in conference, and at trial the lawyers must all speak the same language. The outcome is uncertain, but what must be said and what must be done is predetermined by language and custom. When everyone understands each other and when the system is used properly and ethically, the law, and ultimately justice, is served. It is the same with nursing and medicine: the special language identifies those qualified to participate, it saves time, and it makes possible the common understanding essential for collaboration. Formal professional communication increases the chances that actions will be consistent, that the patient will be evaluated accurately, and that the complications will be observed, understood, and communicated in time.

Nurse managers will not be intimidated by the language of law if they remember that they already possess the knowledge and skills needed to understand it. It is no more difficult to learn the meaning of the terms *defendant* and *respondeat superior* than it was to learn the meaning of the terms *triage* or *ecchymosis*. Learning the language of law is the first step toward understanding the legal environment.

NOTES

1. Roscoe Pound and Theodore F.T. Plucknett, *Readings on the History of Common Law* (Rochester, N.Y.: Lawyer's Cooperative Publishing Company, 1927), 23.

2. Charles Rembar, *The Law of the Land* (New York: Simon and Schuster, 1980), 116–122.

3. Ibid., 68.

4. Ibid., 272.

5. Lief H. Carter, *Reason in Law* (Boston: Little, Brown and Co., 1979), 107.

6. Rembar, *Law of the Land*, 212.

7. Ibid., 168.

8. James Boyd White, *When Words Lose Their Meaning: Constitutions and Reconstitutions of Language, Character and Community* (Chicago: University of Chicago Press, 1984), 231–232.

9. Rembar, *Law of the Land*, 50.

10. "This Constitution and the laws of the United States which shall be made in pursuance thereof, and all treaties made, or which shall be made, under the authority of the United States, shall be the supreme law of the land; and the judges in every State shall be bound thereby, anything in the Constitution or laws of any State to the contrary notwithstanding." U.S. CONST. art. VI, § 2.

11. William T. Schantz, *The American Legal Environment* (St. Paul Minn.: West Publishing Co., 1976), 18.

12. Karl N. Llewellyn, *The Common Law Tradition: Deciding Appeals* (Boston: Little, Brown and Co., 1960), 62–120.

13. Rembar, *Law of the Land*, 53.

14. Ibid.

15. Thomas S. Currier, "Times and Change in Judge Made Law: Prospective Overruling," 51 *Va. L. Rev.* 201 (1965).

16. Carter, *Reason in Law*, 168.

17. Ibid., 184.

18. Ibid., 41.

19. The Preamble to the U.S. Constitution states, "We, the people of the United States, in order to form a more perfect union, establish justice, insure domestic tranquility, provide for the common defence, promote the general welfare, and secure the blessings of liberty to ourselves and to our posterity, do ordain and establish this Constitution for the United States of America."

20. Arthur R. Hogue, *Origins of the Common Law* (Bloomington, Ind.: Indiana University Press, 1966), 7.

21. Definitions: *plaintiff*: the party who brings a civil suit seeking damages or other legal relief; *defendant*: in a criminal case, the person accused of committing a crime; in a civil suit, the party against whom the suit is brought; *respondeat superior*: "let the master answer," the doctrine that states that employers are legally liable for the negligent acts of their employees; *prima facie*: at first view, on its face. A *prima facie* case is made when all the elements of a valid cause of action are alleged to exist.

22. Rembar, *Law of the Land*, 37.

Appendix I

Implications for Nurse Managers

Part I has provided an overview of the law and the American legal system in order to introduce the nurse manager to the legal concepts of law, power, jurisdiction, and process. A clear understanding of the origin, structure, and function of law and government is the essential foundation for the network of legal resources that nurse managers must develop if they are to respond appropriately to the legal requirements of the nursing management role. The following are examples of nurse manager attitudes, behaviors, and activities that should result from an understanding of the fundamentals of law and government:

ORIGIN OF LAW

- Accepting the responsibility to preserve our inheritance of the idea of government ''by the people'' by participating in the political and legal process for the discussion and resolution of today's health care issues

DEFINITION AND SOURCE OF LAW

- Respecting the law and the documents that create and define its substance and form
- Knowing where to find the laws and regulations, developing the ability to read and interpret them and, when necessary, using the system to challenge and change those that have become ineffective or inadequate in meeting the health care–related needs of the people and the nursing profession

BRANCHES OF GOVERNMENT

- Acknowledging the law as a dynamic, moving force
- Knowing the processes that generate movement or change within the executive, legislative, or judicial branches of government and employing the procedures that

activate the checks and balances on government and hold those sworn to uphold the law accountable for their actions

AREAS OF LAW

- Understanding the principles that emanate from the various areas of law and acquiring the ability to relate them to nursing management situations and to consider them when developing and implementing nursing policy

COURT SYSTEM

- Knowing the geographic limits of the state and federal courts in order to be able to distinguish between what is the law, and therefore binding on them and their actions, and what may be of professional interest but having no legal significance in their jurisdiction
- Cultivating the ability to read cases that have an impact on the nursing profession so as to understand how the nursing issues are translated into legal argument and legal reasoning by the attorneys and the courts

LEGAL LANGUAGE

- Learning the language of law to be able to acquire legal information personally, so that they can intelligently and productively discuss and debate the nursing-related legal issues with the business managers, risk managers, and attorneys who comprise a rapidly expanding administrative constituency in today's hospitals

* * * *

LEGAL RESOURCES

GENERAL LEGAL INFORMATION

Legal information is available in most public libraries and in law libraries in the courts, the law schools, the larger law firms, and the libraries of colleges that have paralegal, criminal justice, and political science programs.

LEGISLATION

Constitutions (federal and state)
United States Code (federal law)
State statutes
Code of Federal Regulations

Federal Register (daily publication of new or proposed federal regulations)
State or regional reporter system for court decisions

COURTS

U.S. Supreme Court (nine judges)
State supreme court (name, location, and number of judges)
Intermediate level court of appeals (official name, location for your jurisdiction, and number of judges)
Federal district court (your jurisdiction)
Trial courts of general jurisdiction (official name and location)

PERSONS

Congress and state legislature
   Senators and representatives (names and addresses of your senator and representative)
Health and Welfare Committee members
Appropriations Committee members

NURSE MANAGER'S BOOKSHELF

Law dictionary

Guides and Manuals

Henry, Karen Hawley. *Nursing Administration and Law Manual*. Rockville, Md.: Aspen Publishers, Inc., 1987.

Rowland, Howard S., and Rowland, Beatrice L., eds. *Hospital Legal Forms and Checklists*. Rockville, Md.: Aspen Publishers, Inc., 1987.

American Nurses' Association Publications

- *American Nurses' Association Economic and General Welfare Program*
- *Code for Nurses with Interpretive Statements*
- *New Organizational Models and Financial Arrangements for Nursing Services*
- *Nursing: A Social Policy Statement*
- *Nurses, Politics and Public Policy*
- *Nursing's Influence on Health Policy for the Eighties*
- *Roles, Responsibilities and Qualifications for Nurse Administrators*

Part II

Constitutional Law: Expanding Rights and Remedies

Clauses guaranteeing to the individual protection against specific abuses of power, must have a similar capacity of adaptation to a changing world. . . . "Time works changes, brings into existence new conditions and purposes. Therefore a principle to be vital must be capable of wider application than the mischief which gave it birth. This is peculiarly true of constitutions."

Mr. Justice Brandeis, dissenting
Olmstead v. United States
277 U.S. 438 (1928)

*****

By advocating the proper care of her patients, however, Wrighten was fulfilling her duty as a nurse. Patient advocacy by a nurse is not insubordination.

Wrighten v. Metropolitan Hospitals, Inc.
726 F.2d 1346 (1984)

Constitutional Law

The U.S. Constitution, the world's oldest written constitution, was framed at the Constitutional Convention of 1787 and went into effect on March 4, 1789. This document and the 50 state constitutions set out in formal written terms the structures and powers of government. They also define political relationships, enumerate the rights and liberties of citizens, and place limits on the way those who govern can use their power. A constitution is the organic or fundamental law of a nation or state to which all other laws must conform. A law is considered to be "constitutional" if it is authorized by, and consistent with, the constitution. A law that conflicts with or is in opposition to the fundamental law is considered to be "unconstitutional" and is subsequently void. There are essential differences between constitutions and statutes or ordinances. Constitutions are intended to govern future contingencies. They state principles and establish a foundation for law and government. Statutes and ordinances are enacted to meet existing conditions and, as such, provide detailed and specific information concerning the matter being legislated.[1]

There are two opposing points of view concerning the appropriate role of the U.S. Supreme Court in interpreting the Constitution. Lawyers who are strict constructionists of the Constitution believe that the Supreme Court should interpret the Constitution according to the literal meaning of the words in the document. They argue that when the Court makes a decision that has the effect of making law, it is acting beyond its judicial authority and usurping the legislative function. They accuse the Court of effecting social change through judicial mandate.[2] Others believe that it is necessary and proper for the Court to interpret the Constitution in the light of contemporary issues. They are able to separate the document from the law. As one observer has remarked, "As a *document* the Constitution came from the generation of 1787; as a *law* it derives its force and effect from the present generation of American citizens, and hence should be interpreted in the light of present conditions and with a view to meeting present problems."[3]

The need to resolve the complex and often emotional issues of patient's rights has extended the reach of the Constitution into both public and private hospitals. In the past, hospitals often adopted a paternalistic "we know what is best" attitude that expected and encouraged a passive, uninformed, and unquestioning patient. This attitude was also reflected in the hospital's relationship with its employees, especially nurses, who were also expected and encouraged to be passive and unquestioning concerning their rights as well as those of the patients.[4] Today's hospitals, aware that these attitudes are no longer appropriate or tolerated, are adopting policies that assist patients to actively participate in the health care delivery decisions. The necessary first step is requiring that all hospital employees, including nurse managers, recognize, respect, and protect the rights of hospital patients and employees.

PATIENTS' RIGHTS

Hospital patients have been slow in demanding their basic rights in the treatment process. It has been suggested that they are intimidated by a hospital environment that places nearly all of the control in the hands of managers, physicians, and staff.[5] This disadvantage is being overcome by consumer groups, who have demanded that hospitals acknowledge their duty to identify and preserve the rights of hospitalized patients. At the same time, the number of rights has been expanded through litigation and legislation and by the efforts of hospital medical and ethics committees. It is not enough, however, that hospitals subscribe to the philosophy of respecting patients' rights; as a practical matter on a day-to-day basis, the hospital managers must be able to differentiate the types of rights, recognize the circumstances in which they apply, and identify the category of patients or employees to whom the rights attach. Nurse managers who must tread through this maze need an understanding of the concept of rights so that they can clearly identify the source of patient or employees' rights, which is where all legal accountability begins.

CONCEPT OF RIGHTS

A right is defined as something that is owed, something that is possessed—a claim to which an individual is entitled.[6] It has been suggested that "the concept of rights has its roots in the moral nature of man and its practical expression in the political system he creates."[7] Attempts to trace the origin of rights inevitably reveal an overlapping hierarchy of moral, natural, institutional, and legal rights.[8] Moral rights emerge from the fundamental principles of right conduct rather than on enactment or custom. Natural rights are those that grow out of human nature. They are a derivation from natural law, which is the expression of right reason inhering in nature and humanity.[9] They have an ethically binding force as a rule of civil conduct. Philosophers such as John Locke claimed that life, liberty, and property were natural rights, and this philosophy formed the basis for the "unalienable rights" of "life, liberty, and the pursuit of happiness" enumerated in the Declaration of Independence.

Human rights are those owed to or possessed by all of humanity. They are considered the most basic and fundamental of moral rights. The United Nations' Universal Declaration of Human Rights acknowledges the existence of human rights and attempts to codify the fundamental rights to which all people are entitled, regardless of the form of government under which they live.[10]

Institutional rights are those conferred by the federal government or agencies and associations. Rights granted by the Department of Health and Human Services (HHS) are institutional rights, as are the American Hospital Association's (AHA) Bill of Rights when these rights are adopted by a hospital. These rights are not categorized as legal rights because hospitals can refuse to participate in HHS programs and they can also ignore or selectively incorporate the AHA Bill of Rights.

Legal rights are those conferred by the Constitution, Congress, state legislatures, administrative agencies, and courts. They differ from all other types of rights because they are supported and enforced by the power of the government and the law.

CONSTITUTIONAL RIGHTS

Constitutional rights are the highest level of legal right. The rights guaranteed and protected by the U.S. Constitution and state constitutions cannot be abridged except by an amendment of the constitution. Rights cannot exist without a corresponding duty. The constitutional rights to free speech and privacy create a corresponding duty on the part of government and occasionally on private parties to allow people to speak freely and to respect their privacy. The Constitution and the constitutions of the states create the rights of individuals and limit the power of the government to interfere with those rights. When laws are enacted that threaten these rights, the Supreme Court is empowered to declare the law invalid. It is interesting to note that the doctrine of judicial review, the power of the Supreme Court to declare laws unconstitutional, is not expressly mentioned in the Constitution. The power is derived from the Court's own interpretation of its powers. In the landmark case of *Marbury v. Madison*, 5 U.S. (1 Cranch 137), decided in 1803, the Supreme Court for the first time pronounced an act of Congress unconstitutional, holding that it was within the Court's power to do so.

At the center of every constitutional controversy is the need to maintain the delicate balance between a person's constitutional rights and the extent of the government's duty to respect those rights. Given the tremendous growth in the size of government there is as much need to monitor and evaluate the government's intrusion into private affairs today as there was when the Constitution was first amended to incorporate the Bill of Rights. It is especially important in the area of health care, in which private and intimate decisions are commonplace and any intrusion of the government between the patient and the health care provider is likely to interfere with the provider–patient relationship.

SOURCES OF CONSTITUTIONAL RIGHTS

People who enter the health care system retain their constitutional rights; the admission to a hospital does not act as a waiver or suspension of these rights. Employees of the health care industry retain all the constitutional rights that are guaranteed to public and private employees. There are three sources of constitutional rights. First, there are the rights enumerated in the Constitutional Amendments; second, there are the rights that the Supreme Court has interpreted as emanating from the penumbra of the Constitution; and third, there are the rights conferred by the civil rights statutes enacted by Congress. These rights are not self-enforcing—citizens must be willing and able to assert their constitutional rights. The civil rights legislation enacted by the Congress and the state legislatures provides the means by which citizens can redress their grievances against those individuals or agencies who have ignored or denied them their constitutional rights. In order to protect and promote the constitutional rights of patients and employees, nurse managers must be familiar with the nature and scope of the right. They must also be able to identify the specific area in which the Constitution, the Congress, and the courts have applied constitutional protections to hospital patients and employees.

Bill of Rights

The framers of the Constitution did not believe that it was necessary to enumerate basic individual rights because under the Constitution the national government could exercise only limited power. For example, there was no need to guarantee freedom of press because Congress had no power to regulate the press. They believed that the limited power of the federal government was an assurance of freedom. The states, understandably fearful of a strong national government, demanded the addition of the first ten Amendments as the price for ratification of the Constitution.[11] The first ten Amendments, which are now called the Bill of Rights, were proposed to the state legislatures by the first Congress that assembled under the Constitution in 1789 and were adopted in 810 days.[12] The first ten Amendments apply to only federal government; however, the "due process" clause of the Fourteenth Amendment is frequently used to incorporate the fundamental guarantees and make them applicable to the states. Hospitals and health care agencies that are part of a federal or state system are obligated to respect the constitutional rights of their patients. Just as the reach of the Constitution was extended from the federal government to the states by the Fourteenth Amendment, so has its scope been expanded by the courts and the Congress to include, under certain circumstances, private hospitals and private health care providers.

Substantive and Procedural Rights

The fundamental rights guaranteed by the Constitution are not absolute and can be denied or restricted by the government's successfully claiming a "compelling interest" in protecting the rights of society as a whole. What the Constitution does is protect the individual against arbitrary government action when it denies or restricts a person's constitutional right. This protection is extended to both the substantive and procedural rights guaranteed by the Constitution. Substantive rights are those enumerated or inferred by the Constitution, such as life, liberty, property, and privacy. Procedural rights are those that require fairness in the process that is used by the government to deny or restrict a person's constitutional rights. Procedural rights are the subject of the "due process" clauses of the Constitution. The Fifth Amendment requirement of "due

process'' applies to the federal government, and the Fourteenth Amendment requirement of ''due process'' applies to the states (Exhibit 3-1).

Hospital patients and nurse employees have challenged the authority of the government to deny or restrict their constitutional rights. The Fourteenth Amendment (see

---

Exhibit 3-1 Constitutional Amendments

First Amendment

Congress shall make no law respecting an establishment of religion, or prohibiting the free exercise thereof; or abridging the freedom of speech or of the press; or the right of the people peaceably to assemble, and to petition the government for a redress of grievances.

Fourth Amendment

The right of the people to be secure in their persons, houses, papers, and effects, against unreasonable searches and seizures, shall not be violated, and no warrants shall issue but upon probable cause, supported by oath or affirmation, and particularly describing the place to be searched, and persons or things to be seized.

Fifth Amendment

No person shall be held to answer for a capital, or otherwise infamous crime, unless on a presentment or indictment of a grand jury, except in cases arising in the land or naval forces, or in the militia, when in actual service in time of war or public danger; nor shall any person be subject for the same offence to be twice put in jeopardy of life or limb; nor shall be compelled in any criminal case to be a witness against himself, nor be deprived of life, liberty or property, without due process of law, nor shall private property be taken for public use without just compensation.

Ninth Amendment

The enumeration in the Constitution of certain rights shall not be construed to deny or disparage others retained by the people.

Fourteenth Amendment

section 1.

All persons born or naturalized in the United States, and subject to the jurisdiction thereof, are citizens of the United States and of the states wherein they reside. No state shall make or enforce any law which shall abridge the privileges or immunities of citizens of the United States; nor shall any state deprive any person of life, liberty or property, without due process of law; nor deny to any person within its jurisdiction the equal protection of the laws.

section 5.

The Congress shall have power to enforce, by appropriate legislation, the provisions of this article.

Chapter 4) is the ideal forum for the discussion of substantive and procedural rights of hospital patients and nurses and for the introduction of the legislation that Congress has enacted as a remedy for persons whose rights have been unlawfully restricted or denied. At this point, the reader should be advised that although the constitutional issues relating to health care are generally discussed as arising under a specific amendment or law, the cases themselves may have involved a number of constitutional issues. For example, in *Matter of Karen Quinlan,* 70 N.J. 10, 355 A.2d 647 (1976), *cert. denied* 429 U.S. 922 (1976), Karen's father sought to be appointed guardian of the person with authority to have the life-support systems that were temporarily preserving his daughter's life withdrawn. He appealed to the Court's power of equity and claimed the constitutional right to free exercise of religion, of privacy, and of protection against cruel and unusual punishment.[13] Attempting to expose all of the constitutional issues in each case would unnecessarily complicate a discussion whose main purpose is, first, to demonstrate which rights patients and nurses have litigated and, second, to indicate the decisions of the courts in these areas. Nurses' managers are strongly encouraged to review for themselves cases in which they may have a personal or professional interest (see Chapter 18, Finding and Interpreting a Case).

NOTES

1. 16 C.J.S. Constitutional Law § 2 (b), 22.

2. Mary Delores Helmelt and Mary Ellen Mackert, *Dynamics of Law in Nursing and Health Care* (Reston, Va.: Reston Publishing Co., 1982), 108.

3. Edward S. Corwin, *The Constitution,* 14th ed., revised by Harold W. Chase and Craig R. Ducat (Princeton, N.J.: Princeton University Press, 1978), 1-2; see words of Chief Justice Marshall, 4 Wheat. 316, 421 (1819).

4. Nurses "trained" in a diploma school in the late 1950s, as I was, will probably remember the regulation that nurses were not allowed to give the patients any information about the medications they were taking. Patients who insisted were told that they would have to ask the doctor, and since the patients did not have access to the telephone this meant waiting until the doctor visited. At this point my experience is that the frustrated patient surrendered and took the medication.

5. Eugene I. Pavalon, *Human Rights and Health Care Law* (New York: American Journal of Nursing Co., 1980), 4.

6. Black's Law Dictionary, 4th ed. (St. Paul, Minn.: West Publishing Co., 1968), 1478.

7. Robert M. Sade, "Medical Care as a Right: A Refutation," *New England Journal of Medicine,* 285, no. 23 (December 2, 1971), 13.

8. Gregory Pence, *Medical Options in Medicine* (Oradell, N.J.: Medical Economics Book Co., 1980), 53.

9. Clarence L. Barnhart and Jess Stein, eds., *American College Dictionary* (New York: Random House, 1968), 809.

10. Universal Declaration of Human Rights was adopted by the United Nations General Assembly on December 10, 1948.

11. Jerome A. Barron and Thomas C. Dienes, *Constitutional Law, Nutshell Series* (St. Paul, Minn.: West Publishing Co., 1986), 110–111.

12. Corwin, *Constitution,* 285.

13. *Matter of Quinlan,* 70 N.J. 10, 355 A.2d 647 (1976), *cert. denied* 429 U.S. 922 (1976). The court held that under certain circumstances a right to privacy encompasses the right of a patient or a patient's guardian to decline medical treatment.

Chapter 4

Constitutional Rights: The Fourteenth Amendment

Proposed in 1866 and adopted 25 months later, the Fourteenth Amendment places a significant limitation on state power (see Exhibit 3-1).[1] Over the years, it has become the vehicle through which much of the content of the Bill of Rights is made binding on the states.[2] The due process and equal protection clauses have been the subject of much litigation, and as a result, the courts have often had to define and interpret the words and phrases of each section. In order to understand the specific rights guaranteed by the Fourteenth Amendment it is necessary to examine the judicial interpretation of the words "state," "person," "liberty," and "property" and the phrases "due process" and "equal protection." Of equal importance is the need to identify the standard of review that the federal and state courts apply when they attempt to balance individual rights versus the government's interest in order to make their decision.

PERSON

In order to bring a suit under the Fourteenth Amendment the plaintiff must be a "person" covered by the statute. Corporations, aliens, and illegitimate children have all been found to be "persons" within the meaning of the amendment.[3] In *Roe v. Wade*, 410 U.S. 113 (1973), the Court stated that "The unborn have never been recognized in the law as persons in the whole sense," and concluded that a fetus was not a person entitled to full constitutional protection.[4]

STATE

With the exception of the Thirteenth Amendment (abolition of slavery), the prohibitions of the Constitution apply only to the national and state government. The Fifth and Fourteenth Amendments prohibit the federal and state legislatures from enacting laws that deprive persons of their life, liberty, or property without due process of law. Under the equal protection clause of the Fourteenth Amendment the federal and state legislatures cannot deny equal protection to any person within their jurisdiction, which means they are prohibited from enacting laws that discriminate against a particular class of people. The limitations on federal and state action not only cover legislative acts but also include the actions of administrative agencies, municipal corporations, public schools, and all other units of government.[5] The Fourteenth Amendment has been applied to private persons and private hospitals when the courts have determined that their conduct constituted "state action."

LIBERTY

At common law, "liberty" meant the right not to be physically restrained except for good cause. The Fourteenth Amendment guarantee of physical liberty or freedom from bodily restraint protects the rights of people threatened with involuntary commitment to a mental hospital. The Constitution limits the type of law that the federal and state legislatures can enact, and the courts closely scrutinize both the process and the conditions of federal and state sanctioned incarceration.

Surprisingly, it is in the area of social and economic legislation that the Supreme Court first expanded the Fourteenth Amendment concept of liberty. From 1905 until 1930, liberty was interpreted as protecting the "freedom of contract" of adults in the employer–employee relationship. During these years, the Court, in most cases, considered the "right of property" and the "freedom of contract" from the employer's point of view. Social and economic legislation that sought to regulate the wages and hours of employees was struck down as unconstitutional on the grounds that it denied the employers their property and liberty (freedom of contract) without due process of law.[6] In 1925, the Court extended the Fourteenth Amendment concept of liberty to include certain "fundamental rights" that were already protected against the federal government by the specific language of the Bill of Rights. Freedom of speech and freedom of the press were made applicable to state action via the liberty guarantee of the Fourteenth Amendment.[7]

In the 1930s, changes in the Court and the enactment of the New Deal legislation resulted in a shift in emphasis from employer's to employees' rights. The Court reversed its "freedom of contract" rulings in favor of a "right of labor" to peacefully organize, picket, and strike.[8] At the present time, the Fourteenth Amendment concept of liberty includes, first, the enumerated rights such as speech and press that have been incorporated from the Bill of Rights; second, rights such as association and privacy that have been implied from or read into the Constitution; and third, the fundamental interests that relate to personal autonomy and choice.[9] As the Supreme Court has explained, liberty

> denotes not merely freedom from bodily restraint but also the right of the individual to contract, to engage in any of the common occupations of life, to acquire useful knowledge, to marry, establish a home and bring up children, to worship God according to the dictates of his own conscience and generally to enjoy those privileges, . . . long recognized as essential to the orderly pursuit of happiness by free men.[10]

PROPERTY

At common law, the word "property" signified ownership over private, physical objects and over land. Over the years, court decisions expanded the concept to cover all the elements of ownership and at times allowed it to merge with the indefinite rights of liberty.[11] Under the Fourteenth Amendment the concept of property includes all of the entitlements, benefits, and expectations created by state law. In 1972, the Court held that property interests are not created by the Constitution.[12] Claims of entitlement to a protected property interest arise from state statutes, local ordinances, rules, and mutually explicit understandings.[13] The Court continues to review cases that question whether state employees, whose jobs are created by state law, have a property interest in their jobs that entitles them to a hearing before they are dismissed. In 1976, the Court ruled that public employees whose employment is terminable at will rather than "for cause" do not have a property interest in their jobs.[14] A 1985 decision held that a statute that entitled classified civil servants to retain their positions absent misfeasance, malfeasance, or nonfeasance in office did create a property interest even though the state provided procedures for termination.[15]

Judicial review of constitutional property rights involves both a substantive right of property, which is determined by state statute or regulation, and a procedural right to due process, which is determined by the Constitution. Nurses challenging the state's authority to deny or suspend their professional licenses could invoke a substantive property right in the license, a liberty right to practice their profession, and also challenge the procedures used by the state to deprive them of these rights.[16]

DUE PROCESS

The phrase "due process of law" comes from Chapter 3 of 28 Edward III (1335), a statute that in turn refers to Chapter 29 of Magna Carta (1225).[17] The words "due process" do not have a fixed meaning but expand with the court's interpretation of fundamental fairness. As Justice Frankfurter explained, "Due Process is not a mechanical instrument. It is not a yardstick. It is a delicate process of adjustment inescapably involving the exercise of judgment by those whom the Constitution entrusted with the unfolding of the process."[18] The Constitution contains two due process clauses: the Fifth Amendment due process clause that applies to the national government and the Fourteenth Amendment due process clause that applies to the states. It is through the due process clause of the Fourteenth Amendment that the various "fundamental guarantees" of the Bill of Rights are incorporated and made applicable to the states. Due process challenges to federal and state actions can be made on substantial and/or procedural grounds. Substantive due process involves the purpose or subject matter of the law itself, whereas procedural due process refers to the process or procedures employed by the government in denying or restricting a right.

Substantive Due Process

Substantive due process requires that all state and federal legislation be related to the furtherance of a legitimate government objective. The legislation must also promote the government's interest in a manner that is the least burdensome of a person's rights.[19]

The Supreme Court in the early 1900s held that Acts of Congress must conform to the "fundamental liberties" or "natural rights" of the people. Employers' rights to property and freedom to contract were interpreted by the Court as superior to the government's right to enact wage and hour legislation.[20] Thirty years later, a different Court, in the midst of the Great Depression, began to recognize the "rights of labor" as opposed to the "rights of management" in arriving at their decisions. Since that time, however, economic substantive due process has been on the decline and courts have been reluctant to strike down economic legislation on substantial due process grounds. A 1955 decision clearly revealed the Court's thinking in this area. In *Williamson v. Lee Optical Company*, 348 U.S. 483 (1955), the Court upheld a law that prevented any person except licensed optometrists and ophthalmologists from fitting eyeglass lenses. The Court rejected the opticians' claim that the law denied them their property and stated, "The day is long gone when the Court uses the Due Process Clause of the Fourteenth Amendment to strike down state laws regulatory of business and industrial conditions, because they may be unwise, improvident or out of harmony with a particular school of thought."

Today, substantial due process challenges are appropriate in the areas of civil rights, criminal procedure, marital privacy, and abortion. In these areas, the Court first determines that a fundamental right is involved and then balances the person's fundamental right against the government's interest in enacting legislation to restrict or deny that right. Fundamental rights include all of the express rights and others, such as privacy and association, that have been inferred or read into the Constitution. The determination that a right is fundamental is a Court decision based on its interpretation of the Constitution.

Procedural Due Process

When the government deprives a person of an already acquired life, liberty, or property interest, the due process clauses of the Fifth and Fourteenth Amendments require procedural fairness. Procedural due process looks at the way government acts and the enforcement mechanisms that it uses.[21] The requirement of procedural due process expands each time a court identifies or infers an additional constitutional right. The newly recognized right to privacy binds the government to procedural due process if the right is legislatively constrained or denied. Entitlements, the recognition by government that an individual is entitled to a benefit, creates an expectancy that the right will not be arbitrarily terminated. Entitlement, however, applies only to presently enjoyed benefits, rights, or interests; due process does not protect the person applying for benefits.[22]

WHAT PROCESS IS DUE

A determination of precisely what process is due varies according to the facts of the situation; however, there are certain requirements that support the concept of fairness:[23]

1. The government's power must be limited and based on written, common, or administrative law.
2. A person must have access to a court of proper jurisdiction.
3. A person must be given reasonable notice and the opportunity to be heard.
4. Established rules of evidence and procedure must be followed by the court or agency tribunal.
5. Constitutional rights, including the right to counsel, the right to confront and examine witnesses, the privilege against self-incrimination, and the right to trial by jury, must be safeguarded.

Procedural due process is the concept of "essential fairness" in all proceedings that would restrict or deny a person's rights. It has been suggested that "It is the embodiment of the idea that we are governed by rules and principles and not by unconfined authority; that nothing is timeless in our law except the law itself."[24]

EQUAL PROTECTION

The Fourteenth Amendment guarantees that "No State shall make or enforce any law which shall . . . deny to any person within its jurisdiction the equal protection of the laws" (see Exhibit 3-1). The same limitation is applied to the federal government by the Fifth Amendment due process clause.[25] The equal protection clause requires that all persons similarly situated be treated alike under the law. Laws invariably create distinctions as to how people will be treated. For example, the law permits some individuals to practice nursing and prohibits others from doing so; the law also makes certain persons eligible for benefits such as welfare, while others are not. These legislative distinctions create "classes" of people who are denied certain legal rights. These people may seek to challenge the law as denying them "equal protection" because it unreasonably restricts their rights or unreasonably discriminates against them as a "class." Although legislative classifications are permitted, they must be rationally related to a legitimate state interest. A reasonable classification has been defined as "one which includes all persons who are similarly situated with respect to the purpose of the law."[26]

Suspect Class

A law will not sustain an "equal protection" challenge if it creates a "suspect class." "Suspect classes" arise in two ways. When the legislature enacts a statute that singles out a "discrete and insular group" it creates a "suspect class." Generally these groups have a history of political powerlessness and discrimination that now warrants special protection in the political process. Classifications that have been found to be suspect include alienage, nationality, race, and sometimes women.[27]

Fundamental Right

A "suspect class" is also created when a statute excludes a group from the possession of a "fundamental right," which is expressed or implied by the Bill of Rights. For example, under the equal protection clause indigents have won the right to appointed counsel in a felony case or in any case in which the defendant may be subjected to a period of imprisonment.[28] Challenges to laws on "equal protection" grounds require the courts to determine whether a particular group meets the criteria for a "suspect class" and also whether what they are being denied is considered a "fundamental right."

JUDICIAL REVIEW

Challenges to the due process and/or equal protection guarantees of the Fifth and Fourteenth Amendments provide the focus for judicial review of federal and state legislation. The method of inquiry used by the courts will depend on whether the challenge is based on procedural due process, substantive due process, or equal protection grounds.

Procedural Due Process Review

Procedural due process challenges involve the requirement of "fundamental fairness" in the procedures used by the state and federal government in depriving people of their liberty or property. Under a procedural due process analysis, the court first determines that a liberty or property interest is significantly burdened; then it decides what procedures are required in order to provide "fundamental fairness." Observers have noted that although there is no systematic guidance on the values and objectives used by the court in determining what process is due, primary emphasis has been given to accuracy and avoiding arbitrariness in government decision making.[29] The courts have indicated that once it is determined that due process interests are adversely affected, the person has at least the right to reasonable notice and some form of hearing.[30] Beyond the minimum of reasonable notice and the opportunity to be heard, the type of due process protection that is required is determined by balancing the government's interest in avoiding the loss through additional procedural protections.[31] Courts balance the interests by employing a test that focuses on the following factors:[32]

1. The private interest that will be affected
2. The risk of erroneous deprivation of the interest by the procedure used
3. The probable value, if any, of additional or substitute safeguards
4. The precise nature of the government interest, including the function involved and the fiscal and administrative burden that the additional or substitute procedural requirements would entail

Critics of this balancing approach to due process analysis claim that in practice it:

• Results in subjective value choices rather than an objective measurement of the demands of due process
• Focuses on claimants generally and ignores the effects of government action on a particular person

- Raises serious questions as to the capacity of the courts to weigh the competing interests at stake[33]

Areas subject to frequent challenges to procedural due process protection include criminal law, civil commitment laws, and state laws that create property interests characterized as entitlements, benefits, and expectations. For example, in involuntary commitment proceedings the federal and state courts stress the need for a test of dangerousness, a timely hearing, and the guarantee of an adversary process. The courts have held that an individual cannot be detained in a jail or hospital on an emergency basis pending examination without a timely hearing to ascertain probable cause that he or she is mentally ill. On the issue of confinement for mental illness, courts continue to define not only the specific requirements of the legal proceedings but also the conditions of confinement, including the right of a person to receive treatment in the least restrictive environment.[34]

A person claiming a denial of due process must be able to prove that the damage or injury was suffered because of the denial itself. In *Carey v. Piphus*, 435 U.S. 247 (1978), the Court held that no injuries are presumed to result from a deprivation of procedural due process; rather, a plaintiff must prove actual compensable injury, possibly including emotional distress, in order to recover more than nominal damages.

Substantive Due Process Review

Fourteenth Amendment substantive due process and equal protection challenges require the court to balance the state's interest or purpose in the law versus the importance of the person's constitutional rights. The standard of review of protected rights depends on the importance of the right involved and whether it is constitutional or economic. Also the degree of justification required of the government tends to increase as the severity of the burden on the protected right increases. For example, a law prohibiting the exercise of a right is likely to be tested by a higher standard than a law that only regulates the manner in which the right is exercised.[35] Under the equal protection clause men, women, children, and aliens need not always be treated alike; however, as a "class" they cannot be treated differently on an arbitrary basis. The government must have a legitimate interest in imposing a classification, and the legal classification must be reasonable in relation to the objective of the law.

Three-Tiered Review

The demand for reasonableness in legislative classifications has resulted in a three-tiered system of judicial review.

Strict Scrutiny

"Strict scrutiny" is the phrase used to signify the first tier or highest standard of judicial review. Laws that intentionally employ suspect classifications, such as race, nationality, or alienage, and laws that significantly burden the exercise of a fundamental right are subject to strict judicial scrutiny. The "fundamental rights" that will trigger strict scrutiny include all of the express constitutional rights and some of the nonenumerated rights; however, it is unclear how the latter are determined by the Court.[36]

Under the strict scrutiny standard of review the burden is on the government to establish that the classification is necessary to a compelling government interest. The government must also prove that no less restrictive alternative is available. It has been suggested that a strict scrutiny standard of judicial review generally results in the law being found unconstitutional.[37]

Important Objective

The intermediate tier or middle standard of review involves "quasi-suspect" classifications such as gender and illegitimacy.[38] The Court invoked the new standard in *Craig v. Boren*, 429 U.S. 191 (1976), when they held that the state must prove that the classifications by gender serve an important governmental objective and are substantially related to the achievement of their objectives. In his dissent, Justice Rehnquist objected to the use of the new standard of review, arguing that the phrase "important objective" and "substantial relation" are "so diaphanous and elastic as to invite subjective judicial preferences or prejudices."[39] In 1982, the Court used the intermediate standard of review to strike down a women-only admission policy at a state nursing school. The state had argued that the policy served a compensatory (affirmative action) objective. Justice O'Connor, for the Court, held that the state had failed to establish that this was its actual objective given the lack of disadvantage suffered by women entering nursing. The Court also found that the state had failed to prove that the policy was "substantially and directly" related to its proposed objective.[40]

Rational Basis

The third tier or lowest level of equal protection review is known as the "rational basis" standard. Under this standard the law is presumed constitutional by the court and the challenging party must prove that the legislation is not rationally related to a permissible government objective. If the classification is held to be rationally related to a permissible government objective the requirement of equal protection is satisfied.[41] The rationality standard is used primarily in reviewing socioeconomic legislation, which includes health laws and regulations that are enacted pursuant to the state's power to protect the health and safety of its citizens. The state's police power was used to justify laws requiring compulsory vaccination.[42] It is also the justification for the licensing laws that regulate the health professions.[43] The state's authority to enact health and safety legislation will be restricted by the courts if it interferes with the power of the federal government or if it infringes on constitutional rights.[44] It has been suggested that the rational basis approach to equal protection has been marked by extreme judicial self-restraint and deference to the legislative judgment and that legislative review under the "rational basis" standard is usually upheld.[45]

Observers have concluded that the "law of equal protection has consisted largely in working out the standards for judicial scrutiny of legal classifications."[46] The two-tiered system of review developed during the Warren Court era, and the third, middle level of review emerged during the Burger Court years. Some believe that the rigid three-tiered approach to equal protection review will be abandoned in favor of a "reasonableness" standard in which the degree of judicial scrutiny will vary depending on the identity of the classes, the severity of the burden imposed by the classification, and the nature of the government interest supporting the classification.[47]

NOTES

1. Edward S. Corwin, *The Constitution*, 14th ed., revised by Harold W. Chase and Craig R. Ducat (Princeton, N.J.: Princeton University Press, 1978), 2.

2. Jerome A. Barron and Thomas C. Dienes, *Constitutional Law, Nutshell Series* (St. Paul, Minn.: West Publishing Co., 1986), 110–111.

3. Corporations, *Santa Clara Cty. v. Southern Pacific R.R. Co.*, 118 U.S. 394 (1886); aliens, *Yick Wo v. Hopkins*, 118 U.S. 356 (1886); illegitimate children, *Levy v. La.*, 391 U.S. 68 (1968).

4. *Roe v. Wade*, 410 U.S. 113, 162 (1973).

5. *McCabe v. Nassau Cty. Medical Center*, 453 F.2d 698 (2d Cir. 1971); *Hathaway v. Worcester County Hospital*, 341 F. Supp. 1385 (D.Md. 1969).

6. *Lochner v. New York*, 198 U.S. 45 (1905).

7. *Gitlow v. New York*, 286 U.S. 652 (1925).

8. Corwin, *Constitution*, 388.

9. Barron and Dienes, *Constitutional Law*, 150.

10. Ibid., 148.

11. Corwin, *Constitution*, 387.

12. *Board of Regents v. Roth*, 408 U.S. 564 (1972).

13. *Perry v. Sindermann*, 408 U.S. 593 (1972).

14. *Bishop v. Wood*, 426 U.S. 341 (1976).

15. *Cleveland Board of Education v. Loudermille*, 469 U.S. 1031 (1985).

16. *Arnett v. Kennedy*, 416 U.S. 134 (1974).

17. Corwin, *Constitution*, 386.

18. *Joint Anti-Fascist Refugee Committee v. McGrath*, 341 U.S. 123, 162, 163 (1951).

19. *Mugler v. State of Kansas*, 123 U.S. 623 (1887).

20. *Lochner v. New York*, 198 U.S. 45 (1905).

21. Barron and Dienes, *Constitutional Law*, 145.

22. *Board of Regents v. Roth*, 408 U.S. 564 (1972).

23. William T. Schantz, *The American Legal Environment* (St. Paul, Minn.: West Publishing Co., 1976), 311.

24. Charles Rembar, *The Law of the Land* (New York: Simon and Schuster, 1980), 406.

25. *Bolling v. Sharpe*, 347 U.S. 497 (1954).

26. Tussman and TenBroek, "The Equal Protection of the Laws," 37 *Calif. L. Rev.* 341 (1944).

27. Aliens, *Graham v. Richardson*, 403 U.S. 365 (1971); nationality, *Oyama et al. v. California*, 332 U.S. 633 (1948); race, *McLaughlin et al. v. Florida*, 379 U.S. 184 (1964); sex (women) considered as a suspect class in *Frontiero v. Richarson*, 411 U.S. 677 (1973); (women) not considered as a suspect class in *Mississippi University for Women v. Hogan*, 1035 S. Ct. 3331 (1982).

28. *Gideon v. Wainwright Corrections Director*, 372 U.S. 335 (1963); *Argersinger v. Hamlin Sheriff*, 407 U.S. 25 (1972).

29. Barron and Dienes, *Constitutional Law*, 153.

30. *Goss v. Lopez*, 419 U.S. 565 (1975).

31. *Goldberg v. Kelly et al.*, 397 U.S. 254 (1970).

32. *Matthews v. Eldridge*, 424 U.S. 319 (1976).

33. Barron and Dienes, *Constitutional Law*, 156.

34. *Lessard v. Schmidt*, 349 F. Supp. 1078 (E.D.Wisc. 1972), *vacated on procedural grounds*; 414 U.S. 473 (1974), *vacated on procedural grounds* 421 U.S. 975 (1975); *reinstated* 413 F. Supp. 1318 (E.D.Wisc. 1978).

35. Barron and Dienes, *Constitutional Law*, 124.

36. Ibid., 125.

37. Ibid.

38. Gender, *Craig v. Boren*, 429 U.S. 191 (1976); illegitimacy, *Levy v. Louisiana*, 391 U.S. 68 (1968).

39. *Craig v. Boren*, 429 U.S. 191, (1976).

40. *Mississippi University for Women v. Hogan*, 102 S.Ct. 3331 (1982).

41. *Williamson v. Lee Optical Co.*, 348 U.S. 403 (1955).

42. *Jacobsen v. Massachusetts*, 197 U.S. 11 (1905).

43. *Richardson v. Brunelle*, 398 A.2d 838 (1979).

44. *Jacobsen v. Massachusetts*, 197 U.S. 11 (1905).

45. Barron and Dienes, *Constitutional Law*, 123.

46. Ibid., 159.

47. Ibid., 158, 159.

Chapter 5

Civil Rights Legislation: Constitutional Remedies

The Fourteenth Amendment, section 5, gives Congress the power to enact legislation to enforce the protections of the Constitution (see Exhibit 3-1). This enabling clause allows Congress to provide remedies for violations of the Fourteenth Amendment rights as they have been defined by the Court. In *Katzenbach v. Morgan*, 384 U.S. 641 (1966), Justice Brennan argued that under section 5, congressional power is limited to adopting measures to enforce the guarantees of the amendment and that the power could not be used to restrict, abrogate or dilute these rights. Under this limitation known as the "rachet theory," congressional power under section 5 operates in only one direction, to enforce or extend the rights guaranteed by the Fourteenth Amendment.

CIVIL RIGHTS ACT OF 1871

The Civil Rights Act of 1871, 42 U.S.C. § 1983, one of the civil rights statutes that was enacted after the Civil War, is an example of the use of congressional power to provide a means of enforcing constitutional rights. Many of the civil rights actions brought against government health care providers involve Section 1983, which states

> Every person who under color of any statute, ordinance, regulation, custom or usage of any State or Territory, subjects or causes to be subjected any citizen of the United States or other person within the jurisdiction thereof to the deprivation of any rights, privileges, or immunities secured by the Constitution and laws, shall be liable to the party injured in any action at law, suit in equity or other proper proceeding for redress.[1]

Section 1983 actions remedy the violations of all rights, privileges, or immunities secured by the federal Constitution and the federal laws if the violations are attributable to government action. The statute applies to all of the Fourteenth Amendment rights of life, liberty, property, privacy, due process, and equal protection. Also actionable are violations of the First, Third, Fourth, Fifth, Sixth, Eighth, and Ninth Amendments (see Exhibit 3-1). Corporations are considered "legal persons" under the Fourteenth

Amendment due process and equal protection clauses and as such can qualify as plaintiffs in a 1983 action.[2] The two elements that a plaintiff must allege when bringing a Section 1983 action are (1) that a person has deprived the plaintiff of a federal right and (2) that the person depriving the plaintiff of a federal right acted under color of law.

Color of Law

An action done under color of law is one done with the apparent authority of the law but one that is actually in contravention of the law.[3] Violation of a state law does not automatically give rise to a Section 1983 action. It is only when there is a violation of a federally protected right that a cause of action exists.[4] Persons who act under color of law include state officials, local officials, and private persons whose conduct is found to be state action within the meaning of the Fourteenth Amendment. Examples of medical personnel who have been held liable under Section 1983 include the following:

- A coroner who executed a certificate of commitment of a person who was alleged to be mentally ill and falsely stated that he had examined the person. *Delatti v. Genovese*, 273 F. Supp. 564 (1967).
- A medical officer while acting within his official capacity as a county health officer was held to be suable in a Section 1983 action. *Robinson v. Jordan*, 494 F. Supp. 793 (1974).
- Members of a county health commission were held to be acting under color of law. *Meredith v. Allen County War Memorial Hospital Commission*, 397 F.2d 33 (1968).

In other instances, immunity has sometimes been granted to hospital personnel such as:

- Physicians and hospital authorities who are performing examinations of individuals pursuant to a court order. *Phillips v. Singletary*, 350 F. Supp. 973 (1972).
- Hospital personnel who are carrying out orders from a court for the commitment of a person who has been adjudicated insane. *Campbell v. Glenwood Hills Hospital, Inc.*, 224 F. Supp. 27 (1963).

Absent the finding of state action the conduct of a private person, no matter how wrong or discriminatory, is not actionable under Section 1983.

State Action

Except for the Thirteenth Amendment, the guarantees of the Constitution apply only to national and state government action. Under Section 1983, state action refers to the actions of state and local governments, which often includes the agencies, boards, and commissions that carry out the government's business. In *Morrell v. Department of Social Services*, 436 U.S. 658 (1978), the Court ruled that municipalities and local government units are among those entities to which Section 1983 applies. It indicated that local governing bodies can be sued directly for monetary, declaratory, and injunctive relief, when the action alleged to be unconstitutional implements or executes policy statements or ordinances, regulations, or decisions officially adopted or promulgated by that body's officers. It also concluded that a Section 1983 action may be based on local government custom even though such custom has not received formal approval through the governing body's official decision-making channel. By way of dictum it added, however, that the local governments could not be sued for an injury inflicted solely by its employees or agents. In 1985, the Court in *Oklahoma City v. Tuttle*, 1055 S.Ct. 2427 (1985), reaffirmed the *Morrell* holding that the injuries inflicted must be pursuant to policy or custom of the municipality and not on a theory of *respondeat superior*, which holds the employer responsible for the actions of its employees. This attitude also prevails in private sector litigation. For example, in *Greene v. St. Elizabeth's Hospital*, 487 N.E. 2d 268 (1985), the court of appeals overturned a Human Rights Commission decision that had found a hospital guilty of racial discrimination. The court held that the hospital could not be held liable for the doctor's discriminatory remarks on the basis that it employed the offending doctor, without a finding that the hospital in some way encouraged, condoned, or approved of his illegal acts.

The public sector of the health care industry is subject to Section 1983 actions for violations of patients' or employees' rights. The actions of federal, state, and county hospitals and those of community and public health agencies are considered to be state action for the purposes of Section 1983 litigation. Nurse managers should also know that the courts, under certain circumstances, have found state action in the conduct of private hospitals and private persons.

Private Conduct

Courts have held that the conduct of private parties constitutes state action in situations in which (1) the privately owned corporations have much private power that is attributable to benefits provided by government, (2) the government is significantly intertwined with private groups, and (3) some of the functions performed by these groups are so public in character as to remain essentially governmental even when performed by a private actor.[5] Judicial review of private conduct for the purposes of determining state action revolves around the following five questions or tests:[6]

1. Is the activity a public function?
2. Is the activity significantly or substantially financed with government or public funds?
3. Is the government so significantly involved with the private actions as to make the government responsible for the private conduct?
4. Has the government approved, authorized, or significantly encouraged the challenged conduct so as to be considered responsible for it?
5. Has a private party acted jointly with the state or a state official in wrongful conduct?

These criteria individually or in combination have been used by the courts to review plaintiffs' claims that the conduct of private health care providers should be considered state action and subject to Section 1983 remedies. Courts have found private action to be state action when

- A private hospital received public funds and was found to be subject to pervasive government regulation concerning its operation. *Holmes v. Silver Cross Hospital*, 340 F. Supp. 125 (1972).
- A private hospital had a monopoly in the county. *O'Neill v. Grayson County War Memorial Hospital*, 472 F.2d 1140 (1973).
- A private hospital's policy against abortion rested on what was believed to be a compulsion of state law and the hospital received Hill-Burton funds. *Doe v. Charleston Area Medical Center Inc.*, 529 F.2d 638 (1975).
- A private hospital, pursuant to a contract with the state, provided medical care to involuntarily committed mental patients. *Lombard v. Eunice Kennedy Shriver Center*, 556 F. Supp. 677 (D. Mass. 1983).
- A private hospital's utilization review committee made the determination as to whether a Medicare patient's stay in the hospital is medically necessary. State action is attributed to the hospital because a negative decision by the committee results in the termination of Medicare benefits. *Kramer v. Heckler*, 737 F.2d 214 (1984).

In recent years the courts have been reluctant to find that the actions of a private hospital constitute state action. In *Blum v. Yaretsky*, 102 S.Ct. 277 (1982), the court held that no state action existed when a nursing home discharged and transferred Medicaid patients without a hearing, even though the decision to discharge and transfer resulted in the reduction or termination of the patient's Medicaid benefits. In addition, the court refused to recognize a public function even though the home was state subsidized and the state paid the medical expenses of 90 percent of the patients.

The view that receipt of any taxpayer funds should justify a finding of state action has not prevailed.[7] The courts have not found state action for private hospitals that receive Hill-Burton[8] or Medicare and Medicaid funding.[9] Although both the public function theory and the presence of extensive regulation have led some courts to rule that private hospitals were acting under color of law and subject to Section 1983 actions, no one factor such as receipt of federal funds, tax exemptions, or licensure requirements can achieve this result.[10] There appears to be no precise formula for determining what combination of factors will result in a finding that private conduct constitutes state action within the meaning of the Fourteenth Amendment.[11]

FREEDOM OF RELIGION

The First Amendment states that "Congress shall make no law respecting an establishment of religion, or prohibiting the free exercise thereof . . ." (see Exhibit 3-1). The antiestablishment clause has been interpreted by the courts to prohibit the preferential treatment of any particular sect or religion by the government and to require the separation of church and state.[12] The limitation of the free exercise clause has been interpreted to prevent compulsory acceptance of any religion or form of worship and conversely to safeguard the individual's free choice of any form of religion.[13] This protection was restricted in 1878 when the Court in *Reynolds v. United States*, 98 U.S. 145 (1878), held that the guarantee of religious freedom did not embrace actions that are "in violation of social duties and subversive of good order." The free exercise of religion was held to be a right protected by the Fourteenth Amendment and therefore applicable to the states in *Cantwell v. Connecticut*, 310 U.S. 296 (1940), when the Court struck down a state statute as violating the right of religious freedom. The antiestablishment clause was held to be part of the Fourteenth Amendment rights and applicable to the states in *Everson v. Board of Education*, 330 U.S. 1 (1947). The scope of constitutional protection of religion continues to be reviewed and defined. In 1985, in *Wallace v. Jaffree*, 472 U.S. 38 (1985), the Court held a silent prayer law unconstitutional stating that the First Amendment guarantee of freedom of religion "was adopted to curtail the power of Congress to interfere with the individual's freedom to believe, to worship and to express himself in accordance with the dictates of his own conscience."[14]

Right To Refuse Treatment

State action that results in the violation of the guarantee of freedom of religion can be redressed under Section 1983 of the Civil Rights Act of 1871. For example, in *Winters v. Miller*, 446 F.2d 65, *cert. denied* 404 U.S. 985 (1971), the court held that a psychiatric patient subjected to forced medication and treatment in violation of her freedom of religion had a cause of action under 42 U.S.C. § 1983. The court indicated that before a patient's constitutional right to exercise religious views can be infringed on by the state, a compelling interest must be present. In this case, the patient had given the hospital and the doctor notice that she was a Christian Scientist and had refused all medication and treatment because of her religious beliefs. In reaching their decision, the court indicated that they found "no evidence . . . that in forcing the unwanted medication on Miss. Winters, the state was in any way protecting the interests of society or even a third party."

The patient's right to refuse treatment on the basis of religious freedom had been litigated mainly in the context of Jehovah's Witnesses refusing blood transfusions and Christian Scientists refusing all forms of treatment. In these situations the hospital and the physician are faced with a seriously ill or dying patient who is conscious and will not consent to lifesaving treatment and the hospital seeks an opinion and instructions from the court. The courts have consistently required the state to prove a compelling interest that will justify the administration of the transfusion or treatment over the patient's refusal.

Patient's Refusal Upheld

In *Erickson v. Dilgard*, 252 N.Y. S.2d 705 (1962), the court ruled that a competent adult patient who had agreed to surgery could make the decision to refuse a transfusion even though it seems unreasonable to medical experts. The court in *In re Brooks Estate*, 205 N.E. 435 (1965), held that a competent adult with no minor children could not be compelled to accept a blood transfusion in the absence of some danger to the public health, welfare, or morals. In this case the patient, aware of the consequences, had signed a waiver releasing the hospital and the physician from liability related to her refusal to accept the transfusion. In *In re Osborne*, 294 A.2d 372 (1972), the court upheld the refusal of a patient who had two young children and, aware of the consequences of his refusal, had made adequate financial arrangements for the future care of the children. The court had suggested that the state's concern for the welfare of the children of patients refusing treatment could represent a compelling overriding state interest. In 1985, the Florida Appellate Court, in *St. Mary's Hospital v. Ramsey*, 465 So. 2d 666 (1985), held that a competent adult has the right to refuse a blood transfusion regardless of whether such refusal arises from religious beliefs, fear of adverse reaction, or cost. The court also ruled that the medical authorities could not be held criminally liable if death occurs. The trend is clearly toward judicial recognition of the patient's right to refuse treatment.

Patient's Refusal Overturned

The courts have overridden the patient's or parent's objections in situations in which:

- The patients have indicated that they would not consent to but neither would they resist the transfusion if ordered by the court.[15]
- The patient is a pregnant woman and the treatment is necessary to preserve her life and that of the fetus.[16]
- The patient is a pregnant woman and the treatment is necessary to preserve the life of the fetus.[17]
- The patient is a minor who is not terminally ill but has a life-threatening condition.[18]
- The patient is a minor who is not terminally ill but requires transfusions prior to or during elective or corrective surgery.[19]
- The state's interest in finding the cause of a child's death outweighed the father's religious objections to an autopsy.[20]

The constitutional guarantee of freedom of religion allows patients to refuse treatment that infringes on their religious beliefs. If the state cannot prove a compelling state interest, the patient's right to refuse will be upheld by the courts. Patients can also refuse treatment based on their constitutional right to privacy and their common law right to be free from nonconsensual touching. These two areas that form the basis for the majority of the litigation surrounding the patient's right to refuse or terminate the use of life-support systems will be discussed in Chapter 6 (Privacy: Expanding Constitutional Rights) and Chapter 14 (Consent).

RELIGIOUS DISCRIMINATION IN EMPLOYMENT

Title VII of the Civil Rights Act of 1964, 42 U.S.C. § 2000e, requires that an employer practice nondiscrimination "plus" make "reasonable accommodation" (i.e., adjustments to work schedules) to both applicant's and employee's religious practices. Employers need not make accommodation if doing so would cause "undue hardship" on their business. In reaching a decision as to what constitutes "undue hardship" for the employer the court must consider the facts of each case. In *Brenner v. Diagnostic Center Hospital*, 671 F.2d 141 (1982), the court determined that reasonable accommodation did not require an employer to significantly increase costs, decrease efficiency and service, or unfairly impose on other employees. There are certain organizations that are not bound by the Title VII prohibition of religious discrimination. Title VII contains an exemption applicable to "a religious corporation, association, educational institution or society with respect to the employment of individuals of a particular religion to perform work connected with carrying on by such corporation, association, educational institution or society of its activities."

Conscience Clause

Nurses who are employed by private employers and refuse to participate in abortions, sterilizations, or other procedures because of moral or ethical convictions run the risk of disciplinary action by their employers. Several states have enacted "conscience clause" legislation, which gives nurses, physicians, and other hospital personnel the right to refuse to participate in procedures that violate their ethical and moral principles. These laws also prohibit the employer from discriminating against them for exercising their right to refuse. This issue has been litigated by nurses. In 1980, a New Jersey Court ruled that a hospital did not discriminate against a nurse who refused to participate in an abortion when they transferred her, without changing her seniority, pay, or shift from obstetrics to a medical-surgical unit.[21] In a 1985 case, a registered nurse, who was also a Roman Catholic nun, filed a Title VII action claiming that the hospital had violated her freedom of religion and equal protection rights because they had transferred her off the obstetrics unit in order to lessen her contact with abortion patients. The court, finding that she had been reassigned to obstetrics and reimbursed for lost pay, dismissed her suit on the grounds that she had suffered no damages.[22]

NLRA Religious Exemption

The National Labor Relations Act, 29 U.S.C. § 169 (1982), provides that an employee who is a member of, and adheres to the established teachings of, a bona fide religion that objects to joining or supporting labor organizations shall not be required to join or financially support such an organization as a condition of employment. The objector-employees, however, may be required, by the collective bargaining contract, to pay a sum equal to the union dues to a nonreligious, nonlabor organization or charitable fund. In addition, the union is authorized to charge the objector-employees reasonable costs when they request that the labor organization use its grievance procedure on their behalf.

FREEDOM OF SPEECH

The First Amendment states that "Congress shall make no law . . . abridging the freedom of speech or of the press" (see Exhibit 3-1). This prohibition applied only to the federal government until 1925 when the Court in *Gitlow v. New York*, 268 U.S. 652 (1925), declared that freedom of speech and freedom of the press were among the "fundamental personal rights and 'liberties' protected by the due process clause of the Fourteenth Amendment from impairment by the states." Constitutional freedom of speech guarantees the right of a person to express opinions and facts uncontrolled by any censorship or restriction of government. In addition to protecting the right to oral communication, the amendment has also been interpreted to include activities such as peaceful picketing[23] and certain forms of expression that are referred to as symbolic speech. Like picketing, symbolic speech constitutes *speech plus,* a term that refers to forms of expression that combine both speech and nonspeech elements. In *Tinker v. Des Moines Independent Com. Sch. Dist.*, 393 U.S. 503 (1969), the Court stated that the wearing of armbands for the purpose of expressing certain views is a type of symbolic act that is within the free speech protection of the First Amendment. There are limits to this protection. For example, in 1974 the Court in *Smith v. United States*, 502 F.2d 512 (1974), held that the First Amendment protection did not extend to the wearing of a peace pin by a Veteran's Hospital staff psychologist while on duty working with emotionally disturbed veterans.

The First Amendment applies only to the federal and state government. It does not prohibit private persons from attempting to abridge free speech. As Corwin observed

> Those better placed in society are often able to silence those with whom they disagree. Losing one's job because one has expressed certain opinions or because of one's lifestyle, is nothing new. The reach of the Constitution to protect freedom of expression is sharply bounded, however, by whether the aggrieved individual is publicly or privately employed.[24]

Nurses in Public Employment

In *Pickering v. Board of Education*, 391 U.S. 563 (1968), the Court held that in respect to public employment, in each case, the right to free speech would have to be balanced against the legitimate interest of the government in promoting efficient public services, taking into account two broad considerations: (1) the character of the speech involved and (2) the potential such speech had for disrupting agency operations. The Supreme Court has further refined the principles governing the protection of free speech for public employees who claim the protection of 42 U.S.C. § 1983. In these cases, a determination must first be made as to whether the employee has spoken as a citizen on "matters of public concern" or only as an employee on "matters of personal interest." In general, public employees speaking on "matters of personal interest" are not protected by the First Amendment and will not prevail in a Section 1983 action. If the public employee is speaking as a citizen on "a matter of public concern," the court will balance the competing interests. The state's burden in justifying the employee's discharge will depend on the content and circumstances of the employee's statement.[25] In determining whether the speech is protected, the court in *McPherson v. Rankin*, 736 F.2d 175 (1984), stated that it would consider the "context, manner, time and place" of the speech or activity. In *Buschi v. Kirven*, 775 F.2d 1240 (1985), the court decided that "full consideration" must also be given to the effect of the speech or activity on the efficiency, discipline, and proper administration of the public agency.

Nurses believing they were fired by the hospital because they expressed their views or opinions have sought the freedom of speech protections of the First Amendment. In *Hitt v. North Broward Hosp. Dist.*, 387 So. 2d 482 (1984), a private duty nurse claimed she was denied access to the public hospital because she had posted flyers containing membership information about a nursing organization on the bulletin board. The public hospital did not restrict the bulletin board to administrative notices and allowed intrastaff notices with the permission of administration. The court of appeals determined that the action on the part of the hospital was retaliatory and designed to punish the nurse for posting the flyers on the bulletin board and as such constituted an impermissible abridgement of her First Amendment right to freedom of speech.

Nurses in Private Employment

In *Rozier v. St. Mary's Hospital*, 411 N.E. 2d 50 (1980), a nurse claimed retaliatory discharge for leaking information to the newspaper concerning alleged abuse and improprieties directed at the patients in the hospital. The appellate court held that the hospital was justified in terminating her employment on the basis that she lied with respect to job-related matters and also because there was no basis for her First and Fourteenth Amendment claims that her free speech was violated because the hospital was private and not subject to a "state action" claim. Nurses employed by private hospitals are not protected by the First Amendment and therefore will usually not prevail in 42 U.S.C. § 1983 actions. They may however be protected by other federal statutes that prohibit retaliation against employees who oppose discrimination by engaging in reasonable activities. For example, in *Wrighten v. Metropolitan Hosp. Inc.*, 762 F.2d 1346 (9th Cir. 1984), a federal appellate court held that a black registered nurse had stated a cause of action and could file suit against a private hospital for retaliatory discharge in violation of 42 U.S.C. § 2000e, the Civil Rights Act of 1964. The nurse had claimed she was fired because she complained about black patient care, and the court ruled that this was a protected activity under the statute. Nurses in private hospitals may also be protected by state statutes that prohibit retaliatory discharge of employees who report or complain to government agencies. For example, a New Hampshire statute states, "A nursing home licensee or administrator shall not evict, harass, dismiss or retaliate against a patient, a patient's personal representative or an employee who files a report under this subdivision."[26]

The sharp distinction between the rights of nurses in public and private hospitals with respect to freedom of speech is particularly important for nurses and nurse managers who actively assume the role of patient advocate. Nurses have a professional and ethical responsibility to protect the safety and welfare of their patients. Nurse managers should provide the opportunity and the means through which nurses can report their concerns without fear of losing their jobs.

FREEDOM FROM UNREASONABLE SEARCHES

At the Constitutional Convention of 1789, James Madison, the principal advocate of the Bill of Rights, introduced a proposal to restrict searches that was subsequently adopted with a few minor changes as the Fourth Amendment.[27] Part I of the Fourth Amendment prohibits "unreasonable searches," and Part II sets forth the conditions under which "warrants shall issue." In 1886, the Court in *Boyd v. United States*, 116 U.S. 616 (1886), determined that the provisions of the Fourth Amendment must be read in conjunction with the self-incrimination clause of the Fifth Amendment. The result is that papers or things that are seized as a result of an unreasonable search within the meaning of the Fourth Amendment cannot be received by any court as evidence against the person from whom they were seized.[28]

The prohibition applies only to abuses carried on by the government; therefore, private citizens cannot commit an "unreasonable search" within the meaning of the Fourth Amendment. Evidence turned over to a police officer by a private citizen had traditionally been judged admissible in court.[29]

Searching Hospital Patients

The court in *State v. Gans*, 454 So. 2d 655 (1984), held that the defendant's Fourth Amendment rights were not violated by a hospital emergency department employee who had searched an unconscious patient and having found a vial containing a white powder called the police and turned the vial over to them. The court reasoned that

1. The cocaine was discovered by the employee as part of his hospital duties.
2. The cocaine was placed with the patient's other belongings in a sealed envelope as required by hospital policy.
3. The phone call to the police and the subsequent turning over of the sealed envelope to the police was the act of a citizen suspecting an unlawful act.
4. There was no evidence that the hospital employee was acting as a police agent or that the hospital had an agreement with the police to search for drugs.
5. The emergency department search of an unconscious patient was not an "unreasonable search" within the meaning of the Fourth Amendment.

In this case, the search was upheld; however, this should not suggest that nurses should be allowed to call the police without any regard for hospital policy. Nurses are often required to search patients for medical reasons, such as identification and assessment of the patient's condition and for the safety of the patient and of other patients and staff. The discovery of substances that are suspected to be illegal drugs or contraband poses a particularly difficult situation. Many states have reporting laws if an individual witnesses a felony, but reporting is not required if the offense observed is a misdemeanor. Some states make it a crime to possess an illegal substance only if the amount exceeds certain statutory limits. There is an obvious need to have emergency department policies concerning the disposition of suspicious substances reviewed by hospital counsel so that the policies will be in compliance with the state law. Hospital counsel should assist the emergency department staff in developing protocols so as to avoid any actions that will result in making the hospital personnel appear to be agents of the police for the purposes of the Fourth Amendment.

In 1987, the Fifth Circuit Court of Appeals in *United States v. Borchardt*, 809 F.2d 1115 (1987), ruled on a patient's right to refuse treatment or medication that will make him vomit the illegal drugs that he has ingested. The court also ruled on the admissibility of a patient's answers to questions by nursing personnel that were overheard by the police. The patient, an inmate at a federal penitentiary, had ingested several bags of heroin. The prison infirmary staff, suspecting a drug overdose, had administered three doses of naloxone (Narcan), a drug used to reverse narcotic effects. After the third dose the patient regained consciousness and was transferred by ambulance, in the custody of two officers, to the municipal hospital. At the hospital the patient signed a treatment of consent form and, on being questioned by the nurse, told her that he had ingested heroin. His admission was overheard by an officer who was standing behind a partition. The patient then refused treatment to produce vomiting and also refused the naloxone. Because the patient's condition was deteriorating, the nurse consulted with the staff physician and subsequently administered a dose of naloxone contrary to the patient's wishes. Shortly thereafter, the patient vomited nine full bags and two burst bags of heroin. The nurse refused the patient's request that she dispose of them in the sink; instead, she turned them over to the police officers who were standing nearby. As a result the patient was indicted for possession of heroin in a federal facility, which is a violation of 18 U.S.C. § 1791(A) (2). Prior to trial the patient had filed a motion to suppress the packets of heroin as products of an unreasonable search and seizure. He also filed a motion to suppress the statements to the nurse because he had not been given the Miranda warning before he was questioned. In upholding his conviction the court stated that the

- Drugs given to prevent respiratory arrest and death and the resulting production of evidence were unexpected and incidental to the medical purpose of the treatment.
- Nurses' actions were a reasonable response to a medical emergency.
- Search was reasonable because of the existence of a life-threatening situation.
- Nurses and physicians were not law enforcement officers and therefore were not required to "Mirandize" patients before seeking information for purposes of accurate diagnosis and treatment.
- The nurse did not know that the officers were eavesdropping, and the fact that the prison officers were eavesdropping on the conversation between the patient and the nurse did not transform the conversation into an interrogation for law enforcement purposes.

The findings of this court demonstrate that when there is no concerted action between the police and the hospital personnel, the independent actions of police officers will not result in the court's finding the nurses and emergency department personnel were agents of the police. In *United States v. Newton*, 510 F.2d 1149 (1975), the court took the opposite view and held that state action existed when the hospital employees deliberately searched for evidence at the request of the police.

The Civil Rights Act of 1871, 42 U.S.C. § 1983, provides a remedy for persons whose constitutional rights are violated because of the concert of actions between private persons and public servants. In *Luker v. Nelson*, 341 F. Supp. 111 (1972), the court stated that "Private persons who would not be operating under "color of law" so far as Section 1983 is concerned, if acting alone, are within the statutes purview if they conspire with parties whose actions are deemed to be state action, and consummate the constitutional deprivation that was the object of the conspiracy."

In *Fries v. Barnes*, 618 F.2d 988 (1980), the Second Circuit Court of Appeals held that a patient had alleged a cause of action under Section 1983 for a violation of his civil rights. In this case the hospital personnel, at the request of the chief of police, turned over surgically removed shotgun fragments and tissue and blood specimens, as well as the patient's clothing to the police. These items were given to the police prior to the patient's arrest and without a search warrant. As a result the patient claimed that the hospital employees acted 'under color of state law' in a concerted action with the police that deprived him of his constitutional rights. In *Katz v. United States*, 398 U.S. 347 (1967), the Supreme Court held that the Fourth Amendment protected "people not places" and that what a person "seeks to preserve as private, even in an area open to the public, may be constitutionally protected." Under *Katz*, the person must have exhibited an actual expectation of privacy and the expectation must be one that society is prepared to recognize as reasonable. This certainly gives rise to the expectation that patients will not be subjected to nonconsensual searches by hospital personnel while in the hospital even if they are accompanied by the police.

Police Searches

Under the Fourth Amendment the police may search a person or place if they have a valid warrant issued upon a finding of probable cause. Warrantless searches may be conducted if the person consents and if the consent is given voluntarily and without intimidation. The Supreme Court has determined that a search need not be preceded by a statement from the officer that the person has the right to refuse or by any explanation of the consequences if incriminating evidence is found.[30] The implied consent statutes that have been enacted in many states in order to permit the withdrawal of blood specimens in suspected cases of driving while intoxicated have been held to be constitutional and not an infringement of the Fifth Amendment right against self-incrimination.[31] Many states have statutes that indicate which hospital employees can draw blood alcohol specimens and provide immunity from liability for those individuals who are named in the statute. Some hospitals contract with law enforcement agencies to collect blood alcohol specimens. These contracts may state that the liability is assumed by the law enforcement agency.

The procedures used by the police or their agents to obtain evidence from suspects are often the subject of judicial review. The courts will determine, first, whether the procedure used constitutes a "reasonable search" within the meaning of the Fourth Amendment and, second, whether the evidence that resulted from the search can be admitted at trial in order to gain a conviction. In 1952, in *Rochin v. California*, 342 U.S. 165 (1952), the Court held unconstitutional the attempt by police to force a defendant to regurgitate the drugs he had swallowed. The police officers first put their fingers in the patient's mouth and throat in an attempt to induce the patient to vomit; finally, they transported him to a hospital where the medical personnel pumped his stomach. Justice Frankfurter expressed the view of the Court when he wrote, "The proceedings by which this conviction was obtained do more than offend some fastidious squeamishness or private sentimentalism about combatting crime too energetically. This is conduct which shocks the conscience." Since that time, however, the Court has found a wide spectrum of body searches (i.e., rectal searches, vaginal searches) to be constitutional as long as they are supported by probable cause and are conducted under hygienic conditions, by qualified personnel.[32]

Particular attention has been focused on obtaining blood alcohol specimens from nonconsenting adults in situations where a death has occurred. In *Breithaupt v. Abram*, 252 U.S. 432 (1957), the Court ruled that blood drawn from an unconscious person following a traffic accident could be admitted into evidence if the blood was drawn after the person was arrested with probable cause to believe that the person was intoxicated. In *Schmerber v. California*, 384 U.S. 757 (1966), the Court held that blood drawn from an objecting defendant without a search warrant could be admitted into evidence if five conditions were satisfied: (1) formal arrest, (2) likelihood that the blood will produce evidence, (3) delay would lead to destruction of the evidence, (4) the test is reasonable and not medically contraindicated, and (5) the test is performed in a reasonable manner.

Court-ordered surgery is another area of vital importance to medical personnel concerned with the safety and welfare of the patient. In *United States v. Crowder*, 543 F.2d 312 (1976), *cert. denied* 492 U.S. 1062 (1977), the court approved an order authorizing the removal of a bullet from the forearm of a suspect. They determined that courts in ordering such surgery should make a finding that there is (1) a likelihood that the operation will produce useful information, (2) a minimal risk of permanent injury due to the minor nature of the operation, and (3) evidence that all procedural opportunities have been provided to the defendant prior to the final order for surgery. The court in *State v. Allen*, 291 S.E. 459 (1982), a case in which two defendants had been shot, refused to order surgery for one of the defendants. In ordering surgery for the second defendant the court added the requirement that the sheriff must be in the operating room when the bullet was removed.

Searching Hospital Employees

A hospital must consider the safety and security of its employees, patients, and visitors, and, in doing so, there are certain situations in which it is deemed necessary to stop and search an employee.[33] Nurses employed by federal and state hospitals are protected by the federal and state constitutional guarantees and the federal and state laws that apply to public employees. A private employer's right to stop and search an employee is entirely a matter of state law. The private employer's liability is not one of civil rights violations but rather a liability in tort for charges of battery or false imprisonment, which are civil actions and are discussed in Chapter 14.

NOTES

1. The Civil Rights Act of 1871, 42 U.S.C. § 1983 (Revised Statute 1979 from Act. April 20 1871; Ch. 22, § 1 17 stat. 13). Section formerly classified as Section 43 Title 8, Aliens and Nationality.

2. Chester J. Antieau, *Federal Civil Rights Act*, Civil Practice, 2nd ed., vol 1 (Rochester, N.Y.: The Lawyers Co-operative Publishing Co., 1980), 97.

3. Steven H. Gifis, *Law Dictionary* (Woodbury, N.Y.: Barron's Educational Series, 1975), 36.

4. Jerome A. Barron and Thomas C. Dienes, *Constitutional Law, Nutshell Series* (St. Paul, Minn.: West Publishing Co., 1986), 348.

5. Ibid., 349.

6. Ibid.

7. *Gilmore v. Montgomery*, 417 U.S. 556 (1976).

8. *Modaber v. Culpepper Memorial Hospital Inc.*, 674 F.2d 1023 (1982); *Carter v. Norfolk Community Hospital Assoc.*, 761 F.2d 970 (1985).

9. *Daigle v. Opelousas Health Care, Inc.*, 774 F.2d 1344 (1985).

10. *Ruffles v. Phelps Memorial Hospital*, 453 F. Supp. 1062 (1978); see also Antieau, *Federal Civil Rights Act*, 140.

11. *Burton v. Wilmington Parking Authority*, 365 U.S. 715 (1961).

12. Edward S. Corwin, *The Constitution*, 14th ed. revised by Harold W. Chase and Craig R. Ducat (Princeton, N.J.: Princeton University Press, 1978), 287.

13. Ibid., 297.

14. *Wallace v. Jaffree*, 472 U.S. 38 (1985).

15. *Application of the President and Directors of Georgetown College, Inc.*, 331 F.2d 1000 (D.C. Circuit 1964), *cert. denied* 377 U.S. 978 (1964).

16. *Raleigh Fitkin-Paul Memorial Hospital v. Anderson*, 201 A.2d 537 (1964), *cert. denied* 377 U.S. 985 (1965).

17. *In the Matter of Bentley*, Misc. No. 65-74 (D.C. Super. April 25, 1974).

18. *In the Matter of Ivey*, 319 So. 2d 53 (1975).

19. *In re Sampson*, 278 N.E.2d 918 (1972); however, in *In re Green*, 292 A.2d 387 (1972), the court refused to authorize blood transfusions for the 16-year-old son of a Jehovah's Witness so that an operation could be conducted to correct a severe spinal curvature.

20. *Snyder v. Holy Cross Hospital*, 352 A.2d 334 (1976).

21. *Jeczalick v. Valley Hospital*, No. C-2312-78 (N.J. Super. Bergen County, January 8, 1980).

22. *Ravenstahl v. Jefferson Univ. Hosp.* (D. Pa. Civ. Ac. 83-5790, March 13, 1985).

23. *Teamsters Union v. Vogt, Inc.*, 354 U.S. 284 (1957).

24. Corwin, *Constitution*, 316.

25. Antieau, *Federal Civil Rights Act*, 118.

26. N.H. R.S.A. 151:27 II (Abuse of Nursing Home Patients).

27. John H.F. Shattuck, *Rights of Privacy* (Skokie, Ill.: National Text Book Company, ACLU, 1977) 5, citing Annals of Congress (Washington, D.C., 1834), 1st Cong., 1st Sess., pp. 434–435.

28. Corwin, *Constitution*, 342.

29. *United States v. Blanton*, 479 F.2d 327 (1973).

30. *Scheneckloth v. Bustamonte,* 412 U.S. 218 (1973).

31. *Schmerber v. California,* 384 U.S. 757 (1966).

32. Corwin, *Constitution,* 351.

33. Karen Hawley Henry, *The Health Care Supervisor's Legal Guide* (Rockville, Md.: Aspen Publishers, Inc., 1984), 268.

Chapter **6**

Privacy: Expanding Constitutional Rights

The "right of privacy" was first referred to in an 1890 *Harvard Law Review* article in which Samuel D. Warren and Louis D. Brandeis surveyed cases where damages had been awarded for defamation, breach of confidence, implied contract, and invasion of a property right and concluded that many of the cases were grounded on a broader principle of privacy that deserved to be recognized.[1] The traditional right of privacy encompasses the "right to be left alone," the right to be free from unwanted publicity, and the right to control information about oneself.[2] The concept of privacy concerning information about oneself is considered to be somewhat like a property right, which creates a cause of action for invasion of privacy. The tort of invasion of privacy is recognized in the majority of states either by state statute or judicial decision (see Chapter 15, Confidentiality). In the constitutional sense, the "right of privacy" represents a particular group of interests that the Supreme Court has determined the specific guarantees of the Constitution protect. As with the rights enumerated in the Constitution, a person whose constitutional right to privacy is violated may seek redress by filing a civil rights action under 42 U.S.C. § 1983.

MARITAL PRIVACY

In 1965, the United States Supreme Court in *Griswold v. Connecticut*, 381 U.S. 479 (1965), struck down as unconstitutional a Connecticut statute that made it a crime for married couples to use contraceptives and for persons to counsel the use of contraceptives. In holding that privacy in the marital relationship was a right protected by the Constitution, the Court in effect created a new right to privacy that was related to, but different from, the privacy interests of the First and Fourth Amendments. The Court's majority and concurring opinions offered three constitutional bases for the newly acknowledged right of privacy. Justice Douglas for the majority proposed a penumbra theory. This theory stated that "any important liberty which is not specifically safeguarded by the Bill of Rights can be found in the penumbra or shadow of a specific guarantee and is thus protected as part of that guarantee."[3] The Court determined that the First, Third, Fourth, Fifth, and Ninth Amendments created "zones of privacy" that the government must respect (see Exhibit 3-1). Justice Goldberg, in a concurring opinion, argued that the right of privacy was one of those unenumerated rights suggested by the Ninth Amendment. It was also suggested that marital privacy was part of the "liberty" interest protected by the Fourteenth Amendment and that the Connecticut statute violated the due process clause of the Fourteenth Amendment.

Despite the Court's disagreement as to the origin of the constitutional "right of privacy," the *Griswold* case provided the philosophical and conceptual framework for its birth. The cases examined in this chapter demonstrate the path of judicial reasoning that expanded and extended the constitutional right of privacy to include a woman's right to an abortion and the right of a person to refuse, or request the termination of, life-support systems.

PRIVACY OF INDIVIDUALS

The right of privacy was first expanded in 1972 when the Court extended the protection to unmarried persons. In *Eisenstadt v. Baird*, 405 U.S. 438, 453 (1972), Justice Brennan declared, "If the right to privacy means anything, it is the right of the individual, married or single, to be free from unwarranted governmental intrusion into matters so fundamentally affecting a person as the decision whether to beget a child."

ABORTION

The right of privacy was again expanded in 1973 in the highly controversial landmark case of *Roe v. Wade*, 410 U.S. 113 (1973). In this case, the Court held a Texas penal abortion law unconstitutional on the grounds that it violated the due process clause of the Fourteenth Amendment because it excepted from criminality only a lifesaving procedure on behalf of the mother without regard to the stage of pregnancy and without recognition of the other interests involved. In explaining the basis for the right Justice Blackmun stated that "the right of privacy, whether founded in the Fourteenth Amendment concept of liberty and restriction upon state actions, as we feel it is, or as the District Court determined, in the Ninth Amendment reservation of rights to the people, is broad enough to encompass a woman's decision whether or not to terminate her pregnancy."

The *Roe* Court discussed the three stages of pregnancy and concluded that (1) during the first stage the decision to have an abortion is between the woman and her physician, (2) during the second stage the state can regulate the abortion procedure if the regulations are reasonably related to the mother's health, and (3) during the third stage the state could regulate or even prohibit abortions except in situations in which it was necessary to preserve the life or health of the mother. The third trimester prohibition was based on the Court's finding that, at this stage, the state had acquired a compelling interest in the fetus that could override the woman's right of privacy. In the companion decision, *Doe v. Bolton*, 410 U.S. 179 (1973), the Court declared unconstitutional preabortion requirements including residency, hospital accreditation by the Joint Commission on

Accreditation of Healthcare Organizations, medical committee approval, and mandatory medical consultation.

REMOVAL OF LIFE-SUPPORT SYSTEMS

In 1976, the Supreme Court refused to review a New Jersey Supreme Court decision that had held that the removal of artificial life support systems was permitted pursuant to the patient's right of privacy. In *Matter of Karen Quinlan*, 75 N.Y. 10, 335 A.2d 647, 662, 664 (1976), *cert. denied* 429 U.S. 922 (1976), the New Jersey court held that the right of privacy could be asserted on the patient's behalf by a guardian under the particular circumstances of the case. Chief Justice Hughes speaking for a unanimous court stated, "Presumably the right (to privacy) is broad enough to encompass a patient's decision to decline medical treatment under certain circumstances, in much the same way as it is broad enough to encompass a woman's decision to terminate a pregnancy under certain conditions." The court also declared, "We think the state's interest . . . weakens and the individual's right to privacy grows as the degree of bodily invasion increases and the prognosis dims. Ultimately there comes a point when the individual's rights overcome the state's interest."

SELF-DETERMINATION

In *Superintendent of Belchertown State School v. Saikewicz*, 370 N.E. 2d 417, 426 (1977), the Massachusetts Supreme Court used the doctrine of substituted judgment to approve the guardian's decision to withhold chemotherapy for a profoundly retarded 67-year-old man who had leukemia. The court held that the "Constitutional right to privacy, as we conceive it, is an expression of the sanctity of individual free choice and self-determination as fundamental constituents of life. The value of life as so perceived is lessened not by a decision to refuse treatment, but by the failure to allow a competent human being a right of choice." In *Bartling v. Superior Court*, 209 Cal. Rptr. 220 (Cal. App. 1984), the right of privacy as a right to self-determination was also used as the basis to override a hospital's claim that the patient's ability to make a meaningful decision to terminate life-support systems was questionable because he vacillated about the decision. In rejecting the view that the interests of the state and the medical profession outweighed the patient's interests, the court declared, "If the right of the patient to self-determination as to his own medical treatment is to have any meaning at all, it must be paramount to the interest of the hospital or doctors. The right of a competent adult patient to refuse medical treatment is a constitutionally guaranteed right which must not be abridged." The *Bartling* court specifically held that the right of a competent adult to refuse medical treatment had its origins in the right of privacy, which is guaranteed by the California constitution and the U.S. Constitution.

MINOR'S RIGHT OF PRIVACY

The right of privacy has also been expanded to include minors in certain circumstances. The Court in *Carey v. Population Services International*, 431 U.S. 678 (1977), held that minors are protected by the Constitution and possess a constitutional right of privacy but that "the power of the state to control the conduct of children reaches beyond the scope of authority over adults." Despite this recognition of the state's power to regulate the conduct of children, the courts have closely scrutinized and often overturned such legislation. For example, states cannot enact laws that

- Require parental consent to an abortion for all women under 18 years of age[4]
- Require parental notification to an abortion for minors without making provisions to exclude mature minors and situations where disclosure would not be in the minor's best interest[5]
- Prohibit the sale of contraceptives to minors[6]
- Require notice or consent to the sale of contraceptive devices by county-run family planning clinics or federally funded family planning centers[7]

The courts continue to find that a minor has constitutional rights but that these rights can, under certain circumstances, be limited by the states.

LIMITATION OF PRIVACY RIGHT

The courts have held that the "right of privacy" is a "fundamental right" that cannot be restricted or denied by the state without the showing of a compelling state interest.[8] In reviewing cases involving children and incompetent adults, the courts have found a compelling interest in the state's responsibility to provide for the welfare of its citizens.[9] In the area of contraception the courts have found no compelling interest to justify statutes denying single or married adults access to contraceptives.[10] In the area of abortion the courts have determined that in the third trimester the state has acquired a compelling interest in the fetus that could override a woman's right to privacy and justify stringent regulations or even a total prohibition of an abortion except in situations in which it is necessary to preserve the woman's life.[11]

Federal funding for abortion may create a limitation on the rights of indigent women. The Supreme Court has held that the Constitution does not require the government to provide funds for abortion. Congress can constitutionally forbid the use of federal funds to pay for abortions.[12] On the other hand, several state constitutions have been interpreted to require state funding of abortions. For example, the Massachusetts constitution has been interpreted as prohibiting the state from restricting Medicaid payments for abortions in cases in which the mother's life is endangered by the pregnancy.[13]

In reviewing cases involving the patient's claims of privacy and self-determination in refusing life-sustaining treatment or life-support mechanisms, the state has advanced five separate interests: (1) sanctity of life, (2) protection of third parties, (3) prevention of irrational self-destruction, (4) preservation of the ethical integrity of the health care providers, and (5) protection of the public health and morals.[14] It has been suggested that the state has argued these interests with limited success. There is an evolving judicial policy favoring self-determination that will make it difficult for the state to demonstrate a compelling interest in overriding the intelligent and informed decision of a competent adult to refuse treatment.[15]

Hospital and Physician Liability

As the courts continue to uphold the patient's right to refuse treatment, they are also being asked to determine the liability of the hospital nurses and physicians who accede to the patient wishes. In dismissing the criminal proceedings against the physicians in *Barber v. Superior Court*, 195 Cal. Rptr. 484, 489 (Cal. App. 1983), the court indicated that "A physician has no duty to continue treatment once it is proven ineffective. Although there may be a duty to provide life-sustaining machinery in the immediate aftermath of a cardio-respiratory arrest, there is no duty to continue its use once it has become futile in the opinion of qualified medical personnel." The court also indicated that, absent a legislative enactment, there was no need for a physician or hospital to seek prior judicial approval before a decision to withdraw treatment is made. In *St. Mary's Hospital v. Ramsey*, 465 So. 2d 666 (Fla. App. 1985), the court ruled that no civil or criminal liability could be imposed on the hospital or the doctors for acceding to the refusal of a blood transfusion by a 27-year-old man who was suffering from kidney disease. The immunity granted by the courts will make it easier for hospitals and health care providers to respect a patient's constitutional right of privacy. For a discussion of these issues in relation to the patient's right to consent, see Chapter 14.

NOTES

1. Warren and Brandeis, "The Right of Privacy," 4 *Harvard L. Rev.* 193 (1890); see also Helen Creighton, "The Right of Privacy: Cases and Research Problems," *Supervisor Nurse* 8 (November 1977):62–64.

2. *Olmstead v. United States*, 277 U.S. 438, 478 (1972) (Brandeis, L., dissenting).

3. Edward S. Corwin, *The Constitution*, 14th ed., revised by Harold W. Chase and Craig R. Ducat (Princeton, N.J.: Princeton University Press, 1978), 441.

4. *Planned Parenthood of Central Missouri v. Danforth*, 428 U.S. 52 (1976).

5. *H.L. v. Matheson*, 450 U.S. 398 (1983); the court held that the Utah law requiring that parents be informed of a minor's request for an abortion was constitutional; however, the court declined to rule on whether it would be constitutional if applied to a mature minor.

6. *Carey v. Population Services International*, 431 U.S. 678 (1977).

7. *Doe v. Pickett*, 480 F. Supp. 1218 (1979), federally funded center; *Doe v. Irving*, 615 F.2d 1162 (1980), county run family planning clinic.

8. *Griswold v. Connecticut*, 381 U.S. 479 (1965).

9. *Roe v. Wade*, 410 U.S. 113 (1973).

10. *Griswold v. Connecticut*, 381 U.S. 479 (1965).

11. *Roe v. Wade*, 410 U.S. 113 (1973).

12. *Harris v. McRae*, 448 U.S. 297 (1980).

13. *Moe v. Secretary of Admin. Fin.*, 417 N.E.2d, 388 (1981).

14. Cantor, "A Patient's Decision," 26 *Rutgers Law Review* 228 (1973); see also Robert D. Miller, *Problems of Hospital Law* (Rockville, Md.: Aspen Publishers, Inc., 1983), 229–264.

15. La Rene Oliver Frey, "The Right To Refuse To Treat a Competent Adult Who Refuses Treatment To Prolong Life," 31 *Medical Trial Quarterly* 432 (1985).

Chapter 7

Freedom from Discrimination

CONSTITUTIONAL PROTECTION

The constitutional rights to due process and equal protection guaranteed by the Fifth and Fourteenth Amendments have been interpreted by the courts and the legislatures as prohibiting discrimination on the basis of race, color, national origin, religion, sex, age, pregnancy, handicap, or veteran status. The Constitution prohibits only government action, which, under the Civil Rights Act of 1871, 42 U.S.C. § 1983, means federal, state, or public entities and private agencies whose business is so intertwined with the government as to be considered state action. (See Chapter 5 for a discussion of state action.) In the context of the health care industry, the mere receipt of Medicare or other federal funds by private hospitals will not generally result in a court ruling that state action exists for the purposes of a 42 U.S.C. § 1983 action. As a result, claims of discrimination against a private hospital that are based solely on the Constitution or on a Section 1983 action will not meet with much success. There are, however, a number of other federal and state civil rights statutes that prohibit discrimination by both public and private agencies. For example, Title VII of the Civil Rights Act of 1964, 42 U.S.C. § 2000e, a federal statute that forbids employment discrimination on the basis of race, color, religion, sex, national origin, and pregnancy covers employers in industries affecting commerce that have 15 or more employees. A New Hampshire statute, N.H. Rev. Stat. Ann. 354-A:2, that forbids employment discrimination because of age, sex, race, color, creed, marital status, physical or mental handicap, or national origin applies to all state and government employees and to employers with more than six employees.

Hospitals as private employers may be subject to a variety of federal and state laws, each addressing a different form of prohibited discrimination. In addition, the determination as to who is covered, the enforcement procedures, and the enforcement agency may be different for each statute. A detailed survey of the complex and sometimes overlapping field of federal and state civil rights legislation is beyond the scope of this book; what follows is a description of the major civil rights statutes that are applied, under certain circumstances, to private hospitals and a few examples of the types of litigation that have been maintained by health care employees under the statutes.[1]

Hospitals are particularly vulnerable to charges of discrimination when they (1) refuse to admit patients, (2) segregate patients, (3) reject applicants for employment, and (4) discipline or dismiss employees. All of these activities are covered by some type of federal and/or state legislation.

PUBLIC ACCOMMODATION

Title II of the Civil Rights Act of 1964 prohibits discrimination in restaurants and other places of public accommodation, which includes the cafeteria or restaurant in a hospital. Some states specifically include hospitals within their definition of "public places of accommodation, resort, or amusement." The Massachusetts statute includes hospitals but exempts places owned or operated by any religious, racial, or denominational institution or organization as well as any organization operated for charitable or educational purposes.[2]

RACE, COLOR, NATIONAL ORIGIN

Title VI of the Civil Rights Act of 1964 forbids discrimination on the basis of race, color, or national origin in any institution that receives federal financial assistance.[3] Guidelines published by the Department of Health and Human Services (HHS) pursuant to the statute prohibit the practice of discrimination by any hospital or agency receiving money under any HHS program. This includes all hospitals that are "providers of service" receiving federal funds under Medicare legislation.[4] Medicare and Medicaid and many other federal, state, and local financial assistance programs require, as a condition of participation, affirmative assurances that a hospital will not consider race or ethnic background in admission policies or in the provision of services. Federal statutes are enforced by the federal agency or department that provides the financial assistance. The U.S. attorney general has the responsibility of coordinating the enforcement activities of all of the agencies.

HANDICAP

The Rehabilitation Act of 1973 is a series of laws enacted to assist handicapped persons.[5] Section 504 covers recipients of federal financial assistance and provides that qualified individuals must not be denied the benefits of, or participation in, such programs. The Medicare and Medicaid programs are among the 200 or more programs that the HHS regulations consider as "federal financial assistance." The applicability of section 504 to hospital patient services has generally been accepted; however, the HHS regulations and their attempt to regulate employment practices have been challenged in the courts. The litigation has resulted in two opposing court decisions. In 1978, the Fourth Circuit Court of Appeals ruled that the institution must receive federal financial assistance, "for the purpose of employment," before Section 504 can be applied to the employment decisions of the institution. Other courts have also taken this position; however, in 1982, the Eleventh Circuit Court of Appeals adopted the opposite position, holding that section 504 can be applied to prohibit discrimination on the basis of handicap for both the patient services and the employment practices of hospitals. In 1984, the Supreme Court ruled that any entity receiving federal financial assistance may not discriminate in either services or employment practices.[6] It did not, however, resolve the issue as to whether Medicare and Medicaid constitute "federal financial assistance." One federal court has held that Medicaid is payment for services rendered, not financial assistance, whereas another has ruled that federal financial assistance requires payments in excess of value received.[7] Commentators warn hospitals that "HHS may not have jurisdiction to regulate your facility under section 504, you should not automatically assume this jurisdiction exists, and assistance should be sought if a handicap discrimination suit is filed."[8]

Section 504 of the Rehabilitation Act defines a "qualified handicapped person" with respect to employment, as one who, "with reasonable accommodation can perform the essential functions of the job in question."[9] Activities susceptible to employer discrimination are listed in the regulations and include hiring, upgrading, promotion, and fringe benefits.[10] In *Schor v. St. Francis Hospital*, 490 N.Y.S. 2d 785 (1985), the court upheld the decision of the state division of human rights that a hospital had not engaged in unlawful discrimination when it rejected the application of a nurse for employment as an intravenous nurse. The applicant, who had admitted she was unable to lift more than 15 pounds, was rejected because the hospital regularly required intravenous nurses to substitute for absent or vacationing staff nurses. These nursing positions routinely require the use of physical strength in providing patient care and in handling equipment. Hospitals are not obligated to accept every handicapped applicant; on the other hand, they cannot deny employment to a handicapped person simply because of the handicap. Hospitals are required to reasonably modify their programs or facilities to meet the needs of the handicapped. The regulations allow hospitals to deny benefits or participation to a handicapped person if the hospital can demonstrate that accommodating such a person would result in "undue hardship" on the operation of the program.[11] Factors considered in the determination of "undue hardship" include the overall size of the program, the type of business, and the nature and cost of the accommodation. The Office of Civil Rights (OCR), within the HHS, has the responsibility of ensuring compliance with section 504. The OCR, through its regional field offices, receives complaints, conducts investigations, and initially attempts to obtain compliance by conciliation and settlement of claims. If unsuccessful, the OCR can start proceedings to withhold federal assistance from a facility or it can refer the matter to the Department of Justice, where the attorney general may file a suit against the agency to obtain compliance with the law.[12]

AGE

The Age Discrimination Act, 29 U.S.C. §§ 621–624 (1975), prohibits discrimination because of age against applicants or employees who are between 40 and 70 years old. The law applies to private employers in industries affecting commerce where 20 or more workers are employed during at least 20 weeks in the current or prior year. Federal and state employees are also covered by the statute. There are exceptions for bona fide occupational qualifications related to age, certain apprenticeship programs, and bona fide seniority retirement and benefit systems. In 1979, responsibility for enforcement of the statute was transferred from the Department of Labor to the Equal Employment Opportunity Commission (see Chapter 9, Administrative Agencies).

Buckley v. Corp. of America, 758 F.2d 1525 (1985), is an interesting example of the type of behavior that could subject a hospital to suit based on age discrimination. The plaintiff, a 62-year-old day-shift supervisor, sued the hospital, charging she was terminated because of her age and that the termination was prohibited by the Age Discrimination in Employment Act. The plaintiff quoted the hospital's recently hired administrator as saying that the hospital needed ''new blood.'' She also testified that he had expressed surprise at the longevity of the staff and had indicated that he wanted to attract younger physicians and nurses. She also claimed that he made her work intolerable by having people check up on her and report to him. The administrator had stated that she was under stress because of her advanced age. Eventually she was removed from her supervisory position and was terminated when she refused to accept a staff nurse position. Her supervisory position was eventually filled by a 45-year-old nurse. The appellate court reversed a directed verdict in favor of the hospital and returned the case for trial.

EQUAL PAY

The Equal Pay Act of 1963, 29 U.S.C. §§ 201–209, a subsection of the Fair Labor Standards Act (wage and hour law), prohibits an employer from discriminating in wage payments to employees on the basis of sex for jobs that require substantially similar skill, effort, responsibility, and working conditions in the same workplace. The statute permits wage differentials if they are based on bona fide systems of seniority, merit, output, or some business factors other than sex. Hospitals, as private employers covered by the Fair Labor Standards Act, are also subject to the Equal Pay Act. The question of whether public employees are covered by the law has not been conclusively decided by the Supreme Court; however, most lower courts[13] and the Department of Labor's Wage and Hour Division[14] have taken the position that public employees are covered by the Equal Pay Act. The agency responsible for enforcing the law is the Equal Employment Opportunity Commission.

EMPLOYMENT DISCRIMINATION

Title VII of the Civil Rights Act of 1964, 42 U.S.C. § 2000e, forbids discrimination in employment on the basis of race, color, religion, sex, or national origin. A 1978 amendment to the law added the requirement that disabilities resulting from pregnancy and childbirth be treated the same as other disabilities for employment-related purposes.[15] Title VII forbids discriminatory preferences for any protected class, majority, or minority and requires the removal of artificial, arbitrary, and unnecessary barriers to employment when they discriminate against protected groups. The statute covers employers in industries affecting interstate commerce that employ 15 or more employees and includes employment agencies, unions, and joint labor-management apprenticeship or training committees. In 1972, the act was amended to include state and local government employers and a special provision requiring nondiscrimination in federal employment.[16]

Proving Discrimination

A party who files a Title VII suit must prove a *prima facie* case of discrimination, which means the plaintiff must allege facts that, if true, would establish unlawful employment discrimination. Three theories used to prove unlawful discrimination include charges of the following:[17]

1. Disparate treatment, when plaintiffs attempt to demonstrate that they were treated differently from other employees or applicants because of race, sex, national origin, or religion
2. Disparate impact, when plaintiffs attempt to demonstrate that an employer's practices, which may be facially neutral (i.e., written test), in fact operate to the disadvantage of a protected class
3. Past discrimination, when the plaintiffs attempt to prove that they are in a disadvantageous position because of prior discriminatory practices

Disproving Discrimination

A plaintiff's charge of unlawful discrimination can be rebutted by the employer submitting evidence establishing a defense. Depending on the theory of discrimination, employers' defenses of Title VII charges can include the following:

- Demonstrating that a neutral practice (i.e., written test) does not have a more adverse effect on the plaintiff and other members of their race, national origin, sex, etc.
- Establishing sound business reasons for actions the plaintiff is complaining of and demonstrating that no alternative measures, having less or no adverse impact on the protected class, would have achieved the same results.
- Establishing that national origin, religion, or sex is a bona fide occupational qualification that is reasonably necessary to perform the job correctly. This defense is narrowly construed and cannot be used in race discrimination cases. Under this theory, courts have ruled that patient preferences and patients' privacy rights permit a hospital to deny a male nurse's request to work in the obstetrics and gynecology department.[18] They have also ruled that a hospital's requirement that all employees have some facility in the English language is a bona fide occupational qualification capable of defeating a claim of discrimination based on national origin.[19]
- Demonstrating that the employee's facts are not true and offering alternative explanations and evidence for the employee's termination, such as unsatisfactory performance or inappropriate conduct.[20]

SEXUAL HARASSMENT

Sexual harassment is considered unacceptable behavior in the workplace. Within the past few years the Title VII interpretation of sexual discrimination has been expanded to include sexual harassment. On November 10, 1980, the Equal Employment Opportunity Commission declared "harassment on the basis of sex" to be a violation of section 703 of Title VII of the Civil Rights Act of 1964. The commission has published guidelines that require employers to take affirmative steps to eliminate improper sexual conduct on the job.[21] Of particular importance to hospitals is the section of the guidelines that holds an employer liable for sexual harassment in the workplace by "non-employees." According to the guidelines, employers will be held legally liable if they know or should have known of the harassment and fail to take immediate and appropriate corrective action. This could be interpreted as holding the hospital liable for sexual harassment of its employees by nonemployees, including the medical staff, by employees of contractual services such as security, and even by the patients.[22]

PATIENT ADVOCACY

Title VII protects from employer retaliation employees who oppose discrimination by reasonable action. Under 42 U.S.C. § 2000e-3, an employer cannot discriminate against an employee "because he has opposed any practice made an unlawful practice by this subchapter" or "because he made a charge, testified or assisted or participated in any manner in an investigation, proceeding or hearing under this chapter." In *Wrighten v. Metropolitan Hospitals, Inc.*, 726 F.2d 1346 (1984), the court ruled that a black registered nurse's complaints about black patient care were protected under the statute's nonretaliation clause. The court found that the evidence indicated that the hospital had retaliated against the nurse for engaging in a protected activity. In reaching their decision, the court declared, "By advocating the proper care of her patients however, Wrighten was fulfilling her duties as a nurse. Patient advocacy by a nurse is not insubordination."[23] The court determined that she did not impede the goals of the hospital by advocating good patient care, nor did she abuse her duty as a nurse by advocating the needs of her patients. Patient advocacy by a nurse that may be viewed as insubordination by the employer does not necessarily remove the nurse from the protection of 42 U.S.C. § 2000e.

Title VII is the foundation statute for modern civil rights legislation. It is of utmost importance to hospitals and to nurse managers because it reaches out to the hospital as a public or private employer and protects employees in a variety of areas and activities.

NOTES

1. For a detailed examination of Civil Rights Legislation and Labor Law, see Karen Hawley Henry, *The Health Care Supervisor's Legal Guide* (Rockville, Md.: Aspen Publishers, Inc., 1984).
2. (Massachusetts Civil Rights Statute) Mass. Gen. Laws Ann., ch. 151-B.
3. 42 U.S.C. § 2000d–2000d-6 (1976 and Supp. IV, 1980).
4. 45 C.F.R. § 80.

5. 29 U.S.C. §§ 791–794.

6. *Consolidated Rail Corp. v. Darrone*, 465 U.S. 624 (1984).

7. *Trageser v. Libbie Rehabilitation Center, Inc.*, 462 F. Supp. 424 (E.D. Va. 1977), *aff'd on other grounds*, 590 F.2d 87 (4th Cir. 1978), *cert. denied*, 99 S.Ct. 2895 (1979); *Consolidated v. Darrone*, 465 U.S. 624 (1984).

8. Henry, *Health Care Supervisor's Legal Guide*, 208.

9. 45 C.F.R. § 84.3 (k)(1).

10. 45 C.F.R. § 84.11 (b).

11. 45 C.F.R. § 84.12 (c).

12. 45 C.F.R. § 84.61; 45 C.F.R. § 80.6-10.

13. *National League of Cities v. Usery*, 426 U.S. 833 (1976), struck down an amendment to the Fair Labor Standards Act making state and local governments subject to minimum wage and overtime requirements.

14. Wage and Hour Interpretive Bulletin 29 C.F.R. § 775.2 (e); Labor Department Wage and Hour Division 29 U.S.C. § 206 (d) (1).

15. 42 U.S.C. § 2000e (k).

16. 42 U.S.C. § 2000e-16.

17. Henry, *Health Care Supervisor's Legal Guide*, 174–175.

18. *Backus v. Baptist Medical Center*, 510 F. Supp. 1191 (E.D. Ark. 1981), *vacated as moot*, 671 F.2d 1100 (8th Cir. 1982).

19. *Garcia v. Rush Presbyterian Medical Center*, 600 F.2d 1217 (7th Cir. 1981).

20. Henry, *Health Care Supervisor's Legal Guide*, 175–176.

21. 29 C.F.R. § 1604.11 (1982).

22. Caryn S. Rosen, "Sexual Harassment and Health Care Policy," 31 *Medical Trial Technique Quarterly* 350 (1985).

23. *Wrighten v. Metropolitan Hospitals, Inc.*, 726 F.2d 1346, 1357 (1984).

Appendix II

Implications for Nurse Managers

Part II has provided an explanation of the substance and process of constitutional law and an introduction to the areas of law that are most relevant to nurse managers as health care providers. Constitutional law was purposely selected as the first area of law in this book because it forms the foundation of all other federal and state law and because it affects nurse managers as health care professionals and as private citizens. Constitutional law is extremely complex, and its proper application is dependent on a specialized knowledge of judicial interpretation and an understanding of government legislation and government regulation. The practice of constitutional law is the responsibility of legal professionals, and it is their advice that should be sought when hospitals and private individuals encounter problems in these areas. Nurse managers, as health care specialists, need (1) a basic understanding of the constitutional principles, (2) an awareness of the court decisions affecting hospitals and health care professionals, and (3) an ability to identify and interpret the federal and state laws and regulations that apply to their nursing management and employment situation. Nurse managers who understand the Constitution and the remedies that are available through civil rights legislation and litigation will be better prepared to participate in the development and implementation of health care policies and practices that acknowledge and promote the constitutional rights of patients and employees.

An understanding of the information presented in Part II, Chapters 3 through 7, will assist nurse managers to recognize and apply the following constitutional principles:

CONSTITUTIONS LIMIT GOVERNMENT POWER

- Public employees and patients in public institutions have the full protection of the Constitution.
- Hospital policies must reflect the requirements of federal law.
- Private hospitals are sometimes held to be performing government functions.
- Private hospital personnel who conspire with the government are held to be agents of the government.

CONSTITUTIONS SOMETIMES LIMIT PRIVATE BUSINESSES

- Federal and state statutes dictate the circumstances under which private parties are subject to constitutional prohibitions.
- Absent a statute, patients and employees in private hospitals are not protected by the Constitution (e.g., the free speech protection does not apply to nurses in private hospitals to prevent their dismissal).
- Private hospital policies must reflect the requirements of the state constitution and state law.

HOSPITAL PATIENTS ARE PERSONS UNDER THE CONSTITUTION

- Patients retain all the rights of citizenship when they are voluntarily admitted to private and public hospitals.
- Patients have a right to privacy and self-determination in making their health care decisions.
- Patients have a right to be free from discrimination in hospital practices and hospital services.

NURSES ARE PERSONS UNDER THE CONSTITUTION

- Nurses have a right to be free from discrimination in all aspects of hospital employment.
- Nurses have a liberty interest in the practice of their profession and a property interest in their nursing license that cannot be denied or restricted by the state without due process.
- The scope of nursing practice and the standards of nursing practice are determined by the state's nurse practice act enacted pursuant to the state constitution's safety and welfare clause. (See Chapter 10, Nursing Practice Regulation.)
- Hospital nursing practice policies must conform to and cannot abridge or contradict the state's nurse practice act and the state board of nursing rules and regulations.

CONSTITUTIONAL RIGHTS ARE NOT SELF-EXECUTING

The constitutional guarantee of individual rights wields a force strong enough to defeat a larger, more powerful opponent; however, as with David and Goliath, it is not enough that we possess the five smooth stones—they must be thrown. Nurse managers must be prepared to respect and promote the rights of patients to assert their constitutional guarantees and protections. They must also be willing to assert their own constitutional rights when they are threatened by the unlawful conduct of an employer or the government. A constitution will only protect people who are informed, vigilant, and prepared to demand that their rights be respected. As Judge Learned Hand declared,

"Liberty lies in the hearts of men and women; when it dies there, no constitution, no law, no court can save it." (*The Spirit of Liberty*, 1944).

* * * *

LEGAL RESOURCES

FEDERAL LEGISLATION

U.S. Constitution
The Civil Rights Act of 1871, 42 U.S.C. § 1983
The Civil Rights Act of 1964, 42 U.S.C. § 2000e
The Rehabilitation Act of 1973, 29 U.S.C. §§ 791–794
The Age Discrimination in Employment Act, 29 U.S.C. §§ 621–634
The Equal Pay Act of 1963, 29 U.S.C. §§ 201–219
The Civil Rights Act of 1964, 42 U.S.C. § 2000d–2000d-6

STATE LEGISLATION

State constitution
State civil rights legislation
State labor laws
State patient's rights legislation
State nurse practice act

COURTS, AGENCIES, AND COMMISSIONS

U.S. Supreme Court
U.S. Appellate Court (your circuit, see Chapter 2, Figure 2-2)
Federal district court (your jurisdiction)
State supreme court
State appellate court (your jurisdiction)
Equal employment opportunity commission (your regional office)
State human rights commission

NURSE MANAGER'S BOOKSHELF

United Nations Universal Declaration of Human Rights
American Hospital Association, *Patient's Bill of Rights*
American Civil Liberties Union, *A Model Patient's Bill of Rights*
The National League for Nursing, *Patient's Bill of Rights*
Joint Commission on Accreditation of Healthcare Organizations, *Standards for Rights and Responsibilities of Patients*

American Nurses' Association Publications

Code for Nurses with Interpretive Statements
Affirmative Action Programming for the Nursing Profession through the American Nursing Association
Pay Equity

Guides and Manuals

Mark K. Kander and Robert F. Russell, eds. *Director of Nursing Manual: Federal Regulation and Guidelines*. Owing Mills, Md.: National Health Publishing, 1984.
Grupenhoff, John T., ed. *National Health Directory*. Rockville, Md.: Aspen Publishers, Inc., 1987.
Henry, Karen Hawley, ed. *Nursing Administration and Law Manual*. Rockville, Md.: Aspen Publishers, Inc., 1987.
Rowland, Howard S. and Rowland, Beatrice L., eds. *Hospital Legal Forms, Checklists and Guidelines*. Rockville, Md.: Aspen Publishers, Inc., 1987.

Part III

Administrative Law: Regulating Health Care

The distinctive development of our era is that the activities of the people are largely controlled by government bureaus in State and Nation. . . . A host of controversies as to private rights are no longer decided by the courts.

Chief Justice Hughes
New York Times, February 13, 1931

* * * * *

When (Lunsford) received the privilege of being licensed as a nurse in this State, she entered into a covenant to serve the people of this State with all her professional skills and power. This suit is not brought . . . by one individual who was wronged . . . but is brought by the people of the State for violation of her contractual duties to them to always act in a professional and honorable manner.

Lunsford v. Board of Medical Examiners,
648 S.W. 2d 391 (Tex. Civ. App. 3rd Dist. 1983)

Administrative Law

SOURCE

Administrative Law is the branch of public law that controls the administrative operations of government. It does so by means of the administrative agencies that are created by the Congress and the state legislatures to legislate and adjudicate specific areas of the law. Although 17 of the existing federal agencies, which possess rule making and adjudicatory power, were established before 1900, it is the creation of the Interstate Commerce Commission (ICC) in 1887 that is considered the beginning of our administrative law.[1] Commentators have stated that the ICC represents the first time that a government unit was organized "whose single concern was the well-being in a broad public sense, of a vital and national industry."[2] The ICC was endowed with both legislative and judicial functions, an action highly criticized by those favoring the traditional separation of powers.[3] Present-day administrative agencies generally have the legislative power to issue rules and regulations that have the force of law and the judicial power to decide cases and controversies within their jurisdiction.

TYPES OF AGENCIES

There are two principal types of agencies. The oldest agencies were created to deal with the concentration of economic power and were vested with regulatory authority, such as the licensing power of the Federal Communications Commission, the rate-making power of the Federal Power Commission, and the power to regulate business practices possessed by the National Labor Relations Board. The newer agencies were created for the purpose of promoting social and economic welfare and were empowered to dispense benefits such as pensions and government insurance. Beginning with the old age and unemployment insurance programs enacted by the Social Security Act of 1935, the benefits area of administrative activity has expanded to include programs such as Medicare, Medicaid, aid to dependent children, and workers' compensation.[4]

COMMISSIONS AND DEPARTMENTS

Administrative agencies can function either as independent commissions or as departments, bureaus, or agencies under the executive branch of government. Independent commissions are agencies staffed by groups of people ranging in number from 5 to 11, with all members having basically equal power. A commission is created to accomplish a specific objective, and its members are usually specialists in the area being regulated. The members of a commission are appointed by the President; however, they hold office for a fixed term. Commission members can only be removed from office for such cause as is specified in the applicable statutes. Examples of federal independent commissions include the Federal Trade Commission, created in 1914; the Federal Communications Commission, created in 1934; and the National Labor Relations Board, created in 1935.

Executive departments are headed by a Secretary, who is appointed by the President. Unlike the independent commission members who are appointed because of their particular expertise, the Secretary of an executive department is usually a politician who may or may not have experience in the specific area he or she is appointed to administer. As head of the executive branch of government, the President has absolute power to remove persons whom he has appointed to head an executive department.

The large number of programs administered by the executive departments requires extensive delegation to subordinate officials, who function within a hierarchy of specialized units. For example, funding for nursing research is available from two areas in the Department of Health and Human Services. There are funds available through the Division of Nursing, located in the Bureau of Professions, Public Health Service, Health Resource and Services Administration, and also through the newly created National Center for Nursing Research.[5] The purpose of the National Center of Nursing Research is to conduct, support, and disseminate information regarding basic and clinical nursing research, training, and other programs in patient care research. The director of the center is appointed by the secretary of HHS and reports directly to the director of the National Institutes of Health.[6]

FEDERAL AND STATE LAW

There are 51 systems of administrative law in this country: one federal system and one in each state. Federal administrative law has been centered in the power of Congress to regulate interstate commerce and has resulted in agencies with the power to regulate areas such as railroads, airlines, radio, and television. Federal activity has also been growing in the social welfare areas, with federal agencies directing retirement, survivors, disability, and hospital medical programs under federal law. Congress, however, has not totally displaced the states in the administration of the services themselves. There are a number of programs that are administered by the states with substantial federal assistance. The states have retained the primary administrative role in education, welfare assistance, and areas such as public housing and urban development.[7]

ADMINISTRATIVE PROCEDURE ACT

In 1946, Congress, concerned about what Justice Douglas called the "evolution of administrative agencies as principalities of power," passed the federal Administrative Procedure Act, as an "antidote to that development."[8] The act provided minimum standards of administrative procedures that all agencies were required to follow. Today the Administrative Procedure Act and its amendments regulate the following:[9]

- Rule making process
- Publication of information including rules, opinions, orders, and public records
- Adjudicatory process, including hearings, decisions, and the imposition of sanctions
- Method and scope of judicial review of agency actions

The Federal Administrative Procedure Act does not apply to the states; however, most states have adopted some type of administrative procedure legislation. In general, state administrative procedure laws are based on, or influenced by, either the Model State Administrative Procedure Act, approved by the American Bar Association and the National Conference on Uniform State Laws in 1946, or the Revised Model State Act, which was approved in 1961.[10]

RULE-MAKING POWER

The statute that creates an administrative agency also determines the scope of its rule-making power. Judicial review of agency rules usually begins with a determination of whether the challenged rules are within the power conferred on the agency. There are three main types of agency rules: (1) procedural, (2) interpretative, and (3) substantive.

Procedural Rules

Procedural rules are the rules that govern the procedures and practices of the agency. Agencies are legally bound by their own procedural rules, even if the rules are made informally.[11] Courts have ruled that an agency's violation of its own procedures is considered arbitrary action, which "cannot be reconciled with the fundamental principle that ours is a government of laws."[12] Under the Federal Administrative Procedure Act (APA), agencies are required to state and publish rules of procedure.[13]

Interpretative Rules

An interpretative rule is a classification of existing law or regulation. Interpretative rules advise the public of the agency's interpretation of the law that it administers. They are statements that indicate what the agency thinks the statute or regulation means.[14] The rule-making procedure prescribed by the APA does not apply to interpretative rules; however, interpretative rules must be published.

Interpretative rules are not legally binding. Their legal effect is only that of agency opinion. The statute remains the sole criterion of what the law requires or prohibits.[15] In practice, however, interpretative rules carry great weight because the courts generally defer to the administrator's expertise and experience and seldom overturn the agency's interpretation of the law.[16] Aware of the court's practice, the persons affected by an interpretative rule will generally conform to the agency's opinion.

Substantive Rules

Substantive rules implement a statute and create law by changing existing rights and obligations.[17] Substantive rules have the force of law, and the agency can compel compliance on the part of those affected by the agency's action. Under the APA, agencies are required to follow a rule-making process that involves publishing proposed new rules in the *Federal Register*.[18]

RULE-MAKING PROCEDURE

Under section 553 of the Administrative Procedure Act, agencies are required to

1. Prepare a draft regulation that reflects input from various sources such as legislators, members of the executive branch, congressional committees, officials of local and state government, and representatives of businesses, industry, professional associations and consumer groups
2. Submit the draft regulation for review at all levels of the agency in an extensive clearing process
3. Publish the draft regulation in the *Federal Register*
4. Receive written comments by interested persons. Occasionally, opportunity for comment may take the form of public hearings to obtain testimony. Some statutes, such as the Occupational Safety Act, require public hearings on proposed rules. Section 553 exempts from public participation rule making on matters related to loans, grants, benefits, and contracts; however, the Department of Health and Human Services publishes notices of proposed regulation on exempted matters and provides a period for public comment.
5. Review the public comment and, if necessary, modify the draft regulation and submit it for further internal review
6. Publish the final regulation in the *Federal Register* at least 30 days before the effective date of its application
7. Incorporate the final regulation into the *Code of Federal Regulations,* which contains only regulations in force or those for which a future effective date has been established.

An agency cannot substitute the APA procedure for one of its own invention. Unless an agency is exempt, it must follow the APA requirements in order for its rules to have the force of law.[19]

INVESTIGATIONS

Administrative agencies must have access to the factual materials that are relevant to the matters before them if they are to exercise intelligently and effectively their legislative and adjudicatory powers. Most of the information requested by an agency is obtained without compulsion by voluntary testimony and production of documents and from public records and official reports. Administrative agencies generally have the statutory authority to compel the production of information when their request for such is denied. There are three methods by which agencies can obtain information not voluntarily produced; they have the power to (1) require records and reports; (2) inspect books, records, and premises; and (3) subpoena witnesses and documents.[20]

Administrative inspections are subject to the government principle that a search of private property, without consent, is an "unreasonable search" unless authorized by a valid search warrant.[21] The methods employed by administrative agencies in seeking information from an unwilling person are subject to judicial scrutiny.

HEARINGS

"Notice and the opportunity to be heard are fundamental to due process of law."[22] A person cannot be deprived of life, liberty, or property without an opportunity to be heard in defense of these rights.[23] In the context of administrative proceedings the right to be heard turns on whether the action is one of rule making or adjudication. The Supreme Court has recognized a distinction between "administrative law proceedings for the purpose of promulgating rules and standards, . . . and proceedings designed to adjudicate disputed facts in particular cases."[24] Rule making is normally general and looks to the future, whereas adjudication is specific and looks to the past.[25]

Rule-Making Hearings

Rule-making proceedings are generally informal, resembling hearings held before legislative committees. Courts have held that the purpose of a rule-making hearing "is to allow interested parties to make useful comment, and not to allow them to assert their 'rights' to insist that a rule take a particular form."[26]

A rule-making hearing is the process by which an agency obtains information on the matter at issue. The agency is not bound by the hearing record and can look to other sources of information, including its own knowledge and expertise, in making its rulings. Not all rule making is informal; a few federal statutes require "trial type" hearings. For example, under the Food, Drug and Cosmetic Act of 1938, the agency is required to hold a public hearing before it can issue regulations fixing the identity of foods.[27] The regulations must be based "only on the substantive evidence on the record at the hearing," and the order issuing the regulation must include findings of fact, based on the record, similar to that required in adjudicatory proceedings. Trial type rule making has been criticized by jurists and lawyers.[28] They believe it "imprisons a legislative process in a formal straitjacket that is designed for an entirely different type of process'' and argue that it can substantially impair an agency's ability to provide new regulations that may be needed to protect the public.[29]

Adjudicatory Hearings

An adjudicatory hearing is a forum in which the parties to a dispute are allowed to present arguments and evidence concerning their case to an administrative decision maker. Examples of situations in which adjudicatory hearings are required include the denial of disability benefits, the elimination or reduction of welfare benefits, and the suspension or revocation of a license to practice a profession. The procedures employed by an administrative agency vary according to the agency and the type of problem. At one extreme, an adjudicatory hearing may be identical to a non-jury trial, whereas at the other extreme, it may consist only of a person's explaining his or her position in an informal manner in the administrator's office. The enabling statute that creates the agency determines the type of hearing that is required, and the courts decide which of the elements of due process apply.[30]

Administrative Due Process

The Administrative Procedure Act, 5 U.S.C. §§ 554–556, defines the due process rights that agencies are required to provide to the persons who participate in an adjudicatory hearing. These include the right to

- *Notice.* Section 554 (b) states that notice should consist of the time, place, and nature of the hearing; the legal authority and jurisdiction under which the hearing is held; and the matters of fact and law asserted.
- *Present testimonial and documentary evidence and argument.* Section 555 (d) maintains that subpoenas can be issued upon showing the "general relevance and reasonable scope of the evidence sought." Section 556 (c) 4 permits depositions to be taken, "when the ends of justice would be served."
- *Rebut adverse evidence.* Section 556 (d) states that "a party is entitled to present his case or defense by oral or documentary evidence, to submit rebuttal evidence, and to conduct such cross-examination as may be required for a full and true disclosure of the facts . . . ."
- *Appear with counsel.* Section 555 (d) states that "a person compelled to appear in person before an agency or representative thereof, is entitled to be accompanied, represented and advised by counsel or, if permitted by the agency, by other qualified representatives."
- *A complete record and a decision based solely on the record.* Section 556 (e) states that "The transcript of testimony and exhibits, together with all papers and requests filed in the proceeding, constitutes the exclusive record for decision."

JUDICIAL REVIEW

Statutes generally require that all administrative remedies be exhausted before a court will review the action of an agency.[31] This means that the agency's decision is final and that there is no further review available within the agency. A court can review the agency's decision either by a trial, a procedure that is referred to as a *de novo review*, or by direct appellate review. The type of proceeding that the plaintiff is entitled to is determined by statute. A reviewing court decides all questions of law, interprets constitutional and statutory provisions, and determines the meaning or applicability of the terms of an agency's action.[32] A reviewing court can compel an agency to act, or it can hold unlawful and set aside an agency's action. According to the Administrative Procedure Act, the courts can set aside agency actions, findings, and conclusions in circumstances in which they have been found to be

- Arbitrary, capricious, an abuse of discretion, or otherwise not in accordance with the law
- Contrary to constitutional right, power, privilege, or immunity
- In excess of statutory jurisdiction, authority, or limitation or short of statutory right
- Without observance of the procedures required by law
- Unsupported by substantial evidence
- Unwarranted by the facts to the extent that the facts are subject to a trial *de novo* by the reviewing court.[33]

Judicial review serves as a basic remedy against illegal action. It provides people aggrieved by the decision of an agency their "day in court." What can happen when the agency's decision is reviewed by the courts is illustrated by the following discussion of *Michigan Dept. of Civil Rights, ex. rel. Cornell v. Edward A. Sparrow Hospital*, 377 N.W. 2d 755 (1985).

The plaintiff in this case was employed by the hospital from July 1, 1972, until May 3, 1976, when she was fired for refusing to comply with the hospital's dress code. The hospital dress code required female employees to wear "nurse's uniforms," undergarments of a certain color and white shoes. Male employees were only required to wear "lab" coats over their street clothes. After her dismissal, the plaintiff filed charges with the Michigan Department of Civil Rights alleging her dismissal was based on illegal sex discrimination. Over the next 9 years, the agency and three courts reviewed and ruled on the plaintiff's charge against the hospital.

1976   Civil Rights Commission Referee

The referee for the Michigan Civil Rights Commission who reviewed the case ruled in favor of the hospital. The plaintiff appealed to the Civil Rights Commission.

1978   Michigan Civil Rights Commission

The Michigan Civil Rights Commission reversed the referee's findings and held that the dress code constituted unlawful discrimination on the basis of sex, in violation of the

Michigan Fair Employment Practices Act. The commission issued an order that the hospital cease and desist the illegal practice. It also ordered the hospital to reinstate the employee with backpay. The decision was appealed by the hospital to the Michigan Circuit Court.

1980   Michigan Circuit Court

The Michigan Circuit Court affirmed the Commission's finding of discrimination but reversed on the issue of backpay. The plaintiff appealed to the Michigan Appellate Court.

1982   Michigan Appellate Court

The Michigan Appellate Court upheld the discrimination finding of the Circuit Court and also upheld the withholding of backpay.[34] The decision was appealed to the Michigan Supreme Court.

1985   Michigan Supreme Court

The Michigan Supreme Court held that the hospital employee who was fired following her refusal to comply with a discriminatory dress code was entitled to an award of backpay under the Michigan Fair Employment Practices Act.[35]

After 9 years of litigation the Michigan Supreme Court reinstated the decision of the Michigan Civil Rights Commission. The right to judicial review is an important protection guaranteed by the Federal Administrative Procedure Act[36] and by the state administrative procedure acts. In practice, however, the exercise of this right can be costly and time consuming.

NOTES

1. Bernard Schwartz, *Administrative Law* (Boston: Little, Brown and Co., 1976), 17.

2. Ibid., 18.

3. Ibid., 7.

4. Ibid., 5.

5. 42 U.S.C. §§ 295, 296, 297, 298, 2891 (1982).

6. Cynthia E. Northrop and Mary E. Kelly, *Legal Issues in Nursing* (St. Louis: C.V. Mosby Co., 1987), 343.

7. Schwartz, *Administrative Law*, 24–25.

8. *Renegotiation Board v. Bannercroft Co.*, 415 U.S. 1, 34 (1974) Douglas, W., dissenting.

9. 5 U.S.C. §§ 552, 553, 554, 556, 557, 558, 701.

10. Schwartz, *Administrative Law*, 21.

11. Ibid., 159.

12. *Hammond v. Lendfest*, 398 F.2d 705, 715 (2d Cir. 1968).

13. 5 U.S.C. § 552 (a); Revised Model State Administrative Procedure Act § 2.

14. Schwartz, *Administrative Law*, 154; see also *Gibson Wine Co. v. Snyder*, 194 F.2d 239, 331 (D.C. Cir. 1952).

15. Schwartz, *Administrative Law*, 155.

16. *Brewster v. Gage*, 280 U.S. 327 (1930).

17. Schwartz, *Administrative Law*, 154.

18. 5 U.S.C. § 553.

19. Schwartz, *Administrative Law*, 166.

20. Report of Attorney General's Committee on Administrative Procedure 414 (1941).

21. *Camara v. Municipal Court*, 387 U.S. 523 (1967); see also Schwartz, *Administrative Law*, 93.

22. *Joint Anti-Fascist Refugee Committee v. McGrath*, 341 U.S. 123, 178 (1951) Douglas, W., concurring; see also, *Rees v. City of Watertown*, 19 Wall. 107, 122 (U.S. 1874).

23. *Ray v. Norseworthy*, 23 Wall. 128 (U.S. 1875).

24. *United States v. Florida East Coast Ry.*, 410 U.S. 224, 245 (1973).

25. Schwartz, *Administrative Law*, 183.

26. *Pacific Coast European Conference v. United States*, 350 F.2d 197, 205 (9th Cir. 1965), *cert. denied*, 382 U.S. 958 (1965).

27. 21 U.S.C. § 371 (e), (3).

28. *Long Island R.R. v. United States*, 318 F. Supp. 490, 495 (E.D. N.Y. 1970) J. Friendly; see also Hamilton, "Procedures for Adoption of Rules of General Applicability: The Need for Innovations in Administrative Rulemaking," 60 *Calif. L. Rev.* 1276 (1972).

29. Schwartz, *Administrative Law*, 165.

30. *Matthews v. Eldridge*, 424 U.S. 319 (1976).

31. 5 U.S.C. § 704.

32. 5 U.S.C. § 706.

33. 5 U.S.C. § 706 (1), (2).

34. *Michigan Dept. of Civil Rights ex. rel. Cornell v. Edward A. Sparrow Hospital*, 326 N.W. 2d 319 (1982).

35. *Michigan Dept. of Civil Rights ex. rel. Cornell v. Edward A. Sparrow Hospital*, 377 N.W. 2d 755 (1985).

36. 5 U.S.C. § 702; Model State Administrative Procedure Act, 5 U.S.C. § 15.

Chapter 9

Administrative Agencies

The Federal and Model State Administrative Procedure Acts define an agency as a governmental authority, board, commission, department, or office, other than the legislature or the courts, that is authorized by law to make rules or to determine contested cases.[1] Hospitals, as part of the highly regulated health care industry, are subject to the jurisdiction of a large and ever-increasing number of federal, state, and voluntary agencies.

FEDERAL AGENCIES

At the federal level, the activities authorized by an administrative statute are either administered by an independent board or commission created for that purpose or are assigned to an executive department, which in turn delegates the administrative responsibility to subordinate levels of agencies or boards. Examples of federal agencies created or assigned to regulate activities relevant to the delivery of health care services include the (1) Department of Health and Human Services, Social Security Administration (Medicaid funding); (2) Department of Labor, Occupational Safety and Health Administration, Occupational Safety and Health Review Commission (health and safety regulation); National Labor Relations Board (labor–management relations); Department of Justice, Drug Enforcement Administration (hospital registration and controlled substances records); and Equal Employment Opportunity Commission (employment discrimination).

STATE AGENCIES

States also have executive departments, commissions, boards, and agencies that regulate both the business practices and health care services provided by hospitals. The extent to which a state is involved in regulating the affairs of its citizens is usually determined by its population, its economy, and its politics. As a result, the number of administrative agencies and the scope of regulation varies from state to state. Examples of state agencies authorized to regulate some aspect of hospital services include the (1) department of health and welfare (hospital licensing); Secretary of State's office, corporate division (hospital incorporation); administrative or licensing division, board of nursing, board of medicine, board of pharmacy (licensing of professions); department of labor, workers' compensation division (workers' compensation); and public employee labor relations board, civil rights commission (civil rights complaints).

PRIVATE AGENCIES

Hospitals are also subject to regulation by the private sector. Many hospitals are accredited by the Joint Commission on Accreditation of Healthcare Organizations (Joint Commission), an organization that includes representatives from the American College of Physicians, the American College of Surgeons, the American Dental Association, and the American Medical Association. Hospital accreditation by the Joint Commission is voluntary. Hospitals seeking Joint Commission accreditation are required to participate in an intensive on-site survey that is conducted in order to determine their ability to comply with the Joint Commission's standards, which are published in their *Accreditation Manual for Hospitals*.[2]

LICENSURE AND ACCREDITATION

There are important differences between hospital licensure and hospital accreditation. Hospital licensure is granted by a government agency and is mandatory. State licensing agencies are authorized by the legislature to (1) set standards for licensure, (2) inspect hospitals to ensure compliance with the standards, (3) impose sanctions for standard violations, and, in extreme situations, (4) revoke a hospital's license. A hospital cannot operate unless it is licensed by the state.

Hospital accreditation is granted by a private agency and is not legally mandated. Voluntary accreditation is a widely accepted practice in the health care industry. For example, the Joint Commission accredits a large number of hospitals and the American Osteopathic Association (AOA) sets standards for and accredits osteopathic hospitals. Although the Joint Commission accreditation is voluntary, there are three situations in which the Joint Commission standards are recognized and/or accepted by government agencies.

1. Some states accept the Joint Commission accreditation as a basis for either full or partial licensure without requiring further inspection by the state. For example, the New Hampshire Division of Public Health is required to make annual unannounced inspections of all hospitals; however, the state inspection is waived for "acute care hospitals when the Division and the Joint Commission have agreed to joint inspection standards."[3]
2. Hospitals accredited by the Joint Commission or AOA are deemed to be in compliance with the "conditions of participation" established under Medicare (Title XVIII) and Medicaid (Title XIX) programs of the Social Security Act.

3. The standards established by the Joint Commission have been cited in several leading cases as evidence of the standard of care required by a hospital.[4]

PROFESSIONAL ORGANIZATIONS

Voluntary regulatory activities are conducted by professional organizations in three ways: (1) they set the standards of education for the professional schools and educational programs; (2) they set the standards of practice; and (3) they develop certification programs that certify individual practitioners as having advanced knowledge and skill in specialized areas of practice. Standards of practice promulgated by the American Nurses' Association (ANA) and by specialty nursing organizations, such as the Association of Critical Care Nurses and the Operating Room Nurses' Association, are used as guidelines for nursing practice and in the development of nursing quality assurance programs.[5]

CERTIFICATION

Certification is the process by which a person is recognized as having attained advanced, specialized knowledge and skills beyond what is required of the general practitioner. The person is required to meet certain performance-based criteria, which generally consists of passing a certification test. The ANA has certification programs in each area of practice, including certified nursing administration and certified nursing administration advanced. There are at least ten other specialty nursing organizations with certification programs.[6] It has been suggested that advanced certification by a national certifying agency has become so widespread that in the future it may be included among the requirements necessary for particular jobs within the field of nursing.[7]

Voluntary certification programs can be made mandatory by state law. Acting under the authority of their nursing practice acts, many states have promulgated rules requiring that nurses practicing in the expanded role be certified by a national certifying agency such as the American College of Nurse Midwives, the American Association of Nurse Anesthetists, and the American Nurses' Association.

Certification of physicians by a medical specialty board has become so widely accepted that it may be difficult to practice without such certification. Despite the trend toward certification, the Medicare "conditions of participation" forbid the absolute requirement of board certification as a criterion for granting clinical privileges. This requirement has not always been declared invalid by the courts. In 1976, an Ohio court refused to invalidate a private hospital's requirement that the physicians have board certification or completion of an approved residency before granting clinical privileges; on the other hand, a Tennessee court did invalidate the absolute requirement of board certification by a public hospital.[8] Hospitals can avoid the controversy by requiring board certification or equivalent experience, a policy that recognizes the strengths of private certification but also permits a case-by-case evaluation.[9]

AGENCY: PURPOSE, POWER, PROCESS

All government agencies are creatures of statute—they exist because the legislature created them to address a particular area of the law. Private agencies are created to accomplish the purposes that are designated in the articles of incorporation and bylaws of the agency. Nurse managers, whose responsibilities generally include the development, implementation, and evaluation of hospital policies, need to understand how those policies are affected by the rulings, regulations, and decisions of administrative agencies. It is not possible, nor is it necessary, to examine all of the public and private agencies that regulate or influence a hospital's practices or services. Nurse managers will discover that they can better understand the structure and function of any administrative agency if they develop the habit of isolating and examining the agency's purpose, power, and process. A framework for analyzing the power and process of an administrative agency is provided in Figure 9-1.

Purpose

Purpose refers to the goals and objectives that an agency is created to accomplish. The purpose of a law that has created an agency is determined by examining the following:

1. Constitutional clause (i.e., Health & Welfare, Commerce) that authorizes legislation in this area.
2. Legislature's intent in enacting the legislation
3. Words and meaning of the statute that creates the agency. Exceptions and exemptions also help to define its purpose.
4. Knowledge and expertise of the people who are appointed to serve on the agency board or commission
5. Agency decisions that interpret or clarify its purpose
6. Judicial decisions that interpret the agency's purpose

Power

Power refers to the authority that an agency is granted in order to accomplish its objectives. There are at least four grants of power in an agency structure:

1. The constitutional power that permits the legislature to enact laws in this particular area
2. The legislature's power to enact legislation that delegates its authority to an agency
3. The agency's power to promulgate rules and regulations and to adjudicate cases and controversies
4. The judicial power to review, affirm, amend, and reverse agency action

Process

Process refers to the procedure used by an agency to carry out its objectives. These include

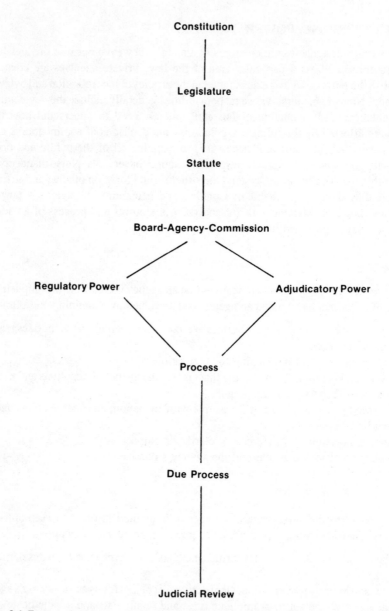

Figure 9-1 Framework of Agency Power-Process. *Source:* Copyright © Carmelle Cournoyer 1986.

1. Procedural requirements of the Administrative Procedure Act
2. Procedural requirements of the enabling statute
3. Procedure for publishing and promulgating the agency's rules and regulations
4. Procedure for beginning and conducting an adjudicatory hearing

5. Procedure for appealing agency decisions within the agency and in the courts
6. Court decisions that interpret and clarify agency procedure

The purpose, power, and process analysis is particularly useful when attempting to understand large and complex federal agencies, such as the Equal Employment Opportunity Commission and the National Labor Relations Board.

EQUAL EMPLOYMENT OPPORTUNITY COMMISSION

The Equal Employment Opportunity Commission (EEOC) was created to interpret and enforce a number of antidiscrimination statutes, including

- Title VII of the Civil Rights Act of 1964 as amended by the Equal Employment Opportunity Act of 1972, which prohibits discrimination in employment on the basis of race, color, religion, sex, or national origin.[10]
- The Equal Pay Act of 1963, which is an amendment to the Fair Labor Standards Act and requires that female and male employees be paid equal pay for equal work.[11]
- The Age Discrimination in Employment Act of 1967, which prohibits discrimination because of age toward applicants and employees who are between 40 and 70 years old.[12]

Power

The power of the EEOC includes the right to

1. Issue guidelines and regulations that contain the EEOC's interpretation of discrimination
2. Issue guidelines and regulations that notify employers of their responsibility to take affirmative steps to eliminate discrimination
3. File charges of unlawful discrimination. A charge can be filed by the person alleging discrimination, by a person on behalf of the person alleging discrimination, or by a member of the EEOC.
4. Investigate, conciliate, and settle charges of employment discrimination
5. Decide whether there is "cause" or "no cause" for believing that the employer violated Title VII
6. Advise the Charging Parties of their right to file a private lawsuit under Title VII
7. Initiate lawsuits in its own name through the Office of General Counsel.

Process

The process by which the EEOC receives, investigates, and resolves charges of employment discrimination provides the agency, the charging parties, and the employer with a variety of approaches and options for resolving the dispute. These choices of action arise during one of the following stages of the EEOC process:

1. Complaint is filed with the EEOC.
2. Employer is notified of the complaint.
3. Employer submits responses to the charge.
4. EEOC investigates the charge and issues related to the charge. The EEOC has subpoena power and can receive evidence and examine witnesses.
5. EEOC staff member visits the employer's facility.
6. A fact finding conference is held. The EEOC staff person conducts the conference and questions the parties. Attorneys for the parties can function only in an advisory capacity.
7. Employer and Charging Party are encouraged to attempt to reach a predetermination settlement; if they do so, an agreement document is drafted.
8. If no predetermination settlement is reached, the EEOC makes a determination of whether the employer violated Title VII. The EEOC staff member attempts to achieve a post-determination settlement agreement by informal conferences, conciliation, and persuasion.
9. If a post-determination settlement is reached, a written agreement is drafted that includes the consent of the employer and the Charging Party to the withdrawal of the charge.
10. If no settlement is reached, the case may be forwarded to the EEOC's General Counsel for a determination of whether the commission will file a suit against the employer in its own name.
11. A letter is sent to the Charging Party and to the employer stating that there is "cause" or "no cause" for believing that the employer violated Title VII. The letter also advises the Charging Party that they have 90 days in which to file a private lawsuit. The Charging Party may file a private lawsuit despite an EEOC finding of "no cause"; however, the agency's negative finding is admissable as evidence at trial.

Judicial Proceedings

When the Charging Party prevails in a lawsuit, courts are permitted to fashion broad remedies. A court can order the employer to change personnel policies and practices and to reinstate or promote an employee or rejected applicant. In addition, courts can order monetary awards, including backpay. They can also award reasonable attorney's fees and costs to the prevailing party. However, in order for the employer to receive attorney's fees, it must prove that the plaintiff's claim was frivolous, unreasonable, and groundless. The EEOC process is both complex and malleable, with the final decision often the result of conciliation, compromise, and consent. It is absolutely essential that all parties avail themselves of legal counsel so that they can be advised of the significance of the options and the consequences of their choices and decisions under the EEOC process.

NATIONAL LABOR RELATIONS ACT

The National Labor Relations Board (NLRB) is the federal agency responsible for interpreting and enforcing the National Labor Relations Act (NLRA), a federal statute that regulates the relationships among employers, unions, and employees. The NLRA refers to a series of federal laws that includes the Wagner Act of 1935; the Labor Management Relations Act of 1947 (Taft-Hartley Amendments), which excluded nonprofit hospital from coverage; the Labor Management Reporting and Disclosure Act of 1959 (Landrum-Griffin); and the 1974 Health Care Amendments that brought the nonprofit hospitals under the act's jurisdiction.

1974 HEALTH CARE AMENDMENTS

The 1974 Health Care Amendments[13] redefined an employer to include nonprofit health care institutions. The following amendments were enacted in recognition of the special services provided by hospitals and are intended to minimize the potential disruption or interruption of hospital services as a result of labor and management disputes.

1. Unions must give at least ten days advance notice of the date and time for a threatened strike.
2. The Federal Mediation and Conciliation Services (FMCS) has the authority to conduct mandatory mediation of contract negotiation disputes.
3. The FMCS can also appoint a Board of Inquiry to make recommendations on issues in dispute during contract negotiations.
4. Unions that wish to renegotiate collective bargaining agreements must give health care employees 90 days notice of their intention to terminate or modify the agreement as well as a 60-day notice to the FMCS. A union need only give a 30-day notice to the FMCS for new contract negotiations.
5. Employees objecting to mandatory payment of union dues on religious grounds have the option of donating equivalent monies to a nonreligious charity.

RIGHTS OF EMPLOYEES

The NLRA defines the protected rights of employees, prohibits the commission of certain unfair labor practices by employers and by unions, and establishes rules governing the determination of appropriate bargaining units and the conduct of elections. The NLRB is responsible for ensuring compliance with the Act in accordance with the enforcement and remedial provisions of Section 10.[14]

Rights guaranteed to employees under section 7 include the right to

- self-organization
- form, join, or assist labor organizations
- bargain collectively through representatives of their own choosing
- engage in concerted activities for purposes of collective bargaining or other mutual aid or protection
- refrain from any or all of the concerted activities unless the collective bargaining contract requires membership or payment of dues as a condition of employment

UNFAIR LABOR PRACTICES

The rights guaranteed by section 7 are protected by the section 8 prohibition of certain unfair labor practices. Section 8 (a) lists employer unfair labor practices as

- Restraining, coercing, or interfering with employees' rights
- Assistance to labor organizations
- Discrimination based on union membership
- Reprisals for participating in NLRB procedures
- Refusal to bargain

Section 8 (b) lists a variety of union unfair labor practices, the most common of which are

- Restraint of employees or employers
- Discrimination based on union membership
- Refusal to bargain
- Secondary boycotts
- Illegal picketing

BOARD COMPOSITION

The National Labor Relations Board (NLRB) comprises five members appointed by the President, subject to Senate confirmation.[15] Members are appointed for a 5-year term. The board operates in three member panels, and each board member has approximately 20 legal assistants who help with the preparation of opinions. The NLRB solicitor is selected by and responsible to the entire board as legal advisor and consultant. The use of the term *NLRB* generally refers to the total agency, including the Office of General Counsel, the approximately 32 regional offices, and the Division of Judges. The Taft-Hartley Amendments require strict separation of the NLRB's adjudication and prosecutorial functions.[16] The General Counsel is not appointed by the board, as is the practice with other agencies; the appointment is made by the President with the Senate's consent. The NLRA gives the General Counsel final authority over the investigation of charges filed by aggrieved persons and over the issuance of complaints and their prosecution before the board. The General Counsel's refusal to issue a complaint is not reviewable either by the board or, in general, by the courts.[17]

ELECTION PROCESS

The NLRB election process begins with the filing of a petition with the nearest NLRB office. The most common reason for filing an election petition is to determine the employees' exclusive collective bargaining representative. Elections may also be called by an employer when a union claims to represent a majority of the employees, to decertify or withdraw recognition from an existing labor organization, and to remove a union shop agreement from an already recognized labor organization. The following is a description of the steps in the petition process:

1. A petition is filed at the nearest NLRB regional office. It must be supported by a 30 percent show of interest.
2. A representation hearing is scheduled at the NLRB offices. If the employer and union consent to an election at this time, the hearing is cancelled.
3. If there is no consent, a hearing is held for the purpose of receiving evidence.
4. The Regional Director issues findings that may
   a. Direct an election on a certain date.
   b. Transfer the hearing record and the case to the NLRB in Washington.

An election is always conducted by an NLRB agent usually at the workplace. Election is by secret ballot, and the union must receive more than 50 percent of the votes actually cast. Parties have five days to file objections to the election with the NLRB.

FILING AN UNFAIR LABOR PRACTICE CHARGE

The NLRB's unfair labor proceedings begin with the filing of an unfair labor practice charge by the employer or by the labor organization or its agents. The following describes the NLRB's procedure for processing unfair labor practice charges:

1. A charge is filed at the regional office closest to where the alleged unfair labor practice occurred.
2. The regional office staff conduct an investigation:
   a. Charging Party submits proof supporting allegations.
   b. Charged Party submits evidence.
   c. Regional office staff questions witnesses and obtains sworn affidavits.
3. The regional office staff conducts predetermination settlement discussion with the charged party.
4. The regional office staff makes a determination. If they find that the unfair labor practice charge is valid, they
   a. Prepare a complaint.
   b. Serve the Charged Party with the complaint.
   c. Set a hearing date.
   d. Notify the Charged Party of the need to respond to the complaint.
   e. After a complaint has been issued the Board may, and in some cases must, apply to the federal district court for a temporary injunction to prevent continuation of the alleged unfair practice.
   f. The regional staff conducts post-determination settlement discussions; if no settlement is reached, a hearing is held before an Administrative Law Judge.[18]

UNFAIR LABOR PRACTICE HEARING

The adjudicatory procedure includes a hearing and an appellate process in which:

1. The attorney for the General Counsel prosecutes the case by presenting witnesses and evidence. The attorney representing the Charging Party may also participate.

2. The attorney for the Charged Party presents evidence and cross-examines the Charging Party's witnesses.
3. A transcript or record of the hearing is made, and briefs are filed by both sides.
4. The Administrative Law Judge issues a recommended decision.
5. The General Counsel or the Charged Party's attorney can file exceptions to the decision.
6. If the Charged Party fails to comply with an NLRB order, the NLRB can file a petition for enforcement of its decision with a federal appellate court.
7. A Charged Party who loses before the Board can appeal to a federal appellate court and ultimately to the U.S. Supreme Court.

The National Labor Relations Board is a formidable administrative bureaucracy that functions under a variety of procedures, some imposed by the statute, others contained in their rules and regulations and in their adjudicatory procedure manuals. Unlike the Equal Employment Opportunity Commission, the NLRB is the only enforcement mechanism for the NLRA. The NLRA does not generally allow private lawsuits for claims involving an unfair labor practice or for questions concerning representation that are subject to the Board's jurisdiction.

NOTES

1. 5 U.S.C. § 551; Revised Model State Administrative Procedures Act § 1 (1).

2. Joint Commission on Accreditation of Healthcare Organizations, *Accreditation Manual for Hospitals* (Chicago: JCAHO, 1986).

3. N.H. R.S.A. 151:6-a.

4. *Darling v. Charlestown Community Memorial Hospital*, 211 N.E. 2d 253 (1965), *cert. denied*, 383 U.S. 946 (1965); *Shilkret v. Annapolis Emergency Hospital Association*, 349 A.2d 345 (1975).

5. Cynthia E. Northrop and Mary E. Kelly, *Legal Issues in Nursing* (St. Louis: C.V. Mosby Co., 1987), 454.

6. Diana Odell Potter, ed. *Practices*, Nurses' Reference Library (Springhouse, Pa.: Springhouse Corp., 1984), 338–339. This text lists all of the nursing specialty organizations and indicates their purpose, process, and eligibility requirements.

7. Northrop and Kelly, *Legal Issues in Nursing*, 455.

8. *Khan v. Suburban Community Hospital*, 340 N.E. 2d 398 (1978), *requirement of certification upheld; Armstrong v. Board of Directors of Fayette County General Hospital*, 553 S.W. 2d 77 (Tenn. Ct. of App. 1976), *requirement of certification overturned.*

9. Robert D. Miller, *Problems of Hospital Law* (Rockville, Md.: Aspen Publishers, Inc., 1983), 127.

10. 42 U.S.C. § 2000e.

11. 29 U.S.C. § 206d (EPA); 29 U.S.C. §§ 201–209 (FSLA).

12. 29 U.S.C. §§ 621–634; for a detailed review of the EEOC and its application to hospitals, see Karen Hawley Henry, *The Health Care Supervisor's Legal Guide* (Rockville, Md.: Aspen Publishers, Inc., 1984), 166–191.

13. 29 U.S.C. § 152, Health Care Amendments to NLRA.

14. Karen Hawley Henry, *The Health Care Supervisor's Legal Guide* (Rockville, Md.: Aspen Publishers, Inc., 1984), 23–115. This text contains a detailed review of the NLRA and its application to hospitals.

15. Bernard D. Meltzer, *Labor Law* (Boston: Little, Brown and Co., 1977), 95–97.
16. NLRA §§ 3, 4.
17. *NLRB v. Sears Roebuck & Co.*, 421 U.S. 132, 138 (1975).
18. Meltzer, *Labor Law*, 97.

Chapter 10

Nursing Practice Regulation

NURSING PRACTICE ACTS

The Tenth Amendment to the U.S. Constitution allows the states to enact legislation in any area that is not prohibited by the Constitution or preempted by federal law.[1] Every state constitution contains a Health and Welfare Clause that authorizes the legislature to enact laws to protect the health, safety, and welfare of its citizens. This power, which is often referred to as the ''police power,'' gives the state legislature the authority to enact licensing laws that regulate hospitals and health care professionals.[2] The practice of nursing is regulated in all states, in the District of Columbia, and in the U.S. territories by statutes that are often called nursing practice acts.[3] Nursing practice acts often contain broad statements of purpose that include the protection of life, the promotion of health, and the prevention of illness.[4] These objectives are usually accomplished by the development of criteria for admission into the profession and by the enactment of rules and regulations that implement, maintain, and enforce the standards of nursing practice.

DEFINITION OF NURSING PRACTICE

The lack of a nationally recognized legal definition of nursing practice may account for the diversity and the confusion surrounding nursing education and the scope of nursing practice. Because occupational licensing is recognized as a state right, every state legislature has the authority and the obligation to determine and enact its own definition of nursing practice. As a result, the scope of nursing practice that the law regulates can vary from state to state. The American Nurses' Association's Congress for Nursing Practice published a revised model definition in 1981, which states

> The practice of professional nursing means the performance for compensation of professional services requiring substantial specialized knowledge of the biological, physical, behavioral, psychological, and sociological sciences and of nursing theory as the basis for assessment, diagnosis, planning intervention, and evaluation in the promotion and maintenance of health; the casefind-

ing and management of illness, injury or infirmity; the restoration of optimum function; or the achievement of a dignified death. Nursing practice includes, but is not limited to, administration, counseling, supervision, delegation, and evaluation of practice and execution of the medical regimen, including the administration of medications and treatments prescribed by any person authorized by state law to prescribe. Each registered nurse is directly accountable and responsible to the consumer for the quality of nursing care rendered.[5]

In 1983, the American Nurses' Association conducted a survey that reviewed the definition of nursing contained in 51 nursing practice acts and compared them with the principles and suggested language of the Model Act.[6] The survey revealed that some combination of the following four general components was used in formatting the state statutory definitions of nursing practice:[7]

1. The nursing functions or acts performed that are clearly nursing practice
2. The teaching, supervision, and delegation of nursing practice
3. The execution of the medical regimen
4. The performance of additional acts by specialty-trained nurses

The study also revealed that although the gross formatting of the components in the state's nursing practice act followed the Model Act's definition, the actual wording within each clause varied considerably from that suggested.[8]

ADVANCED PRACTICE

Expanding the statutory definition of nursing practice has provided the boards of nursing with the authority to promulgate and enforce standards, rules, and regulations in these areas. Since the first "additional acts" clause was enacted in 1971 in Idaho, 24 states have included such language in their statutory definitions of nursing and 4 states have added the language to the definition of the advanced practitioner.[9] A majority of states also regulate specific areas of practice. Rules concerning these areas have been enacted by the states with the "additional acts" clauses and by 5 of the states without such clauses.[10] The expansion of state regulation into the areas of advanced and specialized nursing practice is opposed by the American Nurses' Association, which has endorsed six principles relating to the legal regulation of nursing practice; the sixth principle clearly expresses the reasons for its opposition.[11]

1. The primary purpose of a licensing law for the regulation of the practice of nursing is to protect the public health and welfare by establishing legal qualifications for the practice of nursing. Such legal standards are recognized as minimum standards that are determined adequate to provide safe and effective nursing practice.
2. Every person practicing or offering to practice nursing or practical nursing should be licensed. Protection of the public is accomplished only if all who practice or offer to practice nursing are licensed. The public should not be expected to differentiate between incompetent and competent practitioners.

3. Since nursing is one occupational field, there should be one nursing practice act that licenses both registered and licensed practical nurses. The public and the practitioners may be confused when there is more than one law regulating the practice of nursing and the practice of practical nursing.
4. The enactment of one nursing practice act necessitates only one licensing board for nursing in the state. The board of nursing should be composed of nurses whose practice is regulated by the licensure law and by representatives of the public.
5. Candidates for licensure should complete an educational program approved by the board and pass the licensing examination before a license to practice is granted.
6. The nursing practice act should provide for the legal regulation of nursing without reference to a specialized area of practice. It is the function of the professional association to establish the scope and desirable qualifications required for each area of practice, and to certify a person as competent to engage in specific areas of nursing practice. It is also the function of the professional association to upgrade practice above the minimum standards set by law. The law should not provide for identifying clinical specialists in nursing or require certification or other recognition for practice beyond the minimum qualifications established for the legal regulation of nursing.

The removal of the advanced and area specialty requirements from the state nursing practice acts reverses a trend and; therefore, would require nurses to convince their state legislatures that private certification, totally free of state regulation, would not jeopardize the public safety or confuse or obstruct the board of nursing's power to suspend and revoke the licenses of nurses who have been held to be incompetent while functioning in the advanced or clinically specialized role.

BOARD OF NURSING

The board of nursing is the state agency that is responsible for interpreting and enforcing the nursing practice act. The regulation of nursing practice is delegated to a board of nursing in all jurisdictions except New York, Connecticut, and Illinois.[12] The majority of jurisdictions have one board that regulates both licensed practical and registered nurse practice. California, Colorado, Louisiana, Puerto Rico, Texas, Washington, and West Virginia have separate boards that regulate the practice of practical nursing and registered nursing.

Board composition varies from state to state. For example,[13]

- 33 jurisdictions have practical nurse representation on combined boards
- 7 jurisdictions have boards that are made up only of registered nurses
- 17 jurisdictions have public members representing consumer interests
- 7 boards have physician members
- 5 boards have hospital administrators
- 3 boards have psychiatric technicians
- 1 board has a hospital trustee

Board members are generally appointed by the governor and serve for a fixed term. In many states the governor makes the appointment from a list of candidates provided by the state's nursing association. The nursing practice act may contain specific requirements for the selection of nurse members. Two that occur frequently are the requirements that the nurse member be selected from a particular area of nursing practice or nursing education and the stipulation that the nurse selected must have practiced nursing in the state for a minimum number of years prior to the appointment.

Board of Nursing Power

A board of nursing is a state administrative agency that generally has both legislative and adjudicatory power (see Figure 9-1). It has the authority (1) to develop rules and regulations that govern nursing licensure and nursing practice and (2) to hear and decide cases involving violations of the standards, rules, and regulations contained in the nursing practice act. In most jurisdictions a board of nursing is responsible for the following:[14]

- Determining the eligibility of applicants for licensure
- Administering examinations to applicants for licensure
- Issuing licenses to qualified applicants
- Establishing relicensure procedures
- Establishing minimum standards for approving educational programs preparing a person for licensure
- Overseeing mandatory continuing education programs if continuing education is mandated by the act.
- Investigating complaints against licensees and taking disciplinary action when appropriate
- Promulgating rules that regulate nursing practice

A board of nursing is required to exercise its licensing, rule-making, and adjudicatory power in accordance with the procedures specified by state law.

LICENSING POWER

Nursing licensure regulates the use of the titles registered nurse (RN), licensed practical nurse (LPN), and licensed vocational nurse (LVN) and the scope of nursing practice in each of the areas. In all states the requirements for initial licensure include (1) completion of an academic and clinical program in a board approved school; (2) achievement of a passing grade on the state's licensing examination; and (3) submission of evidence pertaining to citizenship, minimum age, and good moral character.

The four methods by which a board of nursing grants licenses to applicants who hold a valid nursing license in another jurisdiction are (1) examination, (2) waiver, (3) reciprocity, and (4) endorsement. Some states do not recognize licenses issued in other jurisdictions and require all applicants to fulfill all of their requirements, including the state board examination. In other states, specific education, experience, or examination requirements will be waived if the applicant can prove equivalent qualifications. Although the words "reciprocity" and "endorsement" are often used synonymously, a strict interpretation would require two different approaches to licensure. *Reciprocity* refers to a mutual agreement by two states to legally recognize each other's licensees and is only feasible for states whose initial licensing requirements are essentially equivalent. *Endorsement* refers to the process by which a nursing board determines whether the out-of-state nurse's qualifications, including the licensing examination, are equivalent to their own state requirements at the time of initial licensure. A few states have reciprocity or endorsement with some foreign countries. The majority of states have established special training, citizenship, and experience requirements for licensing nurses educated in foreign countries. For example, the qualifications for license by examination in New Hampshire require that the applicant "Be a graduate of an approved nursing education program or demonstrate equivalent educational preparation recognized by the board of nursing including, but not limited to graduation from a foreign nursing program and successful completion of the Commission on Graduates of Foreign Nursing Schools (COGFNS) examination."[15] In most states, temporary licenses are issued to new graduates pending the results of the state licensing examination and to nurses who have a valid license in another state and whose license is being processed.

RULE-MAKING POWER

The number of state agencies with rule-making power and the number of rules formulated by these agencies have increased significantly in recent years. In an effort to control and standardize the many rules and regulations promulgated by these commissions, boards, and agencies, many state legislatures have enacted Administrative Procedure Acts. An Administrative Procedure Act describes in detail the process that all of the state administrative agencies must follow when they want to adopt, amend, or repeal a rule (see Chapter 8).

Rule-Making Process

The Vermont Administrative Practice Act identifies 12 steps that may be required of an agency such as the board of nursing.[16]

1. The board finalizes a draft of the rule.
2. The board completes a form requiring an annotated text showing changes from the existing rule and an economic impact statement.
3. The rule is prefiled with the Secretary of State for review to ensure that it is not arbitrary, beyond the authority of the board, or contrary to legislative intent.
4. The rule is again filed with the Secretary of State and the formal process begins.
5. The rule is published in the state's newspapers.
6. A public hearing is held on the proposed rule.

7. The board considers the public testimony and the written comments and determines their effect on the proposed rule.
8. The board files a final rule with the Secretary of State and with the Committee on Administrative Rules. A new economic impact statement is required if the impact has changed as a result of public comment or because of the board's own reconsideration.
9. The Committee on Administrative Rules schedules a hearing at which members of the board respond to questions by the legislators concerning the proposed rule.
10. The rule is adopted and filed with the Secretary of State and with the Committee on Administrative Rules.
11. The rule becomes effective 30 days after the final filing.
12. All of the submissions and correspondence related to the rule must be kept on file with the board for one year after the rule is adopted.

In many states, rule making has become an elaborate and lengthy process that requires the assistance of legal counsel, which is often available to an agency through the Secretary of State's office. There are usually provisions for emergency rules; however, it is an extraordinary process that requires a showing of imminent peril to public health, safety, and welfare. Emergency rules usually remain in effect for only a few months, during which the agency can adopt the rule through the traditional process.

ADJUDICATORY POWER

A board of nursing has the power to investigate, hear, and decide cases that involve a violation of the state's nursing practice act. They are authorized to discipline nurses by reprimand or by denial, suspension, or revocation of a nursing license. A nurse who is charged with violating the nursing practice act has a due process right to a full and fair hearing before any sanctions or restrictions are imposed on his or her nursing license. He or she also has the right to appeal a board of nursing's decision to a state court. It is within the context of administrative power versus individual rights that the adjudicatory power of a board of nursing is examined and tested.

Grounds for Discipline

The majority of nursing practice acts contain eight categories of grounds for discipline that may be further defined in the board of nursing regulations:[17]

1. Fraud or deceit
2. Criminal acts
3. Unfitness, incompetence, negligence, malpractice
4. Substance abuse
5. Mental incompetence
6. Unprofessional conduct
7. Revocation of a nursing license in another state
8. Violation of the act or scope of practice

Of all of the disciplinary categories, unprofessional conduct is the most difficult to define in a manner that will provide adequate notice of the type of behavior that is prohibited. Some courts have held that the term *unprofessional conduct* gives adequate notice that a wide range of behaviors is forbidden,[18] whereas other courts have held that it is not adequate notice for all possible violations.[19] Many nursing boards are attempting to further define the meaning of unprofessional conduct in their rules and regulations. The clarification usually consists of a list of behaviors that are introduced as "conduct which fails to conform to the accepted standards of the nursing profession." The list is usually preceded by a warning that unprofessional conduct includes, but is not limited to, the behaviors indicated.[20]

Procedural and Due Process Rights

The administrative procedure act in each state determines the procedure that must be followed throughout the adjudicatory proceedings. As discussed in Chapter 8, due process requirements generally include

1. Notice of the time and place of the hearing
2. Hearing before an authorized group or person
3. Definite statement of the charges
4. Right to cross-examine the board's witnesses
5. Right to produce witnesses and documentary evidence
6. Decision based on the facts presented at the hearing as applied to the law (Nursing Practice Act)
7. Right to be represented by counsel
8. Right to a record of the proceedings
9. Right to a judicial review of the board's final decision

JUDICIAL REVIEW

Administrative procedure acts generally require that all opportunities for administrative appeal be exhausted before a court will review the action of an agency. State nursing practice acts usually determine both the process of review and the scope of appeal. Some statutes require a rehearing by the board before a nurse can obtain judicial review of the agency's decision. The language of the New Hampshire statute is typical: "Any person who has been refused a license for any cause, other than failure to pass the licensing examination, shall have a rehearing by the board within 30 days after the original hearing; then within 30 days after the decision not to issue the license on a rehearing, said person may appeal by petition to superior court."[21]

Judicial review generally consists of an appellate proceeding in which the court reviews the record of the agency hearing in making its determination. Some statutes, however, provide for a completely new hearing in a trial court. For example, the Vermont Nurse Practice Act states that any person or institution aggrieved by any action of the board may appeal to superior court. It also states that "the questions raised by such an appeal shall be thereupon heard *de novo* and the parties shall have the right to demand a jury trial.''[22]

Appellate courts usually defer to the nursing board's judgment in determining the facts of a case; some have been criticized for substituting their judgment for that of the board.[23] The major purpose of judicial review is to decide whether the board acted fairly and also to determine whether it interpreted and applied the law correctly. An appellate court will overturn a board of nursing's decision in situations in which the board has acted arbitrarily, capriciously, or unreasonably; abused its discretion; violated the nurse's constitutional rights; made an error of law; or based its decision on insufficient evidence.

If the hearing process was fair and if the board interpreted and applied the law correctly, the court will usually not second guess the board on the facts and will affirm its decision. Observers have found that courts have tended to agree with nursing boards' decisions slightly more often than they have disagreed with them. A survey of 33 cases in which the nurse appealed the board's disciplinary action revealed that in 19 of the cases, the court upheld the nursing board's decision, whereas in the remaining 14 cases, the decision was overturned.[24] (See Chapter 17, Criminal Law: Individual vs. State, for cases involving the court, the nursing board, and the drug impaired nurse.)

CHALLENGES TO BOARD POWER

The right to hold a nursing license and the opportunity to practice nursing are recognized by the courts as constitutionally protected property and liberty interests that a nurse possesses (see Chapter 4). Nurses who challenge a nursing board's authority to deny, restrict, or suspend their licenses are asking the reviewing courts to balance their constitutional right to practice their profession against the board of nursing's statutory responsibility to protect the public from unsafe, incompetent practitioners. Boards of nursing are vulnerable to legal challenges in many areas, including jurisdiction, hearing procedures, investigation, interpretation of the regulations, and interpretation of unprofessional conduct. Challenges have also been aimed at the nurse practice act itself and its ability to expand the scope of nursing practice. In the remainder of this chapter cases are discussed in which these issues have been litigated.

Jurisdiction

In *Leggett v. State Board of Nursing*, 612 S.W. 2d 476 (1980), a nurse challenged the board's decision to suspend her license because she had functioned as a lay midwife. The court of chancery reversed the board's ruling and the board appealed the decision to the Tennessee Court of Appeals. The appellate court upheld the chancery court's decision, holding that the Tennessee Board of Nursing had no jurisdiction over a licensed nurse who rendered services as lay midwife. The court found that she did not represent herself as a nurse midwife or perform as a nurse in her role as midwife. In addition, there was no showing that performing the services of midwife, independently of the profession of nursing, in any way adversely affected the skill or ability of the nurse in the performance of her profession as a registered nurse. Finding that there were no grounds for the board of nursing to conclude that the nurse was any less fit to serve as a registered nurse, merely because she saw fit to practice as a lay midwife from time to time, they ruled that the board had acted beyond its authority in revoking the nurse's license.

Constitutionality of the Law

In *Richardson v. Brunelle*, 398 A.2d 838 (1979), a licensed practical nurse challenged the New Hampshire Board of Nursing's denial of her LPN license on the grounds that she had not graduated from a board-approved school of practical nursing as was required by the New Hampshire Nursing Practice Act. She had originally been licensed in Massachusetts on the basis of educational equivalency after having successfully completed the LPN state board examination. She argued that the New Hampshire statute denied her equal protection of the law and was unconstitutional. The New Hampshire supreme court found that the statute had a rational basis and was therefore constitutional (see Chapter 4). It concluded its opinion with the statement that the appropriate forum for change was in the legislature. In 1979, the New Hampshire legislature amended the Nursing Practice Act to permit educational equivalency as an alternative to graduation from a board-approved school of practical nursing as a criterion for LPN licensure in New Hampshire.

Hearing Procedure

In *Colorado State Board of Nursing v. Hohu*, 268 P.2d 401 (1954), a nurse challenged the number of board members in attendance at the hearing. The statute required that all of the board members be present at the hearing. The court ordered the nurse's license reinstated because the full board had not attended the hearing as required by law.

Board Investigation

In *Wildman v. Axelrod*, 475 N.Y.S. 2d 743 (1984), a nurse challenged the length of time it had taken the office of professional discipline to investigate the complaint. The court held that a delay of five years before scheduling a hearing substantially prejudiced the nurse's due process rights.

Regulation Interpretation

In *Lunsford v. Board of Nurse Examiners*, 684 S.W. 2d 391 (1983), a nurse challenged the suspension of her license for a one year probationary period for "unprofessional conduct likely to . . . injure the public." The board relied on its regulation that requires a nurse to evaluate the status of a patient and institute appropriate nursing care to stabilize a patient's condition and prevent complications. The nurse had performed an assessment on a patient who had come to the emergency department complaining of severe chest pain. Although the nurse suspected cardiac involvement, she did not take the patient's vital signs and, relying on the instructions of a physician, who had not examined the patient, she sent the patient to a hospital 24 miles away. Her concern about the patient's condition did prompt her to advise the patient's friend that he should speed and use his car's emergency flashers and his CB radio to summon assistance. The patient died while on route to the other hospital.

In her defense the nurse argued that (1) hospital policy required the transfer of patients who did not have a physician on staff, unless it was a life or death situation, and (2) that the measuring of vital signs would have been futile because the physician had already ordered the patient transferred. The physician admitted that he ordered the transfer but added that he had received no information as to the patient's instability, having only been told that the patient was having chest pain. Her third argument was that she (3) had no legal duty to the patient because he was not her patient and he was not a patient of the hospital or of the on-call physician. In upholding the Texas Board of Nurse Examiners' decision, the court found that the patient was clearly in a life or death situation and, therefore, not precluded from treatment by the hospital's policy. They also held that a nurse's duty to a patient arises from the privilege of the nursing license and not from a third party relationship, such as between the patient and the hospital or between the patient and the physician. They concluded that neither the hospital's policy nor the physician's transfer order could relieve her of her duty to the patient. They added that the duty to assess the status of the patient and to institute appropriate nursing measures to stabilize the patient's condition and prevent further complications would exist even without the special regulation because the duty stemmed from the privilege of licensure.

Interpretation of Unprofessional Conduct

In *Tuma v. Board of Nursing*, 593 P.2d 711 (1979), a nurse challenged the six months' suspension of her license for unprofessional conduct based on the hearing examiner's decision that she had interfered with the physician–patient relationship by discussing alternatives to chemotherapy with the patient. The nurse's request for a trial *de novo* in district court was denied, and the summary review by the district court upheld the hearing examiner's decision to suspend her license. The Idaho Supreme Court overturned the district court's decision. In ordering the nurse's license reinstated, the Idaho Supreme Court held that the term *unprofessional conduct* was too vague as to adequately warn a nurse that the behavior complained of in this case constituted such conduct. The court stated that if such conduct is to be avoided, the board should provide definitions of unprofessional conduct in its rules and regulations that would give notice to nurses in Idaho as to what type of behavior constitutes unprofessional conduct.

In *Stevens v. Blake, Alabama Board of Nursing*, 456 So. 2d 795 (1984), the Alabama Appellate Court upheld a finding of "unprofessional conduct" for a nurse who self-administered a narcotic while on duty.

In *Ward v. Oregon State Board of Nursing*, 510 P.2d 554 (1973), the Oregon Supreme Court revoked a nurse's license for "conduct derogatory to the standards of professional nursing" because the nurse had instructed and permitted her daughter to perform and serve as a registered nurse.

The statutory definition of "unprofessional conduct" will usually survive a constitutional challenge of vagueness when it is applied to conduct that is widely recognized as unprofessional. Nurses have a legal and ethical obligation to practice safely, reasonably, and competently. They also have the responsibility to safeguard the public from the incompetence of their colleagues. In most states, nurses are required to report violations of the nursing practice act to the state board of nursing. The statutes usually carry penalties for failure to report, but they also provide immunity from civil liability for persons making such reports in good faith and without malice.

Expansion of Nursing Practice

In *Sermchief v. Gonzales*, 600 S.W. 2d 683 (Mo. En banc 1983), the Missouri Board of Registration for the Healing Arts received a complaint that two certified family planning nurse practitioners were practicing medicine without a license. After an investigation, the board recommended the criminal prosecution of the two nurses for the unlawful practice of medicine. It also ordered the five physicians, who were working at the clinic with the nurses, to show cause why their licenses should not be suspended for aiding and abetting the nurses to practice medicine. The nurses and the physicians appealed the board's order to the St. Louis Circuit Court, requesting an injunction to stay the board's order and a declaratory judgment. The circuit court upheld the board's findings, and the nurses and physicians appealed the court's order to the Missouri Supreme Court. In reversing the circuit court's decision the Missouri Supreme Court held that

1. By passing the Nurse Practice Act in 1976, the Missouri legislature indicated its intent to avoid statutory constraints on the evolution of new functions for nurses delivering health care.
2. The functions performed by the nurse practitioners in this case were clearly within the scope of practice as defined by the Missouri Nurse Practice Act.
3. Professional nurses have a right to practice within the limits of their education and experience.

This landmark case represents the first time a court has ruled on the legitimacy of a statute that permits nurses to practice in the advanced role.

NOTES

1. U.S. Constitution, Tenth Amendment: "The power not delegated to the United States by the Constitution, nor prohibited by it to the States is reserved to the States respectively, or to the people."
2. *Dent v. West Virginia*, 129 U.S. 114 (1889). Occupational licensing is held to be a valid exercise of state police power to provide for the general welfare of its citizens.
3. Marie E. Snyder and Clare LeBar, "Nursing: Legal Authority for Practice," in *Issues in Professional Nursing Practice* (Kansas City, Mo.: American Nurses' Association, 1984), 1–20.
4. N.H. R.S.A. 326-B:1.
5. American Nurses' Association, *The Nursing Practice Act: Suggested State Legislation* (Kansas City, Mo.: American Nurses' Association, 1981), 6.

6. American Nurses' Association, *Statutory Definitions of Nursing Practice and their Conformity to Certain ANA Principles* (Kansas City, Mo.: American Nurses' Association, 1983), 1–55.

7. Snyder and LeBar, "Nursing: Legal Authority for Practice," 6–7.

8. Ibid.

9. Ibid., 8.

10. Ibid., 10.

11. American Nurses' Association, *Suggested State Legislation*, 2–3.

12. States that have an agency other than nursing boards regulating the practice of nursing: New York, Regents of the University of the State of New York; Connecticut, State Commissioner of Health; and Illinois, Department of Registration and Education; however, it has an Advisory Board of Opinions on Professional Nursing.

13. Bonnie Bullough, *The Law and the Expanding Nursing Role* (New York: Appleton-Century-Crofts, 1980), 47–50.

14. Snyder and LeBar, "Nursing: Legal Authority for Practice," 15.

15. N.H. R.S.A. 326-B:6 IV.

16. 3 V.S.A. Chapter 25.

17. Cynthia E. Northrop and Mary E. Kelly, *Legal Issues in Nursing* (St. Louis: C.V. Mosby Co., 1987), 409–411. Compares the grounds for revocation of licenses contained in the three model practice acts developed by the American Nurses' Association, the National Council of State Boards of Nursing, and the Model Health Professions Act.

18. *Rayburn v. Minnesota State Board of Optometry*, 78 N.W. 2d 351 (1956).

19. *Tuma v. Board of Nursing*, 593 P.2d 711 (1979).

20. CONN. GEN. STAT. ANN. §§ 20–99 (b) (West 1985).

21. N.H. R.S.A. 326-B:14.

22. Title 26 V.S.A. Chapter 28 § 1582 (c) (1).

23. Ann M. Rhodes and Robert D. Miller, *Nursing & the Law* (Rockville, Md.: Aspen Publishers, Inc., 1984), 30.

24. Northrop and Kelly, *Legal Issues in Nursing*, 213–214.

Appendix **III**

Implications for Nurse Managers

Part III has provided an explanation of the substance and process of administrative law and has examined a few of the agencies through which the business of administrative law gets accomplished. There is no doubt that hospitals, as well as individuals, can be overwhelmed by the complexity and particularity surrounding the requirements of the federal and state agencies. As a result, it is now common practice for individuals and hospitals to seek the advice of legal counsel when they are required to approach or respond to a state or federal agency. This does not preclude a need for hospital management personnel to understand the principles and practices of administrative law. Nurse managers who understand administrative law will be better prepared to participate in the development, implementation, and evaluation of health care policies and practices that are required or influenced by state or federal agencies. In order to function effectively in the management role nurse managers should

- Be aware of the tremendous amount of power that elected legislatures have delegated to unelected officials who are appointed to serve on the government's boards and commissions
- Recognize that a system of checks and balances continues to operate in the form of executive appointment, legislative oversight, judicial review, and consumer involvement
- Understand that agencies are creatures of statute, vulnerable to legal challenges when they exceed their purpose, abuse their power, or disregard their process

Nurse managers who understand these basic principles will be able to integrate them into their management responsibilities. Nurse manager behaviors that demonstrate an understanding of administrative law include the ability to

- Recognize the need for compliance with the rules and regulations
- Adopt an informed, reasonable approach to initiating and monitoring compliance by the nursing staff and other hospital personnel
- Identify the requirements of administrative law as the basis for many of the hospital's policies and procedures. For example, the admission and discharge

policies are influenced by the diagnosis related groups of the Medicare program; the employee grievance procedure may be determined by a collective bargaining agreement under the National Labor Relations Act; the employment interview must consider the requirements of the Equal Employment Opportunity Commission; and the hiring of graduate nurses, pending the result of the state board examination, is subject to the regulations of the state board of nursing.

- Recognize when and how a regulation or decision of an agency or commission should be challenged
- Demonstrate current and accurate knowledge about the state nursing practice act and the rules, regulations, and standards promulgated by the state board of nursing
- Know the state board of nursing's reporting requirements for incompetent and unsafe practitioners and develop and implement hospital policies that identify the situations and the hospital's procedure for reporting unsafe and incompetent practitioners
- Develop, implement, and evaluate nursing practice policies that are based on the standards of nursing practice and on the rules, regulations, opinions, and decisions of the state board of nursing
- Anticipate and attempt to resolve potential areas of controversy between hospital administration and the board of nursing (e.g., telephone orders and LPNs; nurses pronouncing patients dead; nurses taking orders from physicians' assistants)

The health care industry is particularly vulnerable to the elaborate and weighty structure of government regulation. Consumers are beginning to monitor and evaluate the results achieved by regulatory legislation. One study suggests that although licensure exists to protect the public from unsafe practices and incompetent practitioners, it can also operate against the public interest.[1] They argue that licensing schemes can

- Keep information from the public
- Artificially inflate prices by insulating professionals from the influences of consumer preferences
- Unfairly bar competent practitioners
- Limit the opportunities for professionals who gain added expertise to expand their responsibilities

As one observer has remarked, "For the age-old central question of political science, *Quis custodiet ipsos custodes?* (Who will regulate the regulators?) our system has given a new answer: Those who are regulated themselves."[2]

NOTES

1. Baron, "Licensure of Health Care Professionals: The Consumer's Case for Abolition," 9 *Am. J. Law & Med.* 335 (1983).

2. Bernard Schwartz, *Administrative Law* (Boston: Little, Brown and Co., 1976), 23.

* * * *

LEGAL RESOURCES

LEGISLATION

Title VII of the Civil Rights Act of 1964, 42 U.S.C. § 2000e
Equal Pay Act of 1963, 29 U.S.C. §§ 201–209
Age Discrimination in Employment Act, 29 U.S.C. §§ 621–634
The Rehabilitation Act of 1973, 29 U.S.C. §§ 701–794
National Labor Relations Act, 29 U.S.C. §§ 141–187
Social Security Act, Title XVIII (Medicare); Title XIX (Medicaid)
Fair Labor Standards Act, 29 U.S.C. §§ 201–219
Occupational Health and Safety Act, 29 U.S.C. §§ 651–678
Administrative Procedure Act, 5 U.S.C. §§ 552–701
State civil rights act
State labor relations act
State workers' compensation act

AGENCIES

Department of Health and Human Services (federal and state)
Equal Employment Opportunity Commission (regional office)
National Labor Relations Board (regional office)
State workers' compensation board
State civil rights commission
State public health agency
State board of nursing
State board of medicine
State board of pharmacy
State hospital licensing agency
State legislature health and welfare committee
Secretary of state's office
State attorney general's office
Joint Commission on the Accreditation of Healthcare Organizations
American Nurses' Association
State nurses' association
State nursing organizations

NURSE MANAGER'S BOOKSHELF

State administrative procedure act
State nursing practice act

State medical practice act
State board of nursing, rules, regulations, opinions, and decisions
State pharmacy act
Hospital licensing regulations for nursing services
Joint Commission on the Accreditation of Healthcare Organizations, *Standards for an Organized Nursing Service*

American Nurses' Association Publications

- *Affirmative Action Programming for the Nursing Profession through the American Nurses' Association*
- *Boards of Nursing: Composition, Membership Qualifications and Statutory Authority*
- *Code for Nurses with Interpretive Statements*
- *Critical Requirements for Safe/Effective Nursing Practice*
- *Directory of Accredited Organizations, Approved Programs/Offerings and Accredited Continuing Education Certificate Programs Preparing Nurse Practitioners*
- *Enforcement of the Nursing Practice Act*
- *From Accommodation to Self-Determination: Nursing's Role in the Development of Health Care Policy*
- *Hospital Payment Mechanisms, Patient Classifications Systems, and Nursing: Relationships and Implications*
- *Licensure to Practice Nursing*
- *Nurses, Politics and Public Policy*
- *Standards for an Organized Nursing Service*
- *Standards of Nursing Practice*
- *State Nursing Legislation Quarterly*
- *Statutory Definitions of Nursing Practice and Their Conformity to Certain American Nurses' Association Principles*

Guides and Manuals

Kander, Mark K. and Russell, Robert F., eds. *Director of Nursing Manual: Federal Regulation and Guidelines*. Owing Mills, Md.: National Health Publishing, 1984.

Grupenhoff, John T., ed. *National Health Directory*. Rockville, Md.: Aspen Publishers, Inc., 1987.

Henry, Karen Hawley. *Nursing Administration and Law Manual*. Rockville, Md.: Aspen Publishers, Inc., 1987.

Rowland, Howard S. and Rowland, Beatrice L., eds. *Hospital Legal Forms, Checklists and Guidelines*. Rockville, Md.: Aspen Publishers, Inc., 1987.

Joint Commission on Accreditation of Healthcare Organizations. *Accreditation Manual for Hospitals*. Chicago: JCAHO, 1986.

Model Nurse Practice Acts:

- ANA Nursing Practice Act: Suggested Legislation (1981)
- National Council State Boards of Nursing: The Model Nursing Practice Act (1982)
- U.S. Department of Justice, Drug Enforcement Administration, Office of Compliance and Regulatory Affairs: A Model Health Professions Practice Act and State Regulatory Policy (1977)

Part IV

Civil Law: Assigning Legal Liability

1932

. . . there is no branch of nursing where individual intelligence, resourcefulness and initiative are not required and where they are not exercised constantly. The popular idea that the nurse works under the constant eye of a physician and that all she has to do is automatically to carry out his orders, is entirely misleading and is unjust and injurious, not only to the nurse herself, but to those she works with and for. Until we get rid of this idea once and for all, we shall never be able to secure the proper status for nursing or to attract and train enough competent women for the responsible positions in nursing work.

Lavinia L. Dock, *A Short History of Nursing* (1932)

1934

It is common knowledge that the welfare of a patient is as much the responsibility of the nurse as it is the physician.

Norfolk Protestant Hospital v. Plunkett, 173 S.E.2d 363 (1934)

1977

Nurses are specialists in hospital care who, in the final analysis, hold the well-being, in fact in some instances, the very lives of the patients in their hands. In the dim hours of the night as well as in the light of day, nurses are frequently charged with the duty to observe the condition of the ill and infirm in their care. If the patient, helpless and wholly dependent, shows signs of worsening, the nurse is charged with the obligation of taking some positive action.

Utter v. United Hospital Center, 236 S.E.2d 213 (1977)

1983

. . . a nurse may be permitted to assume responsibilities heretofore not considered to be within the field of professional nursing so long as

those responsibilities are consistent with his or her "specialized education, judgment and skill based on knowledge and application of principles derived from the biological, physical, social and nursing sciences."
The broadening of the field of practice of the nursing profession authorized by the legislature and here recognized by the Court carries with it
the profession's responsibility for continuing high educational standards and the individual nurse's responsibility to conduct himself or
herself in a professional manner. The hallmark of a professional is
knowing the limits of one's own professional knowledge.

Sermchief v. Gonzales, 660 S.W.2d 683 (1983)

Chapter 11

Civil Law and
Liability

Civil law is the branch of the law that defines and decides a person's legal rights and obligations. A corporation is recognized as a legal "person" under the law; therefore, hospital corporations also possess these rights and obligations. The areas of tort and contract law are of particular importance to hospitals because it is in these two areas that the majority of civil actions arise. Tort or contract actions are filed by individuals or corporations, including hospitals, that are seeking to protect a right or compel a remedy. A hospital's liability is, to a large extent, determined by the federal and state laws and the court decisions that define and interpret the requirements of their organizational structure and function.

HOSPITAL GOVERNANCE

The power and authority of a hospital originates in the incorporating statute or enabling legislation that creates it. Hospitals are organized in one of five ways. They are either nonprofit corporations, proprietary corporations, partnerships, sole proprietorships, or government agencies. Government hospitals are created either directly by special statute or indirectly by government units that possess the express or implied statutory authority to create hospitals.[1] Most private hospitals are organized as corporations. In many states the general corporation laws authorize the secretary of state or some other state official to create corporations by issuing articles of incorporation. The state statute and the articles of incorporation confer on a business corporation the power and the authority to accomplish its stated purposes. The business practices and ventures of a hospital corporation must remain within the scope of authority that is expressed or implied by the law. A hospital's governing board can be held responsible for *ultra vires* acts, meaning acts that go beyond the scope of their authority. *Ultra vires* acts undertaken by board members for their personal profit or benefit can result in their being held individually and personally liable for any loss or injury to the corporation. Either the state or the members of the corporation can obtain an injunction to prevent the performance of *ultra vires* actions. They can also ask the court to issue an order to remedy the damages caused by a completed *ultra vires* action. Courts can order the sale of property, the termination of services, or any other form of reparation to correct the injury to the corporation.

Governing Board

The basic organization of most hospitals consists of a governing board, an administrator, and an organized medical staff. The governing board usually consists of a board of directors or a board of trustees. The "Conditions for Participation"[2] under the Medicare program and many state licensing statutes require hospitals to have an effective governing body that is legally responsible for the conduct of the hospital. The governing board has the responsibility to

- Adopt bylaws and regulations
- Select corporate officers and agents
- Establish institutional goals, objectives, and policies
- Appoint a qualified administrator or chief executive officer
- Select the medical staff
- Delineate clinical privileges for the hospital staff
- Oversee the welfare of the entire corporation
- Establish mechanisms to retain accountability

Administrator/Chief Executive Officer

The governing board will usually appoint an administrator or chief executive officer (CEO) to assist it in fulfilling its responsibility to supervise and manage the hospital's business practices and health care services. The CEOs have only those duties that are delegated to them by the governing board. The CEO's management responsibilities generally include the following:[3]

- Planning
- Managing human resources
- Delivering quality health care services
- Allocating financial, physical, and human resources
- Complying with regulations
- Influencing legislation and regulation
- Promoting the hospital
- Confronting and resolving crises.

Organized Medical Staff

State licensing regulations, Medicare "Conditions of Participation," and the Joint Commission on Accreditation of Healthcare Organizations' standards all require hospitals to have an organized medical staff. Members of the medical staff are individually and collectively accountable to the governing board for the quality of medical care within the institution. The organized medical staff is usually granted a large degree of self-government. It is generally responsible for[4]

- Implementing policies and procedures to provide patients with satisfactory care
- Recommending appointments to the medical staff
- Recommending the granting, changing, or withdrawal of clinical privileges
- Developing and implementing quality assurance mechanisms
- Providing continuing medical education
- Maintaining a liaison with the governing board

Organized Nursing Service

Many hospital licensing statutes and regulations require hospitals to have an organized nursing service under the direction of a qualified nurse administrator. "Conditions of Participation" for Medicare state that hospitals should have a "well organized departmental plan of administrative authority with delineation of responsibilities and duties of each category of nursing personnel."[5] The American Nurses' Association (ANA) describes nursing services as "all those health care services performed by a registered professional nurse within the scope of professional nursing as defined by state law."[6] The nurse executive is the top ranking administrative nurse appointed by the governing body or CEO to administer the department of nursing.[7] The Commission on Nursing Service of the ANA has established seven *Standards for Organized Nursing Services*.[8] The Joint Commission's *Manual for the Accreditation of Hospitals*, Standard 12, lists eight criteria for nursing services.[9] The standards established by both organizations are similar and include the need for

- An organized nursing service/department
- A qualified nurse administrator as head of the nursing service/department
- A nursing service/department that is appropriately integrated within the administrative structure of the hospital
- Use of the nursing process to provide individual, goal-directed nursing care to patients and clients in the context of their families
- Nursing practice policies and practices that provide for equality and continuity of patient care
- Written policies and procedures that implement the philosophy of the nursing service/department and reflect optimal standards of nursing practice
- Education programs that encourage and support continued growth, competence, and safety in the delivery of nursing services
- An evaluation of the quality and appropriateness of the patient care provided by the nursing service/department as part of the hospital's quality assurance program

- An environment that ensures the effectiveness of nursing practice and contains mechanisms for problem identification and resolution
- Initiation and participation in research studies or projects for the improvement of patient care

CORPORATE LIABILITY

Liability is defined as a duty that must be performed, an obligation to do or refrain from doing something. *Corporate liability* refers to the duty of a hospital as a corporate "legal person" to act as a reasonably prudent hospital would act in the management and supervision of its business practices and professional services. Included within this all encompassing legal obligation are a number of specific duties that the legislature and the courts have determined a hospital must assume. They include the duties that apply individually and collectively to the members of the governing board and officers of the corporation:

- To exercise reasonable care and skill in the management of corporate affairs
- To act in good faith with complete loyalty to the corporation
- To select and supervise a competent CEO

The specific duties also include those that can be delegated to a CEO for implementation through administrative departments and committees:

- To select and supervise a competent medical staff
- To employ qualified nurses and nonphysician staff
- To comply with federal, state, and local laws, rules, and regulations
- To comply with licensing agencies and private accreditation agencies that have jurisdiction over the hospital
- To abide by the hospital's bylaws, rules, and regulations   .
- To provide a safe work environment
- To provide adequate facilities and equipment
- To make proper contracts with subcontractors and vendors
- To provide adequate property or liability insurance
- To provide satisfactory patient care
- To notify the patient or patient's survivors when it is aware of a deviation from the standard of care that caused injury

This last duty is new and controversial. It is based on the premise that a hospital's failure to notify the patient or the patient's survivors of the deviation from the known standard of care that caused the injury constitutes fraudulent concealment.[10]

Charitable Immunity

The duty to provide satisfactory care is an obligation that has just recently been applied to hospitals directly. Historically, hospitals were not held liable for the standard of care within the institution. They were protected by the doctrine of "charitable immunity" first announced in *McDonald v. Massachusetts General Hospital* in 1876.[11] The Massachusetts court held that a charitable hospital would not be held liable for the acts of "inferior agents" if they had been selected with due care. The hospital's immunity was predicated on the belief that because hospitals provided a large amount of charitable care, their funds should not be diminished by lawsuits for negligence. The reasoning was adopted by courts in many states and "charitable immunity" became the rule in this country. Because most hospitals were considered charitable institutions, the doctrine was applied to bar patients from bringing actions based on negligence. In 1914 the doctrine was applied to a case involving a battery or intentional tort. In *Schloendorff v. Society of New York Hospital*,[12] the court investigated the relationship between the physician and the hospital. It concluded that the hospital did not undertake to act through the physicians but merely procured them to act on their own responsibility. The court applied the same reasoning to the actions of the nurses, finding that the hospital procured the services of a nurse and that the nurse did not function as the hospital's agent. The hospital was not held liable for the standard of care provided by the health care professionals.

The development of the hospital as a business, the advent of health care insurance, and the specter of the true victim of hospital negligence barred from compensation are some of the factors that contributed to the demise of the doctrine of "charitable immunity."

Corporate Negligence

The landmark case of *Darling v. Charleston Community Memorial Hospital*, which was decided in 1965, ruled that a hospital could be held negligent for failing to meet the standard of care that was owed to the patient.[13] In this case, which involved an 18-year-old man who had been admitted for treatment of a fractured leg, the hospital was found negligent because it did not require consultation or examination by a skilled orthopedic surgeon and because there were insufficiently trained nurses capable of recognizing a progressive gangrenous condition, which ultimately resulted in the amputation of the patient's leg. The decision abolished the doctrine of "charitable immunity" in Illinois. Hospitals could now be held liable for corporate negligence in the selection and retention of incompetent physicians on their medical staff. In addition, the court held that the hospital could also be held liable for the negligence of the nurses under the doctrine of *respondeat superior*. The decision in *Darling v. Charleston Community Memorial Hospital* surprised and shocked the medical and hospital community. The emergence of the doctrine of hospital corporate negligence, a theory that holds that a charge of negligence could be based on the violation of a duty of care that the hospital owed to the patient was new. As Goldberg noted, "*Darling* was not startling because it invented any new rules of law; it was startling because it applied the rules to hospitals and deprived them of the special privileges they once enjoyed"[14] (emphasis added).

The cases following *Darling* have continued to define and refine the circumstances under which a hospital may be held liable. For example, courts have held that a hospital is liable for the following:

- The injuries caused by an incompetent surgeon whom it had appointed to the medical staff without evaluating his credentials [15]
- The negligent supervision of a surgeon[16]

Trial courts have allowed actions against a hospital based on allegations that it

- Should have known that the operating physician was incompetent and it permitted him to remain on a case that was obviously beyond his ability[17] (Hospital settled)
- Failed to adopt procedures to monitor the quality of medical care provided by a physician[18] (Hospital settled)

Courts have held that a hospital is not liable for

- Failure to ascertain that a surgeon has obtained a patient's informed consent to a unique surgical procedure[19]
- Failure to enforce its rule requiring surgeons to keep progress notes because there was no evidence that this failure contributed to the patient's death from complications following a splenectomy[20]

In addition to court decisions, there are state statutes[21] and Joint Commission standards[22] that acknowledge a hospital's corporate liability and hold it accountable for the standard of care provided to patients within the institution. Springer characterizes the magnitude of the hospital's liability in this way: "The hospital is a place where people expect to be treated with care and competence. The hospital has a duty to see that competent patient care is provided by every physician and department, from surgery to cobalt therapy. The institution is at risk for all activity within its walls."[23]

VICARIOUS LIABILITY

The rule of personal liability holds that every person is responsible for the consequences of his or her actions. This does not preclude the possibility that one or more persons can be held liable for the same action. Joint tortfeasors are individually and jointly responsible to pay the damages for the injury suffered by the plaintiff as a result of their actions.

Vicarious liability is liability without fault. It is liability that is assigned to a person or institution because of the type of relationship that exists with the other person.

Respondeat Superior

The doctrine of *respondeat superior* (let the master answer) is a form of vicarious liability that is based on the master–servant relationship. The law defines a servant as one who is employed to perform services for another, whose conduct in the performance of his or her duties is controlled or is subject to a right of control by the master.[24] Under the doctrine of *respondeat superior*, a hospital is responsible for the negligent acts of its employees if they were acting within the scope of their employment when the negligent act occurred. The justification for the doctrine is one of deliberate allocation of risk.

Employers are able to select, control, and direct the actions of their employees; they are also in a better position to sustain a loss than is the employee or the injured plaintiff. It is suggested that through price rates and liability insurance the employer can absorb and distribute the losses caused by the employee's actions. In the long run, the cost is shifted to the public and ultimately borne by the community at large.[25]

Scope of Employment

Employers are only responsible for the negligent acts of their employees if they are performed within the scope of employment. Scope of employment is a factual determination that allows the court to consider a variety of factors in reaching a decision. The court will generally take into account

- The kind of work the employee has been hired to perform
- The usual time and place of employment
- Whether the act is different from acts usually authorized by the employer
- The extent to which the act is a departure from the normal methods used by the employee
- The employer's ability to foresee or predict the occurrence

The doctrine of *respondeat superior* has been extended to include intentional torts, such as battery, that are committed within the scope of employment. Some authors have suggested that the employees may not be protected by the doctrine for acts of excessive violence or when they are acting solely out of revenge.[26]

Captain of the Ship and Borrowed Servant

The "captain of the ship" doctrine was used mainly for cases of negligence occurring in the operating room. Surgeons were held liable for the negligent actions of the nurses and other hospital employees. Liability was assigned to the physicians on the premise that they had the authority to control and direct the actions of the nurses and other hospital employees in the operating room. Nurses and other hospital employees were considered to be "borrowed servants" of the physician, and liability was imposed under the doctrine of *respondeat superior*. At a time when hospitals were shielded from lawsuits by the doctrine of charitable immunity, the "borrowed servant" doctrine allowed plaintiffs to sue the physician for the actions of nurses and other hospital employees in situations in which the physician was deemed to be in control. The abolition of charitable immunity and the increased recognition that employees receive substantial direction from the hospital's policies and procedures have resulted in the emergence of a dual servant doctrine, based on the concept of joint liability.

JOINT LIABILITY

The doctrine of joint liability holds both the hospital and the physician responsible for the negligent actions of the nurse. The nurse is considered the dual servant of the physician and the hospital, and liability is assigned to both under the doctrine of *respondeat superior*. The doctrine has been applied by the courts to find

- Both the surgeon and the hospital liable for injuries caused by a Kelly clamp that was left in a patient's abdomen following a colectomy. The evidence revealed that the instrument count had not been done.[27]
- Both the anesthesiologist and the hospital liable for the serious brain damage suffered by a patient because the nurse failed to monitor properly the administration of anesthesia, which resulted in the patient going into cardiac arrest.[28]

However, the court refused to find joint liability in a situation in which a 22-year-old postpartum patient who had been put on respirator became paralyzed because the nurses failed to notice that the respirator was not functioning properly. The court held that the physician had a right to assume that the nurses employed by the hospital were competent to perform their duties.[29]

Independent Contractors

Physicians who are not employees of the hospital but are on the medical staff and treat patients at the hospital are generally considered to be independent contractors. Although the hospital is required to select, supervise, and grant clinical privileges to staff physicians, this is not legally equated with them being hired by the hospital. The hospital is not generally held liable for the actions of independent contractors. The hospital may be held liable for its own actions if it knows or should have known that an independent contractor was incompetent and failed to take appropriate action.

Agency and Ostensible Agency

An *agency* relationship is created when one person acts for or represents another by the latter's authority. Vicarious liability for the agent's actions is imposed on the *principal*, a term that refers to the person who hired the agent. Physicians are not usually considered as agents of the hospital; however, one court did find a hospital liable for the negligence of a radiologist who failed to report promptly the results of an x-ray examination to the treating physician. The court ruled that when the radiologist was functioning in an administrative capacity he could be considered to be an agent of the hospital.[30] *Ostensible agency* is the doctrine under which a hospital can be held liable for the actions of independent contractors such as physicians. It has been applied to situations in which the court finds that the patient believed that the physician was an agent of the hospital and relied on that belief in submitting to care. If the circumstances of the case warrant the finding of a general representation to the public that the physician is employed by the hospital, the law will imply an agency relationship between the hospital and the physician and may find the hospital liable for the physician's negligent acts. Liability will not be imposed if there is evidence that the patient knew or should have known that the practitioner was not employed by the hospital. In a 1985 decision, ostensible agency was used to find a hospital liable for the actions of the emergency department physician who was on the hospital staff and covered the emergency department on an on-call basis.[31] Although there are no cases at the present time, it would appear that this doctrine could be applied to nurse midwives, nurse anesthetists, and nurse practitioners who are considered independent contractors at the hospitals where they practice.

TORT LIABILITY

The word "tort" is derived from the Latin word *torquere*, which means "to twist." It is also found in the French language and was, at one time, in common use as a synonym for the word "wrong."[32] A *tort* is a private wrong or injury, independent of contract, that results from the breach of a legal duty. Tort liability is founded on the concept that a person who has suffered insult or injury to his or her dignity, health, body, life, or time has the right to be made whole again. Since the law cannot restore these types of losses, the party committing the wrong is made to pay money damages or compensation.[33]

A *tortfeasor* is a person who commits a tortious act on a person that causes an injury. *Tortious conduct* refers to the type of behavior that will subject a person to tort liability. The three basic types of liability are (1) strict liability, (2) intentional tort liability, and (3) unintentional tort liability.

Strict Liability

Strict liability is liability without proof of fault or negligence. It was first applied to persons who were engaged in activities that had an inherent risk, such as the use of explosives or the harboring of wild animals. The doctrine has been expanded by the legislatures and the courts to include the area of consumer products liability.[34] Most states have adopted or adapted the definition of strict liability, which states that the manufacturers or sellers of defective and unreasonably dangerous products are liable, without proof of negligence or fault, for injuries caused by such products to the user or consumer.[35] There is an exception for products, such as blood or drugs, that are considered to be unavoidably unsafe. In order to make the manufacturer or seller liable for injuries resulting from these products, the plaintiff must prove that the manufacturer or seller had either constructive or actual knowledge of the defect that made the product unreasonably dangerous. To date, hospitals have successfully argued that they are not manufacturers or sellers of products. Hospitals maintain that they provide services to patients and that the products used are incidental to the service and therefore do not constitute the sale of a product.[36]

Courts have adopted the same attitude in refusing to assign liability to hospitals for breach of product warranty. Most courts have held that breach of warranty actions are improper because a patient enters the hospital to be treated for an illness and not to purchase a product. Liability has been assigned, however, in situations in which the hospital could have found the defect by reasonable inspection.[37]

Intentional Tort Liability

An *intentional tort* is a deliberate and conscious action that interferes with an individual's property or person. The required elements are intent and action. The plaintiff must prove that the defendant consciously performed the act in order to accomplish a specific result or that any reasonable person would have known that a particular consequence would occur.[38] The intent does not have to be hostile or based on a desire to harm another person. In fact, the defendant may have meant it as a practical joke or may have honestly believed that he or she would not injure the plaintiff or may even have thought he or she was seeking the plaintiff's own good. In intentional torts, the injury complained of is the intent to interfere or invade the person or property of another in a manner that is unlawful.[39]

The element of intent may also persuade the court to award punitive damages as well as actual damages as a means of deterring such conduct in the future. Intentional torts can arise as a result of the patient–nurse and patient–hospital relationships. The most common intentional torts are assault, battery, and false imprisonment, which are discussed in Chapter 14 in the context of the patient's right to consent, and invasion of privacy and defamation, which are discussed in Chapter 15 in the context of the patient's right to privacy and confidentiality.

Unintentional Tort Liability

An *unintentional tort* is a negligent action that causes personal injury to a plaintiff. There are three essential differences between an intentional tort and a negligent wrong. In a suit for negligence the plaintiff (1) does not have to prove intent, (2) does not have to prove a willful act occurred since failure to act or acting carelessly can constitute negligence, and (3) must prove that he or she suffered a personal injury as a result of the defendant's negligent conduct.

The tort of negligence is based on the belief that certain relationships or privileges impose a duty on individuals to act reasonably toward each other. The standard of care required of everyone is that one should act "as a reasonably prudent person would act under the same or similar circumstances." For example, parents can be held negligent for not taking proper care of their children and drivers can be held negligent for driving in a manner that causes a person to be injured.

Professional negligence or malpractice is concerned with the actions of professionals toward the persons to whom they have incurred a duty. Malpractice is the negligence of a professional person while acting in a professional capacity. In cases of professional negligence or malpractice the jury usually needs the testimony of an expert witness to help it decide how the reasonably prudent professional should have acted under the circumstances presented by that particular case. Negligence is discussed in Chapter 12, and nursing practice litigation is discussed in Chapter 13.

NURSE MANAGER LIABILITY

All of the principles discussed in this chapter apply to nurse managers. Nurse managers, as licensed professional nurses, are personally liable for their tortious actions;

however, because they are also hospital employees, the doctrine of *respondeat superior* makes the hospital vicariously liable for the payment of damages to the injured plaintiff. Nurse managers are accountable for the manner in which they carry out their responsibilities. They are held liable for delegating tasks to individuals who they know or should know are unprepared to carry them out. They can also be held liable for failing to adequately supervise the people and practices under their control. Because nurse managers are not employers, they are not held liable for the tortious acts committed by employees under their direction or control.

There are circumstances in which the decisions of a top level nurse manager could result in the hospital's being held directly responsible for breaching the standard of care. In *Pisel v. Stanford Hospital*,[40] the director of nursing ordered the alteration of the nursing record to cover up an incident in which a psychiatric patient had suffered brain damage as a result of having been left unattended for hours in a locked seclusion room. The director of nursing, without the knowledge of the hospital administration and in violation of hospital policy, ordered all of the nurses who had charted on the record during the time of the incident to alter and rewrite their notations. The original nursing notes were removed, and the falsified nursing notes were substituted in the patient's record. When the substitution was discovered in the course of the trial, the judge told the jury that it could consider the substitution of records as evidence that the hospital was conscious of its negligence. The hospital was found directly liable for a $3.6 million judgment that was upheld on appeal.

Indemnification

The doctrine of *respondeat superior* does not relieve the negligent practitioner of personal liability—it only provides the injured party with another party to sue. Under the doctrine of vicarious liability, hospitals who are themselves blameless are obligated to pay damages to the party injured as a result of their employee's tortious conduct. Indemnification refers to the employer's right to be "made whole again," that is, to recover the amount of damages paid by the employer to the plaintiff on the employee's behalf.[41] To exercise their right to indemnification a hospital would have to file a separate action against the negligent employee asking to be repaid for the money paid to the plaintiff in excess of the hospital's insurance policy coverage. The right of indemnification is only available to employers who are themselves blameless. If the hospital itself is found negligent as a corporation it cannot file an indemnification action to recover its losses. To date, employers have not generally exercised their right to indemnification. The futility of seeking the repayment of a large sum of money from an individual nurse or employee, the chilling effect on employee recruitment and retention, and general public policy considerations are among the major reasons used to explain the employer's reluctance to file indemnification actions against their employees.

NOTES

1. Robert D. Miller, *Problems in Hospital Law* (Rockville, Md.: Aspen Publishers, Inc., 1983), 18.

2. 42 C.F.R. § 405: 1021 (1985).

3. American College of Hospital Administrators, Ad Hoc Committee, "The Evolving Role of the Hospital Chief Executive Officer," in *Hospital Legal Forms, Checklists and Guidelines,* Vol. 1, eds. Howard S. Rowland and Beatice L. Rowland (Rockville, Md.: Aspen Publishers, Inc., 1987), 2:8.

4. Miller, *Problems in Hospital Law,* 116.

5. 42 C.F.R. § 405: 1011 (1985).

6. ANA Commission on Nursing Services, "Standards for Organized Nursing Services" (Kansas City, Mo.: ANA Publications, 1982), 1–10.

7. Ibid.

8. Ibid.

9. Joint Commission on Accreditation of Healthcare Organizations, *Accreditation Manual for Hospitals* (Chicago: Joint Commission, 1986):58.

10. J. Douglas Peters and Jeanette C. Peraino, "Malpractice in Hospitals: Ten Theories for Direct Liability," *Law, Medicine and Health Care* 12 (1984):2.

11. *McDonald v. Massachusetts General Hospital,* 120 Mass. 432 (1876); for a historical perspective on direct liability, see B. Abbott Goldberg, "The Duty to Regulate the Quality of Patient Care: A Legal Perspective," in *Hospital Quality Assurance,* ed. Jesus J. Pena, Alden N. Haffner, Bernard Rosen, and Donald W. Light (Rockville, Md.: Aspen Publishers, Inc., 1984), 25–47.

12. *Schloendorff v. Society of New York Hospital,* 102 N.E. 92 (1914).

13. *Darling v. Charleston Community Memorial Hospital,* 33 Ill. 2d 326, 211 N.E.2d 253 (1965), *cert. denied,* 383 U.S. 946 (1966).

14. Goldberg, "Duty to Regulate," 37.

15. *Johnson v. Misericordia Community Hospital,* 99 Wis. 2d 708, 301 N.W. 156 (1981).

16. *Fridena v. Evans,* 127 Ariz. 516, 622 P.2d 463 (1981).

17. *Corleto v. Shore Memorial Hospital,* 138 N.J. Super. 301 A.2d 534 (1975).

18. *Gonzales v. Nork,* 131 Cal. Rptr. 240, 573 P.2d 458 (1978).

19. *Fiorentino v. Wenger,* 279 N.Y.S. 2d 557, 26 A.2d 693 (1967).

20. *Bost v. Riley,* 44 N.C. App. 638, 262 S.E.2d 391 (1980).

21. Arthur F. Southwick, *The Law of Hospitals and Health Care Administration* (Ann Arbor, Mich.: Health Administration Press, 1978): 411; lists Michigan, Indiana, and Arizona.

22. Joint Commission on Accreditation of Healthcare Organizations, *Accreditation Manual for Hospitals* (Chicago: Joint Commission, 1982) Standard I, 51; Standard IX, 55; Standard X, 56.

23. Eric Springer, "Hospitals at Risk for All Behavior," *QRC Advisor* 1, no. 3 (January 1985):1–3.

24. William L. Prosser, *Law of Torts,* 4th ed. (St. Paul, Minn.: West Publishing Co., 1971), 460.

25. Ibid., 459.

26. Edward E. Hollowell, "Liability for Employees' Intentional Torts: A Growing Concern for Hospitals," *Law, Medicine and Health Care* 12, no. 2 (April 1984):6.

27. *Tonsic v. Wagner,* 329 A.2d 497 (Pa. 1974).

28. *Willinger v. Mercy Catholic Hospital,* 362 A.2d 280 (Pa. Sup. Ct. 1976).

29. *Hill v. Hospital Authority of Clarke County,* 137 Ga. App. 633, 224 S.E.2d 739 (1976).

30. *Keene v. Methodist Hospital,* 324 F. Supp. 233 (D. Ind. 1971).

31. *Paintsville Hospital Co. v. Rose,* 683 S.W.2d 255 (Ky. 1985).

32. Prosser, *Law of Torts,* 2.

33. Salvatore F. Fiscina et al., *A Sourcebook for Research in Law and Medicine* (Owings Mill, Md.: National Health Publishing, 1985), 298.

34. Prosser, *Law of Torts,* 492.

35. RESTATEMENT OF TORTS § 402 A.

36. Cynthia E. Northrop and Mary E. Kelly, *Legal Issues in Nursing* (St. Louis: C.V. Mosby Co., 1987), 547.

37. *Butler v. Northwestern Hospitals of Minneapolis*, 278 N.W.37 (1938).

38. Mary Dolores Helmelt and Mary Ellen Mackert, *Dynamics of Law in Nursing and Health Care* (Reston, Va.: Reston Publishing Company, 1982), 8.

39. Prosser, *Law of Torts*, 31.

40. *Pisel v. Stanford Hosp.*, 430 A.2d 1 (1980).

41. Prosser, *Law of Torts*, 311; see also Helmelt and Mackert, *Dynamics of Law in Nursing*, 25.

Chapter 12

Maintaining the Standard of Care

Nurses have a legal and an ethical duty to practice nursing according to a professional nursing standard of care. Nurses are required to use the same degree of knowledge and skill as reasonably prudent nurses would use under the same or similar circumstances and, if they fail to do so, they can be sued for malpractice by the injured plaintiff. Hospitals can also be sued directly for their failure to provide a reasonable standard of care within the institution and indirectly for the negligent actions of the nurses. Nurses at all levels of management have a responsibility to monitor the quantity and quality of nursing services within the institution. Some nurse managers also have the authority to advise and evaluate the staff nurses to whom the responsibility for the delivery of nursing care has been delegated.

NEGLIGENCE AND MALPRACTICE

Negligence is the failure to exercise the degree of care that a reasonably prudent person would exercise under the same or similar circumstances. *Malpractice* (professional negligence) refers to negligent acts committed by a person in his or her professional capacity. It is defined as any professional misconduct, unreasonable lack of skill or fidelity in professional or fiduciary duties, evil practice, or illegal or immoral conduct.[1] There are fundamental differences between a lawsuit based on a charge of negligence and a lawsuit claiming malpractice. In a malpractice suit

- the act of negligence must have been committed in the course of carrying out a professional responsibility
- the statute of limitations is generally shorter than for negligence
- the standard of care will be tested in reference to the behavior of other nurses
- the testimony of an expert witness is usually required to prove the standard of care

When professionals are sued for malpractice they are accorded these added protections; however, they are not available to nurses in jurisdictions where the courts do not recognize that the nurse's actions are those of a professional. The legal concept of professionalism has traditionally considered a profession to require (1) a rigorous and systematic educational program for practitioners, (2) a code of ethics, (3) a strong research program, and (4) a certain authority and prestige associated with the field.[2] The nursing profession has the altruism and the code of ethics and is improving in the area of research; however, in prestige and authority it is still lagging behind other professions. It has been suggested that the continued existence of a variety of educational paths leading to nursing credentials contributes significantly to the inferior image of nursing.[3] The confusion surrounding the status of nursing sometimes results in the courts having to decide on a case-by-case basis whether registered nurses are, in the legal sense, professionals.

Types of Negligence

Negligence is also categorized according to type and degree.

- Misfeasance is the improper performance of a lawful act.
- Malfeasance is the performance of an act that is wrong or unlawful.
- Nonfeasance is the omission to perform or total neglect of a duty.
- Criminal negligence is wanton or reckless conduct that shows a disregard for the safety of another or a willful indifference to the injury liable to follow. State statutes make it punishable as a crime.
- Ordinary negligence is the failure to do what a reasonably prudent person would do or doing what a reasonably prudent person would not do under the same or similar circumstances.
- Gross negligence is the intentional failure to perform a duty in reckless disregard of the consequences as affecting the life or property of another. It is the degree of negligence that could be considered criminal.

In order to establish a claim of negligence or malpractice, a plaintiff is required to introduce proof of the four elements of negligence: (1) duty, (2) breach of the duty, which is the failure to meet the required standard of care, (3) causation, and (4) injury (Exhibit 12-1).[4]

DUTY

The courts have stated that "in negligence cases, the duty is always the same, to conform to the legal standard of care or reasonable conduct in the light of apparent risk."[5] The plaintiff must first prove that the person charged with negligence is under a legal duty to exercise due care. There is no legal duty to come to the aid of another unless a legal relationship exists. For example, people have a duty to act reasonably toward their dependents, if they caused or contributed to a person's injury, if they own or operate the premises where the injury occurred, and if they have a contractual obligation to come to the aid of another person.

Exhibit 12-1 Negligence and Its Defenses

Negligence

      Duty

      Standard (Breach)

      Causation

      Injury

Defenses/Counterclaims/Immunities

      1.   **Release**

      2.   **Statute of Limitations**

      3.   **Plaintiff's Failure to Prove Negligence**

      4.   **Contributory Negligence**

      5.   **Comparative Negligence**

      6.   **Assumption of the Risk**

      7.   **Immunity Statutes**

      8.   **Unavoidable Accident**

A nurse's duty toward a hospital patient is established by providing evidence that the nurse was employed by the hospital in which the plaintiff was a patient. The nurse's duty arises in the context of the hospital-nurse–patient relationship in which the nurse has a legal and an ethical duty to the patient. Once a duty is acknowledged the plaintiff must establish the scope of the duty that the nurse was obligated to provide. The plaintiff must prove that the nurse failed to act as a reasonably prudent nurse would have acted under the same or similar circumstances. In order to do this, the plaintiff must introduce evidence of the standard of care that was required; in other words, the plaintiff must demonstrate how the nurse should have acted under the circumstances.

STANDARD OF CARE

Although a few jurisdictions continue to treat nursing malpractice as ordinary negligence, the trend is to hold nurses to a professional standard of care.[6] The duty of a professional nurse with respect to the care of patients was recognized in 1979 by a California appellate court, which approved the following instructions for the jury:[7]

It is the duty of one who undertakes to perform the services of a trained or graduate nurse to have the knowledge and skill ordinarily possessed, and to exercise the care and skill ordinarily used in like situations, by trained and skilled members of the nursing profession practicing their profession in the same or similar circumstances.

A number of courts have ruled on the standard of care that should be applied to nurses. They have held that

- A nurse specialist is held to the standard of care observed by those in the same specialty (1972).[8]
- A nurse or person who performs a task that is generally performed by physicians is held to the applicable standard of care for physicians (1971).[9]
- A nurse practitioner is held to the standard of care of other nurse practitioners and not to the physician standard of care (1981).[10]
- A student nurse is held to the standard of care of a professional nurse (1962).[11]

The plaintiff proves the standard of care, and the nurse's failure to meet that standard, by the introduction of documentary evidence and the testimony of expert witnesses.

Documentary Evidence

The type of documents that are usually used to prove the standard of care include the following:

- ANA standards of nursing practice, the standards that are published by the specialty professional nursing organizations, and the Joint Commission's standards
- Statutes and administrative codes such as the nursing practice act and regulations, the federal hospital regulations, and the hospital licensing standards and regulations
- Hospital bylaws and hospital policy and procedure manuals relevant to the standard of nursing practice within the institution

These publications may be introduced at trial if they meet the requirements of the legal rules of evidence. The court determines whether they are admissible and what weight the standards will carry. The jury is instructed as to whether it can use them only as (1) information that can be considered along with all the other evidence in determining the standard of care or whether they can be considered as (2) evidence of the standard of care, unless the defendant can prove otherwise.

Expert Witness Testimony

The standard of care in a nursing malpractice action must be established by expert witness testimony. The general rule is that witnesses can testify only as to the facts; their opinions and conclusions are not admissible. On the other hand, expert witnesses are presented for the purpose of eliciting their expert opinion as to the matter being litigated.

Unlike regular witnesses, expert witnesses seldom have direct, personal knowledge of the actual facts and circumstances of the case. They have generally reviewed the record and formed an opinion as to the nurse's conduct. Both the plaintiff and the defendant may present expert witness testimony. The trial court first determines that the expert witness is competent to testify as an expert on the subject. The court must be satisfied that the testimony to be presented is the kind that requires special knowledge, skill, and experience. The purpose of the expert witness' testimony is to help the jury understand the professional or technical issues that are being litigated. Expert witnesses are subject to cross-examination by the attorney for the opposing side. The jury decides how much weight and credence to give to the expert witness' testimony.

Expert Witness Not Required

There are situations in which the testimony of an expert witness is not required by the court, such as

- When the court finds a legal duty existed. Courts arrive at this determination by considering the burden of preventing the injury as opposed to the severity of the injury incurred. Courts have ruled that an ophthalmologist has a duty, as a matter of law, to test patients for glaucoma because the test is relatively easy and the disease has serious consequences.[12]
- When the court finds a presumption of negligence either by recognizing the principle of *res ipsa loquitur* (the thing speaks for itself) or by the violation of a statute. A student nurse anesthetist was found negligent *per se* (by itself) for violating a state regulation stating that only certified nurse anesthetists could provide anesthesia services.[13]
- When the circumstances of the injury are within the jury's common knowledge. Courts have not required expert witness testimony in situations concerning a patient's fall from a bed when the side bars had not been raised or when the case revolves around the reasonableness of the length of time that a patient's call light went unanswered.
- When the jurisdiction does not recognize nursing negligence as professional negligence. Proof of ordinary negligence does not require the testimony of an expert witness.

The legal requirement of expert witness testimony to prove the standard of nursing care does not necessarily mean that the expert witness must be a nurse. Physicians are sometimes allowed to testify. For example, in *Avery v. St. Francis Hospital*, 442 P.2d 1013 (1968), a case involving the fall of a patient from a hospital window, a physician was permitted to testify as to the standard of nursing care in the community. This practice is criticized by many professional nursing organizations, which take the position that the appropriate expert witness for a nursing malpractice case is a professional nurse. Some courts have agreed with this position; in 1980 a Pennsylvania court refused to let a physician testify as to the nursing standard because he could not demonstrate that he knew the hospital's nursing standard.[14]

Locality Rule

Traditionally, the standard of care required of health care professionals was that degree of care ordinarily exercised by health care professionals of similar knowledge and skills in the same or similar community. The application of a community standard of care, commonly referred to as the locality rule, is rapidly being replaced with the recognition of a national standard of care so that expert witnesses can be hired from anywhere in the country. Some state statutes indicate that, in determining the standard of care, the judge or jury is not bound or limited by the accepted or established standard of care with respect to any particular geographical area. Some of the factors that have influenced this change include the (1) general acceptance of hospital accreditation and professional certification programs based on national standards, (2) increased accessibility and availability of educational resources, (3) improved methods of communication and transportation, and (4) courts' and legislatures' reluctance to continue to permit variable standards for the delivery of health care services that are based on geography.

Respected Minority Rule

The practice of nursing may involve situations in which there are several different, equally safe and efficient ways of performing a procedure. There is no liability if the nurse has followed the approach used by a respected minority of the profession.

CAUSATION

Proximate cause or legal cause requires that the plaintiff prove that a reasonably close connection exists between the defendant's conduct and the plaintiff's injury.[15] Many lawsuits are lost by plaintiffs who are unable to prove the causal relationship. Proximate cause requires a two-pronged inquiry:[16]

1. Is the defendant's conduct the cause "in fact" of the plaintiff's injury?

Two tests are used to answer this question. First, could the injury have occurred "but for" the defendant's conduct. For example, the nurse's negligent administration of an overdose of medication that results in the patient suffering an adverse reaction. Second, was the defendant's conduct a material and substantial factor in bringing about the injury. This issue is critical when there is more than one defendant.

2. How far will the law extend the responsibility for the defendant's conduct to the consequences that have occurred?

Foreseeability of the risk of injury is the criterion used to determine the limits of the defendant's liability. If the defendant's failure to foresee the consequences of the action is proven to be a direct cause of the patient's injury, legal causation is established. For example, in *Laidlow v. Lion Gate Hospital*, 70 W.W.R. 727 (1969), the court determined that the nursing supervisor's knowledge of the operating room schedule and routine made her aware of the number of patients that could be in the recovery room at the same time. She was held liable for allowing two nurses to go to coffee break at the same time, a decision that left only one nurse to monitor three patients in the recovery room; as a result, one of the patients suffered anoxia and brain damage. The court determined that this type of injury was a foreseeable consequence of the nurse's conduct.

RES IPSA LOQUITUR

The doctrine of *res ipsa loquitur*, a Latin phrase that translates as "the thing speaks for itself," is used to satisfy the needs of a plaintiff who has suffered an injury and has no way of knowing how it occurred or who, of several defendants, may be liable. Four conditions must exist in order for the court to apply the doctrine:

1. The injury must be of a kind that ordinarily does not occur unless someone has been negligent.
2. The injury must have been caused by an agency or instrumentality that is within the exclusive control of the defendant.
3. The plaintiff must not have contributed to the injury in any way.
4. Evidence as to the truth of what really happened must be unavailable to the plaintiff.

If these four conditions are met, the law will infer or presume the fact that the defendant's negligence was the proximate cause of the plaintiff's injury.[17] In the context of medical injury, the doctrine is sometimes applied when the patient receives unusual injuries while unconscious or in the course of medical treatment. The first medical malpractice case involving the doctrine concerned a patient who had undergone an appendectomy and, on awakening from the anesthetic, complained of a sharp pain in his right shoulder. The pain increased and eventually resulted in his being unable to lift his right arm due to paralysis of the shoulder muscles. The California Supreme Court reversed the lower court's decision and permitted the application of the doctrine of *res ipsa loquitur*.[18]

INJURY

In negligence actions plaintiffs are required to prove that they suffered physical, emotional, or financial injury.[19] The plaintiff is compensated for the injury by an award of money damages that the defendant is ordered to pay. Types of damages include nominal, actual or compensatory, and punitive damages.

Nominal damages are a minimal sum that is sometimes awarded to vindicate a technical right; however, nominal damages cannot be obtained in a negligence action where no actual loss occurred. Actual or compensatory damages are the losses sustained by the plaintiff and include medical costs, loss of earnings, impairment of future earnings, and past and future pain and suffering. Punitive damages, which are also called exemplary damages, are designed to punish the defendants and deter others from following their example. Some states do not allow punitive damages whereas others will allow them in situations in which the defendant has acted with wanton, reckless disregard for the plaintiff's safety or welfare.

In many jurisdictions, state statutes indicate the persons, other than the plaintiff, who may claim compensatory damages. For example, some states allow family members who suffered emotional distress by having witnessed another family member's injuries to claim damages (negligent infliction of emotional distress). A child can sue for injuries caused while *in utero*. Prenatal injuries are compensable as long as the child was born alive. Representatives of the person's estate may also claim damages under a "wrongful death statute." This includes the wrongful death of a child born alive and has been expanded by the courts to include the wrongful death of a stillborn.[20]

The jury decides the amount of compensatory damages and whether to award an additional amount as punitive damages. Compensatory damages and out-of-court settlements are not taxable to plaintiffs because their purpose is to make the plaintiff whole again, to replace what has been lost. On the other hand, punitive damages are regarded as a "windfall" to the plaintiff and are therefore taxable as income.[21] The plaintiff is entitled to receive the damages awarded in a lump sum payment from the defendant. Jury awards of damages are subject to review by an appellate court.

DEFENSES AND COUNTERCLAIMS

In a civil action for negligence, the plaintiff must prove by a preponderance of the evidence that the defendant was negligent. A *prima facie* case requires that the plaintiff prove the elements of duty, breach of duty (failure to meet the standard of care), causation, and injury. The defendant has a right to present evidence in defense of the conduct under review and a right to institute counterclaims that will require the jury to consider the plaintiff's behavior. Defenses and counterclaims appropriate to professional negligence include release, statute of limitations, the plaintiff's failure to prove a cause of action, contributory negligence, comparative negligence, assumption of the risk, immunity statutes, and unavoidable accident (see Exhibit 12-1).

Release

A *release* is a relinquishment, concession, or giving up of a right, claim, or privilege by the person in whom it exists to the person from whom it might have been demanded or enforced.[22] When the parties agree to a settlement, the plaintiffs are usually required to sign a general release surrendering their right of action against the defendant. The plaintiff's spouse is also required to sign a release surrendering his or her right of action against the defendant. In suits involving a minor, a release signed by a parent surrenders only the parental claims; approval of a court is required in order to surrender the minor's rights. A minor, on reaching the age of majority, may seek to repudiate the release and reclaim the right to institute a cause of action.[23]

A release should not be confused with an exculpatory agreement. In the context of health care services, an exculpatory agreement would require a person to relinquish his or her right to sue or it would limit the amount of damages recoverable against the health care provider *before* the services were provided. Courts reviewing exculpatory clauses between patients and health care providers have held them to be against public policy and have refused to enforce them.[24]

Statutes of Limitation

Statutes of limitation are laws that limit the time period within which a plaintiff may bring a lawsuit. They are designed to accommodate conflicting policy interests. The statutes prevent defendants from having to unreasonably maintain the threat of a lawsuit for an indefinite period of time while permitting the plaintiffs a reasonable length of time within which to assert their claim.[25] Statutes of limitation are largely a matter of state law because state legislatures determine the time limits within which each of the various types of lawsuits must be filed. In many jurisdictions the time period in which a malpractice suit can be filed by a plaintiff has been set at one to two years. It is critical for plaintiffs to be able to identify when the statute "starts to run," a phrase that is used to refer to the date on which the one- or two-year time limit would begin, because they may not be aware of their injury for a number of years after it occurred. The actual time within which the plaintiff must file a medical negligence suit will often depend on the nature of the injury. Hospitals and health care practitioners have been held liable for a variety of injuries, which include (1) localized traumas such as burns, lacerations, and fractures; (2) general traumas such as shock, brain damage, and paralysis; (3) foreign objects left in patients, such as surgical instruments and sponges; and (4) infections and diseases incurred by patients and also by employees. It has been suggested that the discovery rule should be a rule of reasonableness in interpreting statutes of limitation.[26] In 1948, the U.S. Supreme Court refused to apply a strict interpretation of the statute in a case involving job-related silicosis, stating that doing so would imply "that at some moment in time, unknown and inherently unknowable, even in retrospect (the plaintiff) was charged with knowledge of the slow and tragic disintegration of his lungs."[27] The court determined that because diseases are not so readily discernable as accidental injuries, a different accrual time should apply. This view has prevailed, and today in most jurisdictions the statute starts to run when the plaintiff discovers or should reasonably have discovered that his or her injury may have been caused by the defendant's negligence. If the defendant fraudulently conceals the cause of injury, the courts either find that the limitation period of the statute did not apply during the time of concealment or they rule that the defendant's fraud bars the use of the statute of limitation as a defense.[28]

Multiple Statutes

The plaintiff's lawsuit must be filed within a specified time; however, there are situations in which the plaintiff's actions may be subject to more than one statute of limitation. For example, in 1985 a New York court ruled that the two-year statute of limitation for malpractice barred the plaintiff's malpractice suit against the physicians, nurses, and the hospital in its capacity as the nurse's employer. They held, however, that the hospital could be held liable for its own negligence under the three-year statute of limitation for negligence. The plaintiff had claimed that the hospital was negligent because it failed to provide competent medical personnel and also failed to promulgate and enforce appropriate regulations and procedures.[29] In another case decided in 1985, the Illinois Appellate Court held that the plaintiff's suit for medical malpractice against a physician and a hospital concerning an object left in the plaintiff's eye following surgery performed in 1975 was barred by the four-year statute of limitation for malpractice. The court reasoned, however, that because the nurses were not included within the scope of the Illinois malpractice statute, the expiration of the malpractice statute of limitations did not bar a negligence action against the nurses who had assisted the physician in the operating room. The Illinois statute has since been amended to include registered nurses and dentists.[30]

Plaintiff's Failure To Prove Negligence

Defendants can successfully defend a nursing malpractice action if they establish that there was no duty, that the nurse acted reasonably under the circumstances, that the nurse's conduct was not the cause of patient's injury, or that there was no injury. In other words, the defendant claims that the plaintiff did not prove one or more of the elements that are required for a *prima facie* case of negligence or malpractice. Motions to dismiss for failure to prove a cause of action can be maintained before, during, and after the trial. At the close of the plaintiff's evidence the defendant's attorney will usually make a motion to dismiss the case on the basis that the plaintiff failed to prove a cause of action. If the judge affirms the motion, the trial ends at this point; however, if the judge denies the motion, the defense attorney must begin to present the defendant's case. After the defendant has presented the evidence, the defense attorney may again make a motion for a directed verdict on the basis that the plaintiff did not prove his or her case. If the judge agrees, and affirms the motion, the jury will be instructed to return a verdict for the defendant; if the judge denies the motion for a directed verdict, the case goes to the jury. If the jury finds for the plaintiff, the defense attorney can make a motion asking the judge to render a judgment *non obstante veredicto* (NOV), which means a judgment notwithstanding the jury's verdict, which, if granted, would reverse the determination of the jury. Judgments NOV are only granted when it is obvious that the jury verdict had no reasonable support in fact or was contrary to the law. All of the trial judge's decisions are subject to review and reversal on appeal. If a trial court denies the defendant's motion for a directed verdict or for a judgment NOV and the appellate court finds that the ruling was in error, they may reverse the case with directions to enter judgment for the defendant.[31]

Contributory Negligence

The defendant may file a counterclaim alleging that the plaintiff's conduct contributed to the cause of the injury. The two elements that must be established are that (1) the plaintiff's conduct fell below the standard of care to which individuals are supposed to conform for their own protection and (2) there is a causal connection between the plaintiff's negligent conduct and the plaintiff's injury.[32] Contributory negligence is based on the theory that although the defendant violated the standard of care and is liable, the plaintiff cannot recover because his or her own conduct contributed to the injury. In some jurisdictions proof of the plaintiff's negligence, no matter how slight, acts as a total bar to the recovery of damages from the defendant. The harshness of this rule, which allows defendants to totally escape liability, even in situations in which their negligence is far greater than the negligence of the plaintiffs, has prompted some state legislatures to enact comparative negligence statutes.

Comparative Negligence

Comparative negligence is an appropriate counterclaim for situations in which both the defendant and the plaintiff were negligent. In jurisdictions that recognize comparative negligence, the jury is required to find negligence on the part of the defendant and the plaintiff, the percentage of negligence that should be attributed to the defendant and to the plaintiff, and the total amount of damages that should be awarded to the plaintiff.[33]

Under the theory of comparative negligence, the total damage award would be reduced in proportion to the percentage of the plaintiff's liability. For example, if the jury found the defendant to be 80 percent negligent and the plaintiff to be 20 percent negligent, the jury's $100,000 total damage award would be reduced by 20 percent and the defendant would have to pay the plaintiff $80,000. The plaintiff must have been found to be less negligent than the defendant in order to recover an award of damages.

Assumption of the Risk

Assumption of the risk applies to situations in which the person knows of a danger and intelligently and voluntarily assumes the risk.[34] The legal result is that the defendant is relieved of the duty that would otherwise exist. This defense is appropriate in the following instances:[35]

- The plaintiff voluntarily enters into some relationship with the defendant, with knowledge that the defendant will not or cannot protect him or her from the risk. (Nurses who knowingly and voluntarily take care of patients under dangerous conditions such as in outbreaks of communicable disease or radiation hazards or in institutions such as prisons and mental hospitals could probably not sue the patient for their injuries.)

- The plaintiff is aware of the risk already created by the defendant's negligence and proceeds to voluntarily accept it. (Nurses who continue to use unsafe or defective equipment that could injure them as well as the patient.) The nurse's actions could block a suit to the manufacturer or seller of the equipment for their injuries and make the hospital liable for the injuries of the plaintiff.

- The plaintiff, in advance, consents to the relief of the defendant of an obligation of conduct toward him or her and assumes the risk of injury, from a known risk, arising from what the defendant is to do or leave undone. (Patients who sign themselves out of the hospital against medical advice.)

In all of these situations the defendant would be required to establish that the plaintiff (person assuming the risk) knew and understood the risk and assumed it voluntarily. In some jurisdictions, assumption of the risk is not distinguished from comparative negligence except in actions against an employer.[36]

Immunity Statutes

The common law doctrine of charitable immunity is essentially history. Charitable institutions are today held liable for their negligent acts and those of their employees and agents. Immunity conferred by state legislatures in state statutes continues to provide a defense for the defendant charged with negligence. For example, a New York statute grants immunity for errors of professional judgment,[37] whereas a California statute provides immunity to public employees for any injury incurred by a plaintiff that is a result of the exercise of his or her discretion.[38]

Most jurisdictions have enacted Good Samaritan statutes that grant immunity to persons, including health care professionals, who stop and render aid at the scene of an emergency.[39] The statutes vary markedly as to the person protected, the standard of care required, and the types of situations that are covered. Most of the statutes require the person providing the aid do so in good faith and without compensation. Good Samaritan statutes are enacted by legislatures to encourage people to stop and render aid at the scene of an emergency. Despite the vagueness and ambiguity of the statutes there are no reports of successful litigation against a health care professional who has provided aid at the scene of an emergency. The immunity conferred in these statutes does not apply to health care professionals in the hospital setting. In fact, some statutes specifically exempt hospitals from the definition of "scene of an emergency."[40] In addition, the courts have consistently refused to extend the immunity to emergencies that occur in a hospital; therefore, staff nurses, emergency department nurses, physicians, and other hospital employees cannot claim the protection of the Good Samaritan statute for their negligent actions in a hospital emergency.[41]

Unavoidable Accident

An *unavoidable accident* is an unintended occurrence that could not have been foreseen or prevented by the exercise of reasonable precautions.[42] This theory is applicable to situations such as injuries caused by drivers, who without any prior knowledge of a medical condition, suffer heart attacks, fainting spells, or seizures and lose control of their cars. It is also applied to injuries resulting from natural disasters such as hurricanes and earthquakes. Hospitals can claim the defense of unavoidable accident for injuries suffered by patients only in situations that were unforeseeable and completely outside the hospital's control.

ADMISSION

The common law rule that there is no duty to come to the aid of another allows hospitals to legally refuse to admit patients. Courts and legislatures, seeking to ameliorate the consequences of the rule on people needing medical care, are restricting the right of hospitals to deny admission or treatment in an ever-increasing number of situations. Hospitals are required to admit people who have a common law, contractual, or statutory right to be admitted. They are also obligated to treat and/or admit individuals who are in need of immediate or medically indicated emergency care.

Common Law Right to Admission

A person has a common law right to admission in situations in which the hospital has incurred a duty toward them. A hospital is obligated to admit a person if it has caused, or is responsible for, his or her injuries (e.g., if the patient became ill or was injured while on the hospital's premises). A hospital assumes a duty when it exercises control of the person by assessing the patient's condition and providing medical advice and treatment.

Contractual Right to Admission

Contracts between hospitals and employers to provide health care services for their employees and contracts with insurance companies agreeing to accept subscribers, under the terms of their policy, create a right of admission for eligible employees. In hospitals that are run solely for the benefit of one company, employment by that company would create a right of admission if medically warranted.

Statutory Right to Admission

Public hospitals that are run by the state or federal government are obligated by statute to admit patients from a certain population. For example, veterans hospitals must admit veterans who qualify for admission, state psychiatric hospitals are required to admit patients who meet the statutory criteria for admission, and county hospitals are obligated to provide care and treatment for any person who is a resident of the county regardless of ability to pay.

A private hospital's right to refuse admission is subject to the statutes, guidelines, and accreditation standards that regulate its services. The openness of a hospital's admission policy is generally dependent on its legal obligations and on the hospital's perception of its place in the community.

Antidiscrimination Statutes

Federal and state antidiscrimination statutes do not provide a specific right to admission, but they do require that a person who is otherwise eligible for admission not be discriminated against because of race, color, national origin, handicap, diagnosis, or ability to pay. Title VI of the Civil Rights Act forbids discrimination on the basis of race, color, or national origin in any institution that receives federal financial assistance.[43] Department of Health and Human Services regulations make a hospital's participation in Medicare programs conditional on the assurance that the hospital will not use race or ethnic background in admission policies or in the provision of hospital services.[44] The Rehabilitation Act of 1973 forbids discrimination on the basis of handicap in institutions that receive federal funds.[45] Hospitals that are receiving Medicare or Hill-Burton reimbursement cannot deny hospitalization or services because a person is handicapped. The term *handicap* has been interpreted to include substance abuse; therefore, alcohol and drug abuse patients cannot be denied hospital services. A Texas court has ruled that emergency departments must provide acute care to persons with serious alcohol-related illnesses provided the hospitals have adequate treatment facilities.[46] In 1987, the U.S. Supreme Court ruled that a teacher afflicted with tuberculosis, a contagious disease, is a "handicapped person" protected from discrimination by the Rehabilitation Act.[47] It has been suggested that in principle this decision is applicable to the person with acquired immunodeficiency syndrome (AIDS).[48] State child protection statutes give the hospital the authority to detain and, if necessary, admit and treat a child if there is imminent danger to the child's health and life. Some state statutes require hospitals to provide treatment to the victims of sexual abuse or sexual assault. The Hospital Survey and Construction Act of 1944 (Hill-Burton) requires that facilities receiving financial assistance under the act provide a reasonable volume of services to those unable to pay.[49] Under the program, hospitals are obligated to provide, on an annual basis, up to 3 percent of their operating costs or 10 percent of the federal assistance received under Title VI and Title XVI of the Public Services Act.[50]

Right to Emergency Care

A person has a special right to hospital care if his or her condition represents a true or actual emergency. There is a distinction between the public's perception of an emergency and the medical reality of an emergency. An *emergency* has been defined as any condition that the patient, or the person bringing the patient to the hospital, believes requires medical attention.[51] This evaluation is valid until a health care professional has determined that the patient's life or well-being is not threatened. A true emergency is any condition clinically determined to require immediate medical care. These conditions may range from those requiring extensive immediate care and admission to a hospital, to situations that present diagnostic problems that may or may not require admission after examination and testing.[52] The most common emergency situations include heart attacks, hemorrhage, poisonings, shock, pneumonia, severe traumas, burns, fractures, and frostbite.

Since 1962 several courts have recognized a common law right to receive emergency treatment in a hospital. The right has been found to arise from a variety of sources, including

- The hospital's custom of providing emergency care and the patient's reliance on that custom.[53]

- A contractual obligation incurred by the hospital's implied invitation to the public by operating the emergency department.[54]
- Highway and street signs advertising the presence of a hospital that could be considered an offer to provide services that the person accepts when he or she enters the emergency department.
- A hospital's duty to provide emergency services if it is the only hospital in the area.[55]

Many states have enacted statutes that require hospitals to provide emergency services to anyone in need of such treatment. A Texas statute makes it a crime for any officer or employee of a publicly supported hospital to deny a person emergency services available in the facility because of an inability to pay if a physician has diagnosed that the person is seriously ill or injured.[56] California's statute requires every licensed health facility that maintains an emergency department to provide emergency services to any person requesting such services for a condition in which the person is in danger of loss of life or serious injury or illness.[57] In New York, the statute makes it a misdemeanor for a hospital in a city with a population of more than 1 million to fail to provide emergency medical care to all persons who come to the hospital in need of such care. The statute requires ambulance attendants to report a hospital's denial of treatment to the state.[58] In most states, court decisions or state laws require hospitals to provide emergency care to those in need.

Hospital's Right To Refuse Admission

The Joint Commission on Accreditation of Healthcare Organizations requires all accredited hospitals to (1) have a procedure to assess people coming to the emergency department for care and (2) render appropriate services within the defined capability of the hospital.[59] The assessment of the patient must be performed by qualified personnel, and the patient must either be treated or referred to an appropriate facility.[60] A hospital has a right to refuse to admit a nonemergency patient under the following circumstances:

- If the admission is not medically indicated as determined by the physician.
- If space is not available to accommodate the patient. One court has made an exception to this by requiring a mental hospital to admit patients even though the admissions would exceed its bed capacity.[61]
- If the hospital does not and cannot provide the services required by the patient. In these situations the hospital has a duty to transfer the patient to an institution that can provide the services needed.

Transfer

A consenting patient may be transferred to another institution for a variety of reasons, including the need for more specialized care, the need for a more secure environment after appropriate legal proceedings, and the need for the special skills of a chronic care facility. The decision to transfer a patient from one institution to another is a medical decision and the responsibility of the patient's physician. For those instances in which there is a disagreement between the physician and hospital administration as to what is in the best interest of the patient, hospital bylaws and medical committee policies should provide a procedure for third party review of the need to transfer the patient.

DISCHARGE

A hospital incurs liability for negligence if it discharges a patient needing additional care. Areas in which the courts have found hospitals liable include the discharge of an abused infant to the abusing parents without giving the state time to intervene[62] and the failure to provide adequate discharge instructions to the parents of a child who had suffered a head injury.[63] The hospital's right to discharge uncooperative, disruptive patients appears to center around the severity of the patient's condition and the availability of alternate methods of providing the necessary care.[64]

DIAGNOSTIC RELATED GROUPS

Diagnostic related groups (DRGs) is a reimbursement system developed by researchers at the Yale University School of Organization and Management in 1970. The DRG system was approved for Medicare and Medicaid patients by Title VI of the Social Security Amendments,[65] which went into effect on September 12, 1983.[66] The system is based on the selection of a patient's diagnosis from the 470 DRGs that have been identified to date. DRGs form the core of a prospective pricing system in which the hospital's reimbursement for patient care services is computed in advance, according to the DRG formula. The program is premised on the concept that the care of a patient in a DRG category should cost the same as all other patients in that category because the care requirements should be the same. In most instances, the hospital receives one payment for the entire admission based on the DRG and the facility's geographic location. There is no extra payment for longer stays or more procedures, but there is a mechanism by which hospitals can request increased reimbursement for exceptional cases. The goal of the DRG is cost containment. It imposes a financial risk on a hospital when the treatment costs exceed the payment rate. Critics have suggested that DRGs have placed the hospital in the position of health care rationer.[67] They warn that placing the burden of rationing resources on specific health care providers creates a risk that arbitrary, budget-driven decision making will occur.[68] Problem areas have been identified in the preliminary findings of the Senate Special Committee on Aging, which reports that patients are being discharged from hospitals after shorter lengths of stay in poorer health, medical beneficiaries are being told that they must leave the hospital after their coverage is exhausted, and community services are not prepared to handle the "sicker patients."[69]

These conditions will certainly become the basis for litigation by Medicare patients charging the hospital with negligence for failing to provide the standard of care required by their condition. Discharge planning becomes of paramount importance in a system that rewards early discharge to the lowest possible level of care. The responsibilities of nurses for the education and preparation of patients for discharge require their assessment of (1) the patient's condition, (2) the ability of the patient and family to continue the level of care required, and (3) the availability of appropriate community resources. The DRG system has not legally altered the hospital's duty to provide the standard of care that the patient's known or apparent condition requires. Nurses must be able to distinguish situations in which the patient and the family's reluctance to assume the burden of care can be overcome by providing education and encouragement and those in which the patient's capabilities, family support, and community resources are inadequate and could place the hospital at risk for litigation on the basis of patient abandonment or premature discharge.

NOTES

1. *Napier v. Greenzweig*, 256 F. 196 (2d Cir. 1919).
2. Eleanor Tintner Segal, "Is Nursing a Profession?" *Nursing '85* (June 1985):41–43.
3. Ibid., 43.
4. Wiliam L. Prosser, *Law of Torts*, 4th ed. (St. Paul, Minn.: West Publishing Co., 1971), 143.
5. Ibid., 324.
6. Cynthia E. Northrop and Mary E. Kelly, *Legal Issues in Nursing* (St. Louis: C.V. Mosby Co., 1987), 40.
7. *Fraijo v. Hartland Hospital*, 160 Cal. Rptr. 246 (1979).
8. *Webb v. Jorns*, 473 S.W.2d 328 (Tex. Civ. App. 1971), *rev'd on other grounds*, 488 S.W.2d 407 (Tex. 1972).
9. *Thompson v. Brent*, 245 S.2d 751 (La. Ct. App. 1971).
10. *Fein v. Permanente Medical Group*, 121 Cal. App. 3d 135, 175 Cal. Rptr. 177 (1981).
11. *O'Neil v. Glenn Falls Indemnity Co.*, 310 F. 2d 165 (Neb. 1962).
12. *Helling v. Carey*, 519 P.2d 981 (Wash. 1974).
13. *Central Associates P.C. v. Worthy*, 325 S.E.2d 819 (Ga. App. 1984), *aff'd*, 333 S.E.2d 829 (Ga. 1985).
14. *Capan v. Divine Providence Hospital*, 270 Pa. Super. 127, 410 A.2d 1282 (1980).
15. Prosser, *Law of Torts*, 143.
16. Ibid., 236–237.
17. Ibid., 212.
18. *Ybarra v. Spangard*, 154 P.2d 687 (1944).
19. Prosser, *Law of Torts*, 143.
20. Northrop and Kelly, *Legal Issues in Nursing*, 46.
21. William T. Schantz, *The American Legal Environment* (St. Paul, Minn.: West Publishing Co., 1976), 401–402.
22. *Black's Law Dictionary*, 4th ed. (St. Paul, Minn.: West Publishing Co., 1968), 1453.
23. George D. Pozgar, *Legal Aspects of Health Care Administration* (Rockville, Md.: Aspen Publishers, Inc., 1983), 242.
24. *Tatham v. Hoke*, 469 F. Supp. 914 (W.D.N.C. 1979)
25. Theodore Baurer, "Medical Malpractice," *Journal of Hospital Supply, Processing and Distribution* (May/June 1984):62–69.
26. Ibid., 66.
27. *Urie v. Thompson*, 337 U.S. 163 (1948).

28. *Sanders v. H. Nouri*, 688 S.W.2d 24 (Mo. App. 1985).

29. *Bleiler v. Bodnar*, 497 N.E.2d 239, 489 N.Y.S. 2d 885 (1985).

30. *Penkana v. Kasbohm*, 475 N.E.2d 975 (Ill. 1985).

31. Milton D. Green, *Basic Civil Procedure* (Mineola, N.Y.: Foundation Press, Inc., 1972), 176.

32. Prosser, *Law of Torts*, 416–417.

33. Ibid., 436–437.

34. Ibid., 441.

35. Ibid., 440.

36. Ibid., 439; see also *Hagenbar v. Snap-on Tools Corporation*, 239 F. Supp. 676 (1972).

37. *O'Shea v. United States*, 623 F. Supp. 380 (D.C.N.Y. 1985).

38. Cal. Gov't Code § 820.2 (West 1976).

39. Diana Odell Potter, ed., *Practices*, Nurses Reference Library (Springhouse, Pa.: Springhouse Corp., 1984): 198–203; compares the Good Samaritan acts of all the states and Canadian provinces.

40. Arizona Rev. Stat. Ann §§ 32-1471 (1985).

41. *Colby v. Schwartz*, 144 Cal. Rptr. 624 (1978); *McKenna v. Cedars of Lebanon Hospital*, 155 Cal. Rptr. 631 (1979).

42. Prosser, *Law of Torts*, 140.

43. 42 U.S.C. §§ 2000d–2000-6 (1976 and Supp. IV 1980).

44. 42 C.F.R. pt. 80 (1981).

45. 29 U.S.C. §§ 701–709 et seq (Supp. V 1981).

46. *Powell v. State of Texas*, 392 U.S. 514 (1968).

47. *School Board of Nassau County, Fla. v. Arline*, 107 S. Ct. 1123 (1987).

48. Michael R. Brown, "Aids Discrimination in the Workplace: The Legal Dilemma," *Case and Comment* 92, no. 3 (May/June 1987):4.

49. 42 C.F.R. § 53.112.

50. 42 C.F.R. § 124.503.

51. Marguerite R. Mancini and Alice T. Gale, *Emergency Care and the Law* (Rockville, Md.: Aspen Publishers, Inc., 1981), 40.

52. AHA Emergency Services, *The Hospital Emergency Department in an Emergency Care System* (Chicago: American Hospital Association, 1972), vi.

53. *Wilmington General Hospital v. Manlove*, 54 Del. 15, 174 A.2d 135 (1961).

54. *Guerrero v. Copper Queen Hospital*, 112 Ariz. 104, 537 P.2d 1329 (1975).

55. *Stanturf v. Sipes*, 447 S.W.2d 558 (Mo. 1969).

56. Tex. Rev. Civ. Stat. Ann. art. 44382 (Vernon 1976).

57. Cal. Health and Safety Code § 1317 (West 1979).

58. N.Y. Pub. Health Law § 2805b (McKinney 1984).

59. Joint Commission on Accreditation of Healthcare Organizations, *Accreditation Manual for Hospitals* (Chicago: Joint Commission, 1985), 20.

60. Ibid., 21.

61. *Pierce County Office of Involuntary Commitment v. Western State Hospital*, 644 P.2d 131 (Wash. 1982).

62. *Landeros v. Flood*, 17 Cal. 3d 399, 551 P.2d 389 (1976).

63. *Niles v. City of San Rafael*, 42 Cal. App. 3d 230, 116 Cal. Rptr. 733 (1974).

64. *Payton v. Weaver*, 131 Cal. App. 3d 38, 182 Cal. Rptr. 225 (1982); *Modla v. Parker*, 17 Ariz. App. 54, 495 P.2d 494 (1972), *cert. denied*, 409 U.S. 1038 (1972).

65. 97 Stat 65 (April 1983).

66. 42 C.F.R. §§ 405–482.

67. Michael A. Carlucci, "Health Care Systems and Medical Malpractice," *Case and Comment* 91, no. 5 (September/October 1986):36.

68. Ibid., 36.

69. Ibid., 40; see also Michel Clay, "Heinz Raises Specter of Early Discharges," *Hospitals* 15 (April 1985):31.

Chapter 13

Nursing Practice
Litigation

NURSING PRACTICE MANAGEMENT

Hospitals are responsible for the standard of nursing care that is provided within the institution. As corporations they are directly liable to select and maintain a competent professional nursing staff, and as employers they are vicariously liable for the negligent acts of the nurses. The governing board or the chief executive officer usually delegates the implementation and management of nursing services to an executive-level nurse administrator. The American Nurses' Association has defined the role of nurse administrator as it relates to the nursing care within an institution. The Commission on Nursing has stated that "Nurse Administrators are responsible for the quality of nursing care provided within their health care organization. . . . Nurse Administrators are accountable to the consumer, to the nursing profession and to the agency that employs them."[1]

The Commission on Nursing has differentiated three administrative levels, each having a particular focus and contribution within the health care organization. Their publication "Roles, Responsibilities and Qualifications for Nurse Administrators " states that "Nursing Administrators have as their primary objective the timely achievement of patient care goals."[2] They must be able to "conceptualize nursing and operationalize nursing practice."[3] Major objectives for leadership, clinical practice, continuing education, and research are assigned to each level of nursing administration. The following represents the specific clinical practice responsibility assigned to the three administrative levels:[4]

Executive-level nurse managers ensure that nursing practice standards are established and implemented so that sound nursing care is provided to consumers. Specific responsibilities include

- Determining the clinical and administrative goals and directions of the nursing department
- Devising departmental functions and activities to achieve the goals
- Acquiring and allocating resources for the nursing care functions and activities

- Evaluating and revising the organizational goals, structures, activities, and resources of the nursing department

Middle-level nurse managers coordinate activities among nursing units and provide clinical and administrative expertise to the unit's first-line administrators. They also make available the requisite resources for efficient and effective nursing care delivery and provide the nurse executive administrator information that reflects the ongoing state of the department. Specific responsibilities include

- Participating in the development of nursing policy
- Problem solving and supervising the delivery of nursing care
- Evaluating the nursing care provided
- Staffing and scheduling personnel
- Arranging for equipment and supplies
- Evaluating staff for promotion and transfer, disciplinary action, and separation of service
- Providing orientation, training, and continuing education for staff

First-line level nurse managers direct and supervise the nursing staff and ensure the availability of support services that facilitate the delivery of care. They are generally in charge of a unit and have a variety of responsibilities, including

- Providing for the direct nursing care services to patients
- Guiding and supervising the practice of nursing by the nursing staff
- Ensuring that nursing practice is appropriately documented
- Evaluating the nursing staff and taking disciplinary action
- Providing for teaching and ongoing staff development

Nursing administration is primarily responsible for the standard of care within the institution. Charges of nursing negligence or malpractice constitute a legal challenge to that standard of care. Nursing malpractice is a management problem. The malpractice of a professional nurse injures patients, compromises the nurse's license and employment status, and threatens the hospital's assets.

NURSING MALPRACTICE LITIGATION

Nursing malpractice or professional negligence is the failure of a nurse to provide the standard of care that is generally provided by reasonably prudent members of the profession acting under the same or similar circumstances. The standard places a duty on every nurse to possess the same degree of knowledge and skill that is possessed by the average reasonable nurse with the same level of education and experience. Nursing malpractice is the most common type of litigation involving the hospital, the nurse, the patient, and frequently the physician. Nurse managers have been delegated the responsibility of predicting and preventing the occurrence of nursing malpractice. They are responsible for overseeing the safe and competent practice of nursing by nursing professionals who have a legal and ethical obligation to perform according to the standard of care required by the profession. As one author observed, "In supervising the professional, the manager gives up a sometimes considerable measure of direct control in exchange for that person's higher level of responsibility and accountability. This is delegation in its purest and simplest form; the manager surrenders task performance authority and holds the employee responsible for that performance."[5] Nurse managers are administratively required to monitor the delivery of competent nursing care in a manner that will not discourage or disrupt the autonomy of professional practice that is inherent in the individual's license to practice professional nursing. Nurses must be left free to practice nursing yet prevented from practicing nursing negligently. It is a difficult task that requires a balancing of interests based on an intimate understanding of the potential for negligence in the practice of professional nursing.

All authors of legal nursing texts reach the point at which they are required to classify the areas of nursing negligence. The usual approaches include either a "laundry list" of problems, a categorization according to the elements of negligence, or a differentiation according to the stages of the nursing process. My attempts at classification have left me with a profound respect for the intimate and complicated scientific, technological, and sociological services that professional nurses are expected to perform independently, safely, and competently. Nurse managers must manage the nursing care presently being provided; they must also anticipate and prepare nurses for the nursing care that is required when the hospital adopts new types of medical or surgical interventions. New procedures and techniques or areas of patient care should not be implemented until the nursing staff is fully oriented to and is capable of meeting the nursing care needs of the patients. The scope of nursing liability shadows the scope of nursing practice: when the practice increases so does the liability; it is the price the law demands for allowing a profession to expand. Nurse managers should understand that all areas of nursing practice pose a potential threat of litigation and that no approach, including the one to follow, can totally identify all of the risks.

In a nursing malpractice suit, the actions of the allegedly negligent nurse are exposed and examined so that the trier of fact (judge or jury) can determine whether the elements of negligence have been proven by the plaintiff. A review of nursing practice litigation suggests that these actions generally involve challenges to the nurse's professional judgment, as evidenced by the nurse's assessments and interventions, and technical skills in performing procedures and monitoring and using equipment and that they frequently arise within the context of the nurse–physician relationship. The litigation also demonstrates that the failure of a nurse to document properly the standard of care that was provided significantly affects the outcome of the case by weakening or eliminating the hospital's defense. The following is a sampling of the types of litigation that have challenged the standard of nursing practice in hospitals. As a point of interest, the cases for each section are provided in chronological order and the state and date of each case are identified in the text.

ASSESSMENTS AND INTERVENTIONS

The nursing process is a clinical management system that provides individualized goal-directed nursing care to patients. The four steps in the nursing process are assessment, planning, intervention, and evaluation. Most of the litigation involving nursing negligence focuses on the assessment and intervention stages. Planning and evaluation are an important part of the nursing process; however, their potential as a source of legal liability is secondary to the two other stages. The failure to plan or evaluate the care provided will usually result in inadequate or inappropriate assessments and interventions that can be identified by the plaintiffs as a breach of the standard of practice that caused or significantly contributed to their injuries. It is the failure to identify significant changes in the patient's condition, the failure to adequately monitor the patient, the failure to consider the complaints of the patient and family, the failure to take the appropriate nursing action, and the failure to communicate the patient's condition to the physician or to administration that precipitate the plaintiff's lawsuit charging nursing malpractice. The following cases illustrate a few of these situations:

- The nurses failed to properly examine and treat a patient's puncture wound and failed to recognize complications of the injury that would have required referral to a physician (California 1955).[6]

- The emergency department nurse did not examine or provide treatment for a seriously ill infant because she could not contact the child's private physician as was required by hospital policy. Existence of a "true emergency" in the child's condition and the mother's reliance on the custom of the emergency department to provide care overrode the nurse's defense of having adhered to hospital policy (Delaware 1961).[7]

- The nurses ignored the patient's complaint of severe pain following the application of a cast on his foot. They failed to observe and/or recognize the signs of circulatory impairment in the patient's foot and did not inform hospital administration of the progressive gangrenous condition of the patient's leg and of the inappropriate efforts of the attending physician to address the condition (Illinois 1965).[8]

- The nurses failed to seriously consider a patient's protest and refusal to ambulate postoperatively as ordered by the physician. They did not adequately assess the patient's condition and review the order with the physician. The Appellate Court allowed the case to go to trial, overturning the lower court's dismissal of the case on the basis that the nurses had followed the physician's orders (Kentucky 1967).[9]

- The nurses ignored the patient's complaint of a sore throat, failed to recognize the significance of his deteriorating vital signs, and failed to report his deteriorating condition to the physician. As a result, the patient died of a β-hemolytic streptococcal infection. The court ruled that the hospital had a duty to guard against the patient's known physical and mental condition as well as any condition that it should have discovered by reasonable care (Nebraska 1970).[10]

- The nurses failed to recognize the significance of the patient's complaints of dizziness and allowed her to enter the shower alone, where she lost consciousness, fell, and suffered facial injuries. The hospital defended on the grounds that the hospital regulations required a shower for patients every evening and the physician had not indicated that this patient should not shower. The court stated that the presence of a physician's order did not necessarily prevent a hospital from being held liable for the care rendered by the nurses in compliance with these orders (Iowa 1971).[11]

Nursing Supervision

Nurse managers who function as clinical supervisors are not vicariously liable for the negligent actions of the employees under their supervision because they do not have an employer–employee relationship with them, as is required by the doctrine of *respondeat superior*. The staff nurses are liable for their own actions, and the hospital is vicariously liable to pay the damages for the nurse's negligent actions. Nurse supervisors and administrators are responsible for the manner in which they supervise, and the hospital is vicariously liable for the negligent behavior of its supervisors. For example, a hospital was held liable when its nursing supervisor failed to provide a safe level of postoperative care for patients in the recovery room. She had permitted two nurses to go to coffee break at the same time, a decision which resulted in a three patient to one nurse ratio in the recovery room and as a result one of the patients suffered anoxia and severe brain damage (Canada 1969).[12]

Nurse supervisors may rely on the fact that their subordinates are licensed and/or certified as an indicator that they are capable of making the judgments and performing the tasks appropriate to their profession. Nurse managers whose responsibilities include clinical supervision are held liable for (1) inadequate supervision, (2) improper assignments, and (3) failure to take appropriate action if they are personally present and qualified to do so. In malpractice actions, the element of forseeability is critical to the defense of nursing supervisors. They will be held liable if they know or should have known that their subordinates were unprepared, unsafe, or incompetent or if they know that the conditions under which the nurses are functioning are unsafe or inadequate to maintain the proper standard of care.

Patient Abandonment

Claims of negligence due to patient abandonment are a result of the nurse's failure to observe, examine, assess, or monitor a patient's condition. For example, the nurses failed to monitor and provide for the safety of an acutely psychotic patient who was left unattended for several hours in a locked seclusion room. The patient got her head caught between the metal bedframe and the side rails, suffering severe brain damage due to anoxia. The Appellate Court upheld a judgment for $3.6 million (Connecticut 1980).[13] In a case involving a series of negligent actions the nurses failed to provide postoperative care to a patient following an elective laminectomy. They did not take the patient's vital signs nor did they perform neurological checks; in addition, there was no suctioning equipment, although the patient was vomiting. They failed to notify the attending physician of the patient's condition and ignored the legitimate complaints of the patient's family and friends. The nurses did not initiate cardiopulmonary resuscitation when the patient went into cardiac arrest; also their inability to distinguish between a peripheral intravenous line and an atrial catheter resulted in the emergency department physician, who had responded to the emergency call, administering medication directly into the heart. The patient remained in a vegetative state until she died as a result of the nurses' failure to properly care for the balloon cuff of the tracheostomy tube, which eventually worked its way to the posterior of the trachea, eroded part of the left anterior aspect of the thoracic vertebrae, and eroded laterally on the side of the innominate artery, resulting in the patient's bleeding to death. The court held the nurses and the hospital negligent as a matter of law and directed the jury to return a verdict in favor of the plaintiff (California 1981).[14]

Obstetrical emergencies are often the subject of litigation. In one case the nurses failed to adequately examine the patient and to recognize the signs of an obstetrical emergency that would have required the patient to be examined by the physician. The patient had been turned away from the first emergency department after the nurse had contacted a physician by telephone and had been told to advise the patient that the hospital had limited obstetrical facilities and that she should go to another hospital 25 miles away. At the second hospital, the patient was again turned away after a nurse went out to the car, saw that the patient had vomited and was lethargic but, failing to notice any signs of premature labor, advised the family to take the patient to a third hospital. The woman died of a ruptured uterus ten minutes after arriving at the third hospital (Texas 1982).[15] The second hospital was found liable.

An operating room case involved the nurse's failure to follow the hospital policy requiring the circulating nurse to remain in the room and monitor the patient's condition. The patient went into cardiac arrest and suffered deprivation of oxygen that resulted in permanent and total paralysis. The circulating nurse was not in the room when the patient went into cardiac arrest, and the anesthetist was without assistance for two to three minutes. At trial the circulating nurse conceded that she had left the room at a critical time and attempted to defend her action by saying that she had left because she was being "yelled at" by two physicians who had already started surgery in another operating room. The court found that the jury could determine that the nurse had abandoned the patient. They also held that the hospital's failure to provide adequate staff was so obvious that expert witness testimony was unnecessary (California 1983).[16]

In another obstetrical case, the nurses ignored the patient's complaints of pain and neglected to implement the physician's orders for fetal monitoring and intravenous therapy. They also failed to protect the patient's safety and monitor her labor. The woman delivered the infant while she was standing near the bed and the infant fell head first to the floor, sustaining a depressed right parietal skull fracture that left the child mentally retarded. The jury verdict was for $10.5 million (Michigan 1985).[17]

Family Involvement

Ignoring the legitimate complaints and requests of family members has also resulted in hospital liability. Situations in which hospitals were held liable for the nurses' failure to intervene include

- The death of a 13-year-old girl with rheumatic fever and cardiac involvement. Over a six-hour period, the nurses ignored the mother's requests that the physician be notified of her daughter's deteriorating condition. The girl had a fever, blue nail beds, a blue circumoral ring, and bloody froth emanating from her nose and mouth when the mother approached a night supervisor, who finally notified the physician (West Virginia 1965).[18]
- The injuries suffered by a patient who jumped from a hospital window. The nurses had ignored the daughter's warning that she was leaving her father's bedside and that he was still confused and needed supervision. The patient had been transferred from a psychiatric unit to the surgical unit for prostate surgery. The surgical unit nurse was inexperienced in psychiatric care and psychiatric medication and had received no orders to monitor the patient (Kansas 1968).[19]
- The injuries suffered by a patient who jumped from a second floor balcony. The physician had advised watching the patient, and the family had agreed to stay with him; however, the nurses neglected to have someone stay with the patient during the ten minutes it took the family to get to the hospital (New York 1976).[20]

Verdict for Hospital

There are cases in which a hospital successfully defends a nursing malpractice or negligence suit. The following cases represent situations in which the plaintiffs failed to prove that the nurses were negligent. A nurse was not held liable for the complications that a patient suffered while she was on her coffee break. The court found that there was evidence that the patient's condition was much improved before the nurse left for her break and it was not foreseeable that her absence would create an increased risk for the patient (Canada 1969).[21] Nurses were not held liable for failing to perform a vaginal examination on a pregnant patient on her arrival on the obstetrics unit of the hospital. The evidence led the jury to believe that the only available nurses were busy with a complicated delivery and that the decision they made, after externally examining her and determining that she was not in active labor, was reasonable under the circumstances (Utah 1975).[22] The hospital was not held liable for the stabbing death of a man by an adolescent who had jumped out of the car in which he was being transported by his grandmother from one hospital to another. The boy had been brought to the hospital because the grandmother suspected he had taken LSD. The hospital did not have the testing facilities to determine the presence of LSD so they referred her to another hospital in the vicinity. In finding the hospital not liable, the court held that there was no demonstrable evidence that the defendant hospital could have reasonably anticipated the homicidal act of the boy while he was in the emergency department. He had not acted in any bizarre or unusual manner that would have led the emergency department staff to foresee his violent action (Florida 1976).[23] The jury instructions were the focus of the appeal by the plaintiff of a judgment holding the hospital not liable for the death of an asthma patient. The patient had died five minutes after the emergency department nurse had administered a p.r.n. pain medication. The California court allowed the nurse the benefit of the same jury instructions that physicians receive in cases of medical malpractice. The jury was instructed to consider that (1) a nurse is not negligent merely because a therapy does not succeed; (2) a nurse is not negligent if one of several approved methods chosen later proves wrong; and (3) the jury must find the nurse's conduct was the proximate cause of the patient's death. The court held that the nurse was not required to call a physician before administering a p.r.n. medication and that the decision to give a p.r.n. medication is a matter of nursing judgment. In addition, the plaintiff could not prove that the injection was the proximate cause of the patient's death (California 1979).[24]

TECHNICAL SKILLS

The standards of nursing practice require nurses to safely and completely administer medications and perform treatments and procedures that are ordered by the physician and/or required by the nursing process.

Administration of Medication

The standards for the administration of medication are well documented in basic nursing skills courses, in nursing texts, and in the policies and procedures for the administration of medication that are implemented by every hospital. Despite all of these guidelines, errors in the administration of medication remain one of the most frequent areas of negligence litigation. Medication errors arise from nurses giving the wrong substance, giving the wrong dose, using the wrong route, giving the medication at the wrong time, or completely omitting the medication. Examples of litigation involving medication include situations in which the nurse

- Failed to read the label and provided the doctor with a solution of formaldehyde instead of a 1 percent procaine solution (California 1936).[25]
- Failed to follow the standard injection technique, resulting in the patient's suffering wristdrop (California 1955).[26]
- Failed to properly prepare the skin and failed to use a sterile needle, resulting in the development of an abscess in the patient's hip at the injection site (California 1955).[27]
- Failed to read the label and administered hydrochloric acid instead of nose drops in the patient's nose (California 1959).[28]
- Failed to read a new order that changed the route for the administration of the medication from an intramuscular injection to the oral form (Delaware 1962).[29]
- Failed to clarify an ambiguous, incomplete order with the physician and failed to recognize the pediatric elixir form of digitalis and administered a lethal 3-ml intramuscular dose of digitalis to a 3-month-old infant. The physician was also found liable for writing the ambiguous order (Louisiana 1962).[30]
- Administered two units of blood to the wrong patient (Louisiana 1976).[31]

- Failed to read the label and drew up a medication for injection from a vial containing a higher concentration, resulting in the patient receiving 50 times the amount of medication ordered, causing the patient to suffer cardiac arrest. The nurse was experienced in obstetrics and had been transferred to the emergency department where she was not familiar with the medications (New Mexico 1981).[32]

- Injected an intramuscular dose of meperidine (Demerol) and hydroxyzine (Vistaril) three to four inches above the knee, causing nerve damage in the patient's thigh (North Carolina 1983).[33]

- Improperly administered intravenous chemotherapy, resulting in the infiltration of the medication into the patient's forearm, causing severe necrosis and loss of several muscles and tendons (Pennsylvania 1985).[34]

- Erroneously administered an intravenous solution containing potassium chloride, which resulted in the patient's death due to tachycardia (Louisiana 1985).[35]

Equipment

The hospital has a duty to select and maintain adequate equipment. Nurses have a duty to (1) examine the equipment to make sure that it is functioning properly; (2) use the equipment in the manner intended; (3) warn patients of any dangers attendant to the operation of the equipment; (4) remove, isolate, and replace equipment that is malfunctioning; and (5) admit and correct their lack of knowledge and skill or experience with any piece of equipment. Nurse managers are responsible for the development and implementation of training programs to orient nurses to equipment prior to their being required to use it on patients. They are also responsible for the enforcement of the hospital's policies for the selection, maintenance, and use of equipment. Nurses who fail to follow the requirements can become involved in a third party lawsuit with the manufacturer of the equipment. Manufacturers may seek to defend a lawsuit or seek indemnification for their losses on the basis that the nurse (1) failed to inspect or examine the equipment before use, (2) misused the equipment, (3) used the equipment with full knowledge that it was broken or malfunctioning, and (4) lacked adequate knowledge and skill in the use of the equipment.

Nurses are only held responsible for the discovery of defects that are observable or discoverable. This rule was used to find a nurse not liable for burns received by a patient when a defective clamp on proctology equipment allowed hot water to flow unrestricted into the patient's bowel. The court held that "The defect was not patent. The clamp furnished was apparently ready for use and it was not her duty to examine into its mechanical parts for discovery of possible defects" (Minnesota 1938).[36] Examples of litigation involving equipment include situations in which the nurse

- Ignored a patient's complaints of pain and continued to apply the same amount of pressure in using a Stryker saw to remove a patient's cast (Louisiana 1971).[37]

- Failed to monitor the proper functioning and positioning of an electric cautery machine (Oregon 1972).[38]

- Transferred a patient with oxygen equipment that was found to be incompatible with the oxygen wall unit in the patient's room. The hospital was found liable for the patient's death due to anoxia as a result of its lack of standardization of the oxygen equipment (Texas 1974).[39]
- Failed to notice that the patient's respirator was not functioning properly (Georgia 1976).[40]
- Failed to remove the dialysis needles from a patient's arm after disconnecting him from the dialysis machine. The patient had been extremely abusive and disruptive. The nurse supervisor called him a "black son of a bitch" and left the needles in his arm. He refused all offers of assistance by other staff members and left the facility, removing the needles himself and suffering a substantial blood loss. The court, finding extreme provocation, allocated 40 percent of the fault to the patient and 60 percent to the hospital and reduced the patient's damage award by 40 percent (Arkansas 1982).[41]
- Failed to maintain adequate oxygenation levels in a postoperative patient. Testimony revealed that the nurses either failed to respond to the alarm, used malfunctioning equipment, or neglected to provide supplemental oxygen when the respirator could not be properly attached (Washington 1985).[42]
- Failed to monitor the infusion pump on a neonate, who subsequently suffered fluid overload, respiratory arrest, and severe brain damage. The case ended in a $4 million settlement (Arizona 1985).[43]

Procedures

Hospitals are required to follow their bylaws, policies, and procedures. These publications are usually admissible at trial under the business records exception to the hearsay rule. Failure to follow a policy or procedure is not considered absolute proof that the nurse was negligent; however, the jury is allowed to consider such evidence in reaching its decision. Nurse managers are responsible for developing, implementing, monitoring, and evaluating the hospital's nursing policies and procedures. Nurses are responsible for performing the procedures in a safe and competent manner. Examples of litigation in this area include situations in which the nurse

- Failed to properly pad an elbow when restraining a patient for an appendectomy, resulting in injury to the ulnar nerve and causing a permanent numbness in the patient's fingers (Michigan 1968).[44]
- Failed to separate and identify the cyst specimens that were removed from each of the patient's breasts, requiring the patient to undergo a double mastectomy. The physician and the hospital were held to be jointly and severally liable (Florida 1974).[45]
- Failed to perform an instrument count, resulting in a Kelly clamp being left in the patient's abdomen (Pennsylvania 1974).[46]

- Failed to respond to a patient's call light within a reasonable length of time, causing the patient to fall and suffer a back injury when she got out of bed and attempted to walk to the bathroom by herself (Vermont 1975).[47] Falls are a frequent source of litigation. A report by an insurer of the ten most common hospital malpractice claims ranks falls from bed third, walking-related falls ninth, and bathroom-related falls tenth.[48]

- Removed a Foley catheter with the cup inflated, causing a fistula in the patient's bladder. The nurse denied that she had not deflated the cuff; however, a physician testified that, in his opinion, she must have removed it inflated, which caused the fistula. The Appellate Court upheld the jury's finding that the nurse was negligent (Florida 1975).[49]

- Failed to notify the surgeon that a scalpel blade was missing, resulting in the patient's having to undergo additional surgery to have it removed from his bladder. The hospital and the surgeon were found liable on the theory that they both would have benefited by an accurate count of scalpel blades (Kentucky 1977).[50]

- Failed to perform an accurate sponge count, resulting in the hospital alone being held liable because the sponge count was a procedure established by the hospital and the surgeon was not responsible for directing the activity (Texas 1977).[51]

- Failed to recognize that the fetal monitor was indicating fetal distress and failed to notify the physician of the fetal distress, resulting in a profoundly retarded and totally blind child. The case ended in a $2.2 million settlement (Ohio 1984).[52]

- Failed to monitor the patient's contractions and the fetal heart rate every 30 minutes as required by hospital policy and failed to attach an external monitor that was available at the time. The patient delivered vaginally instead of by cesarean delivery, and the fetus was stillborn (Florida 1984).[53]

- Failed to turn on the alarm system on a heart monitoring machine when she left to attend another patient, which resulted in a 70-year-old patient suffering irreversible brain damage. The case ended in a $2.75 million settlement (District of Columbia 1984).[54]

- Failed to correctly suction a newborn who had suffered fetal distress caused by the perinatal aspiration of meconium. The infant had been suctioned by the obstetrician and then transferred to the labor and delivery nurse for further suctioning (Michigan 1985).[55]

Verdict for Hospital

Hospitals win negligence lawsuits filed against nurses in the area of procedure or technical skill if the plaintiff is unable to prove one of the four elements of negligence. For example, an Army hospital nurse injected penicillin into a child's buttocks and the child later demonstrated signs of sciatic nerve injury; however, the jury found that the medical witness testimony failed to prove that the injections caused the injury (Massachusetts 1962).[56] In another case a television antenna wire had been placed so that the patient had to walk around the set to avoid the wire. On the day of discharge the patient stepped over the wire and fell. The jury found that the hospital did not cause the injury because the danger was open and obvious and the patient had the ability to avoid it (Texas 1968).[57] A patient suffered permanent nerve injury to her left shoulder because a Kelly clamp was left in the patient undiscovered for three weeks following a radical mastectomy. The jury found that the sponge and needle counts were the nurse's responsibility but instrument counts were solely the responsibility of the surgeon (Wisconsin 1974).[58] A patient fell from a hospital bed at a time when the protective side rails had not been raised. The court held that the patient failed to establish that the standard of care would ordinarily require the side rails to be raised in her situation. In holding that she failed to prove that the injury was caused by the hospital's conduct, the court stated, "It is the duty of a hospital to provide for the care of its patients, and the degree of care required is such reasonable attention for their safety as their mental and physical condition, if known, requires" (Texas 1980).[59]

NURSE AND PHYSICIAN RELATIONSHIP

Research in the area of professional collaboration has revealed that "the nurse–physician relationship has become a major topic of debate, with particular emphasis placed on the dissatisfaction of nurses with their role, authority and responsibility in health care delivery, and with growing concern on the part of physicians about territorial and economic competition by nurses."[60] Researchers studying the clinical decision making of staff nurses found that there are differences in levels of satisfaction.[61] The data demonstrate that nurses on specialized and critical care units are more satisfied than are nurses who work on general medical-surgical units. The researchers speculate that this is in part because such units promote better nurse–physician communication and afford nurses a greater role in clinical decision making.[62] A 1981 study of factors related to mortality rates in the intensive care units revealed that, "while the type of hospital or the level of technology did not influence patient death rates, positive communication between nurses and physicians, and the nurses' authority to exercise judgment were related to lower mortality rates."[63]

Legal Liability

The manner in which hospitals, nurses, and physicians cooperate and collaborate has always affected the standard of care within the institution. The legal liability for the standard of care provided by hospitals, nurses, and physicians has changed as the public perception and expectation of the role of hospital nurses and physicians have changed.

The development of the nurse's duty has undergone three stages. In the days when hospitals were protected by the doctrine of charitable immunity and physicians could be held liable for the nurse's actions under the doctrine of borrowed servant, the nurse's duty was to simply "follow the doctor's orders."[64] When charitable immunity was eliminated and hospitals could be sued for the negligent actions of the nurses, the nurse's duty was to "follow the doctor's orders unless the nurse knew that in doing so the patient would be seriously injured.'' Nurses were also expected to notify hospital administration when the physician failed to respond to potentially life- or health-threatening situations.[65] Today the doctrine of corporate negligence is applied to hospitals to hold them directly liable for the standard of care within the institution. The hospital's liability has been extended to include actions of nonemployee physicians in situations in which the hospital knows or should have known that the physicians were incompetent. The courts have now held that a nurse's duty is to ''follow the doctor's orders and to take positive action when the orders or the lack of orders create situations in which the patient is not receiving an adequate standard of care.'' For example, when (1) the physician's orders are ambiguous or incomplete; (2) the physician's reaction to the nurse's report is inadequate, in that he or she cannot or will not respond to a life- or health-threatening situation; or (3) the patient is treated in a manner that is a substandard departure from accepted medical practice, the courts have indicated that the nurse has a duty to take some positive action to safeguard the patient, including the notification of hospital administration. The hospitals have been given the responsibility of developing a mechanism for the prompt consideration and resolution of nurse–physician conflicts.[66]

The law introduces an interesting contradiction into the nurse–physician relationship. On the one hand, hospital administrators, nurses, and physicians must cooperate and collaborate in order to maintain a reasonable standard of care within the institution. On the other hand, the hospital's legal obligation to oversee the competence of the nursing and medical staff, the proximity of nurses and physicians to information concerning each other's level of competence, and the conflict created by the nurse employee status versus the physician nonemployee status all contribute to the development of an adversarial relationship between the hospital, the physician, and the nurse. Once a lawsuit is filed, the hospital's insurer, the physician's insurer, and at times the nurse's insurer will all be attempting to prove that it is in their best interest to find the other party primarily liable for the injury. It is on this ally–adversarial relationship that the hospital's policies concerning nurse–physician interaction must be developed and implemented. The litigation surrounding the nurse–physician relationship has focused on the nurse's failure to follow the physician's orders, on the nurse's failure to report significant information to the physician, and on the nurse's duty to take positive action when the patient's welfare is threatened. Many cases have also involved problems arising from telephone communications between the nurse and the physician.

Failure To Follow Physician's Orders

Nurses have always had the duty to follow the physician's orders and are held liable for the patient's injuries if they fail to do so. A nurse was held liable for the injuries sustained by a patient who had jumped out of a window. She had allowed the patient, who had been diagnosed as suicidal, to leave the ward unescorted although the physician had not authorized a change in his status (Alaska 1980).[67] In a case that resulted in a $3.6 million judgment, the nurses failed to obtain and administer the antipsychotic medication that had been ordered for the patient. They did not notify the physician that the medication was out of stock or obtain a substitute for three days, during which the patient grew increasingly agitated. The patient's behavior resulted in her being placed in a seclusion room where she was left unattended for a few hours and as a result suffered an injury that left her brain damaged (Connecticut 1980).[68]

Failure To Report Significant Information

Nurses are not required to make medical diagnoses, nor are they held liable for the negligent diagnosis of a physician. They are, however, expected to assess the patient's condition and to recognize the signs and symptoms that indicate that a patient should be examined and treated by a physician. They are also responsible for identifying the type of information that should be brought to the physician's attention.

- A nurse was found negligent when she wrote, on the patient history section of the x-ray form, that the patient had "diabetic complications" but failed to indicate that the patient suffered from dizziness and blackouts. When the x-ray table was placed in a vertical position, the patient fell and broke his cheekbone. The radiologist was also found negligent (District of Columbia 1967).[69]

- A nurse failed to tell the physician that she had removed two ticks from one of the twin boys that she had admitted to the emergency department for complaints of a rash and high fever. The physician diagnosed measles and discharged the children. One of the boys died, and an autopsy revealed the cause of death to be Rocky Mountain spotted fever. The trial court had rendered a judgment in favor of the hospital and the physician. The Appellate Court affirmed the judgment for the physician but found the hospital liable for the nurse's negligence (Maryland 1977).[70]

- The nurses neglected to tell the physician or administration that an endotracheal tube had been left in a patient for five days when the hospital policy was that the tube should remain in a patient no longer than three days. As a result, the patient suffered complications that required successive surgery and left the patient with a permanent speaking disability. The court held that

  > skilled hospital personnel have a duty to exercise reasonable care in administering services to patients in the hospital. If such personnel know that a licensed attending physician either by his failure to treat a patient or by treating a patient in a manner which is a substantial departure from accepted medical standards is endangering the health and life of said patient then the hospital personnel have a duty to perform such acts as are within their authority to protect the health and safety of said patient (Indiana 1982).[71]

- A nurse was held liable for failing to assess the condition of a patient who had entered the emergency department complaining of chest pain. She also failed to report his condition accurately to the on-call physician. The physician defended his decision to transfer the patient by claiming that he had not been advised of the patient's critical condition by the nurse. The court upheld the board of nursing's suspension of the nurse's license for one year (Texas 1983).[72]

- A nurse was notified by the laboratory that the patient's serum electrolyte levels revealed severe hypokalemia, hyponatremia, and hypochloremia. The nurse unsuccessfully tried to contact the patient's family physician and failed to notify the hospital physician covering in-house emergencies. The patient suffered cardiac arrest and sustained permanent neurological and visual impairments (Illinois 1985).[73]

Nurses Not Held Liable

There are situations in which the court will find that the nurse's actions do not release the physician of liability for the patient's injury. A radiologist attempted to defend his failure to take measures to prevent a patient from falling in the radiology department by claiming that the nurse had not filled out the history form properly. He stated that he had no knowledge of the patient's being unable to walk. The court held that he was negligent for not remaining alert to the reasonable possibility that the patient might faint and fall (Louisiana 1962).[74] In assigning nursing liability, the scope of the nurse's duty must be clearly established. For example, in one case a nurse notified the physician several times that there was swelling and redness in the area of the patient's intravenous tube. The patient sued for damages caused by the infiltration of intravenous fluid into the tissues. The trial court ruled in favor of the hospital and physician; however, the Appellate Court ordered a new trial so that the jury could decide whether the nurse had communicated the seriousness of the condition to the physician when it became markedly worse and also whether the nurse had the authority to discontinue the intravenous infusion without a physician's order (California 1963).[75]

Nurse's Duty for Positive Action

There are a number of cases in which the hospital has been held liable because the nurses failed to take positive action to safeguard the patient's health after they had notified the physician of the patient's condition and received an inadequate response.

- The nurses notified a physician three times that the patient was bleeding excessively after childbirth because the physician had failed to suture the episiotomy. The nurses testified that they knew that the patient's condition was deteriorating but they did not call the physician again because they knew that he would not come. They also testified that they did not contact any other physician. The court held that the nurses' negligence caused the patient's death and held the hospital liable (California 1958).[76]

- A nurse notified the physician that there was a foul-smelling substance draining from under the patient's cast, that the patient's arm was edematous and black, and that the patient had a high temperature. The physician did not act on her report for 48 hours, at which time the patient was transferred to another hospital for treatment, which was unsuccessful and eventually resulted in an amputation. The hospital was found liable because the nurses failed to notify administration of the problem as was required by the hospital's department of nursing manual. The court declared that

> Nurses are specialists in hospital care who, in the final analysis, hold the well-being, in fact in some instances, the very lives of the patients in their hands. In the dim hours of the night, as well as in the light of day, nurses are frequently charged with the duty to observe the condition of the ill and infirm in their care. If that patient, helpless and wholly dependent, shows signs of worsening, the nurse is charged with the obligation of taking some positive action. . . . (B)etter care will result and perhaps more patients will recover   (West Virginia 1977).[77]

- A 41-year-old nurse underwent surgery for a vaginal hysterectomy and a "tummy tuck." Postoperatively she demonstrated signs of restlessness and had a low blood pressure. The nurses notified the physician and requested that he examine the patient, but he took no action. Later a laparotomy revealed that the patient had excessive bleeding due to a ruptured spleen. The patient became comatose and died. The lawsuit charged that the nurses failed to take further action when they knew that the physician's response to their complaints was inadequate. The physician was charged with failure to respond to the nurses' requests that he attend the patient. The parties ultimately settled for $500,000 dollars (California 1983).[78]

- The hospital was found not liable when a woman delivered a stillborn premature infant ten minutes before the obstetrician arrived. The woman was 26 weeks pregnant and had started labor; she called the physician and was told to go to the hospital. She arrived at 3 AM and was attended by two experienced obstetrics nurses, who made repeated calls to the physician during the next eight-hour period. Each time he indicated that he would be right over. The patient sued the hospital for failing to provide another physician or competent medical attendant and sued the obstetrician for failing to provide medical care during her labor and delivery. The court found the hospital not liable, ruling that the nurses were well qualified and provided the patient with skillful and diligent care while they kept the physician informed of her progress. They found the physician liable on a breach of contract claim (Alabama 1981).[79]

Telephone Communication

Telephone communications between patients, physicians, and nurses pose an inherent legal risk. Telephone advice given by the hospital's emergency department personnel to patients is generally considered a medically and legally hazardous undertaking. For the patient, the telephone advice can be anonymous, comfortable, and inexpensive, with the hospital assuming all of the risk by having started a hospital–patient relationship for which it might be held liable to provide a reasonable standard of care. As in all oral communications, there is the danger of being misunderstood, misinterpreted, and misled, and, should legal problems arise, there is the difficult problem of proof if the conversation, order, or advice was not properly documented.

The area of nurse–physician telephone communication creates expectations and exposes concerns about the level of competence of each practitioner. Nurses are required to

- Identify and report significant information promptly.
- Record all telephone orders accurately and promptly.
- Carry out all telephone orders accurately and promptly.
- Question telephone orders that are ambiguous, incomplete, or unusual.
- Report any difficulties encountered in implementing the telephone order.
- Determine whether there is a conflict with orders prescribed by any other of the patient's physicians.

Physicians are required to

- Respond appropriately and promptly to the nurses' assessments, reports, and inquiries.
- Institute and update orders that are appropriate, clear, and complete.
- Promptly amend, correct, or explain ambiguous, incomplete, or unusual orders.
- Sign telephone orders in the manner and in the time frame prescribed by hospital policy.

Hospital policies generally indicate that (1) telephone orders can only be taken by certain authorized persons, (2) orders must be repeated and confirmed before they are recorded, (3) unusual telephone orders must be verified by two nurses, and (4) questions or clarifications concerning an order must be verified with the physician who instituted the order. Most hospitals also have procedures for the prompt reporting and resolution of physician–nurse conflicts. It is possible that the legal risk in telephone communications between physicians and nurses is increased as much by a lack of courtesy as it is by a lack of competence. Physicians who are constantly condescending, rude, and taken to name calling deliver a strong message that they should not be called. Nurses who are consistently condescending, rude, or abrupt may not command the physician's full attention on the information they are attempting to convey. In either case, the patient loses and the liability for all parties is increased.

The following cases illustrate the hazards of nurse–physician telephone communication. In the first case, the patient had just left a bar when he was hit by a car. He was brought to the emergency department at 11:10 PM with an abrasion to the scalp, a complaint of numbness in his right anterior thigh, and an inability to move his right leg. The emergency department nurse checked the patient's vital signs; she then called the physician, notified him of the patient's vital signs, and stated that the patient had been hit by a car. The physician ordered pain medication and told the nurse to admit the patient. After administering the pain medication, the patient's blood pressure dropped to 90/60 mmHg; 20 minutes later it had dropped to 70/40 mmHg. The staff nurse was concerned about the low readings, but the nursing supervisor reasoned that the low readings were because the patient had been drinking and had been given the pain medication; as a result, neither nurse notified the physician. At 2 AM the nurse found the patient had developed Cheyne-Stokes respirations and had no pulse; emergency measures were instituted but the patient died. At trial, the nurse and the physician contradicted each other as to the content of the telephone conversation. The nurse denied that she had told the physician that he did not have to come in to examine the patient. The hospital was held liable for the nurses' failure to notify the physician of the patient's deteriorating condition, and the physician was held liable for not personally examining and treating the patient (Maryland 1972).[80]

In a second case, the patient was in a car accident and was brought to the emergency department at 4:30 PM. He complained of back pain and stated that his back might be broken. The nurse told him to wiggle his toes and then called the physician and stated that she could find nothing wrong with the patient. She also indicated to the physician that the patient and his friends had been drinking. The physician ordered that the patient be given pain medication and released. The next day the patient noticed blood in his urine and went to another hospital where it was discovered that he had a broken back. At trial, the physician at the first hospital denied that the nurse told him that the patient was complaining of a back injury and was unable to walk. The Appeals Court affirmed the lower court's decision, holding the hospital liable (Alabama 1972).[81] As these cases demonstrate, the fact or suspicion that a patient has been drinking may tend to make the health care provider believe less in the plight of the patient and as a result he or she may perform a less than adequate assessment, thus increasing the hospital's liability.

In a third case, the Appellate Court ruled that a jury should decide whether a nurse accurately or inaccurately reported the doctor's telephone orders and whether a failure to accurately report the orders constituted negligence. The nurse had denied hospital admission to a woman who had come to the emergency department in active labor. The nurse testified that she had telephoned the emergency department physician and that he had stated that the patient should get in touch with her own doctor. The physician contradicted the nurse's testimony and stated that he told the nurse to call the patient's doctor and see what he wanted done. The baby was born while the patient was on her way to the other doctor (Texas 1972).[82]

Although there are fewer on-call emergency department physicians in hospitals today, the lessons taught by these cases are still relevant. Nurses should assess the patient's condition accurately and promptly notify the physician of all significant information. They should accurately document the telephone conversation and the physician's response in the nurses' notes and, if appropriate, on the physician's order sheet. Hospitals should have a mechanism for promptly resolving nurse–physician conflicts so that the record is not inappropriately used as a battleground for what may be legitimate professional differences of opinion.

NURSING DOCUMENTATION

The Joint Commission on Accreditation of Healthcare Organizations' standards for the documentation of nursing care for hospitalized patients states that "the nursing process (assessment, planning, intervention and evaluation) shall be documented for each hospitalized patient from admission through discharge."[83] Of the 20 deficiencies most frequently cited during Joint Commission accreditation visits, 3 involve the nurses' responsibility for documentation:[84]

1. A nurse shall note the patient's status in the medical record when a patient is transferred within or discharged from the hospital.
2. Documentation of the nursing care should address the patient's needs, problems, capabilities, and limitations. Nursing interventions and patient responses should be noted.
3. All entries in the medical record should be dated and authenticated.

Nurses' Notes

Inadequate documentation increases the risk of liability for nurses and for the hospital. Nurses have an obligation to practice nursing according to the standard of care, and if they are sued for nursing malpractice, they may be required to rebut the plaintiff's charges of substandard care. The most reliable and convincing defense is the introduction of clear, concise, accurate, and relevant nurses' notes. Nurses' notes are intended to be a complete, accurate, and timely account of the patient's involvement in and response to the nursing process. Medical records are legally classified as business records. All or part of the medical record may be introduced as evidence at trial under the business records exception to the hearsay rule. The rules of evidence require that the records be accurate, complete, relevant, and recorded at or near the time the event took place. The record must also have been produced in the normal course of business and not in anticipation of litigation. This means that there is always the possibility that information that is written in the medical record, after an incident has occurred, may be ruled inadmissible on the belief that it is self serving and written in anticipation of litigation. Nurses' notes are extremely vulnerable to legal challenges. Juries are frequently asked to consider both their form and their content as evidence that the nurse was negligent. Nurse managers are responsible for enforcing the hospital policies that determine the form and content of nurses' notes.

Form

The hospital selects the type of nurses' notes that will be used in the hospital. Traditionally, nurses' notes consisted of a chronological description of the nursing care provided during the three 8-hour shifts. Nurses on each shift charted their notations in different-colored ink (blue, 7 AM–3 PM; green, 3 PM–11 PM; red, 11 PM–7AM). Some hospitals have adopted a problem-oriented record-keeping system in which problems are identified and entries are outlined with reference to the patient's subjective (S) symptoms, objective (O) symptoms, assessments (A) by health care professionals, and plans (P) to further diagnose, treat, or educate the patient. This method is also referred to by the acronym SOAP, derived from the first letter of each element in the recording system. In either recording system, hospital policy requires that the nurses' notes must be

1. *Timely*. Information must be recorded promptly and in proper sequence, avoiding time gaps. Delayed entries are identified by indicating the time and date and the fact that it is a delayed entry.
2. *Complete*. All significant information is recorded for events occurring on each shift or appropriate time period. The record should not have empty spaces or lines. If the record has to be rewritten, the original is kept with the record.
3. *Legible*. Handwriting is legible. Corrections are made without obliterating any of the information on the record. There are no margin notes or notations squeezed between the lines.
4. *Correct*. Grammar and spelling are correct and only standard abbreviations are used.
5. *Accurate*. Errors are clearly identified and explained without obliterating any information on the record. Observations are consistent and logical (e.g., a notation for each time the patient's leg is checked for circulation indicating right or left leg).
6. *Attributable*. The patient is identified by name on each page of the record. The record contains the legal signature, including the title, of all personnel who have made notations. Notations are by authorized practitioners only. Countersigning an entry is legally interpreted to mean that the person is formally attesting to the authenticity of what is written and makes the countersigner as liable as the person who originally signed the report.

Content

The standards of nursing practice require that the nurses' notes reflect accurate and appropriate observations, assessments, interventions, and evaluations. Examples of appropriate observations and assessments include

- Descriptions of the patient's behavior, appearance, and symptoms
- Statements by patients and family that are relevant to the nurses' assessments and observations
- Routine observations of the patient's condition with normal findings
- Changes in the patient's status, especially the initial and ongoing assessments that indicate the patient's condition is deteriorating

Examples of appropriate interventions include

- Identification or description of the test, therapy, or treatment and the patient's status before and after the procedure
- Description of the interventions made in response to the observation of the patient's change of status and/or deteriorating condition
- Notations for each time the physician is notified describing the information communicated and the physician's response

- Identifications of actions taken in response to a change in the physician's orders
- Description of all unusual or unwanted incidents together with the patient's response and the remedial actions undertaken to correct the situation and to prevent further injury. The fact that an incident or variance report was filed does not belong on the clinical record; it is an administrative document that should be submitted to administration and filed in accordance with hospital policy.
- Identification of patient and family teaching activities and discharge information and instructions

Examples of appropriate evaluations include

- Objective statements that reveal the facts that have led to the clinical conclusions concerning the patient's status. Generalizations such as "patient's pulse increased" or "patient uncooperative" and qualifiers such as "appears to be" and "seems to be" should be avoided.
- Notations that reflect follow-up for anticipated effect of interventions such as notations that the patient did obtain relief from pain after the administration of a pain-relieving medication
- Documentation of patient and family's progress in learning to meet their health care needs

The content of the medical record should accurately reflect the events and circumstances of the patient's hospital experience. Extraneous comments concerning the behavior of the physician or nurses, such as "Patient going into shock, unable to contact physician, we never can" or "If nurses could read orders, we'd have fewer problems around here," are totally inappropriate and could significantly compromise the hospital's defense of a negligence suit.

NURSES' NOTES IN LITIGATION

Nurses' notes are often an important factor in determining the nurses' liability for the patient's injury. Nurses' notes have been involved in litigation that included the absence of entries, illegible and conflicting notes, inadequate notes, and records that were altered or replaced.

Absence of Entries

A hospital was held liable for the nurses' failure to monitor the circulation in the leg of a seriously ill patient. The nurses' notes for the seven-hour period prior to the discovery of the ischemia did not reflect any observation of the patient's circulation. The court ruled that the jury could consider that the absence of entries indicated that the observations were not made (Illinois 1974).[85]

An $800,000 verdict was upheld against a hospital for the failure of the nurses to promptly obtain medical assistance for a critically ill patient. At 8 AM the nurse recorded the patient's temperature was 105°F. The record revealed that the patient received no medical attention until 10:45 AM when he was examined by a resident. The court stated that "either the nurse failed in the specified duty of care, immediate notification of an intern or resident, or it took the hospital personnel a totally unexplained and extraordinarily long time to respond" (Pennsylvania 1978).[86]

Illegible and Conflicting Notes

Despite a normal finding on a myelogram, the surgeon, without consultation, performed a laminectomy and spinal fusion on the patient. Immediately following surgery, the patient complained of pain in his back and in his right thigh. There were conflicting notations on the record. On November 30 the physician noted that the patient had "done extremely well, no complaints"; on the same day the nurses' notes stated "ambulated with help for ten minutes, had to be helped to the bathroom, complained of terrible pain, and that his right leg felt paralyzed." The patient's condition continued to deteriorate over the next few days, resulting in his becoming permanently disabled. The physician and the hospital were held liable. The court found the hospital directly liable under the doctrine of corporate negligence, holding that the hospital had a duty to protect patients from medical negligence by the hospital's staff physicians, "If the hospital knows or has reason to know, or should have known such acts were likely to occur" (California 1973).[87]

Incorrect grammar can sometimes make a note incomprehensible. An emergency department nurse, while taking a patient's history, wrote on the admission form "the patient has a puncture type wound obtained while mowing the grass from a broken bottle." The emergency department physician assumed he had cut his leg on the broken glass and did not x-ray the injury to ascertain the presence of foreign bodies. The court held the physician and the hospital liable, stating that the medical standard would have required the wound to be x-rayed. They also stated that if the history had been taken and recorded with proper care the information would have revealed that the injury was caused by a flying object, with the probability that there was a foreign body in the wound (Tennessee 1978).[88]

Expert witnesses are sometimes hampered by the condition of the record. In one case the plaintiff's expert witness, a physician testifying as to the standard of care required of nurse practitioners, reviewed the medical record and complained that he was frustrated by the "very sketchy nature of the (agency's) records." The judge personally reviewed the record and stated that it was impossible to tell how sketchy it was since much of it was totally illegible. The case also involved a series of telephone conversations between the nurse practitioner and the patient; however, there was no record of the calls (Massachusetts 1980).[89]

Inadequate Notes

In a wrongful death suit against a hospital for the death of a patient due to brain damage caused by untreated water intoxication, the Appeals Court upheld the judgment

for the plaintiff. The testimony of the hospital administrator and the nursing staff revealed that the hospital's recording policies had not been followed. The intake and
output records were not accurately compiled or totalled, the emergency department
records were incomplete, the physician's orders did not correspond to the written record
of care provided, and the nurses' notes did not comport with the medication records. The
Appeals Court upheld the trial court's instructions to the jury, which stated that in
deciding the issue of negligence, the jury could consider whether the hospital hired
knowledgeable nurses and whether there had been accurate record keeping (Kentucky
1981).[90]

Inadequate notes do not of themselves cause an injury; therefore, the plaintiff is still
required to prove causation. For example, a hospital was found not liable for the death of
a maternity patient three hours after the uncomplicated delivery of her fourth child. A
nurse expert witness testified that the vital signs were poorly monitored and that the
nurse's notes were poorly kept and possibly written only after the patient's death. In
addition, she stated that the nursing diagnosis should have led the nurses to conclude that
hemorrhage was possible. The court refused to find the hospital liable because an
autopsy had not been performed and there was no expert witness testimony as to the
cause of death. One dissenting judge, however, stated that he would have found the
nurses' abandonment and neglect of the patient as the proximate cause of the patient's
bleeding to death (New Jersey 1980).[91]

Record Altered or Replaced

Occasionally hospital personnel attempt to conceal their actions by altering or replacing the record. Evidence of fraudulent concealment of the hospital's negligent actions
has dire consequences in court. The following four cases illustrate the point. In the first
case the plaintiff had sued the hospital for the intentional infliction of emotional distress
for altering the record of a patient who had been admitted to the emergency department
for injuries received in a fight with the plaintiff. The patient's death was caused by the
negligence of the hospital personnel; however, the records were altered to make it appear
that the patient had died of the injuries inflicted by the plaintiff. As a result the plaintiff
had been charged by the police with third-degree murder and voluntary manslaughter.
The court found the hospital's intentional misstatement as to the cause of death to be
intolerable, extreme, and outrageous unprofessional conduct, which entitled the plaintiff to be compensated for the emotional distress he suffered as a result (Pennsylvania
1981).[92]

In the second case the court ordered a new trial after a physician had won a malpractice
suit because it was discovered that a page of the medical record had been replaced prior
to the beginning of the suit (New York 1979).[93]

In the third case, an appeals court upheld a $3.6 million verdict against a hospital for
the permanent brain damage suffered by a patient because the nurses failed to administer
the antipsychotic medication that was ordered and failed to monitor the patient after she
had been placed in a locked seclusion room. The director of nurses had ordered all of the
nurses who had charted on the record on the day of the injury to revise their notations.

She then ordered that the original notes be removed from the record and the new notes substituted. She acted without the knowledge of the hospital administration and in explicit violation of hospital policy. The substituted record was demonstrably false and conflicted with other portions of the record. In upholding the judgment against the hospital, the appeals court stated that the lower court had correctly instructed the jury that they were entitled to consider the falsified record as evidence that the hospital was conscious of its negligence (Connecticut 1980).[94]

In the fourth case, a $2.5 million judgment was upheld against a hospital for the death of a patient because the nurses failed to assess the patient's postoperative status, to maintain adequate oxygenation levels, and to notify the physician of the patient's deteriorating condition over a nine-hour period from 10 PM until 7 AM. The nurse testified that she had been present the entire time; however, the handwriting in the notes was clearly written by two different people. The nurse later admitted she had made the notations from midnight to 4 AM. No one would admit to making a 6 AM entry that stated that the patient's vital signs were normal. The house physician examined the patient at 7 AM and found that he had a fixed stare and could not be revived (Ohio 1985).[95]

HOSPITAL DOCUMENTS IN LITIGATION

The discovery process allows the plaintiff's attorney to subpoena any documents that are relevant in supporting the charge of negligence or malpractice. The following illustrates the variety of hospital documents that have been found to be of significance in negligence or malpractice litigation:

- The physician's order sheet to demonstrate that the route of medication had been changed from intramuscular to oral (Delaware 1962).[96]
- The hospital's policy and procedure manuals to identify the hospital's procedure for monitoring the circulation in the foot of a patient with a leg cast (Illinois 1965).[97]
- The operating room and recovery room schedule to demonstrate that the nurse supervisor would have known how many patients would be in the recovery room at a certain time (Canada 1969).[98]
- The unit's staffing pattern and routine to demonstrate that there was adequate staff to allow an agitated patient to be watched until his family arrived (New York 1976).[99]
- The department of nursing manual to identify the hospital policy requiring nurses to report the inadequate response of a physician to the chairman of the department (West Virginia 1977).[100]
- The hospital's policy for protective side rails to demonstrate that they would not have been necessary for the plaintiff (Texas 1980).[101]
- The hospital's bylaws and governing board policies to demonstrate the hospital's responsibility to check the credentials of physicians applying for staff privileges (Wisconsin 1980).[102]

- The operating room policy manual to demonstrate that the circulating nurse should have remained in the room to assist the anesthetist (California 1983).[103]
- The emergency department manual to explain the hospital's on-call system for physician specialists (Florida 1985).[104]

NOTES

1. American Nurses' Association Commission on Nursing Services, *Roles, Responsibilities and Qualifications for Nurse Administrators* (Kansas City, Mo.: ANA, 1978), 3.

2. Ibid., 5.

3. Ibid., 3.

4. Ibid., 5–7.

5. Charles R. McConnell, *Managing the Health Care Professional* (Rockville, Md.: Aspen Publishers, Inc., 1984), 50.

6. *Cooper v. National Motor Bearing Co.*, 288 P.2d 581 (Cal. App. 1955).

7. *Wilmington General Hospital v. Manlove*, 54 Del. 15, 174 A.2d 135 (1961).

8. *Darling v. Charleston Memorial Hospital*, 211 N.E.2d 253 (Ill. 1965), *cert denied*, 383 U.S. 946 (1966).

9. *Arnold v. James B. Haggin Hospital*, 415 S.W.2d 844 (Ky. 1967).

10. *Foley v. Bishop Clarkson Memorial Hospital*, 173 N.W.2d 881 (Neb. 1970).

11. *Kastler v. Iowa Methodist Hospital*, 193 N.W.2d 98 (Iowa 1971).

12. *Laidlow v. Lion Gate Hospital*, 70 W.W.R. 727 (Canada 1969).

13. *Pisel v. Stamford Hospital*, 430 A.2d 1 (Conn. 1980).

14. *Sanchez v. Bay General Hospital*, 172 Cal. Rptr. 342 (Cal. App. 1981).

15. *Valdez v. Lyman-Roberts Hospital Inc.*, 638 S.W.2d 111 (Tex. 1982).

16. *Czubinski v. Doctors Hospital*, 139 Cal. App. 3d 361, 188 Cal. Rptr. 685 (1983).

17. *May v. William Beaumont Hospital*, Mich., Oakland County Circuit Court, No. 81-230-540, April 23, 1985; 28 ATLA L. Rep. 419 (November 1985).

18. *Duling v. Bluefield Sanitarium, Inc.*, 142 S.E.2d 754 (W.Va. 1965).

19. *Avey v. St. Francis Hospital* and School of Nursing, Inc., 442 P.2d 1013 (Kansas 1968).

20. *Horton v. Niagara Falls Memorial Medical Center*, 51 A.D. 2d 152, 380 N.Y.S. 2d 116 (1976).

21. *Child v. Vancouver General Hospital*, 71 W.W.R. 656 (Canada 1969).

22. *Nelson v. Peterson*, 542 P.2d 1075 (Utah 1975).

23. *Nance v. James Archer Smith Hospital*, 329 So. 2d 377 (Fla. Dist. Ct. App. 1976).

24. *Fraijo v. Hartland Hospital*, 99 Cal. App. 3d 331, 160 Cal. Rptr. 246 (1979).

25. *Halliman v. Prindle*, 11 P.2d 426 (1932), *rev'd*, 220 Cal. 46, 29 P.2d 202 (1934); *aff'd in part, rev'd in part*, 17 Cal. App. 2d 656, 62 P.2d 1075 (1936).

26. *Bauer v. Otis*, 284 P.2d 133 (Cal. App. 1955).

27. *Kalmus v. Cedars of Lebanon Hospital*, 281 P.2d 872 (Cal. App. 1955).

28. *Neel v. San Antonio Community Hospital*, 1 Cal. Rptr. 313 (1959).

29. *Larrimore v. Homeopathic Hospital Association*, 54 Del. 449, 181 A.2d 573 (1962).

30. *Norton v. Argonaut Insurance Company*, 144 So. 2d 249 (La. Ct. App. 1962).

31. *Parker v. St. Paul Fire & Marine Insurance Co.*, 335 So. 2d 725 (La. App. 1976).

32. *Dessauer v. Memorial Hospital*, 628 P.2d 337 (N.M. App. 1981).

33. *Holbrooks v. Duke University, Inc.*, 305 S.E.2d 69 (N.C. App. 1983).

34. *Ball v. Rolling Hill Hospital*, Pa., Philadelphia County Court of Common Pleas, No. 341, 1983, April 16, 1985; 28 ATLA L. Rep. 467 (December 1985).

35. *Peltier v. Franklin Foundation Hospital*, La., St. Mary Parish, 16th Judicial District Court, No. 73-142F, January 19, 1985; 28 ATLA L. Rep. 182 (May 1985).

36. *Butler v. Northwestern Hospital*, 278 N.W. 37, 39 (Minn. 1938).

37. *Thompson v. Brent*, 254 So. 2d 751 (La. App. 1971).

38. *May v. Broun*, 492 P.2d 776 (Oregon 1972).

39. *Bellaire General Hospital v. Campbell*, 510 S.W.2d 94 (Tex. Civ. App. 1974).

40. *Hill v. Hospital Authority of Clarke County*, 224 S.E.2d 739 (Georgia 1976).

41. *Hall v. Bio-Medical Application Inc.*, 671 F.2d 300 (8th Cir. 1982).

42. *Lindsay v. Mueller*, Wash., Pierce County Superior Court No. 83-2-00271-6 (June 9, 1985); 28 ATLA L. Rep. 276 (August 1985).

43. *Jones v. Samaritan Health Service*, Ariz., Maricopa County Superior Court No. C487995 (April 5, 1985); 28 ATLA L. Rep. 421 (November 1985).

44. *Koepel v. St. Joseph Hospital and Medical Center*, 381 Mich. 440, 163 N.W.2d 222 (1968), *rev'd*, 8 Mich. App. 609, 155 N.W.2d 199 (1967).

45. *Variety Children's Hospital v. Osle*, 292 So. 2d 382 (Fla. Dist. Ct. App. 1974).

46. *Tonsic v. Wagner*, 329 A.2d 497 (Pa. 1974).

47. *Newhall v. Central Vermont Hospital Inc.*, 133 Vt. 572, 349 A.2d 890 (Vermont 1975).

48. "Top 10 Hospital Malpractice Claims: St. Paul Insurance," *Medical Liability Advisory Service*, November 1985:2.

49. *Zach v. Centro Espano Hospital*, 319 So. 2d 34 (Fla. App. 1975).

50. *City of Somerset v. Hart*, 549 S.W.2d 814 (Ky. 1977).

51. *Sparger v. Worley Hospital*, 547 S.W.2d 582 (Tex. 1977).

52. *Dobrzeniecki v. University Hospital of Cleveland*, Ohio, Cuyahoga County Court of Common Pleas No. 17, 843 (May 22, 1984); 27 ATLA L. Rep. 425 (November 1984).

53. *Herrup v. South Miami Hospital Foundation, Inc.*, Fla., Dade County Circuit Court No. 87-37139 (October 24, 1984), 28 ATLA L. Rep. 88 (March 1985).

54. *Slatkin v. Capitol Hill Hospital*, No. 84-0443 (D.D.C. Oct. 18, 1984), Medical Liability Reporter (1985).

55. *Sanders v. Sisters of Mercy*, Mich., Oakland County Circuit Court No. 83-264633 (February 4, 1985); 28 ATLA L. Rep. 183 (May 1985).

56. *Evans v. United States*, 212 F. Supp. 648 (D.C. Mass. 1962).

57. *Charrin v. Methodist Hospital*, 432 S.W.2d 572 (Tex. Civ. App. 1968).

58. *Mossey v. Mueller*, 218 N.W.2d 514 (Wis. 1974).

59. *Hilzendager v. Methodist Hospital*, 596 S.W.2d 284 (1980).

60. Linda Lindsey Davis, "Professional Collaboration in Health Care Administration," *Nursing Administration Quarterly* (Summer 1983):47.

61. Patricia A. Prescott, Karen E. Dennis, and Ada K. Jacox, "Clinical Decision Making of Staff Nurses," *IMAGE: Journal of Nursing Scholarship* 19, no. 2 (Summer 1987):62.

62. Ibid.

63. W. Kraus, E. Draper, D. Wagner, and J. Zimmerman, "An Evaluation of Outcome from Intensive Care in Major Medical Centers," *Annals of Internal Medicine* 104, no. 3 (March 1986):410–418.

64. *McDonald v. Massachusetts General Hospital*, 120 Mass. 432 (1876), Charitable Immunity Doctrine; *St. Paul-Mercury Indemnity Co. v. St. Joseph's Hospital*, 4. N.W.2d 637 (1942) (borrowed servant doctrine).

65. *Goff v. Doctor's Hospital Center*, 236 2d 213 (W.Va. 1977); *Darling v. Charleston Community Hospital*, 33 Ill. 2d 326, 211 N.E. 2d 253 (1965), *cert. denied*, 383 U.S. 946 (1966).

66. *Utter v. United Hospital Center*, 236 S.E.2d 213 (W.Va. 1977); *Poor Sisters of St. Francis v. Catron*, 435 N.E.2d 305 (Ind. Ct. App. 1982).

67. *Abille v. United States*, 482 F. Supp. 703 (N.D. Cal. 1980).

68. *Pisel v. Stamford Hospital*, 430 A.2d 1 (Conn. 1980).

69. *Washington Hospital Center v. Butler*, 384 F. 2d 331 (D.C. CCA 1967).

70. *Ramsey v. Physician's Memorial Hospital*, 373 A.2d 26 (Md. App. 1977).

71. *Poor Sisters of St. Francis v. Catron*, 435 N.E.2d 305 (Ind. Ct. App. 1982).

72. *Lunsford v. Board of Nurse Examiners*, 648 S.W.2d 391 (Tex. App. 1983).

73. *Sinks v. Methodist Medical Center*, Ill., Peoria County Circuit Court No. 82 L 3868 (April 1, 1985); 28 ATLA L. Rep. 466 (December 1985).

74. *Favalora v. Aetna Casualty Co.*, 144 So. 2d 544 (La. 1962).

75. *Mundt v. Alta Bates Hospital*, 223 Cal. App. 2d 413, 35 Cal. Rptr. 848 (1963).

76. *Goff v. Doctors General Hospital*, 333 P.2d 29 (Cal. 1958).

77. *Utter v. United Methodist Hospital Center*, 236 S.E.2d 213, 216 (W.Va. 1977).

78. *Mason v. Lodi Community Hospital*, No. 165743, San Joaquin County Sup. Ct. (August 24, 1983).

79. *Taylor v. Baptist Medical Center Inc.*, 400 So. 2d 369 (Ala. 1981).

80. *Thomas v. Corso*, 265 M.D. 84, 288 A.2d 379 (1972).

81. *Citizens Hospital Association v. Schoulin*, 48 Ala. 101, 262 So. 2d 303 (1972).

82. *Childs v. Greenville Hospital Authority*, 479 S.W.2d 399 (Texas 1972).

83. Joint Commission on Accreditation of Healthcare Organizations, *Accreditation Manual for Hospitals*, (Chicago: Joint Commission, 1985), 98.

84. "JCAH Accreditation Visits (Most Frequent Deficiencies Cited)," *Help News* (currently called *Pulse*) 5 (January 1982):1.

85. *Collins v. Westlake Community Hospital*, 57 Ill. 2d 388, 312 N.E.2d 614 (1974).

86. *Robert v. Chordoff*, 393 A.2d 853 (Penn. 1978).

87. *Gonzales v. Nork and Mercy Hospital*, No. 228566, Sacramento County Sup. Ct. (Cal. 1973); *rev'd on other grounds* 60 Cal. App. 3d 835 (1976).

88. *Baldwin v. Knight*, 569 S.W.2d 450 (Tenn. 1978).

89. *Gugino v. Harvard Community Health Plan*, 403 N.E.2d 1166 (Mass. 1980).

90. *Rogers v. Kasdan and Humana*, 612 S.W.2d 133 (Ky. 1981).

91. *Maslonka v. Hermann, et al.*, 414 A.2d 1350 (N.J. 1980).

92. *Banyas v. Lower Bucks Hospital*, 437 A.2d 1236 (Penn. 1981).

93. *Kaplan v. Central Medical Group of Brooklyn*, 419 N.Y.S. 750 (N.Y. App. Div. 1979).

94. *Pisel v. Stamford Hospital*, 430 A.2d 1 (Conn. 1980).

95. *Duren v. Suburban Community Hospital*, Ohio, Cuyahoga County Court of Common Pleas No. 55142 (Feb. 13, 1985); 28 ATLA L. Rep. 168–169 (May 1985).

96. *Larrimore v. Homeopathic Hospital Association*, 54 Del. 449, 181 A.2d 573 (1962).

97. *Darling v. Charleston Community Memorial Hospital*, 211 N.E.2d 253 (Ill. 1965), *cert. denied*, 383 U.S. 946 (1966).

98. *Laidlow v. Lion Gate Hospital*, 70 W.W.R. 727 (Canada 1969).

99. *Horton v. Niagara Falls Mem. Med. Ctr.*, 380 N.Y.S. 2d 116 (N.Y. 1976).

100. *Utter v. United Hospital Center*, 236 S.E.2d 213 (W.Va. 1977).

101. *Hilzendager v. Methodist Hospital*, 596 S.W.2d 284 (Tex. 1980).

102. *Johnson v. Misericordia Community Hospital*, 99 Wis. 2d 708, 294 N.W.2d 501 (1980).

103. *Czubinsky v. Doctors Hospital*, 139 Cal. App. 361, 188 Cal. Rptr. 685 (1983).

104. *Mark v. Mandel*, 477 So. 2d 1036 (Fla. Dist. Ct. App. 1985).

Chapter 14

Consent

CONSENT AND INFORMED CONSENT

The right to consent to treatment arises from the common law right to be free from unwanted, offensive, or harmful touching by another. The courts have held the health care provider liable for failure to obtain consent even if the therapy, surgery, or procedure improved the patient's condition. The right was first defined and limited in 1914 in *Schloendorff v. Society of New York Hospital* in which Judge Cardozo stated that

> Every human being of adult years and sound mind has a right to determine what will be done with his own body; and a surgeon who performs an operation without his patient's consent commits an assault, for which he is liable in damages. This is true, except in cases of emergency where the patient is unconscious, and where it it necessary to operate before consent can be obtained.[1]

The patient's right to consent presumes the fact that the patient has sufficient information to make a reasonable decision. This presumption evolved into a doctrine of informed consent in which the health care provider has a duty to provide patients with an adequate amount of information concerning the recommended treatment and its risks and alternatives so that they can make an informed decision. In 1980, a California court extended the doctrine of informed consent to require informed refusal when it held a physician liable for the death of a patient from cancer of the cervix because he failed to adequately inform her of the risks of not consenting to a recommended Papanicolaou smear.[2] In this case it was determined that the test would have discovered the cancer early enough to begin treatment that would have extended the patient's life.

There are two sources of liability for violation of a patient's right to consent. In most states, absence of consent makes a health care provider liable for the intentional tort of battery, whereas failure to obtain the patient's informed consent makes the health care provider liable for the unintentional tort of negligence. A minority of jurisdictions continue to treat the failure to disclose adequate information as battery, reasoning that the consent was not a knowing consent; therefore the consent was ineffective, and an ineffective consent is viewed as no consent and thus actionable in battery.[3]

Standards for Informed Consent

In the majority of jurisdictions the law of negligence governs the plaintiff's actions for nondisclosure. There are two standards by which the health care provider's duty may be judged. The traditional standard known as the professional or reasonable physician standard requires the medical care provider to disclose the same type of information regarding the treatment, procedure, or surgery as would customarily have been disclosed to the patient by other medical care providers under the same or similar circumstances. The newer standard, known as the reasonable patient standard, defined in 1972 by the court in *Canterbury v. Spence*, 464 F.2d 772 (D.C. Cir. 1972), *cert. denied* 409 U.S. 1064 (1972), holds that the duty of a physician is to disclose as much information as the average reasonable person in the same set of circumstances needs to know in order to decide if he wants to accept or refuse the proposed surgery or procedure.

The jurisdiction's choice of standard makes a difference in the manner in which the standard is proved. The professional or reasonable physician standard requires the testimony of an expert witness to prove the required disclosure. In the states that have adopted the reasonable professional or physician standard, the provider may defend the nondisclosure on the grounds that the information withheld is not something that is usually told to patients by the professional or medical community. The reasonable patient standard does not require the testimony of an expert witness because it focuses on the information needs of the average reasonable person rather than the standard set by the members of the professional or medical community. The materiality of the disclosure is viewed from the patient's point of view, and the jury decides for itself whether the information disclosed was adequate for an informed decision.

Most of the litigation surrounding informed consent concerns the medical provider's failure to disclose the risks associated with the treatment. The court in *Canterbury v. Spence* indicated that a risk is material "when a reasonable person in what the physician knows or should know to be the patient's position, would be likely to attach significance to the risk or cluster of risks in deciding whether or not to forego the proposed therapy."[4] The malpractice crisis has prompted some legislatures to overturn court decisions establishing the "reasonable patient standard" by enacting legislation that requires the use of the professional or reasonable physician standard in determining whether the nondisclosed risks are material.[5] The plaintiff must be able to prove a causal relationship between the nondisclosed risk and his or her injury in order to win a negligence suit based on the absence of informed consent. The question that the jury must decide is whether a reasonable person with knowledge of the undisclosed risk would have consented to the procedure. If it is determined that a reasonable person, knowing of the risk, would have consented to the procedure, the medical care provider will prevail.

VALID CONSENT REQUIREMENTS

The basic elements of a valid consent are knowledge, voluntariness, and competency.

Knowledge

The patient must have adequate knowledge of the medical condition and of the proposed surgery or therapy. The type of knowledge that patients are entitled to receive in order to make an understanding and informed decision includes at a minimum:[6]

- An explanation of the diagnosis (medical condition or problem)
- A description of the nature and purpose of the proposed treatment, including the identification of those treatments that are experimental
- A description of any expected discomfort, risks, and consequences of the treatment
- A disclosure of the possibility that the proposed treatment will be successful
- A disclosure of appropriate alternative procedures
- An explanation of the consequences if the treatment is not given

The philosophy underlying the doctrine of informed consent is a recognition of the patient's right to decide if he or she wants to risk the treatment or operation. It encourages open and frank communication between the patient and the health care provider, a dialogue in which the health care professional explains the situation, identifies the alternative courses of action, and responds to the questions and concerns of the patient. The law permits the patient to make the decision, which in most cases must be respected by the health care professional.

Voluntariness

The patient must be free to accept or reject the proposed treatment without any physical or psychological coercion. Consent induced by fraud, misrepresentation, or threats is illegal and therefore invalid. The President's commission studying informed consent indicated that "a good deal of routine care in hospitals, nursing homes and other health care settings is provided (usually by health professionals such as nurses) without explicit and voluntary consent by patients."[7] Health care professionals assume that in most instances the patient will simply accept the routine procedures. There is a need for health care providers to recognize the possibility that encouragement and support can turn into coercion and manipulation. The nature and extent of family involvement in the patient's decision-making process should also be evaluated by the health care professionals.

Competency

Patients must be of sound mind and legally and mentally capable of making an informed decision concerning their health care. The consent of an unemancipated minor, a person who has been declared incompetent, or a person who is under the influence of alcohol or drugs is considered invalid. Persons considered competent to make informed decisions concerning their health care include the following:

1. Adults who have not been declared incompetent. Each state determines the age at which a person is considered an adult.
2. An emancipated minor as defined by state statute. Usual requirements are that the minor not be under the control of, nor financially supported by, his or her parents.
3. A mature minor as defined by state statute, which usually requires a consideration of age, maturity, mental status, and the procedure involved in deciding whether the minor is capable of understanding the medical condition and the alternatives and weighing them and choosing accordingly.
4. The parent or guardian of a minor. When the parents are legally separated or divorced, the consent of the custodial parent must be obtained. Parents and guardians have the obligation to act in the best interest of the child.
5. The guardian of a person who has been declared incompetent by the court. Guardians have the obligation to act in the best interest of their wards. If the person, prior to having been declared incompetent, made his or her wishes known, the guardian should honor the decision. Parents and guardians must seek approval of the court before consenting to organ donation or sterilization procedures for minors or incompetent adults.

PROOF OF CONSENT

The nature of the evidence needed to prove the patient consented to treatment will depend on the type of consent and the manner in which the consent was documented.

Implied and Express Consent

The patient's consent can be either implied or express. Implied consent takes into account the conduct of the patient and the circumstances surrounding the situation. For example, a patient's consent was implied when she voluntarily stood in line, extended her arm, and accepted a vaccination without objection.[8] Implied consent has also been recognized in the patient's voluntary admission and voluntary submission to the minor routine procedures of a hospital that no longer use the general blanket consent forms. Consent is generally considered to be implied in emergency situations in which the patient is unable to consent to treatment and immediate action is necessary to prevent loss of life or limb.[9] This does not apply to situations in which an emergency exists and the patient is unwilling to give consent. Implied consent is also used to justify the increased scope of an operation when unexpected conditions arise and the extension is necessary to save the patient's life.[10] Many states have motor vehicle statutes that indicate that there is an implied consent to blood, urine, or breath analysis when a person has been arrested for driving while under the influence of alcohol. The statutes generally contain exemptions for patients who have hemophilia or diabetes or are taking anti-coagulant drugs. Failure to submit to the testing generally results in an immediate suspension of the license for a certain period of time.[11] Some state statutes provide immunity for physicians, nurses, and other employees for any act done or omitted in the course of drawing blood from a nonconsenting adult at the request of a police officer.[12]

Express consent is oral or written consent that is given by direct words. An oral consent is legally valid unless the state has enacted a statute that requires written consent for a certain type of procedure. The major objection to the widespread use of oral consent is the difficulty of proving the consent. The majority of health care providers require that the patient sign a consent form.

Consent Forms

The three basic types of consent forms are the blanket form, the battery form, and the detailed consent form. Some courts have ruled that the blanket consent form is too general to provide adequate evidence of consent to specific procedures.[13] Many hospitals continue to use this form on admission, whereas others have discarded it and rely on the patient's implied consent to hospitalization and routine care as evidenced by his or her voluntary admission and continued acceptance of routine hospital services and procedures.

The battery, or specific procedure, consent form used by most hospitals names and describes the procedure and includes statements indicating that the patient has been told of the risks, consequences, and alternatives and that all of the patient's questions have been answered to his or her satisfaction. Hospital policy also requires that the form be dated and signed by the patient in the presence of a witness. This type of form provides evidence that the patient consented and therefore can shield a hospital from a charge of battery. The form's usefulness as proof that the patient's consent was informed may depend on the availability of corroborative documentation. For this reason some hospitals require the physician to make a notation in the medical record concerning the information that was provided to the patient or the patient's representative.

The third type of form is the specific or detailed consent form that is required when patients are involved in research programs. The forms explain in detail the medical procedures, consequences, risks, and alternatives as well as the patient's right to withdraw consent or discontinue participation without prejudice to the patient.[14] A specific, detailed consent form is required for Medicaid-funded sterilizations: federal regulations require the patient to sign a special consent form at least 30 days prior to the sterilization.[15] A specific, detailed consent form may also be required by hospitals or by physicians for surgery that is elective, such as in some types of cosmetic surgery, and also for medical or surgical procedures that are considered new or experimental.

Period of Validity of Consent Form

The law does not impose a specific time period on the validity of a consent form. Circumstances that may influence or decide whether the patient's written consent is still valid include the following:

- A change in the patient's condition that increases the risks or consequences of the proposed procedure.

- A change in the procedure or equipment that increases the risk or consequences of the proposed procedure.

- A substitution of the physician or person who is to perform the procedure if the patient's consent was obtained with the understanding that a specific person would be performing the procedure. The practice of what is known as "ghost surgery," in which the surgeon who performs the surgery is not the one that the patient consented to, can result in the operating surgeon being held liable for battery.[16] The fact that surgery improved the patient's condition has no bearing in an action for battery.

- Hospital policy indicating a specific time period during which a patient's written consent is valid.

- Hospital policies that extend the original consent indefinitely for procedures that are repetitive and familiar to a patient with a chronic illness or disability.

- Limits contained in state or federal informed consent statutes.[17]

The general rule is that a consent form may be considered as evidence that the hospital obtained the patient's consent but it is not dispositive on the issue of consent. The success of a hospital's attempt to prove that the patient's consent is valid will generally depend on the content of the disclosure and on the circumstances surrounding the patient's expression of consent. The validity of a battery type consent form is more easily defended if the patient's record contains notations that corroborate the objective statements contained on the consent form. Battery consent forms are impersonal, applying to everyone until specific information is added concerning the patient and the procedure. An additional notation in the patient's record as to the specific information that was provided to the patient will individualize and personalize the procedure and serve as convincing evidence that the patient's consent was informed.

Challenges to Consent Forms

A properly executed consent form creates a presumption that the patient understood the nature and risks of the treatment and that he or she freely consented to having it performed by a health care professional. The form can shift the burden of proof of consent from the physician or hospital to the patient, who may now be required to offer evidence that his or her consent was invalid. Challenges to consent forms focus on the sufficiency of their form or content.

Unintelligible Form

The wording of the form is too technical and is written in medical jargon that makes it unintelligible to the lay person. Studies have demonstrated that while the average patient reads at a seventh grade level, most hospital education materials are written at a tenth grade level and some consent forms are written at the level of a scientific journal.[18] Another problem concerns the patient who cannot read the English language. If it is not possible to obtain a form in the language that a patient can read, the form should be translated for the patient. The form should contain the name of the translator and the fact that the information was orally translated for the patient, and it should be dated and certified.

Inaccurate and Misleading Form

The patient may not have received all of the information concerning the procedure, risks, and alternatives that the form indicates were provided. Courts have held that there was no informed consent when the patient had been told the risks of closed reduction surgery for a broken arm but had not been advised of the attendant risks of anesthesia.[19] The form is inaccurate if the person who performed the procedure is other than the person whom the form indicates or implies will perform the procedure or if the surgery was extended or expanded beyond the scope of the patient's consent (e.g., when a patient has consented to an exploratory laparotomy and the surgeon removes the appendix). The form is misleading when additions or alterations are added to the form without the patient's knowledge after obtaining the patient's signature.

Patient's Signature Invalid

The signature of a patient who is incapacitated will invalidate the consent form. In some hospitals it is not unusual for patients to be asked to sign the consent form after they have been given preoperative medications, which often cause drowsiness and confusion. Although most hospitals have a policy that indicates that the consent form should be signed before the preoperative medication is given, nurses frequently complain that hospitals tend to overlook or fail to reprimand the surgeons who violate this policy. If the patient's signature was obtained by the use of coercion or pressure from the medical professionals or the family, it is invalid. The elderly, persons in mental hospitals, and prisoners are particularly susceptible to this type of pressure.

RESPONSIBILITY FOR OBTAINING CONSENT

Courts have responded to the confusion and controversy surrounding the policies and practices for obtaining the informed consent of hospitalized patients by invoking the doctrine of personal liability. Under this fundamental rule of law every person is liable for his or her own negligent conduct.

Physician

Physicians and independent practitioners have the primary nondelegable responsibility to provide the patient with the necessary information and to obtain the patient's informed consent. Hospitals are not held liable for the failure of a physician or other independent practitioner to secure the patient's consent unless the physician or independent practitioner is an employee or agent of the hospital.[20] This policy encourages open and frank communication between the patient and the person best able to explain and answer questions concerning the proposed treatment and its consequences, risks, and alternatives.

Hospital

Hospitals are responsible for adopting and enforcing policies that ensure the patient the opportunity to consent or withdraw his or her consent to treatment. Hospitals are held liable in situations in which it is proven that staff members knew or should have known that the patient's consent was absent or invalid and did not take appropriate action to intervene. Policies that allow or require the nursing staff to secure the patient's signature should specifically limit the nurse's responsibility to screening the form to ensure it is complete and to notifying the physician of the patient's questions and concerns. The policy should clearly state that the nurse does not allow the patient to sign a consent form until his or her questions and concerns have been settled. Some hospitals allow or require the nurse to provide some or all of the information necessary for an informed consent. This type of policy could make the hospital jointly liable with the physician for obtaining the patient's informed consent. Essentially these policies reduce the opportunity for physician–patient interaction and can lead to unnecessary delay and confusion in obtaining the patient's informed consent.

Nurse and Nurse Manager

Nurses are legally and ethically responsible to obtain the patient's consent for the nursing practices and procedures that are part of the nursing process. The patient's consent to the nursing care that is received has traditionally been based in the blanket consent form signed by the patient on admission or on the patient's implied consent as evidenced by his or her acceptance and cooperation in the process. There are those who argue that there is a need to reassess the issue of patient consent to nursing procedures, especially in the area of consent to postoperative care.[21] Some nurses believe that the nurse should inform the patient about the postoperative nursing procedures before consent to the operation is obtained. As one legal reviewer remarked, "An important feature of this process is talking with a patient to assess the patient's understanding of the surgical procedure, answering questions about what to expect after surgery, and allaying anxiety by explaining in some detail the nursing procedures that will be rendered after surgery."[22] Commentators suggest that this function strengthens the nurse's duty to act when the nurse knows or reasonably should know that the patient is uninformed or misinformed about the treatment.[23]

At the present time nurses are responsible for obtaining the patient's express informed consent when (1) the nurse is providing nursing care as an independent practitioner; (2) the nurse is collaborating with another practitioner in providing care that requires informed consent; and (3) hospital policy delegates the responsibility of providing the requisite information material to the decision-making process to the nurse.

Nurses are not responsible for obtaining informed consent for the treatment provided by physicians and other independent practitioners. Their independent duty to protect the patient, however, does make them liable if they are aware that the patient is misinformed or uninformed and they do not take appropriate action. In these situations the nurse should notify the physician of the defective consent and if the physician's response would permit the procedure to be performed without a valid consent, management should be notified. If the nurse knows of the defective consent and takes no further action, the hospital could be held vicariously liable for the nurse's failure to report the situation.

The close proximity of nurses to patients, especially at the critical time prior to surgery and other major procedures, makes it likely that they will be the ones to discover that the patient's consent is inadequate or that the patient wishes to withdraw his or her consent to treatment. It is the nurse manager's responsibility to implement the policies and cultivate the environment where nurses can report their findings promptly, without fear of retaliation or charges of interfering with the patient–provider relationship, problems that have frequently been encountered by nurses who have reported invalid consents.

The focus of the nurse manager's responsibility should be to (1) implement a policy that specifically defines the nurse's role in obtaining informed consent; (2) provide a mechanism for the reporting of inadequate or inappropriate responses on the part of medical care providers when the nurse notifies them of problems with the patient's consent; and (3) require that the nurse document the patient's concerns as well as the nurse's efforts to address the problem. In most cases the problems with consent are promptly corrected by the medical care provider. Nurse managers should be aware, however, that if problems involving failure to obtain informed consent are ignored or improperly handled, they can result in litigation in which the physician, the nurse, and the hospital are all named as defendants.

EXCEPTIONS TO CONSENT REQUIREMENT

Courts have recognized four exceptions to the medical care provider's duty to obtain the patient's informed consent. They include emergency, therapeutic privilege, patient waiver, and prior patient knowledge.

Emergency

An emergency, for the purposes of consent, is a situation in which the patient is (1) unconscious or otherwise incapable of giving consent and (2) in need of immediate treatment to save the patient's life or to prevent loss of an organ, limb, or function. If there is a relative available to consent for the patient and if there is time, the physician or hospital should attempt to secure the consent of this person. The emergency exception does not apply to situations in which the patient is able but unwilling to consent.

Therapeutic Privilege

Therapeutic privilege is used in situations in which the physician believes the risk of disclosure poses such a detriment to the physical condition or well-being of the patient so as to constitute unsound medical practice. This exception is appropriate only when the physician can reasonably predict, from past experience with the patient, that the patient would become so emotionally distraught by the risk disclosure that he or she would be unable to make a rational decision about the procedure. This privilege does not allow physicians to keep silent only because they believe the patient will forego the procedure if they are advised of the risks. The courts are divided as to whether the physician must seek the consent of a spouse or relative before therapeutic privilege is invoked. Some say that the relative must be informed and concur,[24] whereas others say that disclosure to a relative is unnecessary.[25]

Patient Waiver

A patient can waive the right to be informed of any risks, thus relieving the provider of the duty to disclose. The provider may wish to make a reasonable effort to encourage the reluctant patient to become informed; however, a patient's ultimate decision to remain uninformed should be respected. The patient's refusal and the discussion with the health care provider should be documented in the patient's record prior to the treatment or surgery. If the consent form contains objective statements concerning the disclosure of risks to the patient, it should be amended to indicate that the patient chose not to be advised of the risks before the patient's signature is obtained.

Prior Patient Knowledge

There is no liability for nondisclosure of risks that are common knowledge or that the patient has experienced previously if the procedure is simple and the danger is remote and commonly considered to be remote. For example, courts have held that there is no duty to warn a patient of the potential danger of blood clots or infection before taking a routine blood sample.[26]

WITHDRAWAL AND REFUSAL OF CONSENT

Patients may rescind their consent either orally or in writing at any time. An oral withdrawal will rescind a written consent. The legal rules are clear; however, they do not take into consideration the reality of the hospital environment where the nurses and physicians must take into consideration the natural nervousness of patients prior to surgery and major medical procedures or the effects that the preoperative medication may be having in influencing the patient's decision.

Right To Refuse Treatment

The right to consent to treatment implies a right to refuse treatment. The patient's right to refuse treatment is based on the common law right to be free from unwanted touching and the constitutional rights of religion (see Chapter 4) and privacy (see Chapter 6). Constitutional civil rights violations can be filed by patients in instances in which there is federal or state government action or when federal or state law recognizes the patient's right to sue private parties such as private hospitals.

In the past, the courts have considered the patient's right to refuse treatment by balancing the patient's right to privacy, religious freedom, or liberty versus the state's interest in overriding the right. The interests most commonly cited by the state include (1) preservation of society, (2) sanctity of life, (3) respect and preservation of public morals, (4) protection of the individual against irrational self-destruction, (5) protection of third parties such as children, and (6) preserving the ethical integrity of health care providers.[27] The courts today tend to recognize the competent adult patient's right to refusal even when that refusal will clearly result in the patient's death.[28] They have also held that no civil or criminal liability could be imposed on the hospital or doctors for honoring the patient's refusal.[29]

The right to refuse treatment initially also implies the right to terminate or withdraw from treatment. In *Bartling v. Superior Court*, 209 Cal. Rptr. 220 (Cal. App. 1984), the court reviewed a claim by a hospital and a physician that the patient's ability to make a meaningful decision about terminating life support systems was questionable because he vacillated about the decision. The hospital asserted the patient's right to refuse treatment was outweighed by a variety of interests, including those listed above. The court upheld the patient's right to refuse on the basis of the California and federal constitutional right to privacy, stating "If the right of the patient to self-determination as to his own medical treatment is to have any meaning at all, it must be paramount to the interest of the patient's hospital or doctor. This right of a competent adult to refuse medical treatment is a constitutionally guaranteed right which must not be abridged."[30] The right to refuse treatment is also available to minors and persons who have been declared incompetent.

Incompetent Patients and Minors

In reviewing the rights of incompetent patients and minors to refuse or withdraw their consent to treatment the courts have developed a number of approaches that are characterized by the standard that is used by the decision maker in arriving at a decision. The *substitute judgment* approach requires the guardian or parent to determine what the patient would have decided if he or she were competent to make the decision. The *best interest of the patient* approach requires the guardian to ascertain the action that is in the patient's best interest and to decide accordingly. The *benefits and burdens* approach incorporates the substitute judgment approach. In *Barber v. Superior Court*, 195 Cal. Rptr. 484 (Cal. App. 1983), the court held that the determination of the point at which further treatment will be of no reasonable benefit to the patient and the determination of who has the power and authority to make such a decision and terminate treatment "is essentially a medical one to be made at a time and on the basis of facts which will be unique to each case."[31] The court suggested that a rational determination be made as to whether the proposed treatment is proportionate or disproportionate in terms of benefits gained versus burden caused. For example, treatment that is painful or intrusive may be proportionate if the prognosis is complete cure or significant improvement; on the other hand, treatment that is minimally painful and intrusive may be considered disproportionate if the prognosis is virtually hopeless.[32] The court also held that when the patient is incapable of deciding, the family may substitute their judgment, and that legal proceedings of guardianship were not required. The court indicated that the surrogate or guardian should be guided in the decision by the knowledge of the patient's own desires and feelings if they were expressed prior to the patient becoming incompetent. If these wishes are not known, then the surrogate or guardian should make the decision according to what he or she considers to be in the patient's best interest. The court also discussed the duty of physicians to continue to provide life-sustaining measures, holding that "A physician has no duty to continue treatment once it has proven ineffective. Although there may be some duty to provide life-sustaining machinery in the *immediate* aftermath of a cardio-respiratory arrest, there is no duty to continue its use once it has become futile in the opinion of qualified medical personnel."[33]

Finally, the court stated that, in the absence of a legislative enactment, "there is no legal requirement that judicial approval is necessary before a decision to withdraw treatment can be made."[34] In this case the family had requested the termination of all life-sustaining measures for the patient who was in a persistent vegetative coma with virtually no chance of recovery. The physicians honored the family's request and removed the life-sustaining measures without instituting guardianship proceedings. The state district attorney brought murder charges against the physicians for their termination of treatment. The court concluded its findings by ordering the cessation of criminal proceedings against the physicians. This case returns the decision-making authority and power to the family and the physicians, at least in situations in which there is no disagreement among family members as to what course of action should be taken.

Do Not Resuscitate Orders

Orders not to resuscitate a patient, commonly referred to as DNR or NO CODE orders, are common practice in hospitals. The patient has the right to decide whether he or she wants life-sustaining measures initiated; however, it is the physician's responsibility to determine whether the patient's condition warrants the writing of a DNR order.[35] Medical-legal interprofessional committees studying the issues of DNRs have suggested the following principles be considered in formulating a DNR policy:[36]

- A statement that orders to resuscitate are a standing order in the institution and that this procedure should be initiated unless there is an order to the contrary
- A statement regarding the patient's wishes
- A statement of the medical conditions that should be present to justify an order not to resuscitate
- A statement regarding the role of the family or close associates
- A statement regarding entry of the DNR order in the patient's record
- A statement about the scope of the DNR order
- A statement regarding the obligation of various persons responsible for the care of the patient

The nurse's responsibility for calling or not calling a code is determined by the presence or absence of a DNR order. If a DNR order exists, the nurse is required to follow it; if no DNR order has been written, the nurse is advised to institute all emergency measures appropriate to sustain life. The nurse manager's responsibility is to ascertain that the policies are carried out and that a mechanism exists by which the nurses can inform and discuss with the physician their knowledge of the patient's and family's wishes that have come to their attention while caring for the patient. It is not uncommon for patients whose judgment may be impaired by the psychological reactions and metabolic disturbances of critical illness to vacillate in their decision making.[37] Nurses are faced with a professional and ethical problem when they do not have a DNR order and are therefore required to call a code on a patient who has expressed a desire not to receive such treatment. It has been suggested that nurses fully realize that when the code is called the staff will respond and the physician or team member will feel "obligated to start life saving procedures which no one will be brave enough to stop."[38] This can result in the patients surviving on life-support mechanisms for an indeterminable amount of time, giving rise to the ethical and legal dilemma of when these measures can be discontinued and thus creating an emotional, frustrating, and expensive problem for the patient, the family, the physician, the nurse, and the hospital. It is the nurse manager's obligation to ascertain that the hospital's DNR policies take into consideration the fact that nurses often have first-hand and current information concerning the patient's or family's wishes and that this information should be given prompt and serious consideration in deciding whether to institute or rescind a DNR order.

Living Will Legislation

A number of states have attempted to address the problem of the patient's right to refuse life-support systems and other life-prolonging therapy by enacting living will legislation known as natural death acts. The provisions of the natural death acts vary considerably from state to state; however, most of the acts address the following areas.

- The person who may execute a living will; most states restrict it to a competent adult.
- The requirement that the person be diagnosed as terminally ill.
- A directive concerning the termination of treatment. Some states do not indicate whether it includes the withdrawal of food and hydration.
- The time at which the will becomes effective. In many states it is not binding if it is signed before a diagnosis of terminal illness is made.
- The need for witnesses and the disqualification of certain persons as witnesses.
- The means of revocation.
- Sanctions or absence of sanctions for physicians who follow or refrain from following the directive.
- Immunity for a person who acts or refrains from acting in accordance with the document.

Hospitals in states that have enacted living will legislation should adopt policies that reflect the requirements of the legislation. These should include the person responsible for determining whether the patient has executed such a document and whether the document that was executed meets the requirements of state law.

Critics of living will legislation suggest that it adds nothing to the existing constitutional and common law protections while inhibiting the physician's ability to "solve with grace and dignity the problems of the dying patient." [39] They also suggest that the litigation that surrounds the attempts to define the term *terminal illness* would be avoided if the wording were changed to "Life-sustaining measures may be terminated by the attending physician when, in his judgment, based upon a reasonable degree of certainty, according to the usual and customary standards of medicine, it is proper to do so." [40]

Discharge against Medical Advice

The patient's right to withdraw consent to treatment implies a right to withdraw consent to hospitalization. An adult patient who is not drugged, disoriented, or committable has the right to leave the hospital. Nurses who attempt to restrain or unreasonably detain a patient who has expressed an intent to leave the hospital could involve the hospital in litigation based on the patient's claim of false imprisonment. The appropriate response by a nurse to a patient's request to be allowed to leave the hospital against medical advice (AMA) is as follows:

1. Attempt to determine and resolve the problem that is causing the patient's dissatisfaction with the hospital experience.
2. Notify the physician, providing specific information concerning the patient's dissatisfaction if possible.
3. Notify the family and attempt to obtain their assistance in reasoning with the patient.
4. If all attempts at reasoning with the patient fail, resist the temptation to become angry and threaten the patient, which is an understandable reaction on the part of compassionate nurses, who fear for the patient's safety and welfare. Nurses should channel their energies into making certain that the patient and the family have been made aware of the risks and consequences of a premature departure and that the conversation has been properly documented.
5. Request that the patient sign the discharge AMA form. If the patient refuses to sign the form, indicate the fact that he or she refused to sign and place the form in the patient's record. The record will be of vital importance as evidence of the circumstances surrounding the patient's departure and of the information that was provided to the patient. It should contain the reason given by the patient for his or her departure; the persons who were notified of his or her intent to leave, including the time they were notified and their responses; the advice given to the patient as to risks and consequences of early departure, instructions as to the need for follow-up care, and the availability of other health care providers; the name and relationship of any persons accompanying the patient along with any advice or instructions that they were given; and the patient's immediate destination if it is known.

Commentators indicate that the usual AMA discharge form typically states that the patient has been warned of the risks of leaving the hospital prematurely and waives any cause of action against the hospital or health care provider.[41] This type of general waiver of liability will not be enforced by a court because it violates public policy, which prohibits releasing a person from liability for negligence. It has been suggested that this waiver whose invalidity is unknown to the patient is the main reason that patients generally refuse to sign the form.[42] The use of a questionnaire-type elective discharge form that provides information about the patient's complaints and explains the risks and consequences that were told to the patient is believed to be a better approach to obtaining the patient's cooperation.[43] This type of form, which does not contain a release of liability, may be more acceptable to a court as evidence of the hospital's attempt to document and address the patient's problems rather than the typical form, which is often viewed as an attempt to coerce a release of liability from the patient.

TORT LIABILITY: BATTERY AND FALSE IMPRISONMENT

Patients whose rights to consent or withdraw consent for treatment have been violated by health care professionals have a variety of legal causes of action. They may file a civil rights action based on their federal or state constitutional rights of religion, liberty, or privacy. Federal and civil rights actions may not be successful against a private hospital unless government action is found; however, some state constitutions recognize a right of privacy that is actionable against a private person without the requirement of state action.[44]

Patients can also file negligence or malpractice actions based on the provider's failure to meet the duty of information disclosure. State malpractice or informed consent statutes may also impose a duty of disclosure on health care providers. Patients can also sue the health care provider for battery and false imprisonment based on the common law right to body integrity and to freedom of movement. Battery claims have been filed (1) in situations in which the courts have not distinguished between consent and informed consent and have held either to be a battery and (2) in situations in which there is no government action and the constitutional protections cannot be applied to private persons such as physicians or hospitals. Patients do not have to select only one cause of action and can file all of these claims simultaneously in their complaint.

Battery and Assault

Battery is unpermitted touching of another person. The elements that the plaintiff must prove are intent, touching, and absence of consent (Exhibit 14-1). The touching of another person without consent or some other lawful reason is actionable. The legal interest that is protected is the freedom from unpermitted and intentional contacts with one's person; the plaintiff does not have to have suffered physical harm or injury. The protection extends to any part of the body and to anything that is attached or identified with the body, including clothing, canes, objects in hand, cars, spitting, and kissing.[45]

Exhibit 14-1 Assault and Battery/False Imprisonment

Assault: Fear of harmful or offensive touching
Fear
Immediate
Contact harmful or offensive
Plaintiff must prove defendant
intended to commit the act.

Battery: Unpermitted touching of another
Intent
Touching
Absence of consent

Defenses:

Consent: Plaintiff must prove he or she did not consent.
Privilege: Defense of self
Defense of others
Prevention of self-inflicted harm

Qualified Privilege:
Only reasonable force is ever allowed.
Reasonable force: amount of force that can legally be used is that which
is reasonably necessary under the circumstances

False Imprisonment: Unlawful restraint of an individual of personal liberty or unlawful detention of
an individual
Defenses and Immunities: **Mentally ill and dangerous**
Communicable disease

Privilege: Defense of self
Defense of others
Prevention of self-inflicted harm

The person need not be conscious of the contact at the time it occurs. The nonconsensual treatment of an unconscious patient or the nonconsensual surgery or extension of surgery on an anesthetized patient is considered battery. Health care providers should realize that the fact that the treatment or surgery actually improved or corrected the patient's condition does not in any way preclude an action in battery.

The tort of assault is often joined with that of battery. An *assault* is a deliberate threat, coupled with the apparent present ability to touch another person. The elements of assault are fear or apprehension of an immediate harmful or offensive touching (see Exhibit 14-1). An assault consists of any act that gives rise to apprehension that battery is about to be committed; threats to do something in the future do not apply.

Civil and Criminal Assault and Battery

Civil assault and battery cases allow the plaintiff to be paid damages by the defendant who has interfered with his or her rights to not be touched or be put in fear of being touched without his or her consent. Assault and battery are also defined in the criminal code and are generally considered misdemeanors in which the defendant is prosecuted by the state and made to pay a fine to the state if he or she is found guilty. Assault may be classified as a felony if special circumstances exist such as the intent to do great bodily harm or the intent to murder. In these instances the defendant, if found guilty, may be fined and imprisoned.

Defenses

The defenses to assault and battery are consent and privilege (see Exhibit 14-1). The hospital can prove that the patient's implied or express consent was obtained. The hospital can also claim privilege, a superior right that is based on public policy such as the need to hold or restrain a patient to prevent him or her from harm or others from injury. The privilege to touch another person without his or her consent is a qualified privilege. The defendant is only allowed to use the amount of force that is reasonably necessary under the circumstances. The record becomes an important part of a hospital's defense against charges of battery brought by the patient and includes the consent form signed by the patient or the description of the circumstances or behavior that led the hospital personnel to believe that the patient's consent was implied or impossible to obtain (e.g., an emergency). In situations in which it becomes necessary to restrain a patient, the record should contain a description of the type of behavior that led the nurses to believe that the patient had to be restrained and the measures used to restrain the patient.

Litigation

Examples of litigation in which the hospital or the physician and the hospital were held liable for battery include the failure to obtain the patient's consent:

- For repeated physical examinations that were performed on the patient by medical students. A patient testified that she was repeatedly examined several times a day by 10 to 12 men and that when she protested she was told to shut up.[46]
- To administration of a drug used to induce or augment labor.[47]
- To being used as research subjects. Women were unknowingly made part of a double-blind study on the effects of diethylstilbestrol (DES) in preventing miscarriages. They were given DES and told it was a vitamin.[48]
- The administration of medication to a person who had not been found mentally ill, dangerous, or incompetent. A patient was forced to take medications despite her refusal on the basis of her religious beliefs.[49]

A hospital was also held liable for the assault of a patient by one of its employees because the hospital was aware that the employee had a problem with alcohol and continued to employ him despite other incidents involving his alcoholism.[50]

The following cases demonstrate situations in which the physician and the hospital were not found liable. The court found in favor of a physician who had been accused of battery for slapping the cheek of a child who had clamped her teeth down on his middle finger while he was attempting to treat her for a tongue laceration. The court held that the physician had the right to take some action and that the amount of force used was reasonable under the circumstances.[51] In another case, a claim was filed against the hospital for failure to ensure that the plaintiff's complaint was communicated to the physician. The patient had signed a consent form agreeing to a rhizotomy. Shortly before surgery he told the nurse that he wanted to cancel the surgery. The nurse called the operating room but did not talk to the surgeon, who later testified that he never received the nurse's message. In ruling for the hospital, the court found implied consent based on the fact that despite his request for cancellation, the patient, who was awake during the surgery, had cooperated with the surgeon as required by the surgery. The court determined that the medication he had received was not enough to make him unaware of his surroundings because he was alert and able to communicate with the surgeon during the surgery.[52]

False Imprisonment

False imprisonment is the unlawful restraint of personal liberty or the unlawful detention of the individual. The interest that is protected by the law is the freedom from restraint of movement.[53] The plaintiff must prove that there was a direct restraint imposed for a period of time during which he or she was required to stay somewhere or go somewhere against his or her will. There is no need for the plaintiff to prove that damages occurred because of the confinement; the injury is to their freedom of movement. The elements that must be proven include physical restraint or restraint by threat or intimidation and the absence of consent, that is, that the plaintiff did not voluntarily agree to the confinement.[54]

Defenses

Defenses include privilege as discussed in the cases of battery. If the nurses have reason to believe that the person is dangerous and may harm himself or herself or others, they may restrain or detain the patient; however, they must only use the amount of force that is reasonable under the circumstances. The patient's record is an important part of the hospital's defense. It should clearly describe the behavior that led the nurses to believe that the patient was dangerous, as well as the measures used to protect and treat the patient. The hospital's policy concerning the use of restraints should be followed. The record should also reveal the measures taken to protect the patient who is restrained. Physical restraints will require close supervision for circulatory impairment and protection against the dangers of aspiration when taking food or medication. The patient will have to be observed for the common side effects and complications of tranquilizers and other medications that may be administered to treat the patient's condition. An evaluation of the patient's condition in relation to the requirements of the state's voluntary and involuntary commitment statute should be made by the physicians. Hospital policy concerning the patient who is mentally or emotionally ill should reflect all of the due process requirements of the state's commitment statutes. Another defense to false imprisonment are state statutes that permit the detention and treatment of persons for communicable diseases.

Litigation

The following cases demonstrate situations in which a physician or a hospital was involved in defending a charge of false imprisonment. In the first case a court determined that a physician's insurance policy covered his defense against charges of assault and battery and false imprisonment. The preadmission information on an obstetrics patient indicated that she was to be given epidural anesthesia and that she wished to have a tubal ligation performed. After admission, while she was in active labor, the patient did not execute the required consent form for the sterilization. The nurse told the physician that the patient had not completed the consent form because she did not want the procedure done. Words were exchanged between the nurse and the physician and, as the nurse started to walk away, the physician held her and turned her around, stating he was not through talking to her yet; more words were exchanged until others interceded.[55] It is unfortunate when the nurse–physician relationship becomes adversarial; however, professionals do retain the right to sue when their rights are violated. Nurse managers should encourage a cooperative and collaborative relationship between physicians and nurses and provide a forum in which disputes can be resolved promptly and fairly.

A case of false imprisonment can be brought by individuals who are admitted and detained in a mental hospital in violation of the state's statutory requirements for involuntary commitment.[56] The court must also determine when the statute of limitations begins on the plaintiff's charge of false imprisonment. In one case, a patient sued his employer, the security guard, and the hospital for false imprisonment. The patient, while at work, had sought medication for anxiety. The security guard was called and restrained the patient, taking him, against his will, to a hospital where he was confined until the next day and then released. While he was in the hospital he was isolated from other patients and was not allowed to call anyone, including his lawyer. The court held that the tort of false imprisonment continues until the unlawful detention ends; therefore, the statute of limitations did not start to toll until the patient was released from the hospital.[57]

Hospitals that have psychiatric units are particularly vulnerable to charges of false imprisonment when they detain patients against their will. Hospital policies for such units should clearly reflect the requirements of the state's mental health statutes. Nurses and other health care providers should make certain that the patient's due process rights are protected.

The refusal to discharge patients who come to the emergency department for treatment and are under the influence of alcohol may also pose some risk to hospitals for charges of false imprisonment. If the person was discharged and allowed to drive and subsequently injured someone, the hospital could be held liable for the injuries to the third party. The decision to detain the patient until someone can be found to escort him or her home or to allow the patient to leave unescorted calls for a balancing of the risks. These decisions should always be made on the basis of which choice offers the most protection for the patient. In either case, the emergency department record should describe the patient's condition and the facts on which the detention or discharge decision was based. Hospital policy should clearly address the problem of discharging the alcohol-impaired person from the emergency department by indicating who should be notified and what steps should be taken to resolve the problem. It is not appropriate to leave this type of decision to the emergency department nurses to be handled on a case-by-case basis.

NOTES

1. *Schloendorff v. Society of New York Hospital*, 211 N.Y. 125, 129, 105 N.E. 92, 93 (1914).

2. *Truman v. Thomas*, 27 Cal. 3d 285, 611 P.2d 902 (1980).

3. Cynthia E. Northrop and Mary E. Kelly, *Legal Issues in Nursing* (St. Louis: C.V. Mosby Co., 1987):83.

4. *Canterbury v. Spence*, 464 F.2d 772 (D.C. Cir. 1972), *cert. denied* 409 U.S. 1064 (1972).

5. President's Commission for the Study of Ethical Problems in Medicine and Biomedical and Behavioral Research, *Making Health Care Decisions: The Ethical and Legal Implications of Informed Consent in the Patient-Practitioner Relationship* (1983):23.

6. Arnold Rosoff, *Informed Consent: A Guide for Health Care Providers* (Rockville, Md.: Aspen Publishers, Inc., 1981):41.

7. President's Commission, 90.

8. *O'Brien v. Cunard S.S. Co.*, 28 N.E. 266 (Mass. 1891).

9. *Jacovach v. Yocum*, 212 Iowa 914, 237 N.W. 444 (1931).

10. *Kennedy v. Parrott*, 243 N.C. 355, 90 S.E. 754 (1956).

11. N.H. RSA 265:84.

12. New York Vehicle and Traffic Laws Section 1194 (3), McKinney 1970.

13. *Roger's v. Lumberman's Mutual Casualty Co.*, 119 So. 2d 649 (La. Ct. App. 1960).

14. 45 CFR § 46.

15. 42 CFR §§ 441.250–441.259 (1983).

16. *Perna v. Pirozzi*, 96 N.J. 446, 457 A.2d 431 (1983).

17. 42 CFR §§ 441.250–441.259 (1983); Nev. Rev. Stat. §§ 41 A 110 (1981).

18. Regina Walczak, ed., "Managing Hospital Quality Risk and Cost," *QRC Advisor* 1, no. 3 (January 1985):5.

19. *Barth v. Rock*, 674 P.2d 1265 (Wash. App. 1984).

20. *Fiorentino v. Wagner*, 19 N.Y. 2d 407, 227 N.E. 296 (1967).

21. Ann M. Rhodes and Robert D. Miller, *Nursing & The Law* (Rockville, Md.: Aspen Publishers, Inc., 1984), 205.

22. Edith Kelly Politis, "Nurse's Dilemma: When Hospital Staffing Compromises Professional Standards," 18 *University of San Francisco Law Review* (1983):109, 120.

23. Northrop and Kelly, *Legal Issues in Nursing*, 88.

24. *Lester v. Aetna Casualty and Sur. Co.*, 240 F.2d 676 (5th Cir. 1957), *cert. denied* 354 U.S. 923 (1957).

25. *Nishi v. Hartwell*, 473 P.2d 116 (Hawaii 1970).

26. *Cobbs v. Grant*, 104 Cal. Rptr. 505, 515 (Cal. 1972).

27. Eugene Pavalon, *Human Rights and Health Care Law* (New York: American Journal of Nursing Co., 1980), 41.

28. *St. Mary's v. Ramsey*, 465 So. 2d 666 (Fla. App. 1985).

29. Ibid.

30. *Bartling v. Superior Court*, 209 Cal. Rptr. 220, 225 (Cal. App. 1984).

31. *Barber v. Superior Court*, 195 Cal. Rptr. 484, 491 (Cal. App. 1983); for a discussion of this case see Northrop and Kelly, *Legal Issues in Nursing*, 61–62.

32. Ibid., 491.

33. Ibid., 490–491 (emphasis in original).

34. Ibid., 493.

35. Northrop and Kelly, *Legal Issues in Nursing*, 135.

36. President's Commission for the Study of Ethical Problems in Medicine and Biomedical and Behavioral Research, *Deciding to Forego Life-Sustaining Treatment: A Report on the Ethical, Medical and Legal Issues in Treatment Decisions*, pp. 494–497, quoting NO CODE Subcommittee, Medical-Legal Interprofessional Committee, Bar Association of San Francisco Medical Society.

37. Northrop and Kelly, *Legal Issues in Nursing*, 135.

38. Davis, "The Nurse's Dilemma," in *Dilemmas of Euthanasia* (The Euthanasia Educational Council, Inc., 1971), cited in Comment, "Critical Care Nurses: A Case for Legal Recognition of the Growing Responsibilities and Accountability in the Nursing Profession," 11 *Journal of Contemporary Law* 239, 266 n. 110 (1984).

39. Dennis J. Horan, "The Right to Die: Legislation and Judicial Developments," *Forum* 13, no. 2 (Winter 1978):488.

40. Ibid., 491.

41. Howard S. Rowland and Beatrice L. Rowland, *Hospital Legal Forms, Checklists and Guidelines*, (Rockville, Md.: Aspen Publishers, Inc., 1986), 5:26.

42. Ibid.

43. Ibid.

44. *Bartling v. Superior Court*, 209 Cal. Rptr. 220 (Cal. App. 1984).

45. William Prosser, *Law of Torts*, 4th ed. (St. Paul, Minn.: West Publishing Co., 1971), 135.

46. *Inderbitzer v. Lane Hospital*, 12 P.2d 744 (Cal. App. 1932) *aff'd*, 13 P.2d 905 (Cal. 1932).

47. *Kohoutek v. Hafner*, 366 N.W.2d 633 (Minn. App. 1985), *review granted* July 11, 1985.

48. *Mink v. University of Chicago*, 460 F. Supp. 713 (D. Ill. 1973).

49. *Winters v. Miller*,446 F.2d 65 (1971).

50. *Hayes v. State*, 363 N.Y.S. 2d 986 (1975).

51. *Mattocks v. Bell*, 194 A.2d 307 (1963).

52. *Busalacchi v. Vogel*, 429 So. 2d 217 La. (1983).

53. Prosser, *Law of Torts*, 42.

54. Ibid., 44.

55. *Okehi v. St. Paul Fire and Marine Insurance Co.*, 289 S.E.2d 810 (Ga. App. 1982).

56. *Maben v. Rankin*, 10 Cal. Rptr. 353 (Cal. 1961).

57. *Adler v. Beverly Hills Hospital*, 594 S.W.2d 153 (Tex. Civ. App. 1980).

Chapter **15**

Confidentiality

INFORMATIONAL PRIVACY

The right of privacy encompasses two separate concepts: the constitutional right of personal privacy and the common law or statutory right of informational privacy. The constitutional right of personal privacy, which includes the right of autonomy and self-determination, is discussed in Chapters 6 and 14 in relation to a person's right to make choices in private matters, including the right to refuse treatment or to terminate the use of life-support systems. Informational privacy involves the traditional right of privacy that encompasses a person's "right to be left alone," to be free from unwanted publicity as well as the right to keep private information inaccessible to others.[1] Informational privacy, the concept of privacy concerning information about oneself, is considered a property interest rather than a bodily control interest. As a property interest it can form the basis for a cause of action for invasion of privacy and/or defamation, two intentional torts that are recognized either in common law or by statute in a majority of states.

Included in this concept of privacy is the freedom from unwanted disclosure of information, the freedom from actual intrusion into private situations and the freedom to live as one wishes in respect to certain private activities.[2] Privacy has been defined as the ability for people to lead their lives without anyone doing any of the following:[3]

- Interfering with their family and home life
- Interfering with their physical or mental integrity or their moral or intellectual freedom
- Attacking their honor or reputation
- Placing them in a false light
- Disclosing irrelevant embarrassing facts about them
- Misusing private oral or written communications
- Disclosing information given or received in circumstances of professional confidence

208

PATIENTS' RIGHT OF PRIVACY

People who are admitted to a hospital retain their right of privacy. They have the right to expect that the information that is learned about them during the course of administrative or clinical inquiries will be kept confidential. These expectations are supported by the common law and statutory recognition of the right of privacy, by professional codes of ethics, and by professional organization standards that specifically address the patients' right of privacy. For example, the American Nurses' Association Code for Nurses states, "The nurse safeguards the client's right to privacy by judiciously protecting information of a confidential nature."[4] The American Medical Association Code states that "a physician . . . shall safeguard the patient's confidences within the constraints of the law."[5] The American Hospital Association Patient's Bill of Rights states that

> The patient has the right to every consideration of his privacy concerning his own medical care program. Case discussion, consultation, examination, and treatment are confidential and should be conducted discreetly. Those not directly involved in his care must have the permission of the patient to be present.
> The patient has the right to expect that all communications and records pertaining to his care be treated as confidential.[6]

The Standards for Rights and Responsibilities of Patients of the Joint Commission on Accreditation of Healthcare Organizations provide specific guidance as to the patient's right to privacy and confidentiality. The list of personal and informational privacy rights includes the following:[7]

- To refuse to talk to or see anyone not officially connected with the hospital, including visitors, or people officially connected with the hospital but not directly involved in the patient's care.
- To wear appropriate personal clothing and religious or other symbolic items, as long as they do not interfere with diagnostic procedures or treatment.
- To be interviewed and examined in surroundings designed to ensure reasonable visual and auditory privacy. This includes the right to have a person of one's own sex present during certain parts of a physical examination, treatment, or procedure performed by a health care professional of the opposite sex and the right not to remain disrobed any longer than is required for accomplishing the medical purpose for which the patient was asked to disrobe.
- To expect that any discussion or consultation involving a patient's case will be conducted discreetly and that the individuals not directly involved in the patient's care will not be present without the patient's permission.
- To have the patient's medical record read only by individuals directly involved in the patient's treatment or the monitoring of its quality, and by other individuals only

on the patient's written authorization or that of his or her legally authorized representative.

• To expect that all communications and other records pertaining to the patient's care, including the source of payment for treatment, will be treated as confidential.

• To request a transfer to another room if another patient or visitors in that room are causing an unreasonable disturbance by smoking or other actions.

• To be placed in protective privacy when considered necessary for personal safety.

EMPLOYEES' RIGHT OF PRIVACY

The emphasis on the importance of documentation in justifying employment-related decisions has resulted in employers obtaining and retaining a significant amount of information on individual employees. The use of this information to hire, commend, promote, reprimand, and discharge personnel has prompted employees to demand the right to review their personnel files. Employees want the assurance that the information in their files is objective, accurate, and valid. Some states such as California, Connecticut, and Maine have created a general right of employee access, whereas others such as the District of Columbia, Michigan, New Hampshire, Oregon, Pennsylvania, South Dakota, Tennessee, Utah, Vermont, and Wisconsin have legislation that governs employee access to personnel files.[8]

Abuses of Employee Privacy

Abuses of employee privacy can occur when the employer takes part in (1) intrusive data gathering, such as personality or polygraph testing; (2) unfair use of information in employment decision making; and (3) breach of confidentiality by the release of protected data.[9] Employees have the right to have the contents of their personnel file kept confidential. The publication of private facts can lead to suits for invasion of privacy. The Federal Privacy Act of 1974 limits the federal government's acquisition of information about a person to that which is "relevant and necessary to accomplish a purpose of the agency required to be accomplished by statute or by executive order of the President."[10] Under the act, individuals can gain access to the information pertaining to them in federal agency records. They are also entitled to correct, amend, and receive a copy of such records. Under the statute the agency that improperly discloses private information can be subject to a civil suit for any damages that may occur as a result of willful or intentional actions that violate a person's privacy rights. In 1985, 14 Veterans Administration nurses were awarded $1,000 each in damages for "unwarranted invasion of personal privacy."[11] The agency, without their consent, had released reports containing sensitive personal and job performance–related information to a local union.

False or Inaccurate Information

Hospitals must adopt policies that determine when information will be released, to whom it will be released, and the extent of the data that will be provided. If the information that is disseminated to a third party is false or inaccurate, it could cause harm to an employee's reputation and involve the agency in litigation. Prospective employment inquiries and unfavorable job performances carry the greatest potential for suits for defamation. Care must be taken to ensure that the information is given in the form of statements that are truthful, objective, and provable. Although some courts recognize a qualified privilege for employment references provided in good faith, some agencies limit their responses to a simple verification of the dates of employment and the position held.[12] This approach protects the referring agency; however, if it is adopted by a majority of hospitals, it may obstruct or significantly impair the hospitals' duty to screen applicants to ensure that they are hiring competent professional personnel.

INVASION OF PRIVACY

The tort of invasion of privacy (Exhibit 15-1) consists of four distinct kinds of invasion of four different interests of the plaintiff. These include (1) appropriation of the plaintiff's name or likeness, (2) intrusion on plaintiff's seclusion, (3) public disclosure of private facts about the plaintiff, and (4) placing the plaintiff in a false light in the public eye. Each represents an interference with the plaintiff's "right to be let alone."[13]

Exhibit 15-1 Invasion of Privacy/Libel and Slander

Invasion of Privacy	Injury to personal feelings
	The right to be left alone
	Unreasonable publicity of another's private life
	Publication of private facts
Defense:	Reporting and recording statutes—qualified privilege
Libel (Written)	Injury to reputation
	False statement
	Written
	Communicated to a third party
	No need for actual damages
	Public person need to prove malice
Slander (Spoken)	Injury to reputation
	False statement
	Communicated to a third party
	Need damages; however, there are four exceptions when damages need not be proved, one of which is "words that affect a person's profession."
Defenses to Libel and Slander	Truth
	Qualified privilege:
	Superior right—must be in good faith, on the proper occasion, in the proper manner, and to a person who has a legitimate right to know

The law does not require that the plaintiff prove actual damages: the injury is to the person's feelings and to the person's interest in, and right to, privacy. The information that is made public must be one that would be offensive and objectionable to a reasonable person of ordinary sensibilities.[14] It is not difficult to characterize a person's medical history as private information that would meet this criterion.

Litigation

Areas in which hospitals have or could face litigation include the following:[15]

- Releasing patient information to unauthorized parties
- Permitting unauthorized parties to view medical or surgical procedures
- Failing to control visitors in the hospital
- Taking pictures of patients without their consent
- Disclosing or discussing patient problems or situations in public places
- Permitting access to the medical record by unauthorized persons
- Publishing the patient's picture to advertise a product or as part of an article, even for educational purposes, without the patient's permission
- Public disclosure of a person's radiograph or public exhibition of films (such as that of a cesarean section) without the consent of the patient. Even if the patient has consented to a film for educational purposes this does not allow it to be shown to the general public without obtaining additional approval from the patient.
- Publishing a patient's case history in a manner in which the patient is identifiable to the public.

Defenses

Some courts recognize a qualified privilege to release information for purposes that promote the public welfare, such as reasonable investigations for insurance or credit purposes or employment referrals.[16] Reporting and recording statutes such as child protection statutes, communicable disease reporting laws, and criminal law reporting requirements for rape and gunshot wounds create a legal obligation to reveal what is usually considered private information.

Public figures such as film stars and politicians who are often in the public spotlight and ordinary persons who voluntarily adopt a newsworthy course of conduct have less protection than the private person. If a person voluntarily seeks publicity and media attention, he or she will not be allowed to complain if the activity is reported along with his or her name and picture. In the context of the hospital, the patient's right of privacy must be protected. Public relations personnel, nurses, and physicians should not provide detailed statements of the patient's condition. The hospital should appoint a spokesperson, and representatives of the news media should be accommodated within the hospital's policies and the state regulations regarding the release of medical information.

Information may be released with the patient's consent. If the patient has signed a release, the hospital should make certain that the disclosure falls within the scope permitted by the form. A release is always construed against the person or agency that is requesting the completion of a release form.

DEFAMATION

Defamation is made up of slander (oral communication) and libel (written communication), the twin torts that comprise the invasion of interest in a person's reputation and good name.[17] Defamation concerns the opinion that others in the community may have or tend to have of the plaintiff; consequently, it requires that something be communicated to a third person that may affect that opinion.[18] A defamatory communication is one that injures a person's reputation. It has been described as that which tends to diminish the esteem, respect, goodwill, or confidence in which the plaintiff is held or that which excites adverse, derogatory, or unpleasant feelings or opinions against the plaintiff.[19] Defamation requires publication: insults or derogatory words directed only to the plaintiff are not actionable as defamation, although they may give rise to a cause of action for intentional infliction of emotional distress.[20] Any living person may be defamed; no civil action can be taken for the defamation of a person who is dead unless there is a reflection upon individuals who are still living and who are themselves defamed. A corporation is regarded as having no reputation in the personal sense; however, it does have prestige and standing in the business community and therefore language that attacks its honesty, credit, or efficiency may be actionable.[21]

Slander

Slander is an oral defamatory statement that is communicated to a third person. The general rule is that slander is not actionable unless the plaintiff can prove actual damages.[22] Common law and state statutes recognize four exceptions to the rule requiring proof of damage to the plaintiff's reputation: (1) accusing someone of a crime, (2) accusing someone of having a loathsome disease, (3) calling a woman unchaste, and (4) using words that affect a person's business or profession.[23] All of the exceptions involve communications that are considered slander per se, that is, words that are defamatory on their face. Slanderous words that do not fit into the above exceptions are actionable only on specific proof of damages to the plaintiff's reputation.[24]

Libel

Libel is a defamatory communication that is written. Libel is also recognized in the form of signs, photographs, statues, and motion pictures. In some jurisdictions the plaintiff can recover damages in an action for libel without the necessity of proving actual damages. In these states the existence of damages is conclusively assumed from the publication of the libel itself, without any specific evidence of damage to the plaintiff's reputation.[25] The majority of jurisdictions do not require proof of damages when the libelous communication is defamatory on its face or when the publication falls into one of the slander per se categories. They do, however, require proof of damages if the plaintiff must (1) introduce evidence to explain the defamatory nature of the communication or (2) show how the defamatory statement relates to him or her.[26]

Defenses

A *prima facie* case of defamation is established when the plaintiff establishes (1) publication to a third person, (2) the defendant's responsibility for the publication, (3) the recipient's understanding of the defamatory meaning, and (4) its actionable character.[27] Defenses available to the defendant include truth and privilege, which are complete defenses that avoid all liability when they are established. Other defenses such as retraction, bad reputation of the plaintiff, honest belief, or proper motive of the defendant are not complete defenses but can reduce the damages that the plaintiff will recover.[28]

Truth

Truth is an absolute defense to an action for defamation. The law presumes that all defamation is false and places the burden of proving its truth on the defendant. The defense of truth rarely results in pretrial dismissals because the truth or falsity of the statement is often in dispute; therefore, a jury trial is required to settle the issue.[29] It is generally agreed that it is not necessary to prove the literal truth of the accusation in every detail—it is sufficient to show that the imputation is substantially true.[30]

Privilege

The defense of privilege or immunity rests on the idea that conduct, which would otherwise be actionable, is allowed to escape liability because the defendant acted in furtherance of some interest of such social importance that it is entitled to protection even at the expense of uncompensated harm to the plaintiff's reputation.[31] The privilege may be absolute or qualified depending on the importance of the interest that is involved. As the defendant's interest gains in weight in the scale of social values, the privilege becomes greater.[32]

Absolute Privilege. Absolute privilege or immunity applies to situations in which there is an obvious policy in favor of permitting complete freedom of expression without any inquiry as to the defendant's motives. It is generally limited to the following:[33]

1. *Judicial proceedings.* The privilege covers judges, attorneys, petit and grand juries, and witnesses' statements whether they are testifying orally or by deposition. The privilege applies to anything that is said in relation to the matter at issue, whether in the pleadings, affidavits, or open court. It precludes any civil remedy against perjurers as the price that is paid for witnesses who are free from intimidation by the possibility of civil liability for what they say.
2. *Legislative proceedings.* The privilege protects legislators in the course of any legislative functions including debate, voting, reports, or committee work. Wit-

nesses in legislative hearings are given the same protection as those in judicial proceedings. The privilege includes the official publication of the proceedings, such as those appearing in the *Congressional Record*.

3. *Executive communications.* The privilege includes the President and superior officers of the executive departments and branches of the federal and, in a few cases, the state governments.
4. *Consent of the plaintiff.* The privilege covers situations in which the plaintiff invites or instigates the publication of defamatory words. As in all consents, the privilege is limited by the scope of the consent and to the form of publication that was consented to.
5. *Husband and wife.* The confidential nature of the marital relationship confers absolute immunity as to what is said between husband and wife.

Qualified Privilege. The privilege or immunity conferred is referred to as "qualified," "conditional," or "defeasible" because it is conditioned on publication in a reasonable manner for a proper purpose. A publication has been defined as privileged when it is "fairly made by a person in the discharge of some public or private duty, whether legal or moral, or in the conduct of his own affairs, in matters where his interest is concerned."[34] A qualified privilege has been recognized in the following areas:[35]

1. *Interest of the publisher.* The defendant may publish, in a reasonable manner, anything that appears reasonably necessary to defend his or her reputation against the defamation of another.
2. *Interest of others.* The defendant may publish defamatory information for the protection of another who is unable to protect himself or herself. The privilege is usually applied in situations in which some legal relationship exists between the defendant and the person whom he or she is protecting, such as a father advising his daughter not to marry someone, a physician protecting a patient, or a parent protesting to school authorities on behalf of his or her child.
3. *Common interest.* The privilege applies to situations in which there is a common interest between the defendant and the recipient of the communication. The communication must be of a kind that will protect or further the mutual interest. This includes people who are contemplating business dealings with each other in areas such as job references and credit investigations as well as professional, educational, or labor organizations in which the information is pertinent to the interest of the group.
4. *Public interest.* The privilege attaches to communications that are made to those who may be expected to take official action of some kind for the protection of some public interest. This includes reports to licensing boards, accrediting agencies, law enforcement agencies, government agencies such as school boards, and public health agencies.
5. *Constitutional privilege of fair comment.* In 1964, in the landmark case of *New York Times v. Sullivan,*[36] the Supreme Court held that the First Amendment required the recognition of a qualified privilege for the publication of information on matters of public concern. The privilege referred to as "fair comment" covers

the publication of information regarding matters of public concern such as the conduct and qualifications of public officers and public employees, the disbarment of attorneys, the suspension of medical and nursing licenses, and the legitimacy of medical services. The qualified privilege is not limited to comment or opinion but includes false statements of fact provided they were made without malice. *Malice* is defined as the publication of material knowing that it is false or with a reckless disregard for its truth or falsity.

6. *Public figures.* A public figure is defined as a person who, by his or her accomplishments, fame, or mode of living, or by adopting a profession that gives the public a legitimate interest in his or her doings, affairs, and character, has become a "public personage."[37] In 1967, the Supreme Court extended the privilege to cover publications concerning public figures who were not public officers or employees[38] and in a second case ruled that the constitutional qualified privilege applied to tort actions for invasion of privacy.[39]

Litigation

Litigation for defamation has involved patients suing health care providers and health care professionals suing each other or their employer. The following cases illustrate the variety of health care situations in which allegations of slander and libel can arise.

- A physician was treating a 13-year-old girl for a foot infection. On a note to the girl's teacher the physician incorrectly stated that the girl was pregnant. He ignored the parent's repeated phone calls to his office requesting that he correct the notation. Finally his office nurse told the parents to stop bothering him. The jury returned a $7,000 verdict against the physician on the basis of libel.[40]

- The patient did not have syphilis; however, she did have a condition that had caused a false-positive result on a Wasserman test. The patient worked as a caterer and at one of her catering jobs, the nurse told the hostess that the woman was being treated for syphilis. This information destroyed the woman's catering business. An appeal's court upheld the plaintiff's slander suit based on the nurse's defamatory communication.[41]

- A registered nurse at a Veterans Administration hospital sued a licensed practical nurse for both libel and slander. The RN had interpreted a medication order as morphine and told the LPN to administer it to the patient. The LPN refused to give the medication because she did not think that the order was for morphine. The RN checked with the pharmacy and the doctor and discovered that the order was for magnesium sulfate. The RN contended that she then told the LPN to administer the right medication. The LPN contended that she had been ordered to give the wrong medication by the RN. The LPN discussed the correctness of the RN's interpretation of the order with another nurse. The next day the head nurse directed the LPN to make a written report of the incident. The court held that the written report could not be the basis of a libel suit because reports made by federal officials (VA nurses) in the course of disciplinary or other proceedings in which the official is acting under a duty to complete a report are protected by an absolute privilege. The court refused to dismiss the action for slander based on the oral statements. It found that there was a factual dispute as to what the LPN actually said to her colleague and that it was possible to conclude that the statement, on its face, did impugn the plaintiff's professional competence. Since there was more than one plausible interpretation of the statements, the action was allowed to go to trial.[42]

- An RN sued a physician for slander because of statements he had made during the course of a consultation concerning the commitment of her husband to a mental institution. The physician has stated, in a voice loud enough to be heard by patients in another room, that the nurse's husband was an old drunk who should be in jail instead of the hospital. In addition, he again, in a loud voice, told someone he was talking to on the telephone that he would sign the husband's commitment papers if she would also agree to be committed because they were both crazy. The court rejected her claim for $5,000 in damages, holding that the slander did not fall within the slander per se categories that allow plaintiffs to receive damages without proof of specific economic loss. It indicated that the plaintiff had failed to allege that the words were calculated to injure her reputation as a nurse because of the context in which they were spoken. The court ruled that nothing in the words alluded to her professional capacity; therefore, in the absence of special damages, mere insult or contemptuous language alone did not constitute a cause of action for slander.[43]

- A nurse was dismissed for unprofessional conduct because she had been openly critical of the physician's treatment of a postoperative patient. The charges she brought against the physician were dismissed by the hospital's grievance committee. The nurse was later reemployed by the hospital on the condition that she would not discuss hospital business outside the hospital. The physician, on learning of her reemployment, called the administrator and said, "I wanted to ask you if you would stoop so low as to hire that creep, that malignant son of a bitch, back to work for you in the hospital." He also stated that "She was unfit to care for patients . . . he could prove it . . . and that he intended to make an issue of it." She sued the physician for defamation and was awarded $17,500 in a jury verdict that was later reduced to $5,000 by the court, claiming that provocation, although not an excuse for slander, was a mitigating factor in assessing punitive damages.[44]

Qualified Privilege Upheld

In all of the following actions for defamation, a qualified privilege was recognized by the courts, resulting in the plaintiff's being denied the right to recover damages from the defendant hospital or health care provider.

- A hospital pharmacist sued the hospital and its executive director for libel because her annual evaluation stated that she possessed "poor interpersonal relationship skills" and had a "flagrant disregard of others." The court ruled that communication of employee personnel files containing required evaluation material to supervisory personnel within the hospital did not constitute a basis for defamation.[45]

- On an application for employment at a hospital, a nurse anesthetist had indicated that an inquiry could be made of her former employer, an anesthesia service where she had been given a notice of termination. When contacted, the former employer indicated that she lacked professional competence. When her hospital employment application was denied, she sued the anesthesia service for slander. The court found the former employer not liable on the basis that employers and prospective employers have a legitimate interest in employment-related information.[46]

- A physician sent a letter concerning his former physician's assistant (PA) to the Physician's Assistant Licensing Board. The allegedly defamatory letter mentioned missing confidential patient records about which the physician had repeatedly but unsuccessfully attempted to discuss with the PA, who had avoided his calls. The physician forwarded a carbon copy of the letter to the PA's current employer, a physician who had been associated with the defendant physician in a family practice. The court held that both letters concerned interests that were protected by a qualified privilege. The letter to the licensing board was a "communication to one who may act in the public interest," and the letter to the present employer was protected by the "common interest" shared by the plaintiff's new employer and the defendant. The court ruled that the privilege applied to matters of patient care and to their files and that the privilege applied even though the letter was unsolicited.[47]

- A nurse who had been transferred from a dialysis unit sued two physicians and two nurses for interference with prospective employment advantage, intentional infliction of emotional distress, and defamation. The circuit court's dismissal of all of her causes of action was affirmed by the court of appeals. As to the action for defamation, it ruled that the testimony of the physicians before the nurse's review committee that personality conflicts involving nurses who worked in the renal dialysis unit had developed to the extent that they were interfering with the work of the unit was protected by a qualified privilege. The court also held that the nurse's allegations that the physicians' statements were the result of ill will and malice were insufficient to defeat the privilege.[48]

The preceding cases represent situations in which the actions for defamation were litigated and appealed. The hospital is a stressful environment for patients and for health care professionals. It is understandable that in this complex and fast-paced world, tempers and temperaments will at times erupt in a manner that leads to actions for defamation. Exactly how often this occurs is difficult to identify because libel and slander are areas that are especially suitable for a negotiated settlement. At a later time, in a calmer setting, the patient or the nurse or doctor who was allegedly defamed, may be willing to settle for an apology and reasonable compensation. The nurse manager should create and foster an environment of mutual respect and consideration for the contributions and competencies of all types of health care professionals. Of equal importance is the need to adopt and enforce policies that promote and preserve the patient's right to informational privacy.

MEDICAL RECORD

The intimate and sensitive nature of hospital care requires that patients disclose personal, financial, and medical information about themselves to a number of health care clinical and administrative personnel. Once a patient reveals this information, he or she is exposed, vulnerable, and totally dependent on the standards and ethics of the health care community for assurances that the information will be recorded accurately, used effectively, and treated confidentially. The medical record is the primary written means of communication between health care professionals. It must contain sufficient information to justify diagnosis, course of illness, management, and treatment of the patient. The medical record is of importance administratively as evidence of services and procedures that were provided so that the patient's care can be evaluated and the costs identified and billed to the patient or the patient's insurer.[49]

The law considers the medical record as evidence that may be introduced at trial under the business records exception to the hearsay rule. In order to be admissible, the record must be relevant, accurate, complete, and recorded in the normal course of business and not in anticipation of litigation. There is a rebuttable presumption in the law that the statements contained in the medical record are true.

Uses of Medical Record

The medical record serves many purposes. Among the most common are the following:[50]

- Provides a means of communication between health care professionals
- Serves as a data base for planning and evaluating individual care
- Serves as a data base for clinical research and education
- Supplies statistical information for public health care data and state planning agencies
- Documents patient care information that is used by accrediting agencies such as state licensing boards and the Joint Commission on the Accreditation of Healthcare Organizations
- Serves as documentary evidence for the patient's insurance, pension, or workers' compensation claims
- Documents the care received by the patient during the hospitalization and may be used as evidence of care or lack of care in actions charging the hospital or the health care providers with malpractice or negligence (see Chapter 13)
- Identifies patients who have received treatment or medications that have been found to cause a medically induced illness and provides the information that is necessary to notify patients that an iatrogenic effect or technological advancement presently indicates a danger to their health.

The medical record is used for clinical, administrative, educational, and legal purposes. The consequences of inadequate or incomplete records are as varied as its purposes and include

- Errors or delay in the delivery of patient care
- Delayed reimbursement or loss of funds from governmental, insurance or other sources
- Loss of accreditation
- Civil actions by patients when payment of hospital bills is denied by insurers or when their medical disability claim is denied because of inadequate or inaccurate documentation in the medical record
- Loss of internship programs or educational and research grants
- Inadequate data for effective assessment and evaluation of patient care incidents by the hospital's risk management or quality assurance committees
- Significant impairment of the hospital's ability to defend lawsuits resulting in their having to negotiate settlements (see Chapter 13)

The hospital has the responsibility to maintain medical records that are timely, accurate and complete. In addition, it has the obligation to keep the information confidential.

Types of Information

The medical record contains three types of information.

1. *Identification data*: the patient's name, date of birth, sex, marital status, occupation, and next of kin
2. *Financial data*: the name of the patient's employer, the patient's health insurance and policy number, and any other information that is necessary for proper billing
3. *Medical data*: the patient's medical history, the physician's progress notes and orders, the nurses' notes, report of laboratory tests, consent forms, and information concerning medical or surgical interventions

The American Medical Record Association guidelines limit the type and amount of information gathered to that which is needed for patient care. The guidelines specify that supplementary data that are needed for research and education may be recorded with the consent of the patient, following an explanation of the purpose for which the information is requested. The guidelines also require that patient-identifiable secondary information be limited to those indexes required by law or accrediting agencies and to those requested by administration or the medical staff for stated purposes.[51]

Medical Record Security

In order to prevent unauthorized access, theft, destruction, or loss, the hospital must ensure the physical protection of the medical records. Policies and procedures should identify the (1) methods of storage; (2) levels of security for the different types of reports; (3) limited access to sensitive secondary data such as death listings and abortion statistics; (4) availability and access for persons with a legitimate need to know; (5) storage of statistical reports and indexes; (6) financial information, such as active and inactive billing records; and (7) access by the patient or patient's authorized representative.[52]

Computer Records

Guidelines promulgated by the Special Advisory Committee to the secretary of Health and Human Services can assist hospitals in establishing computer systems of data collection.[53] The guidelines suggest that the agency

1. Collect only necessary information that has a lawful purpose
2. Use only data that are relevant, accurate, timely, and complete in making decisions
3. Give the data subject access to the information about self and a procedure by which to challenge and correct the information
4. Use data only for the purpose for which they were collected
5. Protect data against unauthorized loss, alteration, or disclosure.

Observers suggest that the computer offers a number of benefits to the health care system, including improving the quality of care by making readily available protocols for diagnosis and treatment, facilitating surveillance systems designed to protect the public health, and streamlining operational and management systems within a facility.[54] Along with the benefits are concerns that the computer record contains no written record for the physician to sign or initial; the system may be slow to respond to request for information; the data may be inaccurate if patient information gets mixed up; and the lack of an original record may result in reproduction and admissibility problems if the record is subpoenaed.[55]

Confidentiality of Computer Records. A breach of confidentiality can result from accidental or intentional unauthorized entry into the computer system. Computerization of medical records does not diminish the hospital's responsibility to protect and promote the patients' right of privacy. The confidentiality of computer records can be protected by (1) using security codes, (2) identifying authorized users, (3) permitting only limited access to the computer facility, (4) restricting each person's access to a limited scope of information, and (5) monitoring the information being sought by people using the access codes.[56]

The hospital staff needs to be oriented to the uses and potential abuses of the computer. Disciplinary action should be instituted against staff members who disclose their personal access codes or who inappropriately use the computer or the information obtained through computer searches.

Access to the Medical Record

Hospital policies concerning access to the medical record must conform with state law and state regulation. A number of states have laws that recognize and regulate the confidentiality of medical records. Some state statutes prohibit the release or transfer of information on the medical record without the consent of the patient or the patient's representative.[57] In addition, hospitals that are accredited by the Joint Commission on the Accreditation of Healthcare Organizations must conform to the Commission's standards on medical record confidentiality. The general rule is that access to the medical record should be limited to the patient, the patient's authorized representative, the attending physician, and hospital personnel who have a legitimate need to know the information contained in the record.[58]

Patient Access to the Medical Record

The hospital and the patient have a property interest in the medical record. Judicial decisions have determined that the hospital owns the medical record but that the patient has a property right to the information contained in the record.[59] The medical record is considered a business record that is essential to proper hospital administration; therefore, the hospital, as owner, can control access to and release of information. In 1974, an Illinois court ruled that the patient's right of access to the information did not create a right to obtain the original record.[60] The right of access has been interpreted to include the right to inspect and copy the medical record. Commentators suggest that fairness in the hospital's record-keeping relationship with patients should include policies that allow patients to[61]

- Verify whether the hospital has created and is maintaining a medical record pertaining to them
- Discover the nature of any medical information that has been disclosed and the name of the person or agency that received the information
- Correct erroneous information on the record in the form of amendments that do not alter the original entry

Hospitals and physicians have the right to refuse the patient's request to correct or amend the record; however, the patient should be allowed to file a report of any complaint with the hospital.

State statutes also recognize the hospital and the patient's overlapping property rights. For example, in Maryland, patients have the right to receive a copy of their health records within a reasonable time of having presented the hospital with a written request. The statute requires the patient to pay the cost of copying the records.[62] The American Hospital Association (AHA) has recommended that the attending physician be notified before medical records are released. In some hospitals physicians are required to review the record before it is released. The AHA Bill of Rights states that the patient should be able to obtain full disclosure of the information from the physician unless the disclosure would, in the opinion of the physician, be medically contraindicated.[63] There are a number of reasons why patients may want to read their medical records. A 1980 article that reported the reaction of patients who had been permitted to read their charts revealed that among the group

- One third had self-induced or factitious illness and were angry to have been uncovered.
- One third had believed the physician to be unsympathetic to their symptoms. Some found their suspicions confirmed, whereas others gained renewed confidence.
- One third had been worried about their prognosis and feared that their physician was not telling them the truth about the severity of their illness. All of these patients were reassured.[64]

For the most part, patient access to the medical record is recommended as a policy that demonstrates the hospital's respect for, and understanding of, the patient's legitimate interest in the information. Policies permitting review avoid the appearance that the hospital has something to hide and do not burden the patient with the necessity of hiring a lawyer to obtain the records through the legal process.

Denial of Patient Access

There are situations in which the hospital has a right to deny the patient access to the medical record. Included are situations in which the patient cannot legally obtain access, such as minors governed by legal constraints and patients who have been adjudicated as incompetent. Under these circumstances the patient's guardian or representative may be allowed access to the information. The hospital may also deny the patient access in situations in which the attending physician believes that disclosure would be injurious to the patient or to another person. Observers suggest that when the patient's request to review or copy his or her medical record is denied because the physician believes it to be medically contraindicated, the hospital should document the reason for refusal in the medical record, provide the patient or the patient's representative with a summary of the record within a reasonable period of time, and permit the health care record to be reviewed by another comparably licensed health care practitioner who has the patient's written consent to review the record.[65]

Access with Patient Authorization

Commentators suggest that there is an implied consent to keep the immediate family informed of the patient's progress unless the patient has specifically indicated that they should not be informed or unless a statute prohibits the disclosure.[66] In 1985, the American Medical Records Association published a position statement on the release of primary records.[67] The policy states that all information contained in the health record is confidential and that the "release of information from the health record shall be carried out in accordance with all applicable legal, accrediting, and regulatory agency requirements, and in accordance with written institutional policy." According to the policy, a properly completed and signed authorization to release patient information must take into account the requirements of informed consent by including the following information:[68]

1. Name of the institution releasing the information
2. Name of the individual or institution receiving the information

3. Patient's full name, address, and date of birth
4. Purpose or need for information
5. Extent or nature of information with inclusive date of treatment
6. Specific date, event, or condition on which authorization will expire unless revoked earlier
7. Statement that authorization can be revoked but is not retroactive to the release of information released in good faith
8. Date that consent is signed
9. Signature of patient or legal representative

As with all consents, releases, and waivers the person obtaining the patient's consent should ascertain that the patient is signing it freely and willingly and that the patient is not medicated or in such a condition that he or she may not have the present capacity to sign the release. They must also make certain that the patient is able to read and understand the release form.

Alcohol and Drug Abuse Patient's Records

Federal law and regulations concerning patients being treated for alcohol and drug abuse in federally assisted programs prohibit the unauthorized release of any information including the fact that the person is a patient at the facility.[69] The patient's attorney has the right of access to the patient's medical record with the patient's authorization. All other individuals and agencies, including family members, third party payers, and the criminal justice system, must obtain full written consent from the patient.[70] The regulations require that the patient's consent to the release of information be in writing and that the authorization form contain certain information. (The information required is similar to that suggested in the Medical Records Association position statement.) In addition, the federal regulations provide that the facility may make disclosures pursuant to a written consent from the patient if (1) there is no suggestion that the consent was not freely given, (2) the disclosure will not cause substantial harm to the relationship between the patient and the program or to the program's capacity to provide services in general, and (3) the disclosure will not be harmful to the patient.[71]

Access without Patient Authorization

Areas in which a hospital can permit access to or release of information from the medical record without the patient's consent include (1) authorization of the patient's representative, (2) hospital staff access, and (3) external requests for access by persons or agencies with a legitimate interest in the information.

Patient's Representative

Minors. Patient representatives such as parents or guardians are permitted access to, and may consent to the release of, information from the patient's medical record. The U.S. Supreme Court has upheld a Utah law requiring that a physician "notify if possible" the parents or guardian of a minor upon whom an abortion is to be performed.[72] The decision applies to an immature minor but does not address the issue of a mature minor seeking an abortion. A minor's right to access to medical information is governed by state law. State statutes have created exceptions to the rule that parents have a right of access to their child's medical record. Areas that are generally included in the statutes are

- Mature minor statutes that permit the minor to obtain medical care without the consent of his or her parents. As a practical matter the minor who has a right to consent to treatment would also have a right of access to the medical record that could preclude the parent's right of access without the minor's consent.
- Statutes that specifically provide that the minor has a right to treatment without parent consent and without the parent being notified. The conditions most often covered by these statutes are venereal disease, alcohol and substance abuse, family planning, pregnancy, and abortion. Some statutes prohibit the parents from being charged for the treatment.[73]
- Mental health laws or regulations that prohibit or regulate the disclosure of psychiatric or sensitive information in the record of a minor to the parents.

Incompetent Persons. Mental health statutes also determine the right of access to information concerning a person who has been declared incompetent. Generally the guardian of an incompetent patient has the right of access to the medical record and the right to consent to the release of medical information under the same circumstances that the patient would have these rights if he or she were competent. Statutes generally require that the guardian, when making decisions on behalf of the patient, should attempt to identify how the patient would have decided if he or she were competent, an approach that is known as substitute judgment. If this is not possible, the guardian should make the decision in accordance with a determination of what is in the patient's best interest. It has been suggested that for purposes of continuity of care, for decisions concerning entitlement or benefits, or for payment of the patient care charges, the hospital may rely on the authorization of the next of kin in situations in which the patient does not have a guardian.[74] These situations are most likely to occur in relation to the elderly patient seeking medical care.

In the area of substitute consent by patient representatives hospital policy should follow state law. In nonemergency situations the decision to permit access to the medical record or to permit the release of information in which the patient is unable to provide authorization, and no guardian has been appointed, should be referred to the hospital's legal counsel.

Deceased Patients. The release of information concerning a deceased patient should not be permitted without the authorization of the executor or administrator of the estate. If there is no executor, the authorization should be obtained from the next of kin. Generally, authorization of the surviving spouse is sufficient; however, in situations in which there is no surviving spouse and there is disagreement among the children, attempts should be made to obtain authorization from all of the parties. The advice of legal counsel may be necessary to determine, in accordance with state probate or inheritance laws, who among the next of kin has the authority to make the decision.

Hospital Staff Access

Hospital staff access is necessary for medical, administrative, educational, and research purposes. The medical purpose permits access to physicians, including consultants, nurses, and all other health care providers who are currently involved in the patient's care and have a need to know the medical information. The administrative purpose permits access to the governing board, the chief executive officer, the chiefs of the clinical services, the committees of the medical staff, medical records personnel, and all other hospital employees involved in monitoring and evaluating the quality of care. It would also include business office personnel requiring information for the timely and proper billing for patient care services. In-hospital educational and research activities conducted by staff members for legitimate purposes have generally been recognized as appropriate and permissible without the patient's consent. Hospitals may have specific policies concerning these activities, such as (1) the need to obtain permission of the physician if the activity involves contacting the patient, (2) the need to work from the original record and not a reproduction, (3) the need to remove any patient identifiers, (4) a prohibition against redisclosure, or (5) the need for students to have the written permission of their instructors. Not all commentators agree that it is appropriate to conduct these activities without the patient's consent.[75]

External Requests for Access

The general rule is that hospitals should not disclose medical information that is patient identifiable without the patient's consent. Exceptions to the need for patient authorization include the following:[76]

- Access to the medical record pursuant to an agreement between the hospital and a government agency or third party payer authorizing inspection of certain portions of the medical record in the performance of claims processing or financial audit activities
- Compelling circumstances affecting the health and safety of the patient or another person
- The conduct of biomedical, epidemiologic, or health services research. Research or experimentation on human subjects must conform with the requirements of federal law. Some state statutes specifically require patient consent and impose fines and possible imprisonment if proper consent procedures are not followed.

Access by Law

Legally mandated access to medical information occurs in a number of situations. Three of the most frequent are (1) the discovery process of litigation, (2) state reporting statutes, and (3) general or specific access laws such as the Freedom of Information Act or state workers' compensation laws.

Discovery

Parties involved in litigation are permitted access to medical information through the use of subpoenas, interrogatories, depositions, and motions to require mental or physical examinations (see Chapter 18). All of these mechanisms for discovery are subject to the rules of civil procedure promulgated by the state and federal courts. Medical records of parties to the suit can be subpoenaed if the mental or physical condition of the party is relevant to the suit. The courts do not permit the discovery of medical information concerning persons who are not parties to the lawsuit except in cases involving billing fraud by the health care provider or in the adjudication of charges against a health care provider by a licensing board.[77] The courts are divided as to whether to allow access to medical records of nonparties in a malpractice suit if all patient identifiers are deleted. Some courts order access,[78] and others decline to do so.[79]

Reporting Statutes

The hospital or health care provider's statutory duty to report medical information to government boards and agencies varies from state to state. State statutes determine the form, content, and scope of the report. In addition, some statutes contain nonretaliatory clauses that protect the reporter from retaliation from employers and immunity provisions that offer the reporter protection from civil suits. In the absence of statutory immunity, the court may recognize a qualified privilege on behalf of the reporter, if the report is made in good faith and without malice. Among the most common areas in which medical care providers are required to report medical information are

- Birth and death statistics
- Venereal and communicable diseases
- Injuries, including self-inflicted injuries, caused by lethal weapons
- Diseases of the newborn, such as ophthalmia neonatorum and phenylketonuria
- Child abuse and elderly or adult abuse
- All suspicious deaths
- Deaths due to blood transfusions (reportable to Food and Drug Administration)

Because the law mandates disclosure, the failure of the health care provider to report this information can result in criminal penalties being imposed and in civil suits brought by the person who is injured because of the nondisclosure. In 1976, a California court ruled that a physician who had neglected to report a case of suspected child abuse could be held liable for injuries sustained by the child that could have been avoided if the report had been made.[80]

In addition to the mandatory reporting statutes, there are laws requiring that certain kinds of information be made available on request to certain individuals or agencies. In general the information can be released without the patient's consent. For example, the Freedom of Information Act, which applies only to federal agencies (i.e., Veterans Hospitals), exempts medical information from disclosure only when the disclosure would "constitute a clearly unwarranted invasion of privacy."[81] The Freedom of Information Act was enacted to make government-held information public. The release of information about federal employees is subject to the federal Privacy Act[82] and to the Freedom of Information Act. To avoid administrative "gridlock" the federal Privacy Act allows government agencies to disclose information without the employee's consent if the Freedom of Information Act requires disclosure. The Freedom of Information Act gives federal employees a right to obtain the information in their personal record.

Utilization and quality control peer review organizations (PROs) must be permitted access on request to all medical records pertinent to their federal review activities. In addition, a federal court has ruled that Medicare surveyors have the right of access to records of non-Medicare patients as well as Medicare patients.[83]

State workers' compensation statutes, which provide benefits to employees who are injured on the job, differ significantly from state to state. Some statutes compensate only for injuries that result from a specific incident or accident,[84] whereas others compensate for injuries that are caused by continuous trauma or exposure in the workplace.[85] The right of access to medical information also varies from state to state. Some states permit all parties to have access to all the relevant information after a claim is made.[86] In other states, the courts have ruled that an employee is considered to have waived the right to confidentiality by filing a workers' compensation claim.[87] If there is no statutory or common law authorization for the release of information the hospital should not release the information unless the patient consents or the disclosure is made pursuant to a legal mandate such as a subpoena.

Common Law Duty To Disclose

Courts have long recognized a common law duty to warn people of the risk of communicable diseases. This duty has been held to apply to hospital staff, family members, and other people involved in the patient's care.[88] This duty may take on added significance in today's health care environment where health care professionals are facing the dilemma of the rights of patients with the acquired immunodeficiency syndrome to care and confidentiality and the hospital's obligation to provide a safe environment for their employees.

In some jurisdictions the courts have ruled that mental health professionals have a duty to protect third parties from foreseeable harm by a patient.[89] In 1972, a California court ruled that when a psychiatrist determines the patient may pose a serious danger to an identifiable person, the psychiatrist must exercise reasonable care toward that person. In this case the court ruled that the psychiatrist should have either warned the victim or advised others who could apprise the victim of the danger.[90] A subsequent decision clarified the scope of the duty by ruling that only a threat to a readily identifiable person creates the duty to warn.[91] Nebraska law imposes a duty on psychotherapists to initiate whatever precautions are reasonably necessary to protect the potential victim when the psychotherapist knows or should know that the patient poses a danger to others.[92] The courts have not specifically addressed the nurse's duty toward the potential victim; however, as a practical matter it would seem that the patient's disclosure of this type of information to a nurse would create a duty for the nurse to (1) notify the patient's physician of the communication, (2) reassess the patient's status in relation to the least restrictive alternative environment until a decision has been made as to the patient's credibility, and (3) if necessary, assist the physician in carrying out any decisions in relation to notifying the potential victim or contacting people capable of warning and protecting the potential victim. Not all jurisdictions impose a duty to warn. A Maryland court refused to allow a plaintiff to recover damages from a "psychiatric team" for their failure to warn the plaintiff of the patient's unstable and violent condition. The court held that such a disclosure would violate the statute that confers a privilege against disclosure of communications related to the treatment of mental and emotional disorders.[93]

Limitations on Access and Release of Information

Statutory Limitations

Federal laws limit the disclosure of information that is contained in the patient's medical record. Medicare regulations prohibit the release of information without the written consent of the patient.[94] The confidentiality of records maintained by federally assisted drug or alcohol prevention and treatment programs is strictly regulated by federal law.[95] Regulations even prohibit the program from acknowledging the patient's presence in the facility. Information concerning the patient's identity, diagnosis, or treatment can only be disclosed on the specific authorization of the patient. Consent must be in writing and must contain the following:[96]

1. The name of the program that is to make the disclosure
2. The name or title of the organization to which the disclosure is made
3. The name of the patient
4. The purpose or need for the disclosure
5. The extent or nature of the information to be disclosed
6. A statement that the consent is subject to revocation at any time except to the extent that action has been taken in reliance thereon and the date that the consent will expire without express revocation
7. The date on which the consent is signed
8. The signature of the patient or of the patient's authorized representative

The Privacy Act of 1974 was enacted to safeguard the privacy of individuals identified in information systems maintained by federal agencies.[97] The act gives an individual the right to

- Determine what records pertaining to him or her are collected, maintained, used, or disseminated by federal agencies
- Prevent records obtained by the agency for a particular purpose from being used for another purpose without his or her consent
- Gain access to information pertaining to him or her in federal agency records
- Copy all or a portion of the record
- Correct or amend the record

Under the Privacy Act, a federal agency has the right to collect, maintain, and disseminate any record of identifiable personal information in a manner that ensures that such action is for a necessary and lawful purpose, that the information is current and accurate for its intended use, and that adequate safeguards are provided to prevent the misuse of the information. The only exemptions from the requirements are those cases in which there is an important public policy that has been recognized by specific authority. The law permits civil suits for any damages that occur as a result of a willful or intentional action that violates any individual rights guaranteed by the act.

Committee Reports

In some states the courts have recognized a common law qualified privilege that protects peer review activities.[98] A number of states have enacted statutes that protect quality assurance– and risk management–related activities and committee reports from discovery or admission as evidence in legal proceedings.[99] The common law or statutory protection of such activities and information is based on the recognition that effective peer review and candid discussions of hospital incidents and risks can improve the overall quality of care and reduce morbidity and mortality.[100] Hospital policies should clearly indicate the form and content of incident or variance reports and the manner in which they are routed through the hospital. The policy should also determine which committee is to receive and respond to the reports as well as the extent of the involvement of the hospital's legal counsel in quality assurance and risk management activities. The hospital can never be certain the reports will not be successfully subpoenaed by an attorney who claims the report is the only source of evidence or that there is a strong suspicion of fraud or misrepresentation. In addition, not all courts have recognized a common law privilege for peer review activities.[101]

Privileged Communications

Confidential communications are the statements, conversations, and advice that take place between the patient and the health care practitioner in the course of patient care. The codes of ethics of all health care professions prohibit the disclosure of confidential information to unauthorized persons. A confidential communication that takes place between a physician and a patient is only privileged if a statute recognizes the physician–patient relationship as privileged. A privileged physician–patient communication statute confers on the patient the right to prevent the physician from revealing the communication in a legal proceeding. In other words, the physician would be permitted to refuse to testify as a witness concerning information gained during the physician–patient relationship. If the privilege does not exist, the practitioner can be held in contempt of court and incarcerated until he or she is willing to testify. The privilege is usually extended to include privileged information recorded in the hospital record. The only privilege recognized in common law is that of attorney–client; therefore, all other privileges such as nurse–patient, physician–patient, psychotherapist–patient, priest–penitent, and reporter–news source must be established by statute. As a creature of statute the application and scope of the practitioner–patient privilege may vary significantly from state to state. Approximately two thirds of the states have enacted physician–patient statutes. Some states also recognize a psychotherapist–patient privilege.[102] Some states have a nurse–patient privilege, and in some states the nurse is recognized in the physician statute. Some statutes extend the privilege to people working under the supervision of a physician.[103] The existence of a bona fide relationship is required in some states; therefore, information that is obtained by a physician as a result of a court-ordered examination or an examination conducted solely for the benefit of a third party such as an insurance company would not be privileged. Statutes also vary as to the type of communication that is covered. The privilege may apply to all communications and observations[104] or may be limited to that which is customary and necessary for diagnosis and treatment.[105] Statutes may also include exemptions, such as the statement that the privilege does not apply to disciplinary proceedings conducted before the Board of Registration in Medicine.[106]

Waiver. The privilege belongs to the patient; therefore, the patient can waive the privilege and permit the practitioner to testify. A waiver of privilege is also recognized when (1) the patient puts his or her medical condition in issue by suing a hospital or health care provider for injuries allegedly sustained during the course of treatment and (2) when there is a contractual agreement to waive the right, as often appears in insurance contracts.

NURSE MANAGER'S RESPONSIBILITY

Hospital administrators and health care practitioners are the guardians of the patient's right of privacy. The law, the courts, and the professional and administrative codes specifically acknowledge the health care provider's duty to keep the patient's communication and records confidential.

Hospitals have a duty to develop and implement policies and procedures that incorporate the requirements of federal and state law. A hospital's accreditation status is also affected by its ability to adopt and maintain certain standards of patient confidentiality. The nurse manager has a duty to evaluate, monitor, and enforce the hospital's policies as they relate to the rights of both patients and employees. The nurse manager must

- Promote an environment where respect for the patient's privacy is clearly demonstrated. Patient interviews, patient examinations, and treatments are performed in a manner that ensures maximum privacy.
- Create the expectation that nurse-to-nurse communication will always reflect a sensitivity to the patient's exposure and vulnerability and that this awareness will be apparent in each phase of the nursing process.
- Demand that communication between health care practitioners be professional, demonstrating an understanding of the unique and essential contribution that each profession brings to the patient's comprehensive need for health care.
- Promote the implementation and use of mechanisms by which professional disputes between health care practitioners can be handled promptly, discreetly, and fairly.
- Implement and enforce the hospital's policies concerning the privacy and security of the patient's medical record.
- Promptly and fairly institute the hospital's disciplinary procedures when nurses engage in behavior that breaches a patient's right to privacy.
- Create an atmosphere in which nurses are encouraged to report legitimate suspicions of professional incompetence. Investigate the charges in accordance with the hospital's policies, taking into account the need for confidentiality.

The competent delivery of hospital services to patients is dependent on the ability of the institution to communicate information about patients in a manner that is effective and efficient. Computers in the hospital have greatly increased the amount of information that is amassed and the speed with which it is communicated. It is understandable that health care professionals who must daily confront and appropriately respond to this deluge of information may at times forget that at the center of it all there is the patient's right of privacy. Nurse managers have the responsibility to promote and protect the patients' and the employees' constitutional, statutory, and common law rights of privacy.

NOTES

1. *Olmstead v. United States*, 277 U.S. 438, 478 (1972) (Brandeis, L., dissenting).

2. Kent Greenawalt, "Privacy and Its Legal Protections," *Hastings Center Studies* No. 3 (September 1974):45–49.

3. Conclusion of the Nordic Conference on the Right of Privacy, *Privacy and the Law*, A Report by the British Section of the International Commission of Justice (1970):45 (Littman and Carter-Ruchens, 1970).

4. American Nurses' Association, *Code for Nurses with Interpretive Statements* (Chicago: ANA, 1985), 3.

5. American Medical Association, *Principles of Ethics* (Chicago: AMA, August 1980).

6. American Hospital Association, *AHA Patients' Bill of Rights* (Chicago: AHA, November 17, 1972).

7. Joint Commission on Accreditation of Healthcare Organizations, *Accreditation Manual for Hospitals* (Chicago: Joint Commission, 1985).

8. Karen Hawley Henry, *The Health Care Supervisor's Legal Guide* (Rockville, Md.: Aspen Publishers, Inc., 1984), 267; see also Lab. Rels. Rptr. 4 (BNA) (State Labor Laws).

9. Cynthia E. Northrop and Mary E. Kelly, *Legal Issues in Nursing* (St. Louis: C.V. Mosby Co., 1987), 496.

10. 5 U.S.C. §§ 552(a)(e)(1) (1982 & Supp. I 1983).

11. *Andrews v. Veterans Administration* (No. C 84-0459, D. Wyo.), July 17, 1985.

12. Henry, *Health Care Supervisor's Legal Guide*, 267.

13. William L. Prosser, *Law of Torts*, 4th. ed. (St. Paul, Minn.: West Publishing Co., 1971), 803–815.

14. Ibid., 811.

15. Ibid., 803–815; see also Northrop and Kelly, *Legal Issues in Nursing*, 69–70.

16. Prosser, *Law of Torts*, 818.

17. Ibid., 737.

18. Ibid.

19. Ibid., 739.

20. Ibid., 737.

21. Ibid., 745.

22. Ibid., 754.

23. Ibid., 754–760.

24. Ibid., 760.

25. Ibid., 762.

26. Ibid., 762–763.

27. Ibid., 776.

28. Ibid.

29. Northrop and Kelly, *Legal Issues in Nursing*, 798.

30. Prosser, *Law of Torts*, 776.

31. Ibid.

32. Ibid., 99.

33. Ibid., 776–785.

34. Ibid., 786, quoting *Toogood v. Spyring*, 1 C.M.&R. 181, 149 Eng. Rep. 1044 (1834).

35. Ibid., 785–793.

36. *New York Times v. Sullivan*, 376 U.S. 254; *motion denied*, 376 U.S. 967 (1964).

37. *Cason v. Baskin*, 159 Fla. 31, 30 So. 2d 635, 638 (1947).

38. *Associated Press v. Walker*, 388 U.S. 130 (1967).

39. *Time Inc. v. Hill*, 285 U.S. 374 (1967).

40. *Vigil v. Rice*, 397 P.2d 719 (N.M. 1964).

41. *Schessler v. Keck*, 271 P.2d 588 (Cal. 1954).

42. *Malone v. Longo*, 463 F. Supp. 139 (D.D. N.Y. 1979).

43. *Barry v. Baugh*, 111 Ga. App. 813, 143 S.E.2d 489 (1965).

44. *Farrell v. Kramer*, 193 A.2d 560 (Maine 1963).

45. *Ellis v. Jewish Hospital*, 581 S.W.2d 580 (Mo. 1979).

46. *Gengler v. Phelps*, 589 P.2d 1056 (N.M. Ct. of App. 1978); *cert. denied*, 558 P.2d 554 (N.M. Sup. Ct. 1979).

47. *Buckley v. Litman*, 443 N.E.2d 489 (N.Y. App. 1982).

48. *Heying v. Simonaitis*, 466 N.E.2d 1137 (Ill. App. 1 Dist. 1984).

49. Mary Dolores Hemelt and Mary Ellen Mackert, *Dynamics of Law in Nursing and Health Care* (Reston, Va.: Reston Publishing Co., 1982), 176–178.

50. Ibid., 176.

51. *Confidentiality of Patient Health Information: Position Statement of the American Medical Record Association* (Chicago: American Medical Record Association, 1985).

52. Howard S. Rowland and Beatrice L. Rowland, *Hospital Legal Forms, Checklists and Guidelines*, Vol. I (Rockville, Md.: Aspen Publishers, Inc., 1987), 14:2.

53. Special Advisory Committee to the Secretary, U.S. Department of Health, Education and Welfare, *Records, Computers and the Rights of Citizens* (1973); see also Northrop and Kelly, *Legal Issues in Nursing*, 462–463.

54. Miller and Beyda, "Computers, Medical Records and the Right to Privacy," 6 *Journal of Health, Politics, Policy and Law* 464 (Fall 1981).

55. George D. Pozgar, *Legal Aspects of Health Care Administration* (Rockville, Md.: Aspen Publishers, Inc., 1983), 120.

56. Rowland and Rowland, *Hospital Legal Forms*, 14:4.

57. Ibid., 14:9.

58. Ibid.

59. *Pyramid Life Insurance Company v. Masonic Hospital Association*, 191 F. Supp. 51 (W.D. Okla. 1961), hospital ownership; *Wallace v. University Hospital of Cleveland*, 164 N.E.2d 917 (Ohio 1979), patient's right to information.

60. *Cannell v. Medical and Surgical Clinic*, 21 Ill. App. 3d 383, 315 N.E.2d 278 (1974).

61. Rowland and Rowland, *Hospital Legal Forms*, 14:5.

62. Md. Health Gen. Code Ann. § 4-302 (Supp. 1982).

63. American Hospital Association, AHA Patient's Bill of Rights (Chicago: AHA, November 17, 1972).

64. John Altman, "Patients Who Read Their Hospital Charts," *New England Journal of Medicine* 302 (January 1980):169.

65. Rowland and Rowland, *Hospital Legal Forms*, 14:5.

234   THE NURSE MANAGER AND THE LAW

66. Robert D. Miller, *Problems of Hospital Law* (Rockville, Md.: Aspen Publishers, Inc., 1983), 280.

67. *Confidentiality of Patient Health Information: Position Statement of the American Medical Record Association* (Chicago, American Medical Record Association, 1985).

68. Ibid.

69. 42 C.F.R. Part 2 (1983).

70. Rowland and Rowland, *Hospital Legal Forms*, 14:17.

71. Ibid.

72. *H.L. v. Matheson*, 450 U.S. 398 (1981).

73. N.H. R.S.A. 318-B:12-a (Treatment for drug abuse: "Such parent or legal guardian shall not be liable for the payment for any treatment rendered pursuant to this section.")

74. Miller, *Problems of Hospital Law*, 283.

75. Ibid., 279.

76. 45 C.F.R. § 46.102 (e) (1985); 45 C.F.R. § 46.101 (b) (5) (1981); Cal. Health and Safety Code 24170-24179.5, 2668.4.

77. Miller, *Problems of Hospital Law*, 285.

78. *Community Hospital Association v. District Court*, 570 P.2d 243 (Colo. 1977).

79. *Teperson v. Donato*, 371 So. 2d 703 (Fla. Dist. Ct. App. 1979).

80. *Landeros v. Flood*, 17 Cal. 3d 399, 551 P.2d 389 (1976).

81. 5 U.S.C. § 552 (1982).

82. 5 U.S.C. §§ 552 (a) (e) (1) (1982 & Supp. I 1983).

83. *O'Hare v. Harris*, No. 80-457 D.D. N.H. March 12, 1981.

84. Mass. Ann. Laws Ch. 152 § 1 (1985).

85. Fla. Stat. Ann. § 440.151 (West 1985).

86. Iowa Code § 85.27 (1981).

87. *Acosta v. Cary*, 365 So. 2d 4 (La. Ct. App. 1978).

88. *Jones v. Stanko*, 118 Ohio St. 147, 160 N.E. 456 (1928).

89. *Tarasoff v. Board of Regents*, 171 Cal. 3d 425, 551 P.2d 334 (1976).

90. Ibid.

91. *Thompson v. County of Almeda*, 27 Cal. 3d 741, 614 P.2d 728 (1980).

92. *Lipari v. Sears, Roebuck and Co.*, 497 F. Supp. 185 (1980).

93. *Shaw v. Glickman*, 45 Md. App. 718, 415 A.2d 625 (1980).

94. 45 C.F.R. § 1026 (a) (1985).

95. 42 C.F.R. Part 2 (1983).

96. Ibid.

97. 5 U.S.C. §§ 552 (a) (e) (1) (1982 & Supp. I 1983).

98. *Bredice v. Doctor's Hospital, Inc.*, 50 F.D.R. 249 (D.D.C. 1970).

99. Oklahoma Stat. Title 63, §§ 1-1709 (1981).

100. Miller, *Problems of Hospital Law*, 286.

101. *Davison v. St. Paul Fire and Marine Insurance Co.*, 75 Wis. 2d 190, 248 N.W.2d 433 (1977).

102. Fla. Stat. Ann. § 90.503 (West 1985).

103. N.H. R.S.A. 329:26 (1979).

104. Kan. Stat. Ann. § 60-4271 (1971).

105. N.H. R.S.A. 329:26 (1979).

106. Ibid.

Chapter **16**

Contract Law and Liability

Tort law and contract law represent the two main concepts of civil law. The fundamental difference between tort law and contract law is the nature of the interest protected. Tort actions protect a person's interest in freedom from various kinds of harm (see Chapters 11 through 15). Tort liability arises from laws that are based on social policy, such as the public's right to demand that health care professionals provide a reasonable standard of care. Contract actions protect a person's interest in having promises honored. The contractual obligations are owed only to the specific individuals or groups named in the contract and are imposed because the conduct of the parties has manifested consent.[1] Any patient who has suffered an injury as a result of the actions of a hospital or health care provider may bring suit in tort and/or contract. For example, a suit for injuries sustained by a newborn who was delivered by the nurses in the delivery room may allege that the doctor failed to meet the standard of care by not being present in the delivery room; however, the plaintiff may also allege a breach of contract for the physician's failure to be present at the time of delivery. The plaintiff's inability to prove the injury was due to the physician's absence would preclude him or her from winning a negligence suit but it would not defeat a breach of contract suit if the plaintiff had been assured that the physician would be in attendance. Chapters 11 through 15 have dealt extensively with the patient–nurse relationship as it relates to tort liability. The hospital nurse's contractual obligation to a hospitalized patient has not been as clearly identified. Hospitals, physicians, and all independent health care providers, including nurses practicing independently in the advanced role, may incur contract liability toward patients. There are a number of lawsuits by patients against physicians and/or hospitals for breach of contract; however, there are no reported cases of hospital nurses being sued for breach of contract because, as yet, there is a lack of recognition that a direct contractual relationship exists between a nurse employed by a hospital and the patient. The general understanding is that the nurse has a legal obligation to the patients on the unit where the nurse is assigned; however, the nurse's legal obligations to any particular patient cease when the patient is transferred to another unit, or when the nurse goes "off duty," and ends when the patient is discharged. This differs from the physician, who is generally

235

responsible for the patient throughout the course of the hospitalization and after the patient is discharged.[2] The hospital nurse's legal liability is generally based on the person's status as a patient in the hospital. Hospitals that adopt a primary nursing care system may require that a nurse assume responsibility for one or more patients throughout their hospital stay. The hospitals may employ an on-call system in which the primary nurse can be contacted for consultation concerning these patients if he or she is not physically present and a need arises. It could be argued that these situations increase the scope of the nurse's tort liability by extending the time during which the nurse is responsible for providing a reasonable standard of care to assigned patients, but they do not create a direct nurse–patient contractual relationship. It would appear that even when the hospital nurse assumes a primary care nursing relationship he or she still does so under the umbrella of the hospital–patient contractual relationship. At the present time, hospital-employed nurses do not face any appreciable risk of breach of contract suits by patients.

Nurses need to understand contract law in order to recognize the benefits and consequences of the employment relationship that exists between them and their employer. Nursing has lagged behind other professions in recognizing the need to negotiate contractual agreements that promote and protect their employment-related interests. At the present time the majority of nurses are not employed under individual contracts and are considered "employees at will," a status that in the law allows an employer to discharge the employee for any reason or for no reason. Since 1974, a number of nurses have become members of state nursing associations or joined unions for the purpose of collective bargaining and are now covered by collective bargaining agreements that determine their wages, hours, and working conditions. The fundamentals of contract law and the three types of nurse–hospital employment relationships are explained in this chapter. In addition, the court's approach to the defense of patient advocacy in relation to the employer's right to fire a nurse who is considered an employee at will is discussed. The topics of anti-trust litigation, physician–nurse competition, and hospital staff privileges for nurse practitioners are considered, and the types of nursing professional liability (malpractice) insurance are identified with an explanation of the various parts of an insurance agreement.

ELEMENTS OF A CONTRACT

A contract is a promissory agreement between two or more persons that creates, modifies, or destroys a legal relationship.[3] It is a legally enforceable promise between two or more people to do or not to do something. In order for a contract to be valid there must be (1) mutual assent, (2) promise or consideration, (3) two or more parties of competent legal capacity, and (4) an agreement that is lawful and not against public policy.[4]

Mutual Assent

Mutual assent is described as a "meeting of the minds," an understanding by the parties that they have mutually agreed to something and an agreement as to what that something is. The understanding is manifested through an offer being made by one party and acceptance in response to that specific offer by another party. The one who makes the offer (offeror) must make the offer in clear and precise terms and must give the one receiving the offer (offeree) the power to accept the offer. The acceptance must be definite, unequivocal, and in accordance with the specific conditions of the offer. There is no duty to reply to an offer; therefore, a person's silence cannot be considered a form of acceptance. A common exception to the rule that silence is not an acceptance is car insurance contracts in which an existing contract will generally be renewed automatically unless the car owner notifies the insurance company that the policy is being cancelled.[5]

Consideration

Consideration is the "bargained for exchanged" the "something for something" that is exchanged between the parties.[6] One must surrender something or receive something in return—a service, an act, or the exchange of another promise or money. Consideration is recognized when a person refrains from doing an act that he or she otherwise might lawfully do. The need for consideration is what distinguishes a contract from a gift. The promise to give someone a gift is not legally enforceable because the person to whom the gift is made is not giving up anything of value.

Capacity To Contract

In order for a contract to be valid, the parties making the contract must be in full possession of their faculties and not under any legal disability or handicap. They must be able to understand the purpose, nature, and effect of the contract. Areas in which the capacity to contract may be affected include (1) minors, (2) persons who are mentally incapacitated, (3) persons who have been declared incompetent, and (4) prisoners.

Contracts entered into by these persons may be considered void or voidable. A void contract is one in which there is no liability assigned to either party. A voidable contract is one in which one of the parties is allowed to disaffirm or repudiate the contract. Contracts with minors, persons who lack mental capacity but have not been adjudicated incompetent, and persons who are intoxicated or in shock are considered voidable at their option. The result is that these persons are allowed to disaffirm the contract. In some jurisdictions minors are not allowed to disaffirm a contract for necessities such as food, shelter, and clothing. Contracts with persons who have been adjudicated incompetent are considered void and are therefore unenforceable. In some jurisdictions, a person's civil rights may be suspended during a term of imprisonment and taken away completely when a person is sentenced to death or life imprisonment. The prisoner may not enter into valid contracts except to make or acknowledge a sale or conveyance of property. Parole restores a limited series of civil rights, including the right to contract.[7]

Lawful Agreement

In order for a contract to be valid the subject matter of the agreement must be lawful and not against public policy. The traditional examples of illegality include the selling of contaminated meat or the enforcement of gambling debts. It may also include the violation of licensing laws, especially when the licensing statutes specifically state that persons contracting without the licenses may not enforce those contracts.[8]

EXPRESS AND IMPLIED CONTRACTS

An *express contract* is defined as an agreement of the parties in which the terms are stated in distinct and explicit language either orally or in writing. An *implied contract* is one that is inferred by the actions or conduct of the parties, the circumstances surrounding the transaction, or the recognition of a tacit understanding between the parties. Many people enter implied contracts with physicians when they request medical services and receive them without first determining what the physician is going to do and what the charges will be. There is the assumption that if a person requests and accepts the services of a physician he or she will be responsible for paying the bill either personally or through third-party reimbursement.

ORAL AND WRITTEN CONTRACTS

An oral contract in areas not precluded by the statute of frauds is binding and enforceable. The problem with an oral contract is proving that it exists. A person should not be embarrassed about asking the other party to put the terms of the agreement in writing. Without witnesses, defenses that consist of ''I trusted her'' or ''We shook hands on it'' or ''He promised'' do not alleviate the need to prove the existence of an alleged agreement. A written contract does not have to be a formal document. A written memorandum that contains the essential elements of the agreement will constitute a written contract. The memorandum can even consist of several writings if they properly connect and identify the (1) names of the parties, (2) subject matter or nature of the work, (3) terms or conditions, and (4) signature or initials of the party to be charged. This type of writing will satisfy the requirements of the statute of frauds.

STATUTE OF FRAUDS

Every jurisdiction has enacted a statute of frauds that indicates the circumstances in which a contract must be in writing in order to be valid. Although the requirements vary from state to state, all jurisdictions require the following transactions to be in writing.

- A contract that, by its terms, cannot be performed within one year
- A promise to pay the debts of another person
- A contract for the sale of an interest in real estate, including a lease for longer than one year

- A contract for the sale of goods priced at $500 or more
- A contract in consideration of marriage

The statute of frauds is an affirmative defense that must be entered by the defendant when the complaint is answered.[9]

PAROL EVIDENCE RULE

The parol evidence rule states that when a contract has been reduced to a writing which the parties intended to be a complete statement of their agreement, oral or written promises that were made prior to, or contemporaneously with, the signing of the contract, may not be used to add to or contradict the contract. This means that any oral or written statements or promises that are made but are not incorporated into the contract will not be enforced by the courts. For example, if a nurse negotiates a written contract that does not include the oral promise that she would not have to "float" to other units, the nurse would not be able to hold the hospital to that promise. The oral agreements can be added as amendments or as margin notes, but they must be written into the contract to be enforceable. Although prior or contemporaneous oral or written statements cannot be used to add to, modify, vary, or contradict the contract, they may be introduced as evidence to show fraud, misrepresentation, duress, mistake, custom, or prior course of dealing.[10]

TERMINATION OF A CONTRACT

There are five ways in which a contract can be terminated:[11]

1. *Performance*: Most contracts are discharged by the full, complete, and literal performance of the contract.
2. *Termination*: The contract ends when under the terms of the contract the obligations of the parties end.
3. *Accord and satisfaction*: An accord is when the party who has the right to receive the contract performance enters into an agreement with the debtor in which the debtor agrees to perform a different promise instead of the one that is owed.
4. *Impossibility*: Some unforeseeable event may occur that makes performance objectively impossible. This can include the destruction of the subject matter of the contract, the death or incapacity of a person whose personal services were required by the contract, a supervening act of the government that makes the transaction illegal or circumstances in which the purpose of the contract no longer exists and performance of the contract would be futile or valueless.
5. *Rescission*: The two parties to a contract may discharge their respective duties by agreeing to rescind the contract. This cannot be done if there are third parties who have vested rights or an irrevocable assignment of rights under the contract.

Breach of Contract

A breach of contract occurs when there is an unjustified failure to perform the terms of the contract as agreed upon or when performance is due. A contract is a legally enforceable agreement; therefore, when a party fails to perform according to the terms of the contract the nonbreaching party has a right to be compensated for the losses incurred as a result of the breach. There are three distinct remedies for breach of contract: (1) money damages, (2) specific performance, and (3) injunction.

Money Damages

Unlike actions for tort, the amount of damages sustained by a breach of contract must be proven with a reasonable degree of certainty. The purpose of compensatory damages is to make good or replace the loss caused by the wrong or injury. Liquidated damages are damages that have been set forth in advance in the contract. They will be enforced in full unless the court finds them to be unconscionable.

In most situations, the nonbreaching party has a duty to mitigate their damages. This means that the party must take reasonable steps to control or minimize the amount of damages incurred because of the breach. For example, a nurse claiming that the hospital's action in terminating the nurse's employment constituted a breach of contract would be expected to find another comparable nursing position while awaiting the outcome of the litigation. The amount of time the nurse was legitimately unemployed and any loss of income due to differences in salary are some of the factors that would be considered in determining the amount of damages that should be awarded.

Specific Performance

Specific performance of the contract is ordered in situations when money damages are inadequate such as in the case of real estate or in areas such as paintings or antiques in which the item is unique. If the contract involves personal services, the courts will not order a specific person to perform a personal service but may issue an injunction.

Injunction

An injunction is a court ruling ordering a person to do something or refrain from doing something. An injunction can be issued to make a contractor finish work or correct problems that are covered under the contract. Constitutional prohibitions against involuntary servitude and the practical problem of enforcement result in the court being reluctant to order a specific person to perform a personal service. For example, it will not order an opera singer to sing or a hockey player to play hockey. Even if it were permitted to issue such orders, it would have no control over how the person performed the service. The better approach is to issue an injunction that prevents the person from performing the services for anyone else for the duration of the contract.

COLLECTIVE BARGAINING AGREEMENTS

A collective bargaining agreement is a written contract between an employer and a union that sets forth the hours, wages, and working conditions.[12] It is not an employment contract because it does not guarantee continued employment to the covered employee nor does it create an employer–employee relationship.[13] A collective bargaining agreement sets forth the contractual relationship between the employer and the union and governs the relationship between (1) the employer and the employees and (2) the employees themselves.[14]

Collective bargaining activities are covered by three separate areas of law. Federal employees such as nurses working in Veterans Administration hospitals are covered by the Civil Service Reform Act of 1978, 5 U.S.C. §§ 7101–7135. Public employee relation laws for state government workers such as nurses employed by state mental health clinics vary significantly from state to state. Some states, such as Pennsylvania, have one comprehensive statute that includes all state government employees, whereas others, such as California, have five or more statutes, each covering one segment of public employment.[15] Nurses employed in the private sector by either proprietary or nonprofit employers are under the jurisdiction of the National Labor Relations Act, 29 U.S.C. §§ 141–187 (NLRA).

Appropriate Bargaining Units

The National Labor Relations Board (NLRB) employs a "community of interest" standard in determining the composition of collective bargaining units. The members of a collective bargaining unit must have similar interests in wages, hours, and working conditions. The six groups of health care employees that the NLRB considers to be appropriate bargaining units are (1) registered nurses; (2) salaried physicians (excludes house staff); (3) all other professionals; (4) technical employees (identifiable by the requirement of licensure, certification, or registration to perform the work and includes licensed practical nurses and x-ray technicians); (5) service and maintenance employees; and (6) business office clericals (includes clerical employees in the administrative areas and excludes clerical employees such as ward clerks).[16]

The NLRA prohibits the NLRB from including professionals and nonprofessionals in the same bargaining unit unless a majority of the professional employees vote for such inclusion. The NLRA defines a professional employee as "one engaged in work predominantly intellectual in character as opposed to routine; involves independent judgment in its performance; is not susceptible to standardization; requires knowledge of an advanced type personally acquired by prolonged study in an institution of higher learning or in a hospital."[17] Health care employees who are recognized as professionals under this definition include the following:[18]

- Nurses
- Physicians
- Audiologists
- Cardiopulmonary technologists
- Chemists
- Dietitians

- Medical technologists
- Pharmacists
- Physical therapists
- Occupational therapists
- Pulmonary function technologists
- Radioisotope technologists
- Radiologic paramedics
- Recreation therapists
- Speech therapists

"RN Only" Collective Bargaining Units

The right of registered nurses (RNs) to be represented as a separate bargaining unit, apart from all remaining professional employees, is a controversial subject that has frequently been litigated. When the employer and the union cannot agree on an appropriate bargaining unit, the NLRB is required to make the determination. The NLRB's rulings and the varied and contradictory interpretations and orders of the federal courts have centered on the following questions:

- Is an all RN unit an appropriate collective bargaining unit under the NLRA?[19]
- Does an all RN unit contravene the Congressional mandate to avoid the proliferation of bargaining units in the health care industry?[20]
- Can justification for an all RN unit be founded on the conclusion that RNs have distinct interest, duties, and qualifications that warrant separate representation?[21]
- Does a tradition of separate representation make such a unit appropriate?[22]
- Does the NLRB have to evaluate a claim of undue proliferation by the hospital in adequate and specific terms?[23]

The NLRB has ruled that, except for very special circumstances, separate units limited to registered nurses are appropriate. The ruling continues to generate controversy in the health care industry and has resulted in legal challenges that have produced conflicting interpretations and rulings in the U.S. circuit courts. It is probable that the issue will only be resolved by an opinion of the U.S. Supreme Court. For the present time, the question of whether registered nurses are entitled to separate representation in an "RN only" unit is a matter of jurisdiction, entirely dependent on the state in which they are employed.

Exclusion of Nurse Supervisors

Collective bargaining agreements apply to employees and exclude supervisors. The NLRA defines a supervisor as

> Any individual having authority, in the interest of the employer, to hire, transfer, suspend, lay off, recall, promote, discharge, assign, reward, or discipline other employees, or responsibility to direct them, or to adjust their

grievances, or effectively to recommend such action, if in connection with the foregoing the exercise of such authority is not of a merely routine or clerical nature, but requires the use of independent judgment.[24]

Congress, in passing the 1974 health care amendments, specifically declined to define the meaning of "supervisor" for the health care industry. The NLRB does not apply the definition of "supervisor" to a health care professional who gives direction to other employees in the exercise of professional judgment when the direction is incidental to the professional's treatment of patients and not an exercise of supervisory authority in the interest of the employer.[25] The determination of whether nurses such as charge nurses, head nurses, shift supervisors, staff educators, infection control nurses, or nurse coordinators are considered supervisors is made on a case-by-case basis. One court has indicated that the decision as to their supervisory status under the NLRA depends on the "actual job responsibilities, authority and relationship to management."[26]

In *The Health Care Supervisor's Legal Guide*,[27] Karen Hawley Henry provides a list of factors and considerations supporting supervisory status that have been extracted from cases decided between 1975 and 1978.[28] Nurses whose positions include several of the following characteristics would be considered as "supervisors" under the NLRA.

- Supervisory positions that are permanent rather than being rotated among a number of RNs
- Nurses who are required to attend meetings that are not open to nonsupervisory personnel
- Nurses who are told that they are supervisors with supervisory authority
- Nurses who are compensated at a higher rate of pay than nonsupervisory RNs rather than receiving a premium for the occasions when additional duties are performed
- Nurses whose recommendations concerning personnel matters are generally followed rather than their superiors' being free to disregard their recommendations
- Nurses who perform personnel evaluations of other RNs independently for the purpose of providing ratings that are used for disciplinary or pay purposes rather than just offering their input to a superior who determines the content of the actual evaluation
- Nurses who spend the majority of their time performing supervisory and administrative functions rather than direct patient care
- Nurses who are authorized to hire or recommend the hiring of RNs through the use of their own discretion; call in replacements to cover absences rather than just reporting staff shortages to someone else; grant time off or authorize overtime; terminate or recommend the termination of RNs through the use of their own discretion; take or recommend other disciplinary action concerning RNs rather than being limited to counseling them on nondisciplinary matters; and adjust employee grievances

The NLRB classification of an employee as a supervisor makes unavailable the collective bargaining activities guaranteed to employees under the NLRA. Supervisors cannot conduct an election or require an employer to recognize a unit that includes supervisors. In addition, an employer can prohibit its supervisory personnel from obtaining membership in a labor organization. If the supervisory employee joins or refuses to resign, he or she can be disciplined or terminated from employment.[29] It has been determined that nurse supervisors may belong to their state nurses' association even when the association also functions as a collective bargaining representative. Nurse supervisors should be aware, however, that if it is perceived that they are in control of the labor organization functions of the association, the NLRB may decide that a conflict of interest exists and disqualify the association as a collective bargaining representative. If the supervisory members do not participate significantly in the labor organization activities, the employer seeking disqualification of the association must demonstrate that there is a clear and present danger of a conflict of interest interfering with the collective bargaining process.[30]

Duty To Bargain in Good Faith

Once a union has been legally established as the exclusive representative of the employees, the NLRA imposes an obligation on the employer and the union to "bargain in good faith." The refusal of the employer or the union to "bargain in good faith" is considered an unfair labor practice.[31] A 1940 court decision interpreted the duty to bargain in good faith as requiring that the parties enter the negotiations with an open mind and make a sincere effort to reach a mutually acceptable agreement.[32]

COLLECTIVE BARGAINING SUBJECTS

Commentators suggest that "it is difficult to define typical union contract provisions since every contract should be drafted to fit the needs, operations and practices of the affected employer."[33] They caution employers against using standard form contracts drafted by the union without first analyzing the employer's specific needs, practices, and existing contractual obligations.[34] These factors, taken along with the professional employees' right and need to negotiate the wages, hours, and working conditions of their employment, determine the subject areas that will be included in the collective bargaining contract.

The NLRB and the courts categorize the potential subjects of collective bargaining as (1) illegal, (2) mandatory, and (3) voluntary. An illegal subject is one that is prohibited by federal or state laws. For example, regardless of the wishes of either party, it is illegal for a contract to make union membership a precondition of employment or to require employees to become members of a labor organization before they have been employed for 30 days.[35] A mandatory subject is one that falls within the statutory definition of wages, hours, and working conditions. Employers and employees are required to meet, furnish information, and attempt to reach an agreement in these areas. Failure to bargain on mandatory subjects is considered an unfair labor practice. Failure to agree to the inclusion of a mandatory subject on a contract can lead to a finding that an impasse in negotiation exists and creates the potential for a strike. Subjects that are not illegal or mandatory are considered to be voluntary. The employer and the union can bargain about any voluntary subject that they both agree is appropriate to their situation. On the other hand, neither party can (1) insist on bargaining on subjects in the voluntary area or (2) make the reaching of an agreement on other matters conditional on concessions outside the mandatory subject areas. One of the most controversial subject areas frequently requested by health care professionals is the right to participate in decisions involving patient care and the implementation of professional standards. Issues such as staffing patterns and the right to refuse assignments are typical areas requested for voluntary inclusion in the contract. Observers caution that if employers do agree to the inclusion of such areas, they should make certain that the language is drafted with great care. They also advise the employer to exclude these areas from arbitration in order to avoid turning over the power to decide these fundamental issues to a third party.[36]

Common Contract Provisions

A collective bargaining agreement exists as a result of negotiation and compromise between the employer and the union. The contract that emerges from this process is unique to the parties that are bound by it; however, they usually contain a number of provisions that are common to health care industry collective bargaining contracts. The agreements usually begin by recognizing the union as the exclusive representative for all employees through their appropriate bargaining units. The agreement should specifically indicate who is included (e.g., all full- and part-time registered nurses) and who is excluded (e.g., all other employees, head nurses, in-service educators). Collective bargaining contracts between hospitals and registered nurses may contain the following provisions:[37]

- Recognition
- Definitions
- Role of the nurse
- Nondiscrimination
- Hours of work and premiums
- Probationary period
- Evaluations
- Grievance procedure
- Benefits (insurance and retirement)
- Vacations and holidays
- Staff development
- Health and welfare
- Sick leave and leaves of absence
- Discipline or discharge
- Bulletin boards
- Professional performance committee

- Seniority for layoff and recall
- Severability
- No strikes
- Association security
- Call pay
- Job posting
- Termination of employment
- Safety
- Conditions of employment
- Wages
- Nurse clinicians and nurse practitioners
- Labor management consultation
- Duration

Grievance Procedures

Among the most important provisions of the collective bargaining contract is the section that deals with the grievance process. The grievance section describes the process that must be used to settle disputes arising under the agreement. Most grievance procedures consist of a four-step process that determines which parties are involved, what actions are taken, and the time limit in which they are required to function. The employee progresses from one step to the next if the matter remains unresolved or if the deadline for a response is not met. A typical four-step process would require the following:[38]

Step 1

- Employee reports grievance orally to the immediate supervisor.
- Union representative may be present.
- Supervisor must reply within four calendar days.

Step 2

- Employee discusses the grievance with the department administrator.
- Union representative may also meet with the department administrator.
- Discussion must occur within ten calendar days of step 1.
- Administrator must reply within four calendar days.

Step 3

- Standard grievance form is completed, signed, and dated by the employee and the union representative.
- Completed form is submitted to the agency administrator within seven calendar days of step 2.

- Meeting is convened where employee, union representative, and agency administrator are all present.
- Administrator must reply within ten calendar days.

Step 4

- Within ten days of step 3 deadline, the union representative submits a written notice to the employer requesting that the grievance be referred to an impartial arbitrator selected according to the contract requirements.

The contract may also permit the employer to file grievances protesting a union's breach of its contractual obligations. The inclusion of an employer grievance clause may result in the employer being required to submit the dispute to arbitration rather than seek a judicial remedy.[39] There are many variations of this four-step procedure; however, in essence they all (1) impose the order in which the dispute will be examined and resolved, (2) impose a time limit that determines when each step of the process begins and ends, and (3) require that the dispute be disclosed and if possible resolved in accordance with the institution's recognized chain of authority. Adoption of a grievance process should discourage the arbitrary and capricious handling of employee complaints and encourage fair and prompt settlements.

Termination for "Just Cause"

An area vital to the nurse employee's sense of job security is the termination procedure. Collective bargaining contracts often state that the employer may not discharge or discipline an employee except for "just cause." Contracts that include grounds for disciplinary action or termination should clearly indicate the list is not all inclusive. This is usually accomplished by the statement that the grounds for discipline include, but are not limited to, the ones listed in the contract. If the contract is silent on the issue of "just cause" the arbitrator will usually imply a "just cause" limitation on the employer's right to discharge or discipline employees.[40] They will also take into consideration duties such as honesty, sobriety, and punctuality that are considered to be owed by employees to the employer.[41] Collective bargaining agreements usually provide only limited protection to probationary employees. Many contracts permit the employer to terminate the employment of a probationary employee without having to defend a union grievance or prove "just cause."

Nurses who exercise their right to bargain collectively by joining a union or by working in a hospital that is unionized lose the opportunity to personally negotiate their wages, hours, and working conditions with their employer. The employer must negotiate exclusively with the union and cannot negotiate with a second union or with individual employees who are covered by the collective bargaining contract. The union has a duty to represent fairly and fully all employees in the bargaining unit, whether or not they are members of the union.[42]

EMPLOYEE AT WILL DOCTRINE

The law of contracts presumes that an employee who is employed for an indefinite period of time is an employee at will. Traditionally, under the employee at will doctrine, the employer has an absolute right to discharge employees for any reason and without "just cause," as long as the termination does not violate a written contract of employment, a collective bargaining agreement, or a state or federal statute protecting a certain class of workers. The doctrine also allows the employees to resign their positions or quit their jobs without reason and without cause. Although the right to terminate the employment relationship attaches to both the employer and the employee, the harshness of the doctrine is most often felt when the employee is discharged without reason and without "just cause."

The majority of nurses employed in the health care industry are employed for an indefinite period of time and are considered employees at will. The effect of the doctrine on their job security varies from state to state. In most jurisdictions, the doctrine is gradually being undermined by legislative enactments and judicial decisions that are recognizing the employees' right to sue the employer for breach of contract and/or bring an action in tort for wrongful or retaliatory discharge. The three rationales that are most often used to defeat the doctrine and limit the employer's right to discharge employees are (1) public policy, (2) implied contract, and (3) promises of good faith and fair dealing.

Public Policy

Public policy is defined as that principle of law that holds that no person can lawfully do that which has a tendency to be injurious to the public or against the public good.[43] A number of courts have recognized a public policy exception to the employee at will doctrine when an employee is discharged for engaging in some protected activity or for refusing to do something unlawful. The types of activities that have been considered protected by public policy include union membership, filing a workers' compensation claim, or serving on a jury.[44] The following cases illustrate situations in which nurses and other health care providers have successfully claimed that the employer wrongfully terminated their employment:

- The Montana Supreme Court ruled that a nurse-anesthetist's dismissal was invalid because her right to refuse to take part in a sterilization procedure was protected by the state "conscience statute" and outweighed the hospital's business necessities (Montana 1979).[45]

- A Missouri appellate court ruled that a laboratory technician could not be dismissed for reporting to the Food and Drug Administration (FDA) that the laboratory was not performing the tests or applying the hardening treatment on lenses that was required before they could be sold or distributed. The plaintiff was required to initial a form that stated that the eyeglasses had been impact tested and heat treated by the laboratory. When she complained, she was told not to worry about it because the insurance would take care of anyone who was injured. She had warned them that if the practice did not stop she would report them to the FDA (Missouri 1985).[46]

- An Illinois appellate court held that a nurse who had provided information about a patient confined to a state hospital to the Guardianship and Advocacy Commission, and had testified on behalf of the patient at his commitment hearing, was protected by a state statute that prohibited "reporters" and "employees of service providers" from retaliatory discharge. Finding that the nurse's contract was for personal services, the appellate court reversed the lower court's order for reinstatement and remanded the case to the lower court for a determination of the amount and type of damages that the nurse was entitled to receive (Illinois 1983).[47]

- A North Carolina appellate court reversed a dismissal of a nurse-anesthetist's wrongful discharge suit by a lower court that had upheld the employer's right to discharge her under the employee at will doctrine. The nurse alleged that she had been discharged for refusing to falsely or incompletely testify in favor of two doctors at a deposition for a medical malpractice trial that had resulted in a $1.7 million verdict for the patient. The appeals court held that even if the contract were terminable at will, retaliation for telling the full truth in a deposition was against public policy. They sent her tort and contract suit against the hospital back to the lower court for a trial on the merits (North Carolina 1985).[48]

- A federal appellate court remanded for trial a suit by a 62-year-old nurse supervisor who claimed she was discharged because of her age in violation of the Federal Age Discrimination Law. In reversing the lower court's directed verdict in favor of the hospital, the appeals court ruled that the administrator's comment that the hospital needed "new blood" and his statement that the supervisor's "advanced age" caused her stress presented sufficient evidence for a jury determination (11th Circuit 1985).[49]

- A federal appellate court found that the preponderance of the evidence indicated that a hospital had discharged a nurse in retaliation for her complaints about the care that the black patients were receiving. Ruling that employers are prohibited from retaliating against employees who oppose discrimination in a reasonable manner, the court held that her conduct did not exceed the protection of the Civil Rights Act of 1964. It indicated that she did not impede the goals of the hospital by advocating good patient care nor did she abuse her duty as a nurse by advocating for the needs of her patient and stated that "patient advocacy by a nurse is not insubordination" (9th Circuit 1984).[50]

- The Arizona Supreme Court held that in Arizona an employer may fire an employee at will for good cause or for no cause but that an employer cannot fire him or her for bad cause such as in violation of public policy. In finding a nurse had been wrongfully discharged, the court recognized a clear public policy consideration in the state's indecent exposure statute. The nurse has claimed that there was ill will between her and her supervisor and that she was discharged in part because of her disapproval of the behavior (i.e., drinking, public bathing, public urinating) of her supervisor and other hospital employees while on a camping trip. She also believed that the ill will was a result of her refusal to take part in the staging of the song "Moon River," which allegedly concluded with members of the group "mooning" the audience (Arizona 1984).[51]

Risk of Patient Advocacy

Courts have been reluctant to allow nurses to sue their employers for retaliatory discharge in situations in which the nurses' conduct is not protected by a state or federal statute. As one court has stated, "The foundation of the tort [of wrongful or retaliatory discharge] lies in the protection of public policy; the tort serves to curb the employer's otherwise absolute power to terminate an employee at will when that power is exercised to prevent the employee from asserting his rights found in state constitutions, statutes and judicial decisions."[52]

In most of the cases previously discussed the nurses were claiming a statutory right that was found superior to the employer's right to discharge them under the employee at will doctrine. Nurses, who are employees at will, should be warned that "patient advocacy" is not a claim or a defense that is recognized by the courts. Many nurses believe that they will be protected if their intentions are to safeguard the patient and if they earnestly believed that the action was necessary to protect the patient's safety and welfare. Unfortunately, as the following cases demonstrate, charges of wrongful discharge based on the public policy exception supported only by personal, moral, or ethical standards have not defeated the employer's right to fire them under the employee at will doctrine.

- In the case of a nurse who was fired after failing a polygraph test, the Illinois Appellate Court ruled that the employee's claim of retaliatory discharge for having leaked information to a newspaper concerning incidents of patient abuse and improprieties was invalid. They stated that in Illinois, actions for retaliatory discharge were limited to an employee's exercise of his or her rights under the state workers' compensation act. The court found that the hospital was justified in terminating the nurse on the basis that she had lied about job-related matters. They also denied the claim that her First and Fourteenth Amendment rights of free speech had been violated, ruling that the hospital was private and not subject to a state action claim for civil rights violations (Illinois 1980).[53]

- An Illinois court refused to expand the public policy constriction on the employer's right to terminate a nurse's employment to include a situation in which the employer allegedly lied about the reason for the discharge. The nurse had worked for the hospital for two years, during which time her evaluations were satisfactory. Prior to her discharge she had received unsatisfactory performance evaluations and two disciplinary action notices, each of which contained misstatements and lies. Her attempts to correct the falsehoods by means of the problem-solving procedure in the employee handbook were unsuccessful. Finally, she was told that she was being discharged because she had expressed dissatisfaction with the hospital and its personnel policies and because of her attitude toward her peers and her feelings about the nursing profession. The court held that lying about the reason for an employee's discharge was not a compelling reason for imposing liability for wrongful discharge on the employer as it is when the reason for the employee's actions is clearly mandated by public policy. It stated, "It may be a matter of private morality or out of respect for its employees that an employer should be truthful when it gives reasons for terminating employment, however these are personal matters and not matters of public policy" (Illinois 1985).[54] In a subsequent appeal the court also affirmed the lower court's summary judgment of the nurse's defamation suit against the supervisor and upheld the supervisor's qualified privilege to make an allegedly defamatory communication. It found that the supervisor's statement that the nurse's expression of dissatisfaction with the hospital and her peers made continued employment impossible could be read as directed to the employee's relationship with her co-workers and not to the employee's knowledge and ability to practice nursing and were therefore not defamatory per se (Illinois 1986).[55]

- A Colorado court refused to recognize the preamble to the Colorado Nurse Practice Act as a basis for the public policy exception to the employee at will doctrine. The head nurse had been fired for her inability to follow staffing patterns and stay within budget. She sued the hospital for wrongful discharge, claiming the preamble to the Nurse Practice Act required that she safeguard the patients' health and welfare and that her refusal to reduce her staff's overtime work was based on the belief that reducing the staff would jeopardize the health of the patients (Colorado 1978).[56]

Implied Contract

The employer's absolute right to discharge employees at will without just cause or reason can be restricted by an employee's claim that an implied contract has been created between the employer and the employee. Among the factors that have been cited as having the potential to establish an implied contractual relationship are (1) hospital policy, (2) hospital procedure, (3) personnel handbooks, (4) oral promises by supervisors or management personnel, and (5) employer conduct.

In 1980, a Michigan court adopted an expansive view of the potential contractual limitation of the employer's rights when it indicated

> No pre-employment negotiations need take place and the parties' minds need not meet on the subject; nor does it matter that the employee knows nothing of the particulars of the employer's policies and practices or that the employer may change them unilaterally. It is enough that the employer chooses, presumably in its own interest, to create an environment in which the employee believes that, whatever the policies and practices, they are established and official at any given time, purport to be fair and are applied consistently and uniformly to each employee. The employer has then created a situation "instinct with an obligation."[57]

Other jurisdictions have also held that the existence of an implied contract can restrict the employer's rights within the employee at will relationship. For example, in Nebraska a licensed practical nurse (LPN) sued a hospital for wrongful discharge, claiming a breach of contract because the hospital had failed to follow its grievance procedure when it fired her. She had been discharged for dishonesty because she had failed to renew her 1984 nursing license and, as proof of current licensure, had showed a cancelled check that actually was for her 1983 license. In reversing the lower court's dismissal of her claim, the Nebraska Supreme Court held that the fact that the employee does not have an employment contract for a specific term does not deprive her of the benefit of the grievance procedure as set forth in the employer's handbook. The court stated that "She has alleged the existence of an employment contract which, while not guaranteeing her continued, indefinite employment, establishes provisions for discharge and defines procedures to which she and her employer are bound in assessing the validity of her discharge" (Nebraska 1986).[58]

In another case, a nurse in North Carolina sued a hospital for wrongful discharge, claiming that the policy manual was part of her employment contract. In her position as vice-president for nursing, she had transferred an LPN from the emergency department because the state's nurse practice act did not permit LPNs to perform those functions and had instituted a hiring freeze as requested by the administration. She claimed that when public concern arose over the hiring freeze and the transfer of the LPN, the hospital, rather than explain the matter to the public or rescind its decision, discharged her. She had provided evidence that when she was hired she had been required to sign a statement that she had read the personnel manual and agreed to abide by its regulations; the manual stated that an employee may only be separated for cause; and the manual indicated that certain procedures would be followed before an employee was terminated. In reversing the lower court's dismissal of the action and remanding the case for trial, the appeals court ruled that the nurse had sufficiently alleged that the policy manual was a part of her employment contract, which was breached by her discharge (North Carolina 1986).[59]

The issue of whether an employee handbook creates a unilateral contract that can bind the employer to its provisions has been the subject of much litigation, which has produced a variety of responses from the courts.

- The Delaware Supreme Court upheld the hospital's termination of a head nurse who had complained about the hospital's replacing the "syringe method" of feeding patients with the "dry tube" feeding method. She believed that the new method required more time and greater supervision and that there were inherent dangers involved in the dry feeding. In response to her complaints she was told to stop "making waves" and was subsequently given a "false-negative" (unwarranted) job performance evaluation. She also alleged that she was threatened with disciplinary action if she contested the negative evaluation or failed to resign from her head nurse position. The court found that she had not been given a written contract of employment or anything in writing describing the terms and conditions of her employment. It ruled that an employee handbook is a unilateral expression of the hospital's policies and procedures on a number of topics, issued for the guidance and benefit of the employees, and does not alter the employee at will status. It indicated that its adherence to the traditional employee at will doctrine was consistent with the rulings in other jurisdictions, such as Kansas and Pennsylvania (Delaware 1982).[60]

- An Arizona court reviewed the wrongful discharge claim of a director of nursing who had been fired after she sought to transfer back to a previously held supervisory position. The court overturned the lower court's summary judgment in favor of the hospital, stating that there was genuine issue of fact as to whether the employer's policy manual was incorporated into the terms of the employment contract. They remanded the case to the lower court for a trial on the issues (Arizona 1984).[61]

- A 1987 Nebraska Supreme Court decision held that although an employee handbook was not prepared until five years after the employee was hired, its provisions could be enforced against the employer if they met the requirements of a unilateral contract. In the case before the court, however, it found that the language of the handbook was too indefinite to create a unilateral employment contract because it did not limit the reasons for discharge or require that any disciplinary procedures be followed before an employee was discharged (Nebraska 1987).[62]

The determination of whether the hospital's policy and procedure manuals and publications can be used to create an implied contract is very much a matter of judicial interpretation and opinion. Some hospitals have begun to include a disclaimer in their personnel handbooks that states that the contents of the handbook are not under any circumstances to be considered part of any employment agreement with any supervisor or other employee. It remains to be seen how the courts, in jurisdictions that have already recognized the contractual constraint, will interpret the statement.

Promises of Good Faith and Fair Dealing

Some courts have held that the employment relationship can give rise to implied promise of good faith and fair dealing to which the employer can be bound. Under this exception to the employee at will doctrine, a court will uphold an employee's suit for wrongful discharge, if the employee can prove that the employer acted unfairly or arbitrarily or that the employer disregarded or violated its own policies and procedures. In 1980, a California court ruled that length of service and the employer's policy of dealing fairly with employees were two factors that could limit the employer's right to discharge employees without cause. It also found that the existence of specific procedures for the handling of employee disputes revealed the employer's acceptance of the responsibility to act fairly and in good faith when dealing with the employees (California 1980).[63] In 1981, the same court held that an implied promise to avoid arbitrary discharge could be inferred by the totality of the parties' relationship. The type of evidence that could be considered in determining the nature of the employer–employee relationship includes (1) employment policies; (2) employer assurances, commendations, and promotions; (3) absence of any evidence of direct employee criticism; and (4) employees' length of service (California 1981).[64]

Employers have been bound by oral promises that were made by management to employees. One court awarded five certified nurse-anesthetists payment of six months' salary (less the amount they actually earned during those six months) for the breach of an oral promise that they would be given a six-month notice of termination (Louisiana 1979).[65]

The exceptions to the employee at will doctrine may also be available to employees in the probationary stage of employment. For example, a Montana court has held that the probationary status of an employee does not prevent the application of the implied promise of good faith and fair dealing (Montana 1984).[66] In California the court has ruled that the probation period policies may give rise to a contractual restriction of the employer's right to discharge an employee who has completed the probationary period (California 1982).[67]

The employer–employee relationship under the employee at will doctrine will continue to be challenged and changed by the legislatures and the courts. The nurse employee should be aware of the diverse and varied approaches that have been used to restrict the employers' power to terminate employees without reason and without "just cause." Nurse managers, who are responsible for interpreting and implementing the hospital's personnel policies, must understand the risks and consequences of their management behaviors. The major warnings that the preceding cases have sounded are listed below:[68]

- Employees cannot be discharged in retaliation for activities that are protected by law or recognized as carrying out some public policy.
- Personnel manuals, handbooks, and other written materials should not contain employment commitments that the employer is unable or unwilling to fulfill.
- Employment policies and procedures should be strictly adhered to and managers should be cautioned about expanding the meaning of the documents by making oral statements or promises to employees or applicants for employment.
- Grievance and employment termination procedures should be fairly and consistently followed by all management and supervisory personnel.

NURSES' REFUSAL TO PROVIDE NURSING CARE

A nurse's refusal to accept an assignment and provide nursing care for a patient, even when the decision is based on moral and ethical beliefs, has not been regarded favorably by the courts. For example, a New Jersey nurse sought to recover damages for her allegedly wrongful discharge based on a public policy consideration of her right to refuse an assignment she found morally and ethically objectionable. The patient was a terminally ill double amputee who required dialysis treatments. On two previous occasions she had to cease the treatments because the patient had suffered cardiac arrest and severe internal hemorrhaging during the dialysis procedure. She had notified the supervisor that she had "moral, medical and philosophical objections" to performing the procedure because she believed it was causing the patient additional complications. She met with the physician, who stated that the patient's family wanted the dialysis continued and that the patient would not survive without it. When the supervisor once again assigned her the patient she refused to perform the dialysis and was told that if she persisted in her refusal she would be dismissed. In her suit for wrongful discharge she claimed the right to refuse to perform a treatment that was "morally, medically and philosophically" objectionable was supported by the code of ethics for nurses. The court agreed that employees who are professionals owe a special duty to abide not only by federal and state law but also by the recognized code of ethics of their profession. They added, however, that employees do not have the right to prevent the employer from pursuing its business because the employee perceives that a particular business decision violates the employee's personal morals as distinguished from the recognized code of ethics of the employee's profession. In denying the nurse's claim of wrongful discharge the court stated that patients have a fundamental right to expect that medical treatment will not be terminated against their will and that this right outweighs the nurses' right to refuse to participate in treatment which they believe threatens human dignity. It held that the very basis for the nurse's reliance on her code of ethics was her personal opposition to the dialysis procedure. It viewed her action as serving a personal or private interest rather than a public policy interest. In chastising the nurse for her action the court stated, "By refusing to perform the procedure she may have eased her own conscience, but she neither benefited society at large, the patient nor the patient's family" (New Jersey 1985).[69]

Refusing Unsafe Work Assignments

Federal and state statutes and Joint Commission on Accreditation of Healthcare Organizations standards determine a hospital's minimum staffing requirements. The Joint Commission's Standards of Nursing Services mandate that "A sufficient number of qualified registered nurses shall be on duty at all times to give patients the nursing care that requires the judgment and specialized skills of a registered nurse. . . ."[70] The hospital has a duty to maintain an environment in which the patients can receive safe and competent professional nursing care. This obligation requires that the hospital staff the units with a sufficient number of qualified registered nurses, a responsibility that is becoming increasingly difficult at a time when there is a shortage of professional nurses. The legal implications of the current "nursing shortage" are significant and involve the hospital, the nurse manager, and the nurse.[71] The law looks not to the cause of the shortage but to its effect. Under the doctrine of corporate negligence, hospitals are held liable to plaintiffs who are injured as a result of inadequate staffing.[72]

Chronic understaffing, due to a lack of professional nursing staff, can seriously disrupt the relationship between the staff nurses, the nurse managers, and the hospital. Patients who are hospitalized on understaffed units are the ultimate victims of the nursing shortage; however, it is the staff nurses who must daily carry the burden of too much work and too little help who are the first casualties. The questions being asked most often by nurses attending legal seminars are, "Can I refuse a work assignment that I consider unsafe?" and "Can I walk off the unit if I find it is again understaffed and I have previously warned the supervisor that I would not work under these conditions?" The usual answer is that a nurse who refuses an assignment or abandons a patient may face serious contractual and professional consequences. The problem involves the nurse, the nurse manager, and the hospital administration in a scenario that can quickly reach a crisis stage when (1) it is 3 PM and the evening nurse is threatening to leave, (2) the supervisor has no replacement, and (3) there are 20 or more patients who have a right to safe and competent nursing care. In this situation the staff nurses have three choices. The nurses can

1. **Refuse to work and leave the hospital.** The employer cannot force nurses to work; however, if they refuse, they may be fired for insubordination and reported to the state board of nursing for unprofessional conduct in abandoning the patients. In addition, the nurses could be liable in a negligence action for any injury to patients that can be attributed to their having left the unit. It is probably safe to assume that this is never the right action to take. Refusing to work because the nurse believes that the unit is understaffed and that "something might happen" must be distinguished from refusing an assignment because the nurse does not know how to perform the procedures. State nursing practice acts and professional standards require a nurse to refuse an assignment that he or she is not competent to perform.

2. **Stay and request that the supervisor send whatever level of help is or may become available.** This course of action will relieve the nurse of the consequences of breach of contract or insubordination charges; however, it does not address the underlying problem of patient safety and the obligation to provide competent nursing care. The nurse and the hospital would still be held liable for negligence or malpractice if the patient is injured because of a breach of the nurses' and the hospital's duty to provide a reasonable standard of care.

3. **Stay after they have documented their express objections and reservations to the understaffing of the unit.** This course of action will relieve the nurses of the consequences of breach of contract or insubordination charges because they are fulfilling their employment obligations. This approach also emphasizes the view that the acceptance of a nursing assignment on an allegedly understaffed unit is a condition of employment and not a professional nursing judgment.

A few state nurses' associations have prepared assignment despite objection forms that give nurses the opportunity to document the specific grounds for their objections or reservations to the staffing (e.g., staff not oriented to unit, not given adequate staff for acuity).[73] There is no need to use a special form, but there is a need for the nurses to document their specific objections and to submit their objections to the supervisor. They should retain a copy of the complaint. The nurses' written record of the time and nature of their objections and reservations may be used for or against the hospital. For example, the information provides the nursing supervisor and hospital risk managers with specific information on which to assess the potential risk incurred by the level of staffing. If used appropriately, this information could be useful in assisting the hospital to recognize the need to close units or to decrease the number of patients accepted before it is involved in litigation. On the other hand, the information could be used as evidence if the nurse is fired and sues the hospital for wrongful discharge. Also, if the hospital is sued for negligence, it may be used by the plaintiff to demonstrate that the hospital was warned about the lack of adequate staff. Nurses practicing under minimal or inadequate staffing conditions will have to set priorities. They will have to use their professional judgment to determine what will get done and what will be left undone. The standard of nursing practice requires that they practice as reasonably prudent nurses would practice, *under the same or similar circumstances*. In situations in which the shortage of staff could not reasonably have been anticipated, the nurses' documentation of the staffing situation under which they were functioning may help to determine that their actions were reasonable under the circumstances, a finding that could defeat a plaintiff's claim of negligence.

Nurse Manager Implications

The tensions that are created by the lack of adequate staff tend to polarize the nursing staff and the nurse managers. Nurse managers may be perceived as unsympathetic and unwilling, rather than unable, to procure additional professional staff. They are expected to reconcile management staffing policies with what may often be the staff nurses' legitimate requests for additional help. Ignoring the nurses' demands for additional professional help could involve the hospital in a situation in which the hospital is held personally liable for the patient's injury under the doctrine of corporate negligence and is also held liable for the nurses' negligence under the doctrine of *respondeat superior*. Nurse managers can support the hospital's policies and also support the nursing staff if they take positive action. The most obvious approach is to obtain additional nurses from all possible sources, including "floating" nurses who are competent to work on more than one unit and the use of nurses from independent registries and medical pools. Asking nurses to work overtime and double shifts may solve the staffing problem, but tired overworked nurses may only increase the risk of error and substandard nursing care. Nurse managers should make use of the information that is provided by nurses who are documenting their specific complaints. The courts have not yet ruled on the effect that these new assignment despite objection forms will have in relieving the staff nurse of liability. It is possible that these forms, if made available to the plaintiff, could be introduced to prove foreseeability—in other words to demonstrate that the hospital was aware of the risk to the patient's safety and welfare. This points out the need to get the hospital's risk manager involved in identifying possible solutions to the problem and in determining how these written complaints or forms will be routed through hospital administration.

The hospital is responsible for maintaining an adequate level of professional staff, and its failure to fulfill that obligation has resulted in injured plaintiffs winning a number of lawsuits.[74] Nurse managers can obtain and evaluate the staff nurses' perception and opinion of the adequacy of the level of staffing and its effect on the standard of nursing care within the hospital. The willingness of hospital administration to respond promptly and appropriately to the staff nurses' concerns for patient safety is a major factor in promoting a cooperative and productive clinical environment.

The nursing shortage has placed nurses in a better bargaining position. Nurses collectively or individually are drawing up contracts with their employer that specifically address unsafe patient ratios and create contractual protection for nurses who refuse unsafe work assignments.[75]

EXPRESS CONTRACTS

An express written contract sets forth the conditions and terms of employment to which the employer and the employee are bound. In the negotiation of an express contract, the nurse bargains with the hospital as an individual, an approach that is prohibited to employee nurses who are subject to collective bargaining agreements. Express employment contracts generally contain a specific term of employment; therefore, the employee is no longer considered an employee at will and the employer's rights under the doctrine are extinguished. Disagreements arising in the employer–employee relationship will be settled according to the procedures set forth in the contract and, if litigation ensues, the court will interpret the contract in accordance with state law.

NEGOTIATING AN EXPRESS CONTRACT

Three factors that must be considered by a nurse who is considering the negotiation of an individual express written contract with a hospital are (1) opportunity, (2) contract provisions, and (3) legal advice.

Opportunity

A nurse cannot force a hospital to negotiate an individual contract. Nurse educators, directors of nursing services, and nurse specialists such as nurse anesthetists are the nurses who are most likely to have an individual contract with the hospital. It is still unusual to find staff nurses who are protected by individual express contracts. The current nursing shortage may make hospitals more receptive to this type of contractual employment relationship, especially in areas that are in need of permanent, highly qualified staff such as cardiac care units, intensive care units, and emergency departments. The greater the need that a hospital has for specialized nursing skills or for assurances that particular units will be consistently staffed with an adequate number of professional nurses, the greater the chances are that the nurse will be successful in negotiating an individual contract of employment.

Contract Provisions

Nurses who have the opportunity to negotiate individual express contracts must determine the areas that the contract will address. The American Nurses' Association, in conjunction with the Council of Nurse Practitioners in the Nursing of Children, has developed guidelines for the individual nursing contract to assist nurses in obtaining the best contract terms possible.[76] The guidelines contain suggested contract language and justification in the following areas:

- Duties, responsibilities, and authority
- Salary, hours of work, and premium pay
- Holidays and vacation

- Nursing education
- Sabbatical leave
- Sick leave and funeral leave
- Health insurance, life insurance, professional liability insurance, and other benefits
- Transportation expenses including mileage reimbursement
- Procedures for grievances, evaluations, and resignation or termination
- Duration of the contract

The negotiation of a contract is a process of give and take, with both sides attempting to draft an agreement that serves their legitimate self-interest. A contract that is perceived as fair by both sides will encourage a productive, cooperative, and stable employer–employee relationship.

Legal Advice

A valid individual express contract binds the nurse and the hospital to the terms and conditions of the agreement. The contract will be interpreted and enforced by the courts, who have the power to award money damages to the party who is injured by a breach of the contract. It is imperative that both parties clearly recognize the obligations imposed by the contract and the consequences of breaching the agreement. The hospital has administrative personnel familiar with the intricacies of contracts and contract law. The majority of nurses are inexperienced in these areas. This inexperience makes for unequal bargaining power, which is a distinct disadvantage that can be remedied by the nurses obtaining some legal advice and assistance. An attorney can

- Identify all of the potential areas that the contract may cover
- Draft the contract, using appropriate contract language
- Identify and resolve ambiguous, confusing, or conflicting areas
- Ascertain that all oral promises or statements have been incorporated into the written agreement as required by the parol evidence rule
- Determine that all provisions meet the requirements of state contract law
- Make certain that the contract clearly identifies the nurse's employee status as opposed to that of an independent contractor
- Make certain that the contract clearly specifies the hospital's obligation in relation to professional liability insurance
- Include mechanisms to alter, amend, or terminate the contract without having to seek recourse in the courts
- Offer advice as to how to approach the contract negotiations

Knowing that the contract has been reviewed by an attorney and is in accordance with state law will help the nurse to approach the contract negotiations with the positive attitude and professional manner that is essential for a successful outcome.

Need for Nursing Practice Contracts

Nurses, educated to believe that professional nursing is a public service that should be available to everyone in need, have not adapted easily to the contractual realities of bargaining for nursing services. The majority of nurses still practice without a contract and are considered employees at will, a relationship that is almost totally weighted toward the employer's interests. The collective bargaining experience has helped nurses and employers recognize the monetary value of professional nursing services and the feasibility of bargaining for such services.

Respect for the nursing profession and an understanding of its significant contribution to the health care industry have been long in coming and, according to one commentator, have not yet arrived. A 1985 article states:

> There have been many studies of the ambiguous role of the registered nurse, who must function in the crosscurrents of the administrator, the physician, and the patient. The nursing profession has been valiantly striving to establish its turf, but there is little evidence that its situation is changing appreciably. Nurses seem incapable of combining the nurturing aspects of their profession with the high-status, technical and esoteric knowledge characteristics of physicians. The difficult position of the nurse has been exacerbated by the gradual denigration of the service function in modern society.[77]

This attitude must change and is changing as nurses, either through collective bargaining agreements or individual express contracts, negotiate agreements that recognize their contribution to the hospital's prosperity and to the patients' welfare and compensate them equitably for the professional services they provide.

ANTITRUST LAW

Abusive practices by corporate giants in the second half of the nineteenth century resulted in Congress enacting legislation restricting the power of "trusts."[78] Antitrust legislation is designed to preserve the private competitive market by prohibiting anticompetitive activities. The underlying premise of antitrust legislation is that unrestrained interaction of competitive forces will yield the best allocation of economic resources.

Activities or businesses that are exempt from antitrust liability are state actions,[79] activities intended to induce government action such as lobbying,[80] and the "business of insurance."[81] Until the mid 1970s the health care industry was presumed to be immune from certain aspects of antitrust law; however, a series of Supreme Court decisions has brought the health care industry under its jurisdiction. Specifically the Court has held that a hospital's purchasing and reimbursement practices can be used to find that it is involved in interstate commerce and subject to antitrust law.[82] In addition, the Court has held that there is no exemption for the learned professions[83] and that federal health planning laws do not create an immunity to antitrust legislation.[84]

Federal antitrust law consists of the Sherman Antitrust Act, the Clayton Act, and the Federal Trade Commission Act.

The Sherman Antitrust Act, 15 U.S.C. §§ 1–70, makes unlawful every contract, combination, or conspiracy in restraint of trade in interstate or foreign commerce. Commerce that does not involve the crossing of interstate lines is not governed by the Sherman Act; however, virtually every state now has an antitrust statute that governs instate commerce. The Sherman Act also prohibits monopolies or attempts to monopolize.

The Clayton Act, 15 U.S.C. §§ 12–27, 44, prohibits practices that substantially lessen competition, such as price discrimination, tying and exclusive dealing arrangements, corporate mergers of competitors, and interlocking directorates, in which competing companies have common board members. The Robinson-Patman Act, 15 U.S.C. § 13, which is part of the Clayton Act, prohibits discriminatory pricing that lessens competition. The statute exempts purchases by nonprofit institutions "for their own use." In 1976, the Supreme Court[85] held that this exemption applies to hospital pharmacies in nonprofit hospitals that buy drugs from manufacturers at a discount that is not available to commercial pharmacies. The Court, however, defined "for their own use" as limited to drugs for (1) inpatients to be used in their treatment at the hospital; (2) patients admitted to the hospital's emergency facility for use there; (3) outpatients for personal use on the hospital premises; (4) inpatients or emergency facility patients upon their discharge and for their personal use away from the premises; (5) outpatients for their personal use away from the premises; (6) the hospital's employees' or students' (including nurses) personal use or the use of their immediate dependents; and (7) physicians who are members of the hospital staff, but who are not its employees, for personal use or the use of their immediate dependents. The Court excluded from the definition of "for their own use" (1) former patients who wish to renew a prescription given when they were inpatients, emergency facility patients, or outpatients; (2) physicians who are members of the hospital's staff and intend to dispense the drugs in the course of their private practice away from the hospital; and (3) walk-in customers who are not patients of the hospital.

The Federal Trade Commission Act, 15 U.S.C. §§ 41–58, created the Federal Trade Commission, which is an administrative agency that is broadly authorized to enforce the antitrust laws, including the Sherman and Clayton Acts. The Federal Trade Commission Act prohibits unfair methods of competition in or affecting commerce and unfair or deceptive practices affecting commerce.

Judicial Interpretation

The courts will either employ the per se doctrine or the rule of reason in scrutinizing business practices or conduct subject to section 1 of the Sherman Act. Under the per se doctrine of interpretation, any practice found to involve private arrangements and found also to have a restraining effect on trade as to any commodity in interstate commerce is considered unlawful per se, that is, of itself illegal, regardless of its apparent reasonableness, justification, or benefit. When a court holds that certain conduct is unlawful per se, there is no further inquiry into the motive or effect of the conduct. For example, price fixing, division of markets, group boycotts, and tying arrangements have been ruled per se violations of the antitrust laws. When conduct is not considered unlawful per se, the Court will analyze the challenged conduct according to the rule of reason. Under the rule of reason the Court will examine the purposes, nature, and intent of the challenged conduct in reaching its decision. The reasonableness of the conduct is only considered in the context of the competitive process and the resulting impact on competitive conditions. The Court has rejected all arguments that the question of reasonableness should apply to other areas such as public safety.[86]

Penalties

The penalties for violation of antitrust law are significant. A person may be fined up to $100,000 and a corporation may be fined up to $1,000,000. In addition, an individual may be imprisoned for up to three years; however, criminal enforcement of antitrust statutes is generally limited to outrageous and clearly illegal conduct. The federal district courts are empowered to issue injunctions restraining violations. Both the Sherman Act and the Clayton Act allow the injured party to recover treble damages and attorney's fees. This means that the injured party could recover three times the amount of the actual loss sustained and the party found to be in violation would be responsible for paying the injured party's attorney's fees. In addition, in order to neutralize and deny the defendant the profit of illegal practices, the court may order the violator to dissolve or divest itself of any arrangements found to be unlawful under the antitrust laws.[87]

Implications for Health Care Providers

Federal and state antitrust laws promote and protect the competitive aspects of the health care industry. Areas in which health care providers may be vulnerable to antitrust challenges include group purchases, shared services contracts, mergers, agreements not to duplicate services, establishment of wage and salary scales, exclusive contracts with physicians, and exchange of information between hospitals. The Federal Trade Commission has challenged concerted activities by health care providers and professional groups in their reimbursement policies, hiring decisions, and establishment of professional practices on other than a fee-for-service basis and on the dissemination of truthful information to the public.[88]

Antitrust Litigation

Any activity or conduct that threatens to restrain trade or restrict competition is subject to litigation. In reviewing antitrust charges brought against health care providers and insurers the courts have held that

- Hospital trustees could be sued for conspiracy to restrain trade by blocking the expansion of a competing hospital.[89]

- Agreements among organized, competing groups of physicians to set maximum fees for services were a per se violation of the antitrust law.[90]
- Different compensation formulas used by Blue Cross for participating and nonparticipating hospitals did not fall under the "business of insurance" exemption. The formulas were found not to be unlawful because they were reasonable according to the "rule of reason" analysis.[91]
- A hospital that has imposed a moratorium on further medical staff appointments can refuse to grant a physician hospital privileges. The court stated that a moratorium on further medical staff privileges can withstand antitrust challenges if the decision rests on concerns for quality patient care and the needs of the hospital's service areas and not upon the economic self-interest of the present medical staff.[92]
- The denial of a qualified anesthesiologist's application because of an exclusive contract with an anesthesiologist group was a per se violation of the Sherman Antitrust Act.[93]
- Nurse-anesthetists and physician-anesthesiologists are participants in a single anesthesia market. Even though nurses need additional input (physician supervision) they still can be said to compete with anesthetists. The court reasoned that a product should not be excluded from a market simply because it requires additional input in order to be a reasonable substitute for other products in the market. They stated that a "nurse anesthetist administering anesthesia under the supervision of a physician may still duplicate many of the services provided by the M.D. anesthesiologist."[94]
- A nurse-managed health care clinic had a right to proceed to trial for injunctive relief against various physicians and the executive director of the state board of medical examiners on charges that the physicians conspired to boycott the clinic, to fix prices for abortions in the area, and to monopolize the market for providing women's health and abortion services in the area. The actions were primarily aimed at preventing the nurse-run clinic from obtaining the necessary physician backup services.[95]

Nonphysician Staff Privileges

Hospital staff privileges for nonphysician professionals have also constituted an area of antitrust litigation. At present most states permit hospitals to determine the services that will be provided within their institution. A few states have prohibited hospitals from discriminating against an applicant solely because they are podiatrists or psychologists.[96] Court challenges have not favored nonphysician access to the hospital staff. For example, one court has ruled that hospitals are not required to admit podiatrists to their staff; however, if they do the applicant must be provided with due process.[97] Another court has held that hospitals do not have to admit chiropractors or naturopaths to their staff and are not required to have a procedure for reviewing their applications.[98]

The 1985 Joint Commission Standards for accredited hospitals state that the medical staff includes physicians and "may include other licensed individuals permitted by law and by the hospital to provide patient care services independently in the hospital."[99]

Physician evaluation is required of "non-physician members of the medical staff who are granted privileges to admit patients to inpatient services."[100]

Hospitals that permit or are required to permit nonphysicians to practice on the hospital premises should develop policies and procedures that will verify the qualifications of nonphysicians, define their scope of practice, require their compliance with hospital policy and procedure, implement mechanisms for their evaluation and supervision, and process grievances and implement termination procedures.[101]

The American Nurses' Association has published *Guidelines for Appointment of Nurses for Individual Practice Privileges in Health Care Organizations*.[102] The guideline's "Model for Appointment" suggests that all nursing applicants submit their application to the department of nursing services to be reviewed by a nursing credentials committee that would make recommendations to the nursing service department. After considering the credentialing committee's report, the department of nursing services would recommend the appointment to the appropriate governing body.[103] The American Nurses' Association believes that

> Nurses should have the opportunity, through the mechanism of nursing appointments, to gain access to the consumer in health care organizations for the purpose of providing continuity of care in an accountable systematic manner. The nurse appointment is a method of putting into operation the belief that all persons have the right to health care that is accessible, continuing and comprehensive.[104]

The American Nurses' Association has taken the position that "nurse appointments should be based on the need and consent of consumers and their families to have ongoing continuing nursing care at the various levels . . . within the health care system."[105]

INSURANCE CONTRACTS

An *insurance policy* is a contract between the insured and the insurance company. Institutional liability policies are contracts between an institution such as a hospital and an insurance company. A hospital's institutional liability policy will usually cover nurses, up to the maximum policy limit, for injuries sustained by patients as a result of nursing services that were performed by nurses within the scope of their employment. The hospital's insurance policy will not cover nurses

- For nursing services provided outside the employment situation such as private duty, volunteer work, etc.
- For the amount of the judgment that is over the policy's maximum limit.
- If the hospital files an indemnification claim against the nurse asking to be reimbursed for the damages paid to the plaintiff that were in excess of or not covered by its insurance policy.
- If the insurance company files a subrogation claim asking to be reimbursed for sums paid out on behalf of the nurse. For example, if several nurses are found to be negligent and one nurse's insurance company pays the entire judgment, the com-

pany is entitled to file subrogation claims against the other nurses requesting reimbursement for the share of the judgment that was paid on their behalf.

A review of the legal literature in relation to liability for health care professionals reveals that the terms *indemnification* and *subrogation* are often used synonymously to introduce the principle that the hospital or the insurer may ask the nurse to reimburse it for the sum of money that was paid to the plaintiff on his or her behalf. *Subrogation* is defined as the substitution of one person in the place of another with reference to a lawful claim, demand, or right. Most insurance policies contain subrogation clauses as do workers' compensation laws that permit the workers' compensation board to sue the party responsible for the worker's injuries up to the amount of the board's payments to the injured party.[106] *Indemnification* refers to the obligation or duty of one person to make good any loss or damage another has incurred or may incur by acting at his request or for his benefit. Indemnity refers to a total shifting of the economic loss to the party chiefly or primarily responsible for that loss.[107] Indemnification may be sought by the insured for the recovery of expenses or damages paid by the insured that the insurer had an obligation to cover. The employer is also entitled to seek compensation for the damages paid for which it had no insurance coverage.

The doctrine of *respondeat superior* makes the hospital responsible to pay the judgment for the negligent acts of nurses who are working within the scope of their employment. After having paid the damage award for the nurse's negligence, the hospital could file an indemnification claim against the nurse asking to be reimbursed for the amount of money paid in excess of the hospital's insurance policy limits. In practice this is rarely done because of the chilling effect it would have on nurse retention and nurse recruitment and the practicality of obtaining large sums of money from nurses. If the hospital is held liable under the doctrine of corporate liability for its own negligence, it is paying the judgment for its own breach of standard and cannot request indemnification from the nurses. For example, nurses could be found negligent for not having checked the circulation in a patient's leg often enough and the hospital as a corporation could also be held liable for not staffing the unit with an adequate number of professional nurses capable of recognizing circulatory impairment. Nurses should always notify nursing management in writing when they have reason to believe that their work environment is creating a risk that the nursing care will be inadequate and that standards of nursing practice will be breached. A written complaint to nursing management does not relieve the nurses of liability for substandard practice; however, it does make the hospital as a corporation aware of the risk and responsible for taking some corrective action. A hospital that is aware of a risk and does not take any steps to correct the situation can be charged with corporate negligence and made to pay damages for the injuries suffered by the patients as a result of its failure to take appropriate action.

Professional Liability Insurance Contracts

In today's medical-legal climate nurses are advised to carry their own professional liability insurance. The nurse's individual policy can be purchased as a supplement to the employer's coverage. An individual professional liability policy provides the nurse with (1) a specific sum of money that will be used to pay damages that he or she may have incurred because of his or her negligent actions, (2) an attorney–client relationship in which an attorney is professionally bound to defend the suit in a manner that is in the best interest of the nurse, and (3) the obligation of the company to pay the bond that may be required during an appeal of the case.

Insurance policies are contracts that often contain language that is difficult for the lay person to understand. Nurses should discuss their liability insurance needs with an insurance professional so that they will understand the agreement and the type of protection that is available. In order to make an informed decision as to the type and amount of insurance that is needed a nurse must know what protection is offered by the employer's liability policy. An individual liability policy will usually supplement and expand the protection. In addition, the nurse's policy should provide protection from suits by the employer or by other health care professionals in areas such as libel and slander.

A standard professional liability policy has five sections: (1) insurance agreement, (2) defense and settlement, (3) policy period, (4) amount payable, and (5) conditions of the policy.

Insurance Agreement

The professional liability policy protects the nurse from damages arising from rendering or failing to render professional nursing services. Nurses should know whether the policy protects them when they are acting in a managerial or administrative capacity and whether it also covers people who may be working under the nurse's control or supervision. The exclusionary clauses of insurance policies generally exclude from coverage criminal acts, intentional torts, acts that exceed the scope of practice, injuries resulting from a nurse being drug or alcohol impaired and punitive damages.

Defense and Settlement

The insurance company is obligated to arrange for and pay expenses to defend lawsuits brought against the insured. The expenses are generally not limited by or included in the policy limits unless the contract specifically states the limitation. A liability policy that guarantees a defense against all lawsuits binds the company to defend any suit for professional services, including those that are fraudulent, groundless, or false.

In most policies the insurer reserves the right to initiate a compromise or settlement; however, in doing so it must act reasonably and not to the detriment of the insured. The terms of the policy determine whether the insurer must obtain the consent of the insured before agreeing to a settlement. The policy imposes an implied promise of good faith and fair dealing on both the insurer and the insured. Neither party should act in any manner that would prevent the other from receiving the benefits of the contract. Violation of the duty of good faith and fair dealing could make the violator liable for damages in a breach of contract action.

Policy Period

The policy period is specifically stated in the insurance contract. Professional liability policies are either occurrence-based or claims-made policies. An occurrence-based policy provides coverage against any injuries that occurred within the policy period even if the injured person did not file suit until after the policy lapsed or was terminated. A claims-made policy provides coverage only for claims that are actually brought by the injured party during the period of the policy. If the policy is allowed to lapse or is terminated, there is no coverage. In other words, under a claims-made policy, the insurance company has no obligation to a nurse if the patient's injury occurred while the policy was in effect but the lawsuit was not filed until after the policy had lapsed or been terminated. Some insurers allow the nurse to purchase a "gap" policy that will extend coverage for lawsuits filed after the policy terminates for incidents that occurred during the policy period. The policies are renewable each year until the final date of the applicable statute of limitations is reached.

Amount Payable

The amount of money that the insurer is required to pay the injured plaintiff is determined either by a jury after a trial or by the terms of a settlement between the parties. In either case the insurer is only liable to pay the injured party up to the maximum amount that is stated in the insurance policy. The policy usually contains an amount for each occurrence and a maximum amount for all occurrences. For example, a policy with a limit of $100,000/$300,000 would protect the nurse for up to $100,000 on each claim that is filed and up to $300,000 on all claims that are filed. The limits of the liability apply no matter how many people are injured or how many claims are made or suits are brought from any one occurrence. For example, if there are three claims the insurer would pay up to $100,000 on each claim. Should there be more than three claims the aggregate of $300,000 is spread across all of the claims; however, no one claim will receive more than $100,000. The insurance company is only obligated to pay up to the maximum dollar amount contained in the policy. The insured is still obligated to pay the injured plaintiff for the portion of the judgment that is not covered by insurance.

Conditions of the Policy

Most insurance policies contain the following conditions:

1. *Notice of occurrence and notice of claim.* The policy indicates whether the notice should be made orally or in writing. Reports to the insurer can include any unexpected incident or unusual happening, threats of litigation made by patient or family, and any legal papers or letters from attorneys received by the insured.[108] Failure to notify the insurance company promptly can void the insurer's obligations under the policy.
2. *Assistance of the insured.* The insured must cooperate with the insurer by providing whatever assistance is necessary to defend the claim. An insurer may be excused from liability if the insured deliberately and willfully makes false state-

ments or conceals information about matters material to the insurer's defense. The policy imposes an implied covenant of good faith and fair dealing on both parties.

3. *Other insurance*. People are often covered by more than one policy, as is the case when nurses are covered by their employer's policy and by their own professional liability policy. Other insurance clauses are designed to determine which policy provides primary coverage and which provides secondary or excess coverage.

4. *Assignment*. The policy only provides coverage for those individuals named or included in the insurance policy. The protection cannot be expanded or transferred to another party without the insurer's consent.

5. *Subrogation*. Subrogation was discussed earlier in this section. The right of subrogation allows the insurance company to become the beneficiary of all rights of recovery that the insured has against other parties who may also have been negligent.

6. *Changes*. Only the insurance company can alter or amend a term or condition of an insurance policy. The agent must obtain written approval from the company to alter, amend, or modify the policy.

7. *Cancellation*. The cancellation clause spells out the causes and the procedures for cancellation of an insurance policy. Company policy may require written notification or notification by certified mail of the cancellation of the policy.

Malpractice Insurance Litigation

If the judgment is not appealed, the jury verdict awarding a specific amount of money to be paid for injuries suffered by the plaintiff will terminate the lawsuit against the hospital and/or nurse. In situations in which coverage is provided by more than one insurance company the decision as to which company is obligated to pay the judgment may have to be submitted to the courts for a judicial interpretation of the contract terms. For example, a 1981 New Jersey case involved a hospital's insurance policy and a nurse's insurance policy, both of which had excess clauses similar in effect and operation.[109] The patient had alleged that the nurse failed to provide the required standard of care in the recovery room. The parties agreed to settle the case for $350,000. There were three insurance policies:

1. The hospital had an agreement with INA Corporation by which its employees would be indemnified for any claim arising out of rendered professional services up to $100,000 per claim.

2. The hospital was self-insured for sums up to $100,000, with INA Corporation being responsible for any indemnification in excess of the self-insured sum. Section D stated that if other insurance was held by an employee, then INA Corporation would only cover the amount over the excess.

3. The nurse had a policy through the American Nurses' Association by which the National Union Fire Insurance Company would pay $200,000 per claim and $600,000 in the aggregate. This policy also had an excess clause as to other insurance policies.

The court ruled that (1) the hospital's undertaking to indemnify employees to $100,000 for claims arising out of rendered professional services was in the nature of an insurance and (2) the two insurance carriers, each providing only excess insurance coverage, would share equally the burden of funding the loss in excess of $100,000. As a result the plaintiff was paid $100,000 by the hospital, $125,000 dollars by INA Corporation, the hospital's insurer, and $125,000 by the National Union Fire Insurance Company, the nurse's insurer. This case demonstrates that if nurses carry individual professional liability insurance it will be used to compensate the injured plaintiff in situations in which the nurse's insurer is held to have either a primary or a secondary obligation to do so. Some nurses have taken the position that if they do not carry insurance they will not be held personally liable for the economic consequences of their actions. This is a dangerous supposition in an age of increasing litigation; it is also a position that may place all of the nurse's personal assets at risk. On the other hand, it is totally unrealistic for nurses to assume that if they carry professional liability insurance it will not at some time be used toward the payment of the patient's settlement or damage award.

National Nurse Claims Data Base

The loss of malpractice coverage for nurse practitioners for a period during 1987 has pointed out the acute need to obtain statistics to prove to insurance companies that nurses are good risks.[110] The American Nurses' Association has responded by creating the National Nurse Claims Data Base, a centralized system that will monitor professional liability claims for the entire profession.[111] Nurses who experience a liability claim are being asked to submit a reporting form to the National Nurse Claims Data Base. The forms will be available from the American Nurses' Association, the state nurses' associations, and the specialty nursing associations. The data base will provide detailed claims information that the nursing profession can use in negotiating with insurance companies. In time it may become an important factor in ensuring that liability insurance is available at reasonable cost to all nurses.

NOTES

1. William L. Prosser, *Law of Torts*, 4th ed. (St. Paul, Minn.: West Publishing Co., 1971), 613.
2. Ann M. Rhodes and Robert D. Miller, *Nursing & The Law* (Rockville, Md.: Aspen Publishers, Inc., 1984), 184–189.
3. Black's Law Dictionary, 4th ed. (St. Paul, Minn.: West Publishing Co., 1968), 394.
4. Gordon D. Schaber and Claude D. Rohwer, *Contracts* (St. Paul, Minn.: West Publishing Co., 1975), 6–133.
5. Ibid., 52.
6. Ibid., 65.
7. Ibid., 111.
8. Ibid., 115.
9. Ibid., 95–103.

10. Ibid., 157–158.

11. Ibid., 215–223.

12. Karen Hawley Henry, *The Health Care Supervisor's Legal Guide* (Rockville, Md.: Aspen Publishers, Inc., 1984), 75.

13. Ibid.

14. Ibid., 76.

15. Ibid., 141.

16. Gerald Morales, "Unit Appropriateness in Health Care Institutions," 30 *Lab.L.J. (BNA)* no. 3 (March 1974):174.

17. 29 U.S.C. §§ 152 (12) 1982.

18. Henry, *Health Care Supervisor's Legal Guide*, 56.

19. *Addison-Gilbert Hospital*, 253 N.L.R.B. 1010 (1981); *Newton Hospital*, 250 N.L.R.B. 409 (1980).

20. S. Rep. No. 776, 93rd Cong., 2nd Sess. 4, *reprinted in* 1974 *U.S. Code Cong. and Ad. News* 3946–3950; *NLRB v. St. Frances Hospital of Lynwood*, 601 F.2d 404 (9th Cir. 1979), contravenes congressional mandate; *NLRB v. Walker County Medical Center Inc.*, 722 F.2d 1535 (11th Cir. 1984), *reh'g denied*, 726 F.2d 755 (1984), does not contravene congressional mandate.

21. *St. Catherine's Hospital of Dominican Sisters*, 217 N.L.R.B. 787 (1975); see also *Watoman Memorial Hospital Inc. v. NLRB*, 711 F.2d 848, 850 (8th Cir. 1983).

22. Cooper and Brent, "The Nursing Profession and the Right to Separate Representation," 58 *Chi-Kent L.Rev.* (1982):1053.

23. *NLRB v. HMO International California Medical Group Health Plan, Inc.*, 687 F.2d 806 (9th Cir. 1982).

24. 29 U.S.C. § 152 (11) (1982).

25. S. Rep. No. 766, 93rd Cong., 2d Sess. 4, *reprinted in* 1974 *U.S. Code Cong. and Ad. News*, 3946, 3951.

26. *NLRB v. Bell Aerospace Co.*, 416 U.S. 267, 290 (1979).

27. Henry, *Health Care Supervisor's Legal Guide*, 51.

28. Ibid., 68.

29. 29 U.S.C. § 164(a).

30. *Abington Memorial Hospital*, 250 N.L.R.B. 682 (1980); see also Henry, *Health Care Supervisor's Legal Guide*, 53.

31. 29 U.S.C. § 158 (a) (5); (b) (3).

32. *NLRB v. Highland Park Mfg. Co.*, 110 F.2d 632, 637 (4th Cir. 1940).

33. Henry, *Health Care Supervisor's Legal Guide*, 75.

34. Ibid.

35. 29 U.S.C. § 158 (a) (3).

36. Henry, *Health Care Supervisor's Legal Guide*, 110.

37. Howard S. Rowland and Beatrice L. Rowland, *Hospital Legal Forms, Checklists and Guidelines*, vol. I (Rockville, Md.: Aspen Publishers, Inc., 1987), 31:16.

38. D. Peterson, J. Rezlee, and K. Reed, "Grievances: Forerunners to Arbitration," *Arbitration in Health Care* (1981):23.

39. *Eberle Tanning Co. v. Food & Commercial Workers International Union*, 682 F.2d 430 (3rd Cir. 1982).

40. Henry, *Health Care Supervisor's Legal Guide*, 110.

41. Ibid.

42. *Vaca v. Sipes*, 386 U.S. 171 (1967).

43. *Warthen v. Toms River Community Memorial Hospital*, 488 A.2d 229 (N.J. Super. AD 1985).

44. 12 A.L.R. 4th 544 (1982).

45. *Swanson v. St. John's Lutheran Hospital*, 597 P.2d 702 (Mont. 1979).

46. *Boyle v. Vista Eyewear Inc.*, 700 S.W.2d 859 (Mo. App. 1985).

47. *Witt v. Forest Hospital*, 450 N.E.2d 811 (Ill. 1983).

48. *Sides v. Duke University Medical Center*, 328 S.E.2d 818 (N.C. App. 1985), *rev. denied,* 335 S.E.2d 13 (N.C. 1985).

49. *Buckley v. Hospital Corporation of America*, 758 F.2d 1525 (11th Cir. 1985).

50. *Wrighten v. Metropolitan Hospital Inc.*, 726 F.2d 1346 (9th Cir. 1984).

51. *Wagenseller v. Scottsdale Memorial Hospital*, 74 P.2d 412 (Ariz. App. 1984); Ariz. Sup. Ct. No. 17646, June 17, 1985.

52. *Mein v. Masonite Corporation*, 464 N.E.2d 1137, 1138 (1984).

53. *Rozier v. St. Mary's Hospital*, 88 Ill. App. 3d 994, 44 Ill. Dec. 144, 411 N.E.2d 50 (1980).

54. *Powers v. Delnor Hospital*, 481 N.E.2d 968 (1985).

55. *Powers v. Delnor Hospital*, 499 N.E.2d 666 (Ill. App. 2 Dist. 1986).

56. *Lampe v. Presbyterian Medical Center*, 590 P.2d 513 (Colo. App. 1978).

57. *Toussaint v. Blue Cross & Blue Shield of Michigan*, 882 Mich. Sup. Ct. 1980, 292 N.W.2d 880 (1980).

58. *Jeffers v. Bishop Clarkson Memorial Hospital*, 387 N.W.2d 692 (Neb. 1986).

59. *Trought v. Richardson*, 338 S.E.2d 617 (N.C. App. 1986).

60. *Avallone v. Wilmington Medical Center, Inc.*, 553 F. Supp. 931 (1982).

61. *Liekvold v. Valley View Community Hospital*, 688 P.2d 201 (Ariz. App. 1983), *vacated,* 688 P.2d 170 (Ariz. 1984).

62. *Johnston v. Panhandle Co-op Association*, Nebraska Supreme Court No. 85-676, June 26, 1987.

63. *Cleary v. American Airlines*, 168 Cal. Rptr. 722 (Cal. App. 1980).

64. *Pugh v. See's Candies*, 171 Cal. Rptr. 917 (Cal. App. 1981).

65. *Hebert v. Woman's Hospital Foundation*, 377 So. 2d 1340 (La. Ct. App. 1979).

66. *Crenshaw v. Bozeman Deaconess Hospital*, 693 P.2d 487 (Mont. 1984).

67. *Walker v. Northern San Diego County Hospital District*, 135 Cal. App. 3d 386 (1982).

68. Henry, *Health Care Supervisor's Legal Guide*, 264–265.

69. *Warthen v. Toms River Community Memorial Hospital*, 488 A.2d 229 (N.J. Super. Ct. App. Div. 1985).

70. Joint Commission on the Accreditation of Healthcare Organizations, *Accreditation Manual for Hospitals* (Chicago: Joint Commission, 1985), 97–98.

71. Edith Kelly Politis, "Nurses' Legal Dilemma: When Hospital Staffing Compromises Professional Standards," 18 *Univ. San Francisco Law Review* (Fall 1983):109–126.

72. Helen Creighton, "Law for the Nurse Manager: I. Understaffing," *Nursing Management* 17, no. 4 (April 1986):24–28; "II. Understaffing," *Nursing Management* 17, no. 5 (May 1986):14–16.

73. North Carolina Nurses' Association, *Guidelines for the Registered Nurse in Giving, Accepting, or Rejecting a Work Assignment* (Raleigh, N.C.: NCNA, 1986).

74. Creighton, *Law for the Nurse Manager*, 24–27.

75. Cynthia Northrop, "Refusing Unsafe Work Assignments," *Nursing Outlook* 35, no. 6 (1986):302; see also Newscaps, "In a first, Maryland contract sets RN ratios," *American Journal of Nursing* 87 (July 1987):980. Maryland Nurses' Association has negotiated guaranteed nurse–patient ratios for the general medical-surgical and critical care areas at Baltimore's Liberty Medical Center.

76. Diana Odell Potter, ed., *Practices*, Nursing Reference Library (Springhouse, Pa.: Springhouse Corp., 1984), 684–691.

77. Odin W. Anderson, *Health Services in the United States: A Growth Enterprise since 1875* (Ann Arbor, Mich.: Health Administration Press, 1985), 265.

78. Ernest Gellhorn, *Antitrust Law and Economics* (St. Paul, Minn.: West Publishing Co., 1976), 15.

79. *Parker v. Brown*, 317 U.S. 341 (1943).

80. *United Mine Workers of America v. Pennington*, 381 U.S. 657 (1965).

81. 15 U.S.C. § 1012 (b) 1976 (McCarran-Ferguson Act).

82. *Hospital Building Company v. Trustees of Rex Hospital*, 42 U.S. 738 (1976).

83. *Goldfarb v. Virginia State Bar Association*, 421 U.S. 773 (1975).

84. *National Gerimedical Hospital & Gerontology Center v. Blue Cross of Kansas City*, 452 U.S. 378 (1981).

85. *Abbott Laboratories v. Portland Retail Druggists Association, Inc.*, 425 U.S. 1 (1976).

86. *National Society of Professional Engineers v. United States*, 435 U.S. 679 (1978).

87. 15.U.S.C.S. § 1; 88 Stat. 1706 (Antitrust Procedures and Penalty Act).

88. Pollard and Schultheiss, "FTC and the Professions: Continuing Controversy," 1 *Nursing Economics* (November–December 1983):158–159.

89. *Hospital Building Company v. Trustees of Rex Hospital*, 425 U.S. 738 (1976).

90. *Arizona v. Maricopa County Medical Society*, 457 U.S. 332 (1982).

91. *St. Bernard Hospital v. Hospital Services Association of New Orleans, Inc.*, 618 F.2d 1140 (5th Cir. 1980).

92. *Williams v. Kleaveland et al.*, 534 F. Supp. 912 (W.D. Mich. 1981).

93. *Hyde v. Jefferson Parish Hospital District No. 2*, 686 F.2d 286 (5th Cir. 1982).

94. *Bhan v. NME Hospitals, Inc.*, 772 F.2d 1467 (1985).

95. *Feminists Women's Health Center v. Mohammed*, 586 F.2d 530 (5th Cir. 1979), *cert. denied*, 444 U.S. 924 (1979).

96. Nev. Rev. Stat. §§ 450.005 and 450.430 (1981), podiatrists and psychologists; Cal. Health and Safety Code § 1316 (West 1979), podiatrists.

97. *Shaw v. Hospital Authority of Cobb County*, 614 F.2d 946 (5th Cir. 1980).

98. *Samuel v. Curry County*, 639 P.2d 687 (Or. Ct. App. 1982).

99. JCAHO, *Accreditation Manual for Hospitals*, 1.

100. Ibid., 10.

101. Robert D. Miller, *Problems in Hospital Law* (Rockville, Md.: Aspen Publishers, Inc., 1983), 155.

102. American Nurses' Association, Commission on Nursing Service, *Guidelines for Appointment of Nurses for Individual Practice Privileges in Health Care Organizations* (Chicago: ANA, 1978), 1–4.

103. Ibid., 3.

104. Ibid., 1.

105. Ibid., 2.

106. Steven H. Gifis, *Law Dictionary* (Woodbury, N.Y.: Barron's Educational Series, Inc., 1975), 203.

107. Ibid., 101.

108. Cynthia E. Northrop and Mary E. Kelly, *Legal Issues in Nursing* (St. Louis: C.V. Mosby Co., 1987), 101.

109. *ANA et al. v. Passaic General Hospital*, 445 A.2d 448 (N.J. 1981).

110. "ANA System Ready for Claims Data," *The American Nurse*, Official Newspaper of the American Nurses' Association (February 1988):12.

111. Ibid.

Appendix **IV**

Implications for Nurse Managers

Part IV has examined the two major concepts of civil law: torts and contracts. These areas form the foundation of the nurse's relationship to the patient, the physician, the hospital, and the nursing profession. In this section the focus has been on the nurse's and the nurse manager's responsibility for maintaining a reasonable standard of nursing care and for promoting and protecting the patients' rights to consent and confidentiality. The status and rights of nurses as employees were also examined, and potential areas of nurse and nurse manager confrontation were introduced. The specific responses and responsibilities of nurse managers were discussed in each section because the diversity and scope of the information demanded it. The two major legal responsibilities that civil law imposes on nurses and nurse managers are to (1) maintain the standard of nursing care and (2) respect the rights of patients and staff. The following behaviors demonstrate some of the responsibilities that nurse managers must assume in order to fulfill their legal obligations to the patient and to the employer:

- Hire, supervise, and evaluate the nursing staff
- Evaluate interaction with the non-nursing staff
- Develop mechanisms for resolving professional conflicts
- Participate in the credentialing and evaluation process
- Implement and maintain the current standard of nursing practice
- Provide for nursing staff competency through education
- Evaluate the nursing staff and the level of nursing care being provided to patients
- Discipline nurses found to be incompetent, reporting to the state board when necessary
- Participate in the risk management process
- Respect patients' rights to consent or to refuse to consent to treatment
- Respect nurses' rights to fair and equitable treatment under the employment agreement

- Respect the nurses' and the patients' constitutional rights
- Promote an environment of mutual respect and cooperation between health care professionals
- Promote an environment of mutual respect and cooperation between nursing and hospital management

Oscar Wilde once remarked, "Nowadays, to be intelligible is to be found out." The major objective of this section is to make tort and contract law intelligible to nurses and nurse managers. It is critical that they "find out" about the law so that they can identify and confront areas of potential risk and conflict and promote current, competent nursing practice. The law of tort and contracts, the civil law, defines the relationship between individuals. It can be understood and fostered by individuals.

* * * *

LEGAL RESOURCES

LEGISLATION

Social Security Act, Title XVIII (Medicare); Title XI (Medicaid)
Equal Pay Act of 1963, 29 U.S.C. §§ 201–209
Age Discrimination in Employment Act, 29 U.S.C. §§ 621–634
National Labor Relations Act, 29 U.S.C.
Federal Privacy Act of 1974, 5 U.S.C. 552 (a)
Federal Drug Abuse and Treatment Act, 21 U.S.C. 1175
Freedom of Information Act, 5 U.S.C. 552
State medical injury (malpractice) statute
State comparative negligence statute
State immunity (Good Samaritan) statutes
State civil assault and battery statute
State invasion of privacy statute
State defamation statute
State privileged communication statutes
State right to know law
State medical records laws
State reporting and recording statutes
State statute of frauds

FEDERAL AND STATE COURTS

U.S. Supreme Court
U.S. Court of Appeals (Circuit)
U.S. District Court

State supreme court
State appellate courts
State trial courts
State malpractice panels

PEOPLE AND AGENCIES

Hospital administrator and hospital management personnel
Hospital risk manager
State board of nursing
State board of medicine
State board of pharmacy
National Labor Relations Board (regional office)
State civil rights commission
State workers' compensation board
State hospital licensing agency
State nurses' association
State nursing organizations
Joint Commission on the Accreditation of Healthcare Organizations

NURSE MANAGER'S BOOKSHELF

State nurse practice act
State board of nursing, rules, regulations, opinions and decisions
Hospital licensing regulations for nursing services
Joint Commission on Accreditation of Healthcare Organizations, Standards for an
  Organized Nursing Service
Hospital policy and procedure manuals
Hospital personnel policies
AHA Patient's Bill of Rights
National League for Nursing, Patient's Bill of Rights
American Medical Records Association, Confidentiality of Patient Health Information,
  Position Statement, 1985

American Nurses' Association Publications

- *Roles, Responsibilities, and Qualifications for Nurse Administrators*
- *Standards for an Organized Nursing Service*
- *Standards of Nursing Practice*
- *A Plan for Implementation of the Standards of Nursing Practice*
- *Specialization in Nursing Practice*
- *The Scope of Practice of the Primary Health Care Nurse Practitioner*
- *The Role of the Clinical Nurse Specialist*

- *Credentialing in Nursing: Contemporary Development and Trends*
- *Guidelines for the Appointment of Nurses for Individual Practice Privileges in Health Care Organizations*
- *DRGs in Nursing Practice*
- *Code for Nurses with Interpretive Statements*
- *Guidelines for Implementing the Code for Nurses*
- *Collective Bargaining and the Nursing Profession*
- *American Nurses' Association Guidelines for the Individual Nurse Contract*
- *Hospital Payment Mechanisms, Patient Classification Systems, and Nursing: Relationships and Implications*
- *Guidelines for Use of Supplemental Nursing Services*
- *Nursing Staff Requirements for In-Patient Health Care Services*
- *New Organizational Models and Financing Arrangements for Nursing Services*
- *Pay Equity*
- *Magnet Hospitals: Attraction and Retention of Professional Nurses*
- *The Economic and Employment Environment: Recent Developments and Future Opportunities*

Guides and Manuals

Henry, Karen Hawley, ed. *Nursing Administration and Law Manual*. Rockville, Md.: Aspen Publishers, Inc., 1987.

Kander, Mark K. and Russell, Robert F., eds. *Director of Nursing Manual, Federal Regulation and Guidelines*. Owing Mills, Md.: National Health Publishing, 1984.

Roach, Chernoff, and Esley. *Medical Records and the Law*. Rockville, Md.: Aspen Publishers, Inc., 1985.

Rosoff. *Informed Consent, A Guide for Health Care Providers*. Rockville, Md.: Aspen Publishers, Inc., 1981.

Rowland, Howard S. and Rowland, Beatrice L., eds. *Manual of Nursing Quality Assurance*. Rockville, Md.: Aspen Publishers, Inc., 1987.

Rowland, Howard S. and Rowland Beatrice L, eds. *Nursing Administration Handbook*. Rockville, Md.: Aspen Publishers, Inc., 1987.

Rowland, Howard S. and Rowland, Beatrice L., eds. *Nursing Forms Manual*. Rockville, Md.: Aspen Publishers, Inc., 1985.

Stull and Pinkerton, eds. *Current Strategies for Nurse Administrators*. Rockville, Md.: Aspen Publishers, Inc., 1987.

Swansburg et al., eds. *The Nurse Manager's Guide to Financial Management*. Rockville, Md.: Aspen Publishers, Inc., 1987.

Criminal Law: Individual vs. State

. . . a nurse's proximity to a suspicious death makes her a likely "first choice" when [the] interrogations begin.

Loy Wiley, *Nursing '81* (September 1981):37

* * * * *

The privilege against self-incrimination . . . is the essential mainstay of our adversary system and guarantees to the individual the right to remain silent unless he chooses to speak in the unfettered exercise of his own will during a period of custodial interrogation, as well as in the courts or during the course of other official investigations.

- You have the right to remain silent;
- Anything you say can and will be used against you in court;
- You have a right to consult with an attorney and to have an attorney present during interrogation;
- If you are indigent, an attorney will be appointed to represent you.

Miranda v. Arizona, 384 U.S. 436 (1966)

Part V

Criminal Law: Individual vs. State

Criminal Law:
Individual vs. State

Criminal law defines a particular relationship between the individual and the state. The term *individual* includes entities such as corporations, partnerships, and other forms of association. Criminal law establishes rules of conduct, identifies, defines, and prohibits various types of crimes, and prescribes the punishment. In a criminal case, the state or federal government is a litigating party referred to as the prosecution. There is a fundamental difference between a civil case and a criminal case. In a civil trial, the outcome is a remedy; in a successful tort or contract action the plaintiff has translated the personal and/or economic injury into dollars in the form of compensatory damages. Occasionally, an injunction is issued and the court orders the defendant to do, or refrain from doing, a particular act. The criminal law is not directed toward compensating the victim's personal or economic loss. The interest protected is the public health, safety, morals, and welfare of society at large. Criminal penalties include fines, incarceration, and the death penalty in states where the statute meets the constitutional test. The money collected from the fines is paid to the government; the victim is not compensated for the loss of money or property unless the jurisdiction has enacted a victim compensation program.

Criminal law and criminal procedure are intimately involved with a person's concept of justice. As one observer explains, "Justice, of course, is a two-sided thing. Part of us—part of all of us and usually part of each of us—thinks of justice as fairness to those accused, while the other part thinks of it as law enforcement and retribution."[1]

The involvement of health care providers in the area of criminal law and criminal liability reveals the same ambivalence and vacillation, depending on the position of the parties involved. For example, hospitals or nurses may be criminal defendants being prosecuted by the state for having acted in a manner prohibited by state or federal criminal statutes. On the other hand, nurses or hospitals may be responsible for providing medical care to a convicted criminal or an alleged perpetrator of a crime. In these situations, their actions may be found to be aiding the police and treated as a police action. In Chapter 5 judicial decisions were discussed concerning the effect of the Fourth Amendment on interrogations of patients by health care personnel. Another possible area of involvement is in the care of the victim of a crime such as rape, child abuse, or assault in which the nurse's ability to handle the evidence correctly may be critical to the outcome of the criminal proceedings. Whether the nurse and the hospital are involved in the defense of a crime, in the prosecution of a crime, or in preserving the evidence of a crime, it is essential that they understand the criminal justice system identifying what it must do, what it can do, and what it cannot do. In this chapter the criminal process is explained, selected areas of nurse criminal liability are examined, and the legal foundations of appropriate police–hospital relationships are reviewed.

CRIMINAL PROCESS

A *crime* is defined as a positive or negative act in violation of criminal law—an offense against the state.[2] It is a wrong that the state or federal government has determined is injurious to the public and subject to prosecution in criminal proceedings. The two major categories of crimes are felonies and misdemeanors. A felony is a crime punishable by death or by imprisonment in a state penitentiary or prison for more than one year. A misdemeanor is a lesser offense, punishable by a fine and/or by incarceration in a local or county jail for a maximum period of a year.

Prosecution

Crimes are offenses against the citizens of a state or against the citizens of the nation. Federal crimes are prosecuted by the Attorney General of the United States, the Federal Bureau of Investigation (FBI), and the regional United States Attorney offices. Federal crimes include all routine crimes in federal enclaves such as the District of Columbia and specific federal offenses that have nationwide application such as income tax evasion and the robbery of a federally insured bank.[3] Federal cases are entitled *United States v. Jane Doe*, for example, and are filed in the U.S. District Courts.

The majority of crimes are defined by state legislatures and prosecuted at the state or local level. These cases are entitled the *State v. Jane Doe* or the *People v. Jane Doe*. State crimes are investigated by state and local law enforcement officers and are prosecuted by the state attorney general or by local district attorneys and county prosecutors.[4] Although criminal law is a matter of state jurisdiction, the U.S. Supreme Court has often ruled that the U.S. Constitution is binding on the state's criminal investigation and prosecution procedures.

Criminal Defendant

The two elements that are necessary for the commission of a crime are a criminal act (*actus reus*) and criminal intent (*mens rea*). A person commits a crime by an action or omission; bad thoughts such as the desire to rape or steal do not constitute criminal conduct.

Criminal Act (Actus Reus)

Conduct that is most often recognized as sufficient to constitute a criminal act includes the following:[5]

- *Acting*: stealing, lying under oath, hiring someone else to perform a crime.
- *Not acting*: failing to file an income tax report or failing to stop at the scene of an accident in which the person is involved. A person is only liable for failure to act under circumstances when there is a duty to act. Legal duties are imposed by family and employment relationships and by statute.
- *Attempting*: engaging in a course of conduct, beyond mere preparation, that is planned to culminate in the commission of a crime.
- *Soliciting*: intentionally enticing, advising, inciting, ordering, or encouraging another person to commit a crime.
- *Conspiring*: agreement by two or more persons to commit a crime. The unlawful combination or agreement constitutes the offense—no other act is necessary.
- *Assisting*: assisting a criminal in the form of an accessory before the fact, aiding and abetting or as an accessory after the fact. Also included are harboring a fugitive and obstructing justice.

Criminal Intent (Mens Rea)

Criminal statutes require the state to prove that the defendant intended to commit the crime of which he or she is accused. A person who accidentally or mistakenly takes someone's property does not have the *mens rea*, or intent, that is necessary for a criminal indictment for larceny. Statutes frequently state that persons are guilty of receiving stolen property only if they know it was stolen when they accepted it.[6] A person who is threatened or placed in a state of fear and forced to commit a crime may be excused from criminal liability on the basis that the behavior is involuntary and therefore lacks the element of intent. Criminal law recognizes the principle that people ''intend'' the natural and probable consequences of their actions. For example, proof that the accused broke into a building and committed larceny may be sufficient to establish a specific intent to steal.[7]

Motive is not an essential element of a crime. It makes no difference whether the person has a good motive, a bad motive, or no motive at all. For example, in cases of euthanasia (mercy killing) the person's motive of relieving the patient of intractable pain does not negate or ameliorate the finding of an ''intent to kill,'' which is necessary for a criminal homicide conviction.[8]

Exceptions to the requirement of a finding of specific intent are generally found in criminal statutes in the areas of negligence and strict liability. For example, it is not necessary for the state to prove specific intent to kill in order for a person to be found guilty of negligent homicide. In negligent homicide actions the statute generally requires the state to prove that the person acted with reckless disregard for the standard of conduct required for the protection of others. Under strict liability statutes, motorists who drive in excess of the speed limit or with absent or defective equipment may also be convicted without proving specific intent.[9]

Types of Crimes

The identification and definition of crimes and the punishments decreed are essentially a matter of state law. Although the state criminal codes may vary, the general principles and applications are similar. There are many types of crimes, and many states identify different degrees within a particular crime such as first- and second-degree murder. The following list of offenses demonstrates how crimes can be classified according to the interest that is affected:[10]

- *Offenses against the person*: murder, manslaughter, assault, battery, rape, sexual offenses, kidnapping
- *Offenses against property*: larceny, burglary, robbery, arson, criminal trespass, theft of services
- *Offenses involving fraud and deception*: forgery, fraudulent use of credit cards, negotiating a bad check, falsifying a business record, issuing false financial statements, misrepresentation of age by a minor
- *Offenses against the public order*: riot, disorderly conduct, carrying a concealed weapon, loitering, public intoxication, misconduct with emergency telephone calls
- *Offenses against public health and decency*: prostitution, promoting prostitution, compelling prostitution, furnishing obscene material to a minor, criminal activity in drugs, criminal use of drugs, liquor prohibition
- *Offenses against state and public justice*: bribing a public servant (giving and/or receiving a bribe), perjury, escape, bail jumping, bribing a witness, hindering the prosecution, initiating a false report to a law enforcement officer or emergency agency (false fire alarm), obstructing government administration

Defenses

There are a number of excuses and justifications that defendants may use to defend the criminal charges that have been brought against them. The following defenses have developed from the common law and are frequently included in the state's criminal statute, which is generally referred to as the criminal code.

Insanity

The insanity defense is appropriate for persons who were mentally ill at the time they committed the crime and, as a result of the mental illness, were unable to realize that their actions were wrong and were unable to control their behavior. If they are found to be "not guilty by reason of insanity," they are usually hospitalized in a state mental hospital. They have been found not guilty; therefore, they cannot be tried again should they recover their sanity. Persons who are mentally ill to such an extent that they are unable to understand or participate in the criminal proceedings and are incapable of assisting the defense attorney in their defense cannot be tried, convicted, or sentenced for a crime. Persons who are held to be incompetent to stand trial are usually hospitalized in a state mental hospital until such time as they are diagnosed as competent. If they recover their sanity, it is possible, but unlikely, that they would be tried for the crime of which they are accused.

Alcohol Intoxication and Drug Impairment

Some courts may find that a person who was under the influence of alcohol or drugs at the time he or she committed the crime lacks the specific intent (*mens rea*) necessary for criminal liability. Other courts, however, consider the ingestion of alcohol or drugs as "voluntary" and therefore insufficient to excuse criminal acts such as the possession of narcotics or burglary.[11] The fact that the defendant is addicted to drugs or alcohol may be relevant in mitigating the punishment. The intoxication defense is of no value when intoxication is an element of the crime, such as for driving while under the influence of alcohol or public intoxication.

Mistake or Ignorance

A defendant may claim mistake of fact or a mistake of law.

Mistake of Fact. Ignorance or mistake of fact is a defense that negates the criminal intent (*mens rea*) element required for the commission of a crime. For example, in most states a person would not be guilty of bigamy if he or she honestly believed that the first spouse had died. In some states the law will only find persons guilty of receiving stolen property if they knew that it was stolen when they accepted it. Ignorance of the facts is not a defense for crimes for which the legislature has imposed strict liability. For example, in most jurisdictions an honest, mistaken belief that the girl was of legal age is not a defense against a charge of statutory rape. The mistake, however, may be considered by the court in mitigating the punishment.

Mistake of Law. Traditionally, ignorance of the law or the mistaken belief that the conduct is not prohibited by law has not been considered a valid defense. Some jurisdictions have recognized an exception to the rule when (1) the statute has not reasonably been made available and the defendant claims that he or she did not know the statute had been enacted and (2) the defendant has reasonably relied on an official statement of the law that later proves to be incorrect or invalid.

Entrapment

Entrapment is an appropriate defense in situations in which government agents or private persons acting as government agents instigate a crime by implanting a criminal idea in an innocent mind and thus bring about a crime that would not have otherwise been committed. The entrapment defense is most often used in relation to government "sting" or undercover operations. Proof by the prosecution that the defendant had a predisposition to commit the crime and that the police only provided the opportunity for its perpetration will defeat the defense of entrapment.

Duress

The duress defense is available to defendants who have committed criminal acts while in a state of fear created by an unlawful threat and under the reasonable belief that it was the only way to avoid imminent death or serious bodily injury to themselves or others.

The law considers the defendant's actions to be involuntary, thus negating the criminal intent (*mens rea*) element essential for criminal conduct. Duress cannot be used as a defense for the intentional killing of an innocent third person or for crimes committed by employees claiming that they were only carrying out orders.[12]

Alibi

Although alibi is not strictly considered a defense, it is referred to as such in criminal procedure. The defense of alibi means that the defendant is claiming that at the time the crime was committed he or she was at a different place, so remote or distant that under the circumstances the defendant could not have committed the crime. Court rules may require that defense counsel file notice of the intention to rely on an alibi defense. The rule will generally require that the notice be filed within a specific period of time (10 days) after the entry of a not guilty plea. In addition, the court may require that the parties disclose the names and addresses of witnesses relevant to the alibi defense.[13]

In general, defenses to crimes are described in the state's criminal code. In some states the court may have a notice requirement for criminal defenses. For example, New Hampshire Superior Court Rule 102 states: "Absent good cause shown, the defense counsel must file within 10 days after the entry of a not guilty plea a notice of his intent to claim any defense specified by the Criminal Code. Failure to do so may result in a forfeiture of the defense."

The insanity defense poses a particular problem. A defense counsel who suspects that the defendant may be suffering from a mental illness may request that the defendant be committed for pretrial psychiatric evaluation. Such requests are made in the form of motions for psychiatric evaluation. The procedures for pretrial commitment for psychiatric evaluation are usually determined by the state's commitment statutes.

Criminal Procedure

The consequences of a criminal conviction are extremely serious. A person may be imprisoned for months, years, or even life. In some states, the criminal may be put to death. The law of criminal procedure is designed to protect the innocent from conviction, imprisonment, and sometimes death, even if, as a result, some of the guilty go free.[14] It has often been stated that "In a free society, it is more important to guarantee that those of us who do not commit crimes are not arrested, convicted and sent to jail than it is to put away those who do."[15]

The prosecutor, the defendant, the crime, the prosecution, and the defense form the nucleus of the criminal process. Their actions, interactions, and reactions are prescribed by the criminal procedures and constitutional protections that must be implemented and maintained throughout the pretrial, trial, and appellate proceedings (Figure 17-1).

PRETRIAL PROCEDURES

The criminal process begins when a crime is committed and reported to the police. Pretrial procedures consist of the arrest, booking, investigation, preliminary hearing, indictment or information, and arraignment (see Figure 17-1).

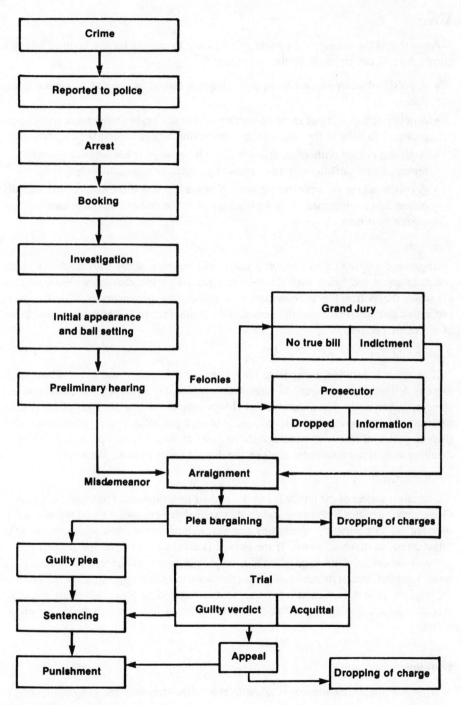

Figure 17-1 Criminal Procedure

Arrest

An *arrest* is the taking of a person into custody to answer for the commission of a crime. Arrests can be made by the following:[16]

- A police officer pursuant to an arrest warrant issued by a judge or justice of the peace.
- A police officer without an arrest warrant if he or she has probable cause (reasonable grounds) to believe the suspect was committing or had committed a crime.
- A private citizen without an arrest warrant if the suspect has actually committed a felony. Some jurisdictions also require that there be a breach of the peace.
- A police officer or a private person without a warrant if the suspect has actually committed a misdemeanor or has attempted to commit one in the presence of the citizen or officer.

Warrants

The two circumstances in which a judge will issue an arrest warrant directing the police to arrest and bring before the court a named person charged with a crime are (1) when the police file a complaint that sufficiently demonstrates that they have probable cause to arrest a specific person and (2) in response to a grand jury indictment of a specific person.

Reasonable Force

If an arrest is justified, reasonable force is permitted to effect the arrest. *Reasonable force* is defined as the amount of force that is reasonably necessary under the circumstances. Whether the force that was used was reasonable is a question of fact that is determined in the light of the circumstances of each particular case.[17] In most jurisdictions, a police officer who has the right to make an arrest is also permitted to enter a dwelling and, if necessary, break open the door in order to make the arrest.

"Hot Pursuit"

The arrest power of the police is limited to their geographic and political jurisdiction. One exception to this limitation is when they are in "hot pursuit" of a felony suspect. If they are in "hot pursuit" of a felony suspect, they can cross into adjoining towns or jurisdictions to make an arrest. If the pursuit is across a state line, the suspect can be arrested and confined in a local jail until a judge determines that the arrest is lawful. If the arrest is lawful, interstate rendition proceedings are instituted requesting the governor of the asylum state to return the fugitive to the demanding state. Interstate rendition proceedings are analogous to the extradition process that exists between sovereign nations.

Booking

After the arrest, the suspect is taken to the police station in the geographic area in which the arrest took place. *Booking* is a procedure in which the person's name, address, and the time, place, and reason for arrest are recorded. Practices vary among police departments. Some keep a log and an arrest book or "blotter"; others just have the arrest book. The suspect is usually fingerprinted and photographed at this time.

Investigation

Following the booking procedures, the defendant is ordinarily subjected to an interrogation conducted by one or more police officers. The interrogation is designed to (1) secure the defendant's admission or confession to the offense for which he or she has been arrested, (2) obtain the names of others that may be involved in the offense, and (3) obtain an admission to other offenses that he or she may have committed. In addition to interrogation, there are many other investigative procedures that the police may want to subject the defendant to, the most common of which are

- Exhibiting the defendant in a lineup before witnesses
- Requesting that the defendant reenact or demonstrate what happened
- Requiring the defendant to don special clothes
- Asking the defendant to speak certain words or sentences
- Obtaining specimens of the defendant's hair, blood, or body scrapings for laboratory analysis

All of these procedures are geared toward obtaining evidence that can be used against the defendant at trial. Defendants may have the right to refuse to participate in some of these procedures, or they may have the right to have the procedure such as a lineup take place only when their attorney is present.

The extent and manner of police interrogation and investigation techniques are strictly controlled and limited by the defendant's constitutional rights. In *United States v. Miranda*, 384 U.S. 436 (1966), the Supreme Court established the warnings that must be provided to a defendant prior to any custodial interrogation. Police advising a defendant of his or her Miranda rights must state

1. You have the right to remain silent;
2. Anything you say can and will be used against you in court;
3. You have the right to consult with an attorney and to have an attorney present during interrogation;
4. If you are indigent, an attorney will be appointed to represent you.

In addition, many police departments require that the police ask the defendant if he or she understands what has been stated. They may also ask the defendant to sign the form on which the rights are printed as an acknowledgment that the rights were read and understood. The Court has indicated when the Miranda rights apply:

> The privilege against self-incrimination . . . is the essential mainstay of our adversary system and guarantees to the individual the "right to remain silent unless he chooses to speak in the unfettered exercise of his own will" during a

period of custodial interrogation, as well as in the courts or during the course of other official investigations.

Custodial interrogations are also subject to the defendant's Fifth Amendment right not to be compelled to testify against himself or herself. The Fifth Amendment prohibition against compelled self-incrimination taken in conjunction with the Fourteenth Amendment right to due process prevents the use of coerced or involuntary confessions or statements as evidence in criminal trials.

Constitutional protections attach to many of the investigative procedures and techniques. Searches and seizures must be conducted in accordance with the Fourth Amendment guarantee of freedom from unreasonable and warrantless searches. The constitutional mandate that involuntary information or illegally obtained evidence is inadmissible at trial is known as the exclusionary rule. The patient's rights to be free from unreasonable searches by police and by health care professionals acting under the direction of the police are discussed in Chapter 5. In this chapter a variety of court opinions on hospital searches are examined. For example, in 1975 the Supreme Court held that state action existed when hospital employees deliberately searched for evidence at the request of the police;[18] however, in 1987, the Fifth Circuit Court of Appeals ruled that when there is no concerted action between the police and hospital personnel, the independent actions of the police officers will not result in the court's finding the nurses or emergency department personnel were agents of the police.[19]

Bail

Bail is the security that a defendant gives to assure the court that he or she will be available at every stage of the criminal proceeding. Depending on the circumstances, bail can be set at the police station or the defendant may be required to make an initial appearance before a judge who will determine the amount of bail. A person arrested for a criminal misdemeanor can usually be released by posting bail in the designated amount or on personal recognizance (personal bond) by signing a form promising to appear before the court as required. If the person fails to appear, he or she will be held liable for the amount of the personal bond. A person arrested for a felony has a more difficult time obtaining bail, and the amount of bail may be set at the time of arraignment. Factors frequently used in deciding the amount of bail are listed below:[20]

- The nature of the crime
- The physical or mental condition of the defendant as related to the possibility of danger to himself or herself or to the public
- Whether the defendant has sufficient contacts with the state
- The defendant's prior failure to appear
- Any other circumstances bearing on the possibility of the defendant's failure to appear.

If the crime is of a very serious nature, the defendant may not be eligible for bail.

Preliminary Hearing

In most states, prosecutions that have been initiated by a complaint or information require a preliminary hearing before a judicial officer to determine whether there is probable cause to hold the defendant. In the federal system and in states that use the grand jury system a preliminary hearing may be held to determine whether there is probable cause to hold the defendant for the grand jury. The courts have stated that probable cause means that at the moment of arrest the police had facts within their knowledge, of which they had reasonably trustworthy information sufficient to warrant a prudent person to believe that the defendant had committed or was committing a crime.[21] The right to a preliminary hearing can be waived by the defendant.

Grand Jury Indictment

The Fifth Amendment of the Constitution requires a grand jury hearing in all federal felony cases: "No person shall be held to answer for a capital or other infamous crime unless on a presentment or indictment of a grand jury, except in cases arising in the land or naval forces, or in the militia, when in actual service, in time of war or public service." A grand jury is a "board of inquiry" consisting of a number of persons who are summoned and sworn to determine whether the facts and accusations presented by the prosecution warrant an indictment and eventual trial of the accused. The jury is called "grand" because of the relatively large number of jurors that are impaneled. Traditionally, a grand jury consists of 23 members as opposed to the 12-member "petit" jury that is impaneled for civil and criminal trials. A grand jury has subpoena power and can compel witnesses to testify. It can sometimes act as an investigative body and determine that a person whom the police have not charged with a crime should be charged. A well-known example of the investigative function is the Watergate grand jury. When a grand jury determines that the defendant should be prosecuted it returns an indictment or true bill, which is a formal written accusation that a person has committed a crime. If the accused has not already been taken into custody at the time of the indictment, the judge will issue an arrest warrant.

Prosecutor Information

In states that do not use the grand jury system, the police officer presents a complaint to the prosecutor. The complaint is a sworn written statement that states the offense and outlines the basis of evidence for the crime. Once the arrest and the complaint are made, the prosecutor draws up a formal written accusation, which is called an information. The information must reasonably apprise the defendants of the charges against them so that they may prepare and present their defense.

Arraignment

The *arraignment* is the first formal court appearance after the information or indictment has been filed. It is a public hearing in which the defendants are informed of the charges against them and of their constitutional rights, including the right to counsel. The indictment or information is read to the defendants and they are asked to enter a plea. If the defendants plead "not guilty," the prosecutor is required to prove at trial every charge that is specified in the indictment or information. As a matter of practice, defendants who are charged with serious crimes usually plead "not guilty." A guilty plea is a complete admission of the charge. Some states do not permit a guilty plea to crimes punishable by death or life imprisonment. The prosecution is required to prove all of the charges against the accused. If the defendant pleads guilty and the plea is accepted by the court, no trial is necessary; all that remains is for the sentence to be determined and imposed. By pleading guilty the defendant waives all of the due process guarantees of the constitution and the right to appeal. The federal and state rules of criminal procedure require that the judge, prior to accepting a guilty plea, must ascertain that the defendant understands the nature of the charges and the consequences of pleading guilty. The judge must also make certain that the defendant's guilty plea is being made voluntarily.

Plea Bargaining

Plea bargaining is the process by which the prosecutor and the accused negotiate a mutually satisfactory disposition of the case.[22] The judge may or may not be a party to the plea bargain, depending on the jurisdiction. In all jurisdictions the decision to accept or reject the plea bargain agreement is within the discretion of the judge. Plea bargaining means that the defendant will plead guilty to a lesser offense; plead guilty to one or some of a multicount indictment; or plead guilty to one or some of a series of overlapping charges. In return for the defendant's plea of guilty, the prosecutor recommends to the judge a reduction of the charge or a more lenient sentence. In essence, the defendant is receiving some concessions in exchange for his or her waiver of the right to trial. In some states, the criminal rules of procedure require that the plea bargain be entered on the record in open court at the time the defendant pleads guilty.

Plea bargaining is an extremely controversial practice, and there are those who believe that it serves the guilty better than the innocent.[23] The innocent are faced with the dilemma of deciding whether to stand trial and expect no leniency if convicted. They argue that plea bargaining puts a price tag on the exercise of one's right to trial.[24] In defense of the practice, one court has stated that "properly administered it is to be encouraged."[25] They stated that plea bargaining can[26]

- Lead to prompt and largely final disposition of most criminal cases
- Avoid much of the corrosive impact of enforced idleness during pretrial confinement for those who are denied release pending trial
- Protect the public from accused persons who are prone to continue criminal conduct even while on pretrial release
- Shorten the time between the charge and the disposition
- Possibly enhance whatever may be the rehabilitative prospects of the guilty when they are ultimately imprisoned

Proponents of plea bargaining suggest that the plea bargaining system is essential to prevent the courts from being overwhelmed by defendants exercising their right to trial. They indicate that at the present time 70 percent to 85 percent of defendants plead guilty, either at the arraignment or at some subsequent time.[27] Under the plea bargaining system, the victim is spared the trauma and uncertain outcome of a trial and the prosecutor can guarantee a conviction with almost no possibility of reversal on appeal.[28]

Discovery

The U.S. Constitution requires the prosecutor to turn over to the accused evidence that is material to the defendant's guilt or innocence and evidence of the defendant's statements to law enforcement officers.[29] This can include the following:[30]

- A copy of records, statements, or confessions signed or unsigned by the defendant to any law enforcement officer or his or her agent
- A list of tangible objects, papers, documents, or books from, or belonging to, the defendant
- A statement as to whether the foregoing evidence or any part thereof will be offered at the trial

The U.S. Supreme Court has held that the withholding of evidence material to the guilt or punishment of the defendant is a violation of due process of law irrespective of the good or bad faith of the prosecution.[31] The federal rules of criminal procedure provide for broad discovery techniques; however, the state rules of criminal procedure vary widely as to the types of evidence, in the possession of the prosecution, that the defense may see. The prosecutor's opportunity for discovery is limited by the defendant's Fifth Amendment privilege against self-incrimination. Defendants do not have to testify nor do they have to help the state prove the charges against them. The defense attorney's duty to defend the client may require the filing of a variety of motions. Motions that are frequently made by the defense include a motion for expert services, a motion for attendance of material witnesses, and a motion for the suppression of evidence that was taken in violation of the defendant's Fourth, Fifth, or Sixth Amendment rights.[32]

The court may also require the parties to exchange or otherwise inform each other of, or permit each other to inspect, copy, or photograph (1) statements of witnesses; (2) reports or results of physical or mental examinations; (3) reports or results of scientific tests, experiments, or comparisons; and (4) any other reports or statements of experts.[33] Court rules or regulations may require that certain notices be filed by the defense. For example, in some jurisdictions the defense must file a notice of intent to use the alibi defense and must include the names and addresses of witnesses relevant to the defense.[34] It is also customary to require the defense to file a notice of intent to use the insanity defense.[35]

TRIAL

The Sixth Amendment to the Constitution states

> In all criminal prosecutions, the accused shall enjoy the right to a speedy
> and public trial, by an impartial jury of the State and district wherein the crime
> shall have been committed, which districts shall have been previously ascer-
> tained by law, and to be informed of the nature and cause of the accusation; to
> be confronted with the witnesses against him; to have compulsory process for
> obtaining witnesses in his favor, and to have the assistance of counsel for his
> defense.

Burden of Proof

The basic principle of criminal law is that the defendant is considered innocent until
proven guilty. In a criminal trial the government must prove that the defendant is guilty
beyond a reasonable doubt. The term *reasonable doubt* is often used but difficult to
explain. *Black's Law Dictionary* defines reasonable doubt in the following manner:

> It does not mean a mere possible doubt, because everything related to
> human affairs, and depending on moral evidence, is open to some possible or
> imaginary doubt. It is that state of the case which, after the entire comparison
> and consideration of all the evidence, leaves the minds of jurors in that
> condition that they cannot say they feel an abiding conviction to a moral
> certainty of the truth of the charge.

In a criminal case, the prosecution must create in the mind of the jury an "abiding
conviction to a moral certainty" that the person charged with the crime actually
committed it. The degree of proof required in criminal trials is much greater than the
"preponderance of the evidence" standard required in civil trials. For example, in professional negligence (malpractice) trials the jury balances the weight of the evidence
presented by the injured plaintiff against that which is presented by the defendant health
care professional.

Jury Selection

The jury is selected in a process that is called the *voir dire*. The judge alone or the
judge and the attorneys involved question the jurors in order to discover their qualifications. Potential jurors can be dismissed for cause or on a peremptory challenge. A juror is
dismissed for cause when the judge is convinced that the person cannot serve as an
impartial, attentive juror. A peremptory challenge means that the attorney can have a
juror dismissed without having to state the reason. The defense and the prosecution each
receive a number of peremptory challenges that are automatically granted; however,
because the challenges are strictly limited, they must be used very carefully. In recent

years, attorneys sometimes employ specialists in sociology and psychology to assist them in the selection of jurors.

Rights of the Accused

The rights of the defendant must be protected during the trial. The trial judge decides the questions of law by sustaining or overruling the attorney's motions in accordance with the law and the rules of evidence. The jury listens to the evidence and the instructions of the judge and decides the questions of fact and ultimately renders a verdict as to the defendant's guilt or innocence. The U.S. Constitution guarantees the accused:

- *The right to an attorney*: The right extends only to criminal proceedings that may lead to imprisonment.
- *The right to a speedy trial*: State statutes generally set specific time limits.
- *The right to a fair and impartial trial*: A change of venue is granted when publicity or other factors might deny the defendant a fair trial in the community.
- *The right to a trial by jury*: The right does not extend to cases in which the maximum penalty for conviction is a monetary fine or imprisonment for less than six months.
- *The right to a public trial*: In extremely sensitive cases and in situations in which children are testifying, particularly if the defendant agrees, the public may be excluded. The exclusion does not generally apply to friends and relatives of the accused.
- *The right against self-incrimination*: The defendant in both the federal and state courts may refuse to take the stand and testify.
- *The right to confront witnesses*: The defendant has the right to be physically present in the courtroom when a witness testifies and also the right to cross-examine the witness. The right to be present in the courtroom can be forfeited by a defendant whose behavior is found to be disruptive and disorderly.

Trial Procedure

A criminal trial is an extremely complicated legal proceeding. The rules of evidence and the rules of criminal procedure vary from jurisdiction to jurisdiction; however, the overall process is the same. A trial comprises eight major events, consisting of (1) opening arguments by the prosecution, (2) opening arguments by the defense, (3) presentation of evidence by the prosecution, (4) presentation of evidence by the defense, (5) closing arguments by the defense, (6) closing arguments by the prosecution, (7) instructions to the jury, and (8) jury deliberation culminating in a jury verdict. During the presentation of the evidence the witnesses are subject to direct examination by the party calling them and to cross-examination by the opposing party. There are provisions for redirect examination and recross-examination of the witnesses, and each side has the opportunity to present rebuttal evidence in the same format. Exhibits that meet the criteria for admissibility can be introduced as evidence, and counsel may request that it be passed to the jury. In most cases, the closing argument is made by the defense first with the prosecutor getting the last word.

Jury Instructions

Prior to its deliberations the jury receives instructions from the judge on the rules of law that apply to the case. These instructions may include the essential elements of the crime, the definition of reasonable doubt, and an explanation of the defenses that have been raised. Attorneys on either side can request that the judge give the jurors specific instructions concerning the case. They may also object to portions of the jury instructions and request that something be added.

Jury Verdict

In most jurisdictions a jury verdict, whether guilty or not guilty, must be unanimous. The Supreme Court, however, has approved nonunanimous verdicts (9 to 3 and 10 to 2) established by law in a few jurisdictions.[36] If the jurors cannot agree on a verdict, the judge declares a mistrial and the defendant will stand trial again unless the prosecution drops the charges. If the jury acquits the defendant, the government cannot appeal the verdict or retry the case.

Postconviction Procedures

In a criminal case the sentence is always imposed by the judge, although some states allow the jury to recommend the punishment. The judge will usually set a date for a sentencing hearing at which the defense can submit evidence as to the defendant's background and special circumstances. In determining the sentence the judge may also consider the information that is contained in the pre-sentence report, which is usually prepared by a probation officer. The report provides information concerning the defendant's background, prior criminal record, family, and financial circumstances. The report may contain a recommendation for probation or for incarceration for a specific period of time. The amount of discretion a judge has in sentencing the convicted person varies from state to state. The Constitution prohibits ''cruel and unusual punishment,'' and a judge's sentence can be set aside by an appeals court if it is found to be too severe or not suited to the crime. Some state statutes provide that any person sentenced to a year or more in a state prison may file an application for a sentence review before a board of judges.[37]

APPEAL

The appellate process begins with the defendant's post-trial motion for a new trial. These motions are seldom successful but are required in most states. Once the trial judge has denied the motion for a new trial, the defendant can file an intent to appeal and request that the court reporter prepare an official record of the case. The appellate court will review the official trial record and the appellate briefs filed by both sides. When the appellate court permits or requests oral arguments, the attorneys have the opportunity to make oral presentations and the judges can ask questions about the case. Appellate courts are reluctant to overturn the decisions of the judge who presided over the trial. They will only order a stay of sentence awaiting the appellate decision if the defendant appears to have a substantial appellate issue. The issues on appeal are those that have been preserved during the trial by the attorneys' objections to the trial judge's rulings. If the defense counsel did not object to the judge's ruling during the trial, the appellate court may refuse to consider the issue on appeal. An appellate court can affirm or overturn a conviction. Frequently, it finds that an error has been committed by the trial judge but holds that the error was harmless. A finding of harmless error means that the court has decided that the error, when weighed against all the other evidence presented, did not prejudice the defendant's right to a fair trial. The right to appeal a criminal conviction is a due process right that cannot be denied simply because a person is indigent. If a person cannot afford to pay for a copy of the trial transcript and cannot afford to hire an attorney to handle the appeal, both must be provided for him or her.

Habeas Corpus

Once the appeal process has ended, defendants may seek a review of their conviction by filing a writ of habeas corpus. The writ is also available to defendants who have been convicted following a guilty plea. *Habeas corpus* literally translated means "you should have the body" and is basically a procedure for obtaining a judicial determination of the legality of an individual's custody. The petition of habeas corpus is filed with the court and specifies in writing why the petitioner should not remain in jail. The court determines whether the writ should issue and, if it does issue, whether the prisoner should be released. The court's decision can usually be appealed to a higher court. A writ of habeas corpus is an extraordinary procedure that in practice is rarely successful.

CRIMINAL LIABILITY

Crimes committed by health care institutions and health care personnel are subject to the same criminal process and criminal penalties as crimes committed by ordinary citizens. Areas of health care that carry an inherent risk of criminal prosecution for nurses and physicians include practicing or aiding and abetting a person to practice medicine without a license, the termination of life-support systems, and the administration of narcotic medication to terminally or critically ill patients. Although the number of criminal prosecutions has increased over the past 20 years the number of convictions has not been significant. For example, there are four reported cases of physicians being charged with hastening the death of patients by injecting lethal substances and in all four cases the physicians were acquitted by the jury.[38] Nurses have not fared as well, however; of the seven reported cases of nurses having been charged with causing the death of patients, four cases were dismissed for lack of evidence, in one case the nurse was acquitted, and in two cases the nurses were convicted. As one observer has commented, "a nurse's proximity to a suspicious death makes her a likely first choice when [the] interrogations begin."[39]

Murder and Manslaughter

In the American criminal justice system, murder and manslaughter are categories of homicide, which is defined as the killing of one human by another. A homicide can be justifiable and not subject to prosecution or unjustifiable and subject to prosecution. Homicide is considered justifiable when it is committed in war; self-defense, which includes the killing of a person by a police officer in the prevention of a felony in which the suspect was armed; and capital punishment, in which the state statute decrees it as punishment for certain crimes.[40]

Unjustifiable homicide includes

1. Murder, which is defined as the unlawful killing of a human being with deliberateness and malice aforethought.[41] In some jurisdictions murder is further defined as to degree.
2. Manslaughter, which is the unlawful taking of human life without malice and includes

   • Involuntary manslaughter: the unintentional death of a human as a result of an unlawful act (e.g., death resulting from a person driving while intoxicated)[42]

   • Criminal negligence/involuntary manslaughter: the death of a person because of a failure to act when there was a duty to act (e.g., failure of a parent to get medical attention for a critically ill child)[43]

   • Voluntary manslaughter: the killing of a human being while in a state of passion or while under some provocation on the part of the victim (e.g., in a sudden quarrel in which two persons fight and one of them kills the other).[44]

In cases involving health care providers the term *euthanasia* is often used in describing the death of the patient. Euthanasia is the act or practice of painlessly putting to death a person who is suffering from an incurable or distressing disease.[45] Under federal law euthanasia is considered murder.[46]

Corporate Murder

A 1985 Illinois Circuit Court decision extended the risk of criminal liability to the business community. In *People v. Film Recovery Systems*, three corporate executives were found guilty of murder in the death of an employee from cyanide poisoning as a result of the regular exposure to cyanide at work.[47] Evidence introduced at the nonjury trial proved that the defendants knew about the danger and failed to properly warn or protect the employees from the hazards of working with the cyanide gas. The three executives were found guilty, and each was sentenced to 25 years in prison and fined $10,000; the corporation was also fined $10,000. The case demonstrates the need for appropriate warnings and procedures to protect employees from hazardous substances in the workplace. Many states have hazard communication standards covering workplaces that are subject to occupational safety and health laws. All hospitals must comply with the federal Occupation Safety and Health Act (OSHA) standards, such as the standard concerning the short-term exposure limits for ethylene oxide, a common sterilant used in many hospitals.

Prosecution of Nurses for Murder

The administration of narcotic medications to terminally ill patients who are in pain is a frequent and routine responsibility of nurses. The following case demonstrates how orders that permit the nurse to adjust the dosage or that indicate that the patient should be "kept comfortable" may involve the nurse in criminal proceedings. In Massachusetts a licensed practical nurse was charged with murder for having administered an overdose of morphine (195 mg) over a period of seven hours to a terminally ill cancer patient who subsequently died.[48] The physician testified that he had ordered the morphine limited to 45 mg; however, the nurse testified that the orders were to "keep the patient comfortable," which she interpreted as meaning she could administer whatever amount was necessary to relieve the patient's pain. After a highly publicized trial, the jury acquitted the nurse. The difficulty in bringing a murder charge based on the administration of lethal doses of medication is that the prosecutor must prove the nurse's criminal intent to kill the person. The most obvious and most probable explanation for overdosing a patient would be that the nurse was negligent in not identifying that the dose or accumulated doses were lethal or that the patient's physical condition resulted in a retention of the medication with the cumulative effect being lethal. Either explanation may be enough to create a reasonable doubt in the minds of the jurors. It should also be noted that the acquittal of murder does not necessarily mean that the conduct is within the standard of nursing practice. In the above case, following the acquittal, the Massachusetts Board of Nursing held a hearing that resulted in the nurse's license being suspended.

In a controversial Michigan case, two nurses who were Philippine citizens in the United States on work visas were indicted by a grand jury on five counts of murder, ten counts of unlawfully mixing a poison in the food or medicine of certain patients, and conspiring to commit those offenses.[49] The indictments stemmed from incidents that had occurred at the Ann Arbor Veterans Hospital in July and August of 1975. During that time 34 patients had suffered 51 cardiopulmonary arrests and 11 of the patients had died.[50] The anesthesiologist was convinced that someone had caused the arrests by administering a muscle relaxant to the patients.[51] The Veterans Administration hospital officials contacted the Federal Bureau of Investigation (FBI), whose investigation revealed that the patients had been poisoned by the administration of pancuronium bromide (Pavulon), a curare-like muscle relaxant. They also determined that the victims had been in the intensive care unit and that most of the cardiopulmonary arrests had occurred during the 3 PM to 11 PM shift. These findings made Perez and Narciso, two nurses who worked that shift, the prime suspects. There were other possible suspects, including a psychiatric patient who had been near one of the victims prior to his death and a "man in a green suit."[52] The FBI investigation was criticized by the Michigan Nurses' Association as focusing solely on the nurses. A statement by the Association claimed that a "witness testified in court that she was told by the FBI that they had five nurse suspects and that it was going to be a nurse on the afternoon shift. She asked 'why does it have to be a nurse? Why can't it be a doctor?' The FBI agent allegedly replied that the hospital chief of staff didn't want the doctors harassed." There were also charges that the investigation demonstrated a sex bias. A 1977 journal article on the trial stated that although the FBI claims that it did question many men, "there can be no doubt that men were questioned differently: as witnesses not as suspects."[53] During the first month of the investigation the two nurses had cooperated with the investigation and endured interrogations that lasted four or more hours. They continued to cooperate during the spring of 1975 and 1976. They did not seek the advice of a lawyer during this time because, as they later told reporters, in the Philippines, "only the guilty have lawyers."[54]

The grand jury indicted the two nurses on murder and conspiracy charges that could have resulted in life sentences if they were convicted. They were permitted to remain free on bail during the two-year period prior to the trial. At trial the prosecution did not prove that the defendants knew more about pancuronium bromide than other staff members, had more access to the patients than other staff members, or had injected the drugs into the patients.[55] The government claimed that the motive for the crime was the shock value that the case would have in aiding the nurses' protest of the nursing shortage in the Veterans Administration.[56] After 13 days of deliberation, Perez was found guilty of conspiracy and poisoning three patients and Narciso was found guilty of poisoning three patients and of murdering one patient. After the trial the defense, citing serious errors in the trial, filed a motion for a new trial. The trial court granted the motion and ordered a new trial; however, the prosecutor chose to dismiss the indictments against the nurses. The Michigan Nurses' Association publicly criticized the prosecution's approach to the case, which led the jury to find the nurses guilty. It argued that the prosecution did not prove that the nurses had administered the poison but had merely placed the nurses at the patient's side at the time of the respiratory arrests, which is where the standard of nursing practice requires that a nurse be at this time. It stated that if "a nurse is now under suspicion because she [or he] is in the proper place, fulfilling a basic responsibility for nursing practice, what does that do for nursing care and the role of all nurses."[57]

Conviction of Nurses for Murder

The following cases demonstrate two shocking and extraordinary situations in which the overt criminal action of nurses resulted in their conviction and incarceration for first-degree murder:

A Los Angeles nurse was found guilty of the murder of 12 elderly patients at two county hospitals.[58] The prosecution provided evidence that

- The nurse worked the night shift at the hospitals.
- The patients began dying during the late hours of the night.
- Each patient had been under the care of the defendant nurse.
- Autopsy performed on the bodies of the victims that had been exhumed revealed the bodies contained ten times the normal dose of lidocaine.
- When analyzed, three syringes used on the victims were found to contain ten times the normal dose of lidocaine.

The defense contended that

- There was no evidence that the drug was used purposely to kill the patients.
- The high level of lidocaine was due to a buildup of the regular doses given over a long period of time.

The judge following a nonjury trial convicted the nurse of 12 counts of first-degree murder. In sentencing the defendant, the court, citing California's multiple murder rule, found the special circumstances required to make the defendant eligible for the death penalty.

The second case concerns a licensed vocational nurse who had been the subject of a year-long investigation into the deaths of ten infants and into the cause of an undisclosed number of seizures that the patients had sustained on the night shift in the intensive care unit at the San Antonio, Texas, hospital where she had worked from 1980 to 1982. The investigation had been impeded by the hospital's shredding of pharmaceutical documents. The hospital contended that the shredding was a routine procedure and that the documents had nothing to do to with the intensive care unit or with the defendant. In 1982, the nurse left the San Antonio hospital and was employed by a pediatrician who had set up an office in Kerrville, Texas. While working for the pediatrician, children under her care started having seizures, which required their hospitalization. Following the death of a 15-month-old child while in her care, the nurse was indicted on seven counts of causing injury as a result of seizures suffered by the children at the office of the local pediatrician and one count of murder.[59] The murder charge alleged that she had injected the 15-month-old child with succinylcholine chloride (Anectine), a muscle relaxant with the potential for causing respiratory arrest and death. At trial the prosecution provided evidence that

- The nurse had given the infant the injection, stating it was a "baby shot."
- Immediately after receiving the injection, the child went limp and had difficulty breathing.
- The child was transferred to the hospital where the emergency department physician decided to transfer her to another hospital.
- The nurse decided to accompany the child, and a witness testified that she saw her give the infant another shot just before placing her in the ambulance.
- The nurse testified that it was the diazepam (Valium) that had been ordered by the physician; however, a registered nurse in the emergency department testified that she had already administered the diazepam to the child.
- The pediatrician who had employed the nurse testified that a bottle of succinylcholine was unaccounted for and that later, when it was found, there were unexplained holes in the stopper.

The state contended that the nurse had injected the medication that caused respiratory arrest in six children and the death of one child in order to demonstrate the need for a pediatric intensive care unit at the Sid Peterson Hospital in Kerrville, Texas. According to the prosecution she had hoped to end up "a heroine and the head of a pediatric

intensive care unit by injecting the children with a powerful drug and then curing them.''
The nurse was convicted of one count of murder and sentenced to a 99-year prison term.

Manslaughter Conviction and Reversal

In 1981, a nurse in New Jersey was found guilty of ''reckless manslaughter'' for the
death of a patient resulting from her having administered a transfusion of incompatible
blood.[60] The prosecution presented evidence that the patient, who had undergone open-
heart surgery, had type B negative blood and had died of a reaction to a transfusion of
type A positive blood. Testimony revealed the physician had ordered two units of clear
plasma and that the type A blood had been delivered to the patient's room by mistake.
The nurse denied having administered the transfusion and testified that she had put the
blood that was delivered to the patient's room in a hospital refrigerator. Her testimony
was contradicted by the patient's children, who testified that they saw the nurse
administer a transfusion to their mother on the night in question. The prosecution
presented evidence that she concealed her actions, disposed of the remainder of the
blood, and altered the medical record. The nurse's surreptitious behavior was used by
the prosecution to support an inference of criminal intent. The Newark Superior Court
Jury acquitted the nurse of the ''aggravated manslaughter'' charge, which carried a
maximum sentence of 20 years, and found her guilty of ''reckless manslaughter,''
which carried a 5- to 10-year sentence. The nurse appealed her conviction to the New
Jersey Superior Court, and on July 2, 1984, the court reversed her conviction on the
basis of prejudicial error.

Withholding and Withdrawing Life-Sustaining Treatments

The withholding and withdrawal of life-support mechanisms and treatments and the
injection of potentially lethal doses of medication with the intent to kill the patient is
conduct that is subject to criminal prosecution for murder. These overt unlawful acts
must be distinguished from the withholding and withdrawal of life-sustaining mechanisms on a terminal patient in response to the patient's constitutional right to refuse
treatment or in response to the physician's judgment that the treatment is no longer
medically appropriate and should be terminated.

Nurses may be held criminally liable if they terminate or adjust life-support mechanisms without proper authorization. A Baltimore nurse stood trial for the first-degree
murder of a ventilator-dependent cancer patient who had died after a 26-hour coma.[61]
The director of nursing service had been informed by the staff nurses that they suspected
the defendant had killed the patient by shutting off the ventilator and subsequently
reconnecting it to avoid detection. The hospital's investigation of the allegations
uncovered no evidence against the nurse, who subsequently resigned without confirming
or denying the charges. After a year-long investigation by the district attorney's office
the nurse was indicted on several counts of murder. She was accused of having
disconnected three patients' respirators and of having turned down the oxygen flow on
the fourth. During the trial on the first count, the nurse admitted to disconnecting the

ventilator without authorization but insisted that the patient had no pulse or blood pressure and was already dead. Under Maryland law, the prosecutor had to prove that the patient lost spontaneous function after the nurse disconnected the ventilator. Expert witnesses argued about the definition of spontaneous death. The case ended in a hung jury, and the prosecutor chose not to try the case again and dismissed all charges against the nurse. In Nevada, a nurse was indicted for murder in the death of a patient in the intensive care unit.[62] The prosecution alleged that she had caused the patient's death by turning down the oxygen on the ventilator. The court, finding insufficient evidence to support the charge, dismissed the case.

The risk of criminal liability for physicians and for nurses who withhold or withdraw life-sustaining mechanisms in accordance with physician's orders and hospital protocol is minimal. Cases involving the withholding or withdrawal of life-sustaining treatment to a terminal patient are rarely prosecuted because of the difficulty in establishing a duty of health care providers to provide such treatment, especially when the termination is being done with the patient's and/or family's consent. In 1984, a California court ruled that a competent patient may refuse treatment even if the refusal will lead to death.[63] The court also stated that the health care professionals who withhold or withdraw life-sustaining treatment in accordance with the patient's wishes are not subject to criminal prosecution. In 1983, the same court had dismissed murder charges against two physicians.[64] The charges stemmed from their having discontinued intravenous therapy and nasogastric feedings on a patient who was diagnosed as hopelessly comatose. The court held that the physicians had no duty to continue treatment in this case and added that the decision to terminate treatment "is essentially a medical one to be made at a time, and on the basis of facts which will be unique to each case."

Practicing Medicine without a License

State medical licensing statutes generally make it a crime to practice medicine without a license. It is also a crime to aid and abet a person to practice medicine without a license. In most states the same criminal sanction exists in relation to the practice of nursing without a license and to aiding and abetting a person to practice nursing without a license.

In the 1983 landmark case of *Sermchief v. Gonzales*,[65] the Missouri State Board for the Healing Arts filed a complaint charging two nurse practitioners with practicing medicine without a license and four physicians with aiding and abetting the nurses to practice medicine without a license. The physicians and nurses were employed by a Missouri obstetric and gynecology clinic. The trial court ruled in favor of the board and ordered the nurses and physicians to cease and desist in their activity. The Missouri Supreme Court, aware of its position as the first court to rule on the legality of nurse practitioners, reviewed the Missouri Nurse Practice Act and determined that the nurses were practicing professional nursing. This decision points out the necessity of ensuring that nurse practice acts are amended or redrafted to accommodate the expanding knowledge, skills, and responsibilities of the nursing profession. There is a need to admit the fact that there are areas in which the practice of nursing and medicine may overlap.

There are some states in which the practice of midwifery is strictly regulated. For example, in California a registered nurse who practiced midwifery without having obtained a midwifery certificate was convicted for the illegal practice of medicine and the conviction was upheld on appeal.[66]

Fraud

Fraud is defined as the false representation of a matter of fact, whether by words or conduct, by false or misleading allegations, or by concealment of that which should be disclosed, which deceives, and is intended to deceive another so that he or she shall act upon it to his or her legal injury.[67] State statutes define fraud as a tort and also as behavior that is prohibited under the state's criminal code. In 1984, an Ohio appellate court overturned a lower court dismissal and recognized a family's right to sue a hospital in tort for fraud.[68] The court ruled that the hospital could be held liable for fraud for failing to inform the plaintiff of the irreversible nature of the patient's condition. The patient had been receiving care for a progressive, terminal disease when she suffered a cardiac arrest that left her in a chronic vegetative state. The court indicated that the hospital could be made to pay for the expenses that occurred during a five-month period in which the patient was being treated against the family's wishes and that they could also claim damages for their pain and suffering during this time. The husband had to resort to instituting guardianship proceedings in order to have the life-support mechanisms removed.

Acts that constitute fraud are defined by state statute. For example, the New York Penal Law, section 175.10, states that a person is guilty of falsifying a business record when, with the intent to defraud, they (1) make or cause to be made a false entry; (2) alter, erase, obliterate, delete, remove, or destroy a true entry; (3) omit to make a true entry in violation of a duty to make such an entry; and (4) prevent the making or cause the omission of a true entry. In 1978, a New York court upheld the indictment of a physician and a nurse on charges of falsifying business records.[69] The indictment charged that the physician failed to make a true entry in his operative report and the nurse failed to make a true entry in the operating room log. These omissions were held to be in violation of a duty imposed on them by the nature of their positions and by the law.

Medicare Fraud and Abuse

The Federal Civil Money Penalties Law implemented in 1983 authorizes the secretary of Health and Human Services (HHS) to impose substantial penalties and program suspensions against health care providers who submit false or improper Medicare and Medicaid claims.[70] For example, in one case involving $145,000 in false Medicare claims, the maximum penalty that could have been assessed under the law was $5.7 million. The HHS sought $2.9 million in penalties and assessments and was awarded $1.79 million and the judge imposed a 25-year suspension from the program.[71] The hearings are conducted before an Administrative Law Judge with an optional review of the proceedings by the secretary of HHS. An appeal to the federal court is available;

however, the review is based on the administrative record and is limited to whether the secretary's final decision is supported by "substantial evidence."

Criminal Assault and Battery

Assault and battery are classified both as torts (see Chapter 14) and as crimes. Criminal assault is an attempt with unlawful force or violence to inflict a physical injury, accompanied by the apparent ability to carry out the attempt if not prevented.[72] Criminal battery is the unlawful application of force to another person.[73] Some jurisdictions have by statute defined criminal assault to include what was in common law a battery. In these jurisdictions a criminal assault requires actual physical touching and/or injury.[74] Assault is generally classified as a misdemeanor. It is classified as a felony in situations of "aggravated assault" (1) in which the assault is particularly fierce, (2) the intent is to commit serious bodily harm, (3) when a dangerous or deadly weapon is used, or (4) when the assault is committed intentionally concomitant with further crime.[75]

Nurses who threaten patients or use unwarranted or unreasonable force could be held accountable for the conduct in both civil and criminal proceedings. Patients could sue the nurse in civil assault or battery to recover damages for their injuries, and they could also file criminal charges of assault and battery in which the punishment is a fine and/or imprisonment, depending on the nature of the assault. In a 1984 Massachusetts case, the family of a critically ill patient filed a criminal complaint against a private duty nurse who was caring for the patient in his home.[76] The family claimed that the nurse had turned off the patient's respirator, causing his death. The prosecutor charged the nurse with assault and attempted murder. During the nine-day trial the jury watched a videotape in which the patient testified that he had watched the nurse pull the respirator out of his reach. He also testified that the nurse had stated, "You are going to die." On cross-examination the nurse revealed that she had a drinking problem that had resulted in her resigning or being fired from a number of hospitals and nursing homes over the past few years. The defense argued that there was no motive, that the case was based solely on the testimony of a very sick and confused man. They also suggested that in the confusion surrounding the incident one of the family members could have shut off the respirator. The prosecution did not want the jury to characterize the incident as a mercy killing and instead attempted to make the jury believe that the nurse had been drinking that night and had not been thinking clearly. The jury found the nurse not guilty. A juror who was questioned concerning the verdict stated that the jury was not entirely convinced by the nurse's testimony but that it had just as much difficulty believing the patient.[77]

Theft

Theft is the popular name for larceny, which is the taking of another's property unlawfully with the intention of depriving the owner of its use.[78] In some state penal statutes it includes swindling, embezzlement, obtaining property by false pretenses, and issuing bad checks.[79] Nurses can be prosecuted for stealing the patient's or the hospital's property. The suspicion that the nurse has stolen either the patient's or the hospital's property places the hospital manager in the position of having to obtain proof of the criminal act.

Detention and Search of Employees

The detention and search of hospital employees is a matter of state law, and observers suggest that it is important to seek expert legal advice in developing a uniform policy and procedure to be used whenever the problem arises.[80] Managers who act reasonably within the hospital's policies will minimize the risk of being sued by employees claiming that the search constituted an assault, false imprisonment, or a civil rights violation. For private employers, the following management behaviors, if not precluded by state law, have been considered reasonable:[81]

- Asking an employee to submit to a search only when there are reasonable grounds (e.g., a bulge in the pocket similar to the missing object) to suspect the person has committed a theft
- Warning employees that if they refuse the request for a search they will be subject to disciplinary action
- Posting or distributing notices that searches may be required periodically upon entering or leaving the facility as a means of preventing pilfering or other unlawful activity. The notice should warn employees that disciplinary action will be taken against employees who refuse to submit to a reasonable search.

Nurses employed by federal and state hospitals are protected by the federal and state constitutional guarantees and the federal and state laws that protect the individual from unreasonable searches by the government.

CONTROLLED SUBSTANCE DIVERSION IN HOSPITALS

Controlled Substances Act

The Comprehensive Drug Abuse Prevention and Control Act of 1970, which is commonly referred to as the Controlled Substances Act, replaced all of the preexisting federal laws dealing with narcotics, depressants, stimulants, and hallucinogens.[82] Since 1970, most states have enacted state substance control acts that regulate intrastate drug transactions in areas not controlled by the federal law.

Substances regulated by the Controlled Substances Act include narcotics, central nervous system stimulants, depressants, hallucinogenic drugs, and some tranquilizers. The act classifies drugs into five categories, referred to as schedules. Schedule I, which is the most strictly controlled, includes drugs that have no accepted medical use in the United States and are therefore rarely encountered by health care professionals.[83] Schedule V, the least controlled category, includes what were formally known as "exempt narcotics," such as codeine-containing cough syrups.[84] Controlled substances listed in schedules I through IV can only be dispensed on the lawful order of a practitioner. People authorized to prescribe or dispense controlled substances are required to register with the Drug Enforcement Administration of the Department of Justice. Hospitals are considered "institutional practitioners" under the Act, whereas state law determines which health care professionals have the right to prescribe and dispense controlled drugs. Regulations that implement the Act require practitioners to maintain complete an accurate record of all controlled substances received, administered, or otherwise disposed of. The regulations also require the keeping of accurate and complete inventory records and the taking of a physical inventory every two years. The Controlled Substances Act creates a closed system of distribution for legitimate handlers of controlled drugs. It was enacted for the purpose of reducing their widespread diversion from legitimate channels to the illicit market.[85] Violators of the Controlled Substances Act can be subjected to substantial criminal penalties, including fines and imprisonment. Practitioners who violate the Act lose their authority to possess, prescribe, or dispense controlled substances. Despite the enactment of comprehensive federal and state legislation, strict law enforcement efforts, and widespread public education, the illegal sale, use, and abuse of controlled drugs continue to permeate our society. A major problem for patients, hospitals, and health care professionals is the diversion of controlled substances from hospitals by health care personnel.

Incidence of Drug Diversion in Hospitals

A 1979 and a follow-up 1980 survey of hospitals with over 100 beds exposed the magnitude of the problem.[86] The 1979 study consisted of a small systematic random sample of 285 short-term hospitals, while the 1980 study surveyed 3,466 hospitals or virtually all U.S. hospitals with 100 or more beds. Statistics and projections were based on the 162 (57 percent) usable responses of the 1979 study and the 1,359 (39 percent) usable responses of the 1980 study. The researchers projected that 400,000 unit doses per year are diverted from hospitals with 100 beds or more and estimated that another 50,000 to 100,000 dosage units per year may be diverted from the over 3,000 U.S. hospitals with fewer than 100 beds. Taken together these statistics suggest that in U.S. hospitals one-half million dosage units of medication are diverted every year.

Drug Diversion by Nurses

In both the 1979 and 1980 surveys registered nurses were found to be involved in 70 percent of all reported incidents of controlled substance diversion from the hospitals.[87] Physicians were found to be responsible for 3 percent, whereas pharmacists and pharmacy technicians were responsible for 13 percent and 8 percent, respectively. Although nurses were most often implicated in the incidence of diversion, the total number of dosage units stolen by pharmacists and pharmacy technicians exceeded those taken by nurses. The 1980 study revealed that the pharmacists and pharmacy technicians diverted over 42,000 dosage units of controlled substances compared with the 34,000 units that were diverted by registered nurses and licensed practical nurses. The dosage unit per incident statistics revealed that pharmacists and pharmacy technicians diverted an average of 144 and 85 dosage units, respectively, per incident to the nurses' 10 dosage units per incident. The researchers suggested that the difference was due to the pharmacist and pharmacy technician having access to larger quantities of controlled substances than did the nurses. The statistics revealed that other diverters of controlled substances included unit clerks; housekeeping personnel; pharmaceutical sales representatives; patients; paramedics; and medical, pharmacy, and nursing students. In addition, in the 1980 survey, 11 percent of the reported incidents listed the diverters as "unknown." The drugs most often diverted by nurses include the following:[88]

- Meperidine (Demerol), 25.7 percent
- Diazepam (Valium), 18.9 percent
- Codeine products, 9.6 percent
- Flurazepam, 6.6 percent
- Morphine, 6.5 percent
- Propoxyphene products, 5 percent
- Pentazocine, 4 percent
- Barbiturates, 3 percent
- Cocaine, 1 percent

The study revealed that only a few select drug products are involved in the majority of diversions, with meperidine and diazepam accounting for almost one half of all hospital controlled substance diversions. Researchers suggest that the hospital institute control methods designed to ensure accountability of the more commonly diverted drugs.[89]

Drug-Impaired Nurse

Nurses are not immune to the stresses and conditions that result in drug misuse and abuse. The problem of the nurse impaired by drugs or alcohol has been the subject of much discussion. Some authors report that one nurse in seven is at risk,[90] whereas others indicate that the incidence of nurse chemical dependency is 50% higher than in the general population.[91] In an article on drug abuse by nurses, the author, a state board of nursing investigator, suggests that the profile of the nurse drug abuser is markedly different from that of the lay drug abuser.[92] A comparison of the characteristics of nurse drug abusers versus lay drug abusers reveals that nurses[93]

- Begin their abuse in adulthood rather than in adolescence
- Use drugs to escape pain or distress or to function in the face of pain and disease rather than for kicks
- Use drugs alone rather than in association with other people
- Obtain their drugs from physicians, hospitals, or through forged prescriptions and orders rather than through the lay addict's sources, which include the black market, shoplifting, and prostitution
- Have closer family ties than the lay addict

- Seek treatment voluntarily more often than lay addicts
- Have a higher cure from treatment than lay addicts
- Have little trouble with the law until they are apprehended for falsification of narcotics logs or for forging prescriptions, as opposed to lay addicts, who generally have frequent encounters with the law

The problem of the nurse drug abuser is significant. The early identification of a nurse who is suspected of using or diverting drugs is often hampered by the reluctance of employers and peers to report all but the most overt cases because they fear the adverse publicity or the possibility of being sued by the nurse for libel or slander. Unfortunately, the failure to identify and report the nurse drug abuser generally results in the continuation and increase of the nurse's addiction.[94] Failure to promptly identify the nurse drug abuser also increases and prolongs the risk to the patients' safety and welfare. Nurses who are practicing nursing while alcohol or drug impaired should be identified and reported to the appropriate agency. Nurses are liable to criminal prosecution under state criminal statutes that make it a felony to knowingly and unlawfully manufacture, cultivate, transport, possess, furnish, prescribe, administer, dispense, or compound a narcotic or dangerous drug.[95] In some states the judge can reduce the felony charge to a misdemeanor by taking into consideration the history and character of the defendant and the nature and circumstances of the crime.[96] Nurses whose drug conviction represents a first encounter with the law may be sentenced to probation. The most frequent legal proceeding involving alcohol- and drug-impaired nurses is an administrative hearing conducted by the state board of nursing for the purpose of determining whether there are grounds to suspend the nurse's license to practice nursing. There has been a significant increase in the number of disciplinary hearings conducted by state boards of nursing in relation to substance abuse by licensed nurses. Most state nurse practice acts list a variety of drugs that may be involved in a disciplinary proceeding. Some states include the use or abuse of any drug as grounds for discipline.[97] The nurse practice act in some states permits the state board to demand that the nurse submit to a medical and/or mental examination.[98] The statutes also specify that the nurse's refusal to submit to an examination that is ordered by the board constitutes immediate grounds for license suspension.[99] Some statutes provide for an automatic license suspension when a nurse is hospitalized for mental illness or substance abuse.[100] Most state boards of nursing have the power to suspend a nurse's license if they find that the nurse has violated the state's nurse practice act. The nurse has a right to due process and a fair hearing and in most states can obtain a judicial review of the board's final decision (see Chapter 10). In the following cases the board of nursing's decision to suspend the nurse's license was overturned by the court:[101]

- A charge of fraud for making a false statement in the hospital narcotics log was overturned because the nurse's entries were correct. She had recorded the right amount of medication in the log; however, she had given the patient a fraction of the dose and self-administered the remainder. If there was fraud, it would have been when she recorded the amount she had given the patient on the medication sheet and not in the log, which did accurately represent the amount taken from stock.[102]

- A charge of addiction was overturned because the evidence only supported a finding of occasional use rather than evidence of addiction, which the board was required to prove.[103]
- A charge of distribution was overturned because the nurse's actions in taking the drugs home did not support a finding of distribution.[104]
- A charge of drug misappropriation (taking drugs for one's own use) was overturned because the evidence only supported a finding that the nurse could not reasonably account for the wasted narcotics but did not prove she actually used them.[105]

As these cases demonstrate, the board of nursing must prove the specific offense with which the nurse is charged. In most jurisdictions, the board's order to suspend a nurse's license must include a statement of law, a specific reference to the section of the nurse practice act or regulations that the nurse has violated, and a statement of fact, which is a citing of the evidence on which it based its decision (see Chapter 10).

Nurse managers must consistently and lawfully confront the problem of an alcohol- or drug-impaired nurse practicing in the hospital. The nurse must be identified and disciplined according to the hospital policy and state law. The appropriate action taken discreetly and promptly will protect the patients from being injured by a drug-impaired nurse and lessen the hospital's risk of liability for corporate negligence in continuing to employ a nurse it knew or should have known was impaired. In addition, it will eliminate the nurse's drug source and remove him or her from practice. It may also encourage the nurse to admit the problem and seek medical assistance. Commentators suggest that nurses often seek treatment voluntarily because there is an incentive in having a profession that they may return to after they have been rehabilitated.[106]

REPORTING AND RECORDING STATUTES

The health and safety clauses of the U.S. Constitution and the state constitutions permit the government to exercise police power in protecting the safety and welfare of its citizens. As a result, the Congress and the state legislatures can determine that certain conditions pose such a serious threat to the public health or safety that they must be exposed despite the potential loss of individual privacy that may accompany such disclosures. In all jurisdictions there are a number of laws that require all persons, or those named in the statute, to report information to law enforcement or social service agencies. Areas most often made subject to reporting or recording requirements include (1) vital statistics, (2) newborn diseases, (3) communicable diseases, (4) child and elderly abuse, (5) suspicious deaths and injuries, and (6) criminal acts.

Vital Statistics

All states require the reporting of births and deaths. In addition, some states mandate the reporting of fetal deaths, abortions (within the guidelines provided by the United States Supreme Court in 1976),[107] and births to single (unwed) mothers.[108]

Diseases of the Newborn

In protecting the newborn's safety and welfare many states have enacted legislation that mandates the reporting and the treatment of certain diseases. The newborn diseases for which reporting and treatment are often required are ophthalmia neonatorum, an infectious disease that can cause blindness, and phenylketonuria, a congenital disease that can result in mental retardation. The basis for the state's authority to order treatment, in addition to the identification and reporting of these diseases, lies in its interest in maintaining the child's health and in the recognition of the need for prevention. In most states, the care and treatment of blind and mentally disabled children and adults is funded by public money. The statutes generally require the physician, midwife, nurse, or person attendant at the childbirth to make or cause to be made the standard tests and/or to institute the preventive treatment required by the health regulations. Some states recognize the parent's right to object to or refuse the testing and treatment of their newborn for phenylketonuria. Statutes may indicate that only a parent may object and only on religious grounds. In some states the statute will exempt a newborn from examination or testing for the discovery of preventable mental disorders if either parent files a written objection with the person or institution responsible for the examination or tests.[109]

Communicable Diseases

The reporting of communicable diseases is mandated by both federal and state law.

Federal Law

The Centers for Disease Control (CDC) were created by Congress under the Public Health Service (PHS) for the purpose of surveillance, data collection, and analysis.[110] The law requires all states and U.S. territories to report, on a weekly, monthly, and annual basis, the occurrence of certain diseases. Diseases which the statute indicates must be reported include gonorrhea, syphilis, chickenpox, hepatitis, tuberculosis, salmonellosis, shigellosis, rubeola (measles), mumps, aseptic meningitis, and acquired immunodeficiency syndrome (AIDS).

The U.S. Public Health Service has declared AIDS as its number one priority. It has published information in the *Facts about AIDS* and instituted a Public Health Services AIDS hotline (1-800-447-AIDS).[111] Issues that continue to generate controversy are the constitutionality of government-mandated screening and maintaining confidentiality in the reporting process.

State Law

In all jurisdictions the public health department is authorized to obtain and maintain reports on communicable diseases, determine the prevalence of each, and devise the means to control the spread of the disease.[112] State public health laws and regulations provide public health officials with specific powers in relation to communicable diseases, which include the right to investigate the disease, enter the premises and inspect the person, order a physical examination to be conducted on the person suspected of having the communicable disease, order tests such as blood analysis or chest x-ray films, confine and quarantine contagious individuals, and disinfect the property.[113]

State statutes generally indicate that physicians, hospitals, and laboratories are required to report the occurrence of certain communicable diseases to specific state health officials.[114] In most states the list of diseases that must be reported includes gonorrhea; viral hepatitis types A and B; meningococcal, streptococcal, and viral meningitis; meningococcemia; yellow fever; scarlet fever; chancroid; typhoid or nontyphoid salmonellosis; syphilis; and tuberculosis.[115] The reports generally include the patient's name, address, age, race, and sex and the identity of the disease. The legal mandate that this information be collected by the state overrides, to a certain extent, the patient's right to privacy. Statutes generally require that the information received by the health department remain confidential within the department.[116]

Child Abuse

The Child Abuse Prevention and Treatment Act provides funds for the identification, treatment, and prevention of child abuse.[117] States are eligible to receive the federal funds if they have enacted a child protection law that meets the federal requirements. All of the states and the District of Columbia have child protection legislation that is generally referred to as a child abuse law. These statutes require the reporting of suspected cases of child abuse and neglect to a law enforcement or social services agency. The statutes also[118]

- Define abuse, neglect, and abandonment
- Indicate who must report incidents of child abuse. Health care professionals and teachers are usually considered mandatory reporters, although the statutes often indicate that anyone may report.
- Identify the standard to be used, which in most cases is a person who has "reason to suspect" that a child is being abused
- Identify the nature and content of the report and the agency to which it is submitted
- Provide immunity from criminal or civil liability for anyone who in good faith (1) makes a report, (2) participates in the investigation, and (3) participates in the legal proceedings
- Abrogate all privileged communications except the attorney–client privilege. This permits spouses to testify against each other and also permits health care professionals to testify as to their patient or client
- Permit photographs, medical tests, and x-ray films (if medically indicated) to be taken without the parent's consent
- Determine the process that is to be followed by officials who are responsible for investigating the report
- Set penalties (usually misdemeanor) for violating the statute by failing to report as required

- Require the social service agency to report all serious cases of bodily injury to the attorney general's office for possible criminal prosecution
- Provide that court records of child abuse proceedings be kept separate from all other court records. The records are not open to public inspection but may be inspected by the parties, child, parent, guardian, custodian, attorney, or other authorized representative of the child.

A review of the case law has failed to reveal any case in which a nurse has been sued either for reporting or for failing to report a case of child abuse. In 1976, a physician was found liable for discharging an abused 11-month-old child from the emergency department without reporting the abuse and giving the state an opportunity to intervene.[119] The court also ruled that persons who are required to report and fail to do so could be held liable in a civil suit for future injuries to the child that could have been prevented by the report. In 1984, a physician's negligent breach of the child abuse reporting statute resulted in a jury awarding the child $186,851 in damages.[120]

Elderly Abuse

Elderly abuse statutes resemble child abuse statutes in that they require certain individuals to report suspected incidents of abuse and provide immunity for all persons who report in good faith. The nature of the legislative protection of the elderly varies depending on the state. Some states have enacted elderly abuse statutes, whereas others have enacted statutes that cover any adult involved in abusive situations or environments. *Elderly abuse* is a broad term that can include a variety of situations, including mistreatment, battering, physical violence, psychological abuse, denial of basic human needs, violation of civil rights, medical neglect, financial exploitation, misuse and abuse of drugs, unsanitary environment, and destruction of personal property or pets.[121]

Most states have enacted separate statutes to protect the rights of children and the elderly who are institutionalized. These statutes require individuals to report incidents of abuse or neglect in the institution to a state agency. The statute may contain a nonretaliatory clause. For example, N.H. R.S.A. 151:27 states that "A nursing home licensee or administrator shall not evict, harass, dismiss or retaliate against a patient, a patient's personal representative, or an employee who files a report under this section." In addition, the statute provides for the assessment of damages against a nursing home for all injuries proximately caused by the violation of the statute.

Domestic Violence

Many states have enacted domestic violence statutes to prevent and deter violence in the home. Domestic violence statutes attempt to preserve and protect the safety of the family unit for all family or household members by entitling victims of domestic violence to immediate and effective police protection and judicial relief.[122] The statutes generally cover spouses, parents, persons related by blood or affinity, and persons who cohabit with each other. Children are usually excluded because they are protected under the state's child abuse statute. Domestic violence statutes generally[123]

- Require police officers responding to a domestic disturbance to notify the victim of abuse of his or her right to file a petition in district court requesting a restraining order against the attacker and to sign a complaint at the police station
- Waive the fee for filing a petition and also waive the fee required to have the defendant notified of the restraining order (service of process)
- Allow the plaintiff to proceed *pro se*, which means the plaintiff can represent himself or herself and does not have to hire an attorney in order to file the petition
- Provide for the relocation of the plaintiff to a safe house and require that the new address of the plaintiff not be revealed except by court order. The files involving domestic violence proceedings are generally segregated from other files and closed to public inspection.

The filing of a domestic violence petition does not preclude the plaintiff from filing criminal and civil charges against the defendant. In some states the courts have permitted a battered spouse to join a tort action with a divorce proceeding.[124] In these cases the battered spouse would be able to receive compensatory and punitive damages in addition to the amount awarded for alimony or in a property settlement. Emergency department personnel should be familiar with their state's domestic violence law so that they can notify the victims of battery who are treated in the emergency department of their right to protection.

Suspicious Deaths and Injuries

All states require the reporting of suspicious deaths and injuries that are inflicted by lethal weapons or illegal acts. The statutes vary from state to state; however, in most states the attending physician is required to report to a medical examiner or coroner, any death from other than normal causes. These include

- Persons who are diagnosed as dead on arrival at the hospital
- Suicides
- Deaths resulting from violent acts
- Deaths from poisonings
- Deaths occurring in the course of a pregnancy
- Deaths occurring without prior medical care
- Deaths occurring within 24 hours of admission to a hospital when a diagnosis has not been made
- Deaths resulting from accidents

Federal regulations (C.F.R. § 606.170 [b]) require that all deaths due to blood transfusions be reported to the Food and Drug Administration. The report to the medical examiner or coroner indicates the person's name and the time, place, manner, circumstances, and suspected cause of death. The medical examiner or coroner conducts an investigation and issues a report. The report will generally indicate the actual cause of death and help determine whether there is a need for a criminal investigation.

Injuries Caused by Lethal Weapons

State ''gunshot wound'' laws require the reporting of all injuries, including self-inflicted injuries, that are caused by lethal weapons. In addition to firearms, the definition of a lethal weapon can include knives, icepicks, or any sharp-pointed tool or instrument.[125] In some states an automobile is considered a lethal weapon and injuries resulting from car accidents are reportable.[126]

Injuries Caused by Criminal Acts

State statutes require the reporting of injuries that are the result of unlawful or criminal acts. Criminal acts that usually result in reportable injuries include assaults, rapes, attempted suicides, unlawful dispensing or taking of drugs and controlled substances, drug overdoses, and suspected criminal abortions.[127] The laws also mandate the reporting of animal bites, as a precaution against rabies, and the reporting of all cases of food poisoning that are traceable to a commercial vendor in order to prevent further injury to the public.[128]

OBTAINING AND PRESERVING EVIDENCE

The admissibility of evidence in civil or criminal proceedings is dependent on its being able to pass a three-part test that asks if it was (1) lawfully obtained, (2) properly collected and preserved, and (3) if the chain of custody was maintained. All of these questions will be asked by the defense attorneys when they evaluate the evidence that was obtained while the person was hospitalized. It is an inquiry that focuses attention on the relationship between the police and the hospital.

Police and Hospital Relations

The most likely area for a confrontation between the police and hospital personnel is the emergency department. The first priority of the emergency department nurses and physicians is to provide competent treatment to the patient who is injured regardless of whether the person is a victim or an alleged perpetrator of a crime. Patients who receive medical care in the emergency department of a hospital have the same rights as other patients to consent or refuse to consent to all or part of the medical treatment. Patients who are under arrest are in the custody of the police and subject to the officer's legal authority to search and detain them. Police officers have a legal obligation to accompany victims of crimes or criminal suspects who are in need of medical care to the emergency department. They are also required to continue their investigation into the crime by interrogating parties or witnesses and by collecting evidence. Their investigation must be conducted in accordance with the state rules of criminal procedure and the state and federal constitutional requirements. Hospital personnel and law enforcement officers are

314 Te Nrse Mnaer ad te Lw

bound by the legal and ethical requirements of their respective professions and can become involved in litigation if they fail to meet their legal responsibilities. Nurses and physicians can be held liable for assault and battery if they treat a patient without his or her consent and for civil rights violations if they act under "color of law" and perform nonconsensual procedures at the request of the police. Commentators suggest that the risk of liability for civil rights violations is minimal because no cases have been reported in which a hospital or hospital personnel were held liable for acting under police orders.[129] They also suggest that if liability were found, the fact that the personnel were acting under police direction would preclude a finding of intentional wrongdoing on the part of the practitioner or institution and point out that several courts have recognized a good faith defense to civil rights violations that were unintentional.[130] Finally they argue that

> Medical personnel are entitled to rely on the police officer's determination of how far his or her legal authority extends and need not conduct their own inquiry or analysis. Upon this reasoning, recovery against medical personnel, if any, would likely be limited to nominal damages unless the procedure is patently unreasonable or unless the subject were physically harmed because the procedure had been performed negligently.[131]

A hospital does not generally have any legal obligation to assist police officers in their investigation; however, it cannot take any action that might be considered an obstruction of justice. Hospital personnel could be charged with obstruction of justice if they attempt to prevent, or prevent the execution of, the legal process. Conduct that is considered as an obstruction of justice includes stifling, suppressing, or destroying evidence that a person knows is being sought by law enforcement officers or is needed in judicial proceedings.[132]

Police officers can incur legal liability for false arrest if they detain a person without probable cause. If they have probable cause to arrest a person, they can be sued for assault and battery if they use unreasonable force in effecting the arrest. Law enforcement officers can be charged with civil rights violations if their investigative techniques are found to have been unconstitutional. Evidence obtained as a result of unconstitutional interrogations or searches would most likely be ruled inadmissable by the court under the exclusionary rule.

The hospital has a responsibility to develop policies that guide the professional personnel in maintaining an appropriate relationship with the police. Emergency department nurses and physicians are skilled in making nursing and medical decisions concerning their patients. The decision to assist or refuse to assist the police is not a clinical decision, and it should not have to be made individually, by each practitioner, every time the problem arises. The extent to which health care professionals should cooperate with the police is an administrative decision that should be made by the practitioners according to clearly defined administrative guidelines that reflect the state's criminal and constitutional law. The guidelines should identify:

- The scope of the police officer's responsibility within the institution
- The areas in which the hospital will provide assistance
- The right of individual practitioners to refuse the request for assistance
- The appropriate response when the patient is under arrest
- The appropriate response when the patient is not under arrest
- The professionals who are authorized to perform nonconsensual tests and their potential involvement as witnesses in legal proceedings
- The procedures for collecting and preserving the evidence
- The procedures for maintaining the chain of custody
- The mechanism for getting prompt legal advice from the hospital legal counsel as to how to proceed in unusual cases

The tension in hospital and police relations is created by the existence of a number of conflicting responsibilities. Law enforcement officers are sworn to uphold the law and to protect the public by investigating crimes and arresting people who commit crimes. Hospitals and the health care professionals have a legal and ethical duty to promote and protect the rights of their patients. There are also public policy considerations, in which the state's reponsibility to protect the safety and welfare of the people by discovering and apprehending persons suspected of engaging in criminal acts would impose a general obligation on all citizens and corporations to cooperate with the police in their lawful investigation of crime.

Lawful Searches and Seizures

The constitutional issues and court decisions surrounding the interrogation and searches of patients by police and hospital personnel are discussed in Chapter 5. The general principles of patient searches by hospital personnel are listed below:

- Hospitals may be held liable for violating the civil rights of patients if they search for evidence at the request or order of the police. Searches performed for the benefit of the police could lead the court to find that the health care personnel were agents of the police and that the search constituted state action that was subject to constitutional limitations.
- Hospitals may not be held liable for violating the civil rights of patients if there is no concerted action between the police and the health care employee. For example, a court upheld the admission into evidence of a shirt that had been taken by a nurse for safekeeping and subsequently turned over to the police, without their requesting it.[133] It found there was no government intrusion and therefore no constitutional violation. A court has also upheld the admissibility of evidence found during a routine search of an unconscious patient's pockets, finding that the search was proper because of the need to obtain identification and medical information.[134]

Hospital policy should clearly define the nurse's responsibility for searching patients and for the disposition of evidence that is found as a result of a search. Unless precluded by state law the general guidelines for searches provide that

- The police can search a person who consents to a search.
- The police can search a person and the immediate environment of a person who has been arrested (search incident to arrest).
- The police can seize evidence that is in plain view.
- The nurse can search an unconscious or otherwise unresponsive patient for identification and/or for medical reasons and can make an inventory of the patient's belongings and place them in the temporary custody of the hospital.
- The nurse can search a patient who is suspected of being in possession of a substance or object that could potentially harm the patient or others. It is prudent for nurses to seek the assistance of staff trained in dealing with threats of violence (hospital security) before requesting patients to turn over any weapons in their possession.
- Hospital policy determines whether a nurse can assist the police in searching a patient who is under arrest. This type of assistance will significantly affect the nurse–patient relationship and should be avoided except in extreme circumstances.

Disposing of Evidence Obtained in a Search

How nurses dispose of substances and objects that are found on patients depends on a number of variables. Objects such as guns and knives that they have reason to believe were used in the commission of a crime can usually be turned over to the police. If there is no reason to believe that the objects have criminal significance (hunting accidents, injuries to a person who is licensed or legally authorized to carry firearms), then the objects should be removed and kept in the hospital's custody until they can be returned to the patient or family. The disposition of suspected illegal substances is a matter of state law. In some states it is not a crime to possess otherwise illegal substances unless the amount exceeds a certain statutory limit.[135] State law also determines whether the amount possessed is a felony or misdemeanor.[136] Some states have a mandatory reporting law if a citizen witnesses a felony, but no reporting is required, if the offense is a misdemeanor. The nurses' actions concerning the seizure and disposition of these substances should be determined by seeking the opinion of the hospital's legal counsel. A nurse's reasonable suspicion that a patient may take the drugs or substances in his or her possession in conjunction with the medication that is being prescribed would probably justify the nurse's removing and taking temporary custody of the substance. All articles that are removed from patients should be considered the patient's property and be properly identified and inventoried. Hospitals should retain a record of all articles that are turned over to the police. The receipt should indicate the date and time, the patient's name, a description of the article, the name and badge number of the police officer receiving the article, and the name and title of the person releasing it from the hospital.

Collecting and Preserving Evidence

Evidence is defined as any article, object, medical photograph, statement, visual or olfactory observation which may assist in the solution of a crime.[137] It includes clothing, objects in an unusual state, aspects of physical injury, x-ray films, blood or other body fluids, observation of odors on or about the patient, statements made by the patient, and the emotional condition of the patient.[138] The guiding principle of all procedures to collect and preserve evidence is that it should be done in a manner that maintains the evidence in as close to its original condition as possible. The procedures to achieve this are developed by forensic experts. Health care professionals need to be properly instructed on the purpose and methods of evidence collection and preservation. The general principles underlying the preservation of the condition of the evidence include the following:[139]

- Limiting the number of people who handle objects to diminish the chances of destroying evidence such as fingerprints.
- Requiring the documentation of any procedure or occurrence that alters the original condition of the evidence. The report should indicate who altered the condition, how it was altered, and the reason why it was altered.
- Establishing specific procedures for the removing and handling of clothing worn by victims of assault (e.g., avoid cutting through bullet holes or stab tears; avoid shaking the garment; and place it in a clean paper bag to preserve any substances that may have adhered to it).
- Developing procedures for marking, packaging, and labeling evidence such as bullets that are surgically removed from patients. Every medical and legal person that handles the object must be identified.

There is also the need to distinguish between evidence obtained for legal purposes and evidence that is considered part of the patient's medical treatment, such as laboratory tests. These reports should only be released with proper authorization in accordance with the hospital's medical record release policies.

Obtaining Evidence of Driving While Under the Influence of Alcohol

The liability of hospital personnel for performing blood alcohol tests on persons suspected of driving while under the influence of alcohol (DWI) is entirely a matter of state law. The majority of states have enacted implied consent statutes that provide that by operating a motor vehicle an operator gives his or her consent to submit to a breath or blood test to determine whether he or she was intoxicated while driving. It has been suggested that law enforcement personnel tend to adopt a liberal interpretation of the statutory language concerning hospital assistance to the police.[140] The absence of a clear administrative directive as to how to respond to the police requests for testing can result in a major confrontation between the police officers and the health care professionals. Police, who are aware that the traces of alcohol in the blood sample dissipate rapidly, may resort to threatening hospital personnel with a charge of obstruction of justice.[141] These scenes can be avoided by a clear hospital policy that reflects the provisions of state law. The state's DWI statute may indicate that[142]

- The implied consent is only valid if the person is under arrest.
- A person may refuse to be tested. In most states, refusing the breath or blood test results in an automatic loss of license for a specific period of time.

THE NURSE MANAGER AND THE LAW

318

- Only certain health care professionals are authorized to draw blood samples for DWI. The statutes usually include physicians, laboratory technicians, and nurses.
- The person drawing the sample will have to testify in court or the statute may state that the court will accept an affidavit and not require the person drawing the sample to testify in court.
- The person who draws the blood sample is immune from civil or criminal liability as long as the test is done in a reasonable manner in a hospital, or medical clinic environment, according to accepted medical practice and without violence.

In addition, the statutes generally exempt from testing, under the implied consent provision, persons who are suffering from blood disorders or who are taking certain medications. The law may also indicate that a person who is dead or unconscious is deemed to have consented to the testing.[143] The statutes may also contain uniform standards for the drawing, handling, and preserving blood samples for analysis and may indicate the method of transferring them to an approved testing facility.

Hospital policy should address all of these issues. Because the drawing of blood samples in DWI cases is a procedure in which time is of the essence, it is suggested that the hospital develop a form to document the officer's request, the circumstances for which the test is requested, and the patient's consent to the test.[144] If the person refuses to consent (withdraws implied consent), the police officer should be notified so that the procedure that is required to activate the law's automatic penalty provisions can be instituted. There is also a need to develop a separate policy to address the action that is to be taken when a blood sample is obtained for the purpose of providing treatment. The patient's consent to a blood analysis for the purpose of diagnosis and treatment does not necessarily mean that he or she consents to having the results of the analysis revealed to the police.

Maintaining the Chain of Custody

Maintaining the chain of custody (chain of possession) is a legal procedure that ensures that the evidence is always accounted for and always under the control of a specific person. The state must be able to prove that the evidence introduced during a criminal trial is in its original state and that it has not been switched, altered, or tampered with in any way. There must be a record that identifies every person who had custody of the evidence from the time it was collected until its admission at trial. The responsibility of hospitals to collect and preserve evidence encompasses the need to maintain the chain of custody. The hospital should

- Have locked and secure places for the storage of evidence
- Specify how the various types of evidence will be routed and stored in the hospital
- Provide only a limited number of personnel with the authority to obtain, transport, and release evidence
- Develop a protocol that requires a signature every time a person handles, receives, or releases the evidence.

- Designate the administrative person who is authorized to release evidence to the police.

This chapter has concentrated on the admission of evidence in criminal trials; however, the need to collect and preserve evidence for admission in civil proceedings is of equal importance and failure to do so can have significant consequences for the plaintiff. For example, in an action against a nightgown manufacturer for injuries sustained when an 11-year-old girl's nightgown caught fire as she attempted to escape a house fire, the federal court found that there was insufficient evidence to identify the manufacturer of the nightgown. The court stated that the child's nightgown was either totally destroyed in the fire or it had been thrown away at the hospital.[145]

Attorneys have a legal and ethical obligation to question the authenticity, accuracy, and reliability of the evidence that is used against their clients in criminal or civil proceedings. The discovery of any improprieties, inaccuracies, or uncertainties requires them to file a motion to have the evidence excluded by the court. If the motion is denied by the judge, and the evidence is admitted over the attorney's objection, the admission of the evidence at trial becomes an issue for appeal.

NOTES

1. Charles Rembar, *The Law of the Land* (New York: Simon and Schuster, 1980), 152.

2. *Black's Law Dictionary*, 4th ed. (St. Paul, Minn.: West Publishing Co., 1968), 444.

3. Chester S. Weinerman, *Practical Law, A Layperson's Handbook* (Englewood Cliffs, N.J.: Prentice-Hall, 1978), 194.

4. Ibid., 195.

5. William T. Schantz, *The American Legal Environment* (St. Paul, Minn.: West Publishing Co., 1976), 466–467.

6. Ibid., 468.

7. Ibid.

8. Ibid.

9. Ibid.

10. Ibid., 447–466.

11. Weinerman, *Practical Law*, 198.

12. Cynthia E. Northrop and Mary E. Kelly, *Legal Issues in Nursing* (St. Louis: C.V. Mosby Co., 1987), 394.

13. New Hampshire Superior Court Rule 101.

14. Schantz, *American Legal Environment*, 294.

15. Ibid.

16. Ibid., 297.

17. William L. Prosser, *The Law of Torts*, 4th ed. (St. Paul, Minn.: West Publishing Co., 1971), 134.

18. *United States v. Newton*, 510 F.2d 1149 (1975).

19. *United States v. Borchardt*, 809 F.2d 1115 (1987).

20. N.H. R.S.A. 597:6-a

21. *Beck v. Ohio*, 379 U.S. 89 (1964).

22. Steven H. Gifis, *Law Dictionary* (Woodbury, N.Y.: Barron's Educational Series Inc., 1975), 153.

23. Weinerman, *Practical Law*, 215.

24. Ibid.

25. *Santobello v. New York*, 404 U.S. 257 (1971).

26. Ibid., 260–261.

27. Weinerman, *Practical Law*, 214.

28. Ibid.

29. *Clewis v. Texas*, 386 U.S. 707, 712 (1967).

30. N.H. Superior Court Rule 99.

31. *Brady v. Maryland*, 373 U.S. 83 (1963).

32. N.H. Superior Court Rule 99.

33. N.H. Superior Court Rule 100 (reciprocal discovery).

34. N.H. Superior Court Rule 101.

35. N.H. Superior Court Rule 102.

36. Weinerman, *Practical Law*, 230.

37. N.H. R.S.A. 651:37.

38. Ann M. Rhodes and Robert D. Miller, *Nursing and the Law* (Rockville, Md.: Aspen Publishers, Inc., 1984), 245.

39. Loy Wiley, "Liability for Death: Nine Nurses' Legal Ordeals," *Nursing '81* 11, no. 9 (September 1981):34–43.

40. *Black's Law Dictionary*, 867.

41. Ibid., 1170.

42. Ibid., 1116.

43. *Craig v. State*, 155 A.2d 684 (Md. 1984).

44. *Black's Law Dictionary*, 1116.

45. Ibid., 654.

46. Helen Creighton, *Law Every Nurse Should Know* (Philadelphia: W.B. Saunders Co., 1981), 239.

47. *People v. Film Recovery System*, Cook County Ill. Cir. Ct., June 14, 1985.

48. Wiley, "Liability for Death," 41.

49. *United States v. Narcisco*, 446 F. Supp. 252 (E.D. Mich. 1977) and see Wiley, "Liability for Death," 34–43, for a discussion of the investigation's irregularities and biases.

50. Wiley, "Liability for Death," 37.

51. Ibid., 34.

52. Northrop and Kelly, *Legal Issues in Nursing*, 398.

53. Wiley, "Liability for Death," 36.

54. Ibid.

55. Northrop and Kelly, *Legal Issues in Nursing*, 398.

56. Ibid.

57. Wiley, "Liability for Death," 37.

58. Wiley, "Liability for Death," 42; see also Northrop and Kelly, *Legal Issues in Nursing*, 386.

59. *Jones v. State*, 716 S.W.2d 142 (Tex. App. 1986).

60. *State of New Jersey v. Winter*, N.J. Super. Ct. A-35, decided July 2, 1984.

61. Wiley, "Liability for Death," 37.

62. Wiley, "Liability for Death," 40.

63. *Bartling v. Superior Court*, 209 Cal. Rptr. 220 (Cal. App. 1984).

64. *Barber v. Superior Court*, 195 Cal. Rptr. 484 (Cal. App. 1983).

65. *Sermchief v. Gonzales*, 660 S.W.2d 683 (Mo. en banc 1983).

66. *Bowland v. Municipal Court for Santa Cruz Cty.*, 556 P.2d 1081 (Cal. en banc 1977).

67. *Black's Law Dictionary*, 788.

68. *Estate of Leach v. Shapiro*, 469 N.E.2d 10 (Ohio App. 1984).

69. *The People v. Smithtown General Hospital, et al.*, 402 N.Y.S. 2d (1978).

70. 42 U.S.C. §§ 1128 A, 1128 (c); Social Security Act §§ 1320a-7a, 1320a-7 (c).

71. "Medicare Fraud: Tracking the CMP Law," *Civil Money Penalties Reporter 1*, no. 1 (November 1986):1.

72. Gifis, *Law Dictionary*, 16.

73. Ibid., 21.

74. Ibid., 16.

75. Ibid.

76. *Commonwealth v. Knowlton*, No. 84-7322 (Mass. 1984), reported in the *National Law Journal*, October 29, 1984, p. 13.

77. Ibid.

78. Gifis, *Law Dictionary*, 116.

79. N.Y. Penal Law §§ 155.05 (McKinney 1980).

80. Karen Hawley Henry, *The Health Care Supervisor's Legal Guide* (Rockville, Md.: Aspen Publishers, Inc., 1984), 268.

81. Ibid., 269.

82. Pub. L. No. 91-601; 84 Stat. 1236 (codified as amended in scattered sections of U.S.C. §§ 7, 15, and 21).

83. Creighton, *Law Every Nurse Should Know*, 250.

84. Ibid.

85. Ibid., 251.

86. William C. McCormick, Ronald C. Hoover, and Joseph B. Murphy, "Controlled Substance Diversion from U.S. Hospitals," *Registrant FACTS*, U.S. Department of Justice, Drug Enforcement Administration, Vol. 10, no. 1 (1985):1–5.

87. Ibid., 2.

88. Ibid., 3–4.

89. Ibid., 5.

90. Melinda Beck and Jerry Buckley, "Taking Drugs on the Job: Nurses with Bad Habits," *Newsweek* (August 22, 1983):54.

91. Kapp, "Chemical Dependency, Helping Your Staff," *Journal of Nursing Administration* 14 (November 1984):18.

92. McCormick et al., *Registrant FACTS*, 8 (Guest Article, Teri Hutson Salane, "The Nurse Drug Abuser").

93. Ibid.

94. Ibid.

95. Schantz, *American Legal Environment*, 464–465.

96. Ibid.

97. N.C. Gen. Stat. §§ 90–171.37 (3) (1985).

98. S.D. Codified Laws Ann. §§ 36-9-49 (Supp. 1984).

99. Ibid.

100. R.I. Gen. Laws. §§ 5-34-26 (Supp. 1985).

101. Northrop and Kelly, *Legal Issues in Nursing*, 413–414; describes 19 cases in which the denial, revocation, suspension, or reprimand decisions of the board of nursing were upheld by the appellate courts and 14 cases in which the nursing board's decisions were overturned.

102. *Application of Sutton*, 207 N.Y.S. 2d 550 (1960).

103. *Carruthers v. Allen*, 239 N.Y.S. 2d 756 (1963).

104. *Garrison v. Washington State Nursing Board*, 550 P.2d 7 (Wash. 1976).

105. *Hogan v. Mississippi Board of Nursing*, 457 So. 2d 931 (Miss. 1984).

106. McCormick et al., *Registrant FACTS*, 8.

107. *Planned Parenthood of Central Missouri v. Danforth*, 428 U.S. 52 (1976).

108. N.D. Cent. Code §§ 50-20-03.

109. Nev. Rev. Stat. §§ 422:115.

110. 42 U.S.C. §§ 236, 289a-4, 247d, 4362a (1982) (Centers for Disease Control).

111. Public Health Service, U.S. Department of Health and Human Services, *Facts About Aids* (August 1985); see also "AIDS: Precautions for Health Care Workers and Allied Professionals," *Morbidity and Mortality Weekly Report* 32 (1983):450.

112. MD. HEALTH-GEN. CODE ANN. §§ 18-103 (1982).

113. MD. HEALTH-GEN. CODE ANN. §§ 18-102 (2) (b) (1982).

114. MD. HEALTH-GEN. CODE ANN. §§ 18-201, 202, 205 (1982).

115. MD. HEALTH-GEN. CODE ANN. §§ 18-205 (1982).

116. MD. HEALTH-GEN. CODE ANN. §§ 18-205 (e) (f) (h); §§ 18-322 (b) (1982).

117. 42 U.S.C. §§ 5103 (b) (2) (1982).

118. N.H. R.S.A. 169-C:2 (1979) (Child Protection Act).

119. *Landeros v. Flood*, 551 P.2d 389 (Cal. 1976).

120. *O'Keefe v. Osario*, Ill. 27 ATLA. L. Rep. 39 (Nov. 1984).

121. Marshall B. Kapp and Arthur Bigot, *Geriatrics and the Law* (New York: Springer Publishing Co., 1985), 6.

122. N.H. R.S.A. 173-B (1981).

123. Ibid.

124. *Trevis v. Trevis*, 155 N.J. Super. 23 (1978), *reversed*, 79 N.J. 422 (1979); *Merenoff v. Merenoff*, 76 N.J. 535 (1978).

125. N.Y. Penal Law §§ 265.25 (McKinney 1980).

126. Marguerite R. Mancini and Alice T. Gale, *Emergency Care and the Law* (Rockville, Md.: Aspen Publishers, Inc., 1981), 160.

127. Ibid.

128. Ibid.

129. Arnold Rosoff, *Informed Consent* (Rockville, Md.: Aspen Publishers, Inc., 1981), 20.

130. Ibid.

131. Ibid.

132. *Black's Law Dictionary*, 1228.

133. *State v. Perea*, 95 N.M. 777 (1981) App.).

134. *United States v. Winbush*, 428 F. 2d 357 (6th Cir. 1970).

135. Kathleen Driscoll, "Search and Seizure in the Emergency Department," *Journal of Emergency Nursing* 12, no. 2 (March/April 1986):77.

136. Schantz, *The American Legal Environment*, 463, citing the Oregon Criminal Code, Or. Rev. Stat. Ann. 161.600 (1971).

137. Howard S. Rowland and Beatrice L. Rowland, eds. *Hospital Legal Forms, Checklists and Guidelines*, Vol. I (Rockville, Md.: Aspen Publishers, Inc., 1987), 25:4.

138. Ibid.

139. Ibid.

140. Ibid., 25:9.

141. Ibid.

142. Cal. Vehicle Code § 23158 (West Supp. 1986).

143. N.H. R.S.A. 265:91 (1982).

144. Rowland and Rowland, *Hospital Legal Forms*, 25:10.

145. *Brown v. Stone Mfg. Co.*, 660 F. Supp. 454 (S.D. Miss. 1986).

Appendix V

Implications for Nurse Managers

Part V has examined the involvement of health care professionals in the area of criminal law. The criminal law exposes the individual to the legitimate, yet ominous, police power of the state. A criminal investigation and indictment can significantly compromise a person's professional reputation, and a criminal conviction can result in a loss of personal freedom. The spectacle of a nurse accused of murdering a patient makes for sensational headlines in which the nurse is characterized as an angel of death or an angel of mercy. The dismissal of the charge for lack of evidence does not generate the same amount of public exposure or public interest. The emotional, professional, and economic injury to a nurse who must face the criminal process and the press is significant and enduring. In addition, a highly publicized murder trial makes the public aware of the potential danger that nurses, intent on committing criminal acts, could inflict on the public. These situations generate suspicion and distrust of the nursing profession.

Nurse managers who understand the criminal law are better prepared to function effectively within the requirements of the criminal process. The attitudes and behaviors of nurses involved in the criminal process frequently reflect an uncertainty and ambivalence that is due to the existence of overlapping or conflicting responsibilities. There is the expectation that the nurse manager will (1) avoid unnecessary and/or premature charges and investigations of nurses; (2) preserve the rights of the patients; (3) protect the patients' safety and welfare; and (4) if appropriate, cooperate with the police in the investigation of the crime.

This chapter has examined seven areas in which the nurse manager is involved in the criminal law: (1) the nurse as a suspect, (2) the patient as a suspect, (3) the patient as a victim, (4) the patient whose medical condition is subject to a reporting statute, (5) the nurse whose behavior is subject to a licensing statute, (6) the authority of the police within the institution, and (7) the state reporting and recording requirements. The following describes the specific knowledge, attitudes, and behaviors that will assist nurse managers to recognize and assume their responsibilities.

- The substance of criminal law is for the most part defined by the state.
- The federal and state constitutions and the federal and state courts define criminal procedure.

- The federal and state constitutions guarantee specific rights to the accused during the investigation of a crime.
- The nurse manager must investigate reports of suspected nurse criminal conduct promptly, discreetly, methodically, and fairly.
- The investigation must be aimed at uncovering the facts and at discouraging rumor, innuendo, and unsupported accusations.
- The nurse manager must notify administration of the problem promptly, discreetly, and accurately.
- The evidence must be obtained lawfully and carefully collected, preserved, and transferred in accordance with hospital procedures.
- The nurse manager must promote a relationship with the law enforcement officials that recognizes the rights of the police and of the patient or nurse suspect.
- The nurse manager must implement hospital policies that promote and preserve the rights of the patient who is a victim of a crime.
- The nurse manager must ensure that nurses follow the hospital procedures that are mandated by state reporting and recording laws.
- The nurse and nurse manager who are involved in the criminal process as suspects should promptly seek legal representation.

The area of criminal law is perhaps the most unfamiliar and the most hazardous for nurse managers. All hospital managers need an understanding of criminal law and the guidance of specific hospital policies, procedures, and protocols that incorporate the law. Clear and precise directives will enable them to act promptly and appropriately and to avoid decisions that could compromise the hospital, the nurse, the patient, and the police.

****

LEGAL RESOURCES

LEGISLATION

U.S. Constitution
Comprehensive Drug Abuse and Prevention Act of 1970, 84 Stat. 1236
Civil Money Penalties Law, 42 U.S.C. §§ 1320 (Medicare fraud)
State constitution
State criminal code
State motor vehicle statute (DWI provisions)
State substance abuse act
State child protection act
State elderly abuse act
State domestic violence act

State disease reporting and recording statutes
State death and injury reporting statutes

FEDERAL AND STATE COURTS

U.S. Supreme Court
U.S. Court of Appeals
U.S. District Court
State supreme court
State appellate court
State criminal trial courts

PEOPLE AND AGENCIES

Hospital administrator and hospital managers
Hospital risk management personnel
Hospital security personnel
Hospital pharmacy personnel
State board of nursing
State board of medicine
State board of pharmacy
U.S. attorney (federal crimes)
State attorney general
Local law enforcement agency
State and local medical examiner
State forensic laboratory
State medical testing facilities

NURSE MANAGER'S BOOKSHELF

State nurse practice act
State board of nursing rules, regulations, opinions, and decisions
Hospital policy and procedure manuals
ICU/CCU policies for removal of life-support mechanisms
Emergency department policies on police/hospital relations
Emergency department policies for evidence collection and preservation
Joint Commission on Accreditation of Healthcare Organizations Standards for Emergency Department
Hospital pharmacy controlled substances policies and regulations
Hospital policies for obtaining assistance of security personnel

Guides and Manuals

Blanchet Kevin D., ed. *AIDS: A Health Care Management Response.* Rockville, Md.: Aspen Publishers, Inc., 1987.

Henry, Karen Hawley, ed. *Nursing Administration and Law Manual*. Rockville, Md.: Aspen Publishers, Inc., 1987.

Kander, Mark K. and Russell, Robert F., eds. Director of Nursing Manual, *Federal Regulations and Guidelines*. Owing Mills, Md.: National Health Publishing, 1984.

Lewis, Angie, ed. *Nursing Care of the Person with AIDS/ARC*. Rockville, Md.: Aspen Publishers, Inc., 1988.

Roach, William H., Chernoff, Susan N., and Esley, Carole Lange. *Medical Records and the Law*. Rockville, Md.: Aspen Publishers, Inc., 1987.

Rosoff, Arnold J. *Informed Consent, A Guide for Health Care Providers*. Rockville, Md.: Aspen Publishers, Inc., 1981.

Rowland, Howard S. and Rowland, Beatrice L., eds. *Nursing Administration Handbook*. Rockville, Md.: Aspen Publishers, Inc., 1987.

Rowland, Howard S. and Rowland, Beatrice L., eds. *Nursing Forms Manual*. Rockville, Md.: Aspen Publishers, Inc., 1985 (police/hospital relations and evidence).

Legal Skills: Participating in the Legal Process

I am not trying to reveal to the layperson the unique world of lawyers and judges. I am trying to tell lawyers, judges and laypersons alike that they live and work in the same world—that is what too many of us do not understand.

Lief H. Carter, *Reason in Law*, 1979:5

* * * * *

The basic legal skills and information that nurse managers need in order to participate intelligently and effectively in the legal process are described in this chapter.

Skill 1 Finding and Interpreting a Statute
Skill 2 Finding and Interpreting a Case
Skill 3 Understanding the Civil Trial Process
Skill 4 Participating in Discovery
Skill 5 Testifying As a Witness
Skill 6 Retaining an Attorney
Skill 7 Understanding the Legislative Process
Skill 8 Lobbying

Chapter **18**

Legal Skills: Participating in the Legal Process

SKILL 1: FINDING AND INTERPRETING A STATUTE

FINDING A STATUTE

In order to locate a specific state or federal statute it is necessary to have a complete citation. For example, the appropriate citations for the federal Administrative Procedure Act and for Vermont's Nurse Practice Act are shown in Figure 18-1. A complete citation includes the following:

- Name of the statute (e.g., Nurse Practice Act).
- Volume number or title number that indicates the subject classification within the legal reference. Federal law is organized into 50 titles.
- Abbreviation of the legal reference that contains the federal or state law.
- Numbers following the legal reference abbreviation that indicate the chapter and/or the section (§) in the reference volume where the law is located.

INTERPRETING STATUTORY REFERENCE ABBREVIATIONS

Finding a statute requires the ability to interpret the abbreviation of the legal publication in which the statute is found. The following lists frequently cited legal publications.

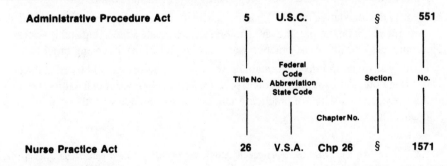

Figure 18-1 Statute Citation

Federal Statutes

L.W.   *United States Law Week*: recently enacted statutes
Stat.   *United States Statutes at Large*: a chronological list of all statutes enacted
          during a single legislative session
U.S.C.   *United States Code*: all federal statutes*
U.S.C.A. *United States Code Annotated*
U.S.C.S. *United States Code Service**

Federal Regulations

C.F.R.   *Code of Federal Regulations*: federal regulations arranged by title.
F.R.   *Federal Register*: published daily and updates the C.F.R.

State Statutes

State statutes are published in official state sets using the standard state abbreviation (e.g., UTAH CODE ANN., KAN. STAT. ANN., N.H. REV. STAT. ANN.).

State Regulations

State regulations are published in official state sets using the standard state abbreviation (e.g., MASS. REGS. CODE).

READING A STATUTE

A law should be read in the context of the words and phrases, in the context of the total statutory scheme, and in the context of the times in which it was written. The reader should

- Identify the legislative purpose. What end did the legislature want to accomplish by enacting the law? For example, the child abuse statutes are enacted to protect children and nurse practice acts are enacted to protect the public.
- Identify the legislative intent. What means did the legislature employ to accomplish its purpose? For example, the child abuse statutes create a reporting and investigating process and the nurse practice acts create a mandatory licensing process.
- Identify any exemptions to the statute. The exemptions are usually listed at the end of the statute. For example, medical practice acts exclude from mandatory medical licensure, nurses who are practicing nursing in accordance with the state's nurse practice act.

---

*U.S.C., U.S.C.A., and U.S.C.S. represent three different publishers. Each publication contains the federal statutes arranged by title.

Basic Principles of Statutory Construction

According to the basic principles of statutory construction a person reading a statute can assume that

- The statute has a single true meaning.
- The preamble to the statute is not law unless the statute indicates that it is.
- The statute should be read literally with the words given their common ordinary meaning.
- The statute distinguishes words of permission and mandatory words. In general the word ''shall'' is considered mandatory and the word ''may'' is considered permissive.
- The statute is complete. If something is not expressly mentioned, it should be assumed that the legislature did not want it included.
- The statute sections are consistent. One part of the statute should not contradict any other part of the statute.
- The statute is consistent with the constitution, with other statutes, and with the common law.

JUDICIAL INTERPRETATION

In enacting legislation, the legislature is attempting to formulate rules that will govern future situations. Ambiguity in a statute may occur as a result of legislative compromise, careless draftsmanship, or the legislature's inability to anticipate all of the circumstances in which the statute may be applied. If a statute has ambiguous sections it is the responsibility of the court to interpret the meaning. The judicial interpretation of a statute can include

- A literal reading and interpretation of the words and phrases of the statute.
- A review of the context in which the disputed word or clause occurs. The court will look at the overall structure of the statute, the name, the titles and subheadings, and the relationship of the disputed word or clause to other clauses.
- A search for evidence of legislative intent. The court will examine the act's legislative history, which includes the records of the legislative debates and hearings and all relevant documents.

SKILL 2: FINDING AND INTERPRETING A CASE

FINDING A CASE

In order to locate a specific federal or state case it is necessary to have a citation. The appropriate citation for a state and a federal court decision is shown in Figure 18-2.

A citation includes the (1) names of the parties, (2) volume number, (3) reporter abbreviation, (4) page number, and (5) date on which the case was decided.

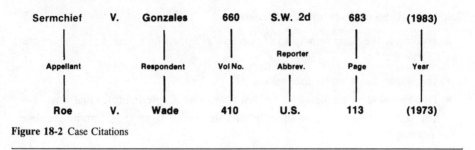

Figure 18-2 Case Citations

Interpreting the Case Citation

Names of the Parties

Case names consist of the last names of the parties. The name of the appellant (the party bringing the appeal) is usually listed first and the respondent (the opposing party) is listed second. In some jurisdictions the plaintiff's name is listed first regardless of which party (plaintiff or defendant) is bringing the appeal. Corporations are listed by their full name, including first names or initials; however, common abbreviations such as Co., Inc., Bd., and HMO are used to shorten the title. When there is more than one party or when several cases have been consolidated, the citation uses only the name of the first party listed on each side or the first case listed. When the state is a party to a case in its own courts, it is usually listed as the *People v.* _____ or the *State v.* _____. When the state is a party in a federal court it is cited as state name v. _____. For example, if Ohio were a party it would be cited as *Ohio v.* _____.

Numbers before and after the Reporter Abbreviation

The numbers before the reporter abbreviation indicate the volume in which the case is found, and the numbers after the reporter abbreviation indicate the page number where the case begins. The number in parentheses indicates the year in which the case was decided. Some citations also identify the court. For example, (1st Cir. 1986) would indicate that the First Circuit Court of Appeals decided the case in 1986; (Cal. 1987) would indicate that the California Supreme Court decided the case in 1987; and (Ill. App. 1976) would indicate that the Illinois Appellate Court decided the case in 1976.

Case Reporter Abbreviations

A court case on the state level may have two sets of identifying numbers and abbreviations, as in *Collins v. Westlake Community Hospital*, 57 Ill. 2d 388, 312 N.E.2d 614 (1974). The first set is the official citation, which indicates where the case can be found in the state's official publication of court case decisions. The second set is the unofficial citation, which indicates where the case can be found in a commercially published set of court case decisions that are classified by geographic region. Federal cases are published in a reporter system that includes the Supreme Court, the U.S. Courts of Appeals (formerly called the U.S. Circuit Courts of Appeals) and selected decisions of the U.S. district courts. The initials 2d refer to the second series of the reporter. For example, F. 2d indicates the case is located in the second series of the *Federal Reporter*. If the U.S. Supreme Court has refused to hear an appeal (*denied certiorari*), this will appear in the citation. For example, the full citation for the frequently cited hospital negligence case in which the court refused to hear the appeal is *Darling v. Charleston Community Memorial Hospital*, 33 Ill. 2d 326, 211 N.E.2d 253 (1965), *cert. denied* 383 U.S. 946 (1966).

INTERPRETING CASE REFERENCE ABBREVIATIONS

Federal Court Decisions

F.	*Federal Reporter*: U.S. Courts of Appeals decisions
F. Supp.	*Federal Supplement*: U.S. district court decisions
L.Ed.	*Lawyer's Edition, United States Supreme Court*: Supreme Court decisions
L.W.	*United States Law Week*: recently issued unofficial Supreme Court decisions
S.Ct.	*Supreme Court Reporter*: Supreme Court decisions
U.S.	*United States Reports*: Supreme Court decisions

State Court Decisions

About two thirds of the states publish state court decisions in official state sets that are cited by the standard state abbreviation. The official report is the authoritative text and must be cited in legal briefs. The official report is cited before the unofficial report. The unofficial reports consist of the commercially published National Reporter System, which collectively contains most of the decisions issued by the appellate courts of the 50 states every year. The National Reporter System divides the country into seven regions. The decisions of the appellate courts of the states in each of these regions are published together in one series of reporters.

A.	Atlantic Reporter Maine, New Hampshire, Vermont, Connecticut, Rhode Island, Pennsylvania, New Jersey, Delaware, Maryland
N.E.	North Eastern Reporter Illinois, Indiana, Ohio, New York, Massachusetts
N.W.	North Western Reporter North Dakota, South Dakota, Nebraska, Iowa, Minnesota, Wisconsin, Michigan
P.	Pacific Reporter Kansas, Oklahoma, New Mexico, Colorado, Wyoming, Montana, Idaho, Utah, Arizona, Nevada, Oregon, Washington, California, Alaska, Hawaii
S.E.	South Eastern Reporter West Virginia, Virginia, North Carolina, South Carolina, Georgia

So.   Southern Reporter
         Louisiana, Mississippi, Alabama, Florida
S.W.   South Western Reporter
         Kentucky, Tennessee, Missouri, Arkansas, Texas

UNDERSTANDING THE CASE FORMAT

The West Publishing Company has adopted a format that is used throughout the federal and state reporters. The format for each case includes the following sections:

1. The title or name of the case.
2. Identifying data such as the docket number, the name of the court or jurisdiction, and the date of the decision.
3. A case synopsis, which consists of a brief descriptive paragraph of the case including the facts, the judicial history, and the lower court decision.
4. A brief statement of the appellate court decision and, if there are concurring or dissenting opinions, a notation to that effect.
5. A series of headnotes summarizing the points of law that are discussed in the case. Each headnote is classified in accordance with the West Key Number System, which has assigned a permanent number to specific points of case law.
6. The names of the lawyers for each party and the names of the judges who have heard and decided the case.
7. The complete text of the opinion, which includes a recitation of the facts, the identification and discussion of the issues, and the judicial reasoning.
8. The holding or court ruling on each issue. The holding is considered law in this case and is binding on the courts in subsequent cases. The holding should be differentiated from *dictum*, a term that refers to the statements, remarks, or observations in a judicial opinion that are not necessary for the decision of the case. Dictum is not binding on the courts in subsequent cases.
9. The disposition of the case. The court can affirm the lower court decision, reverse the lower court decision, or affirm in part and reverse in part the lower court decision. If the case is remanded to the lower court with instructions, the lower court is bound to follow the instructions.
10. The full text of the concurring and dissenting opinions of the judges. A judge may indicate that he or she agreed (concurred) with one part of the opinion but disagreed (dissented) with another part of the opinion. A judge may indicate that he or she agrees with the holding of the majority opinion but for different reasons.
11. The names of the judges who were absent.

READING A CASE

The reading of a case may seem complicated to the layperson; however, he or she should be able to obtain the information being sought if the data are isolated and organized. The following steps suggest one way in which this can be done:

1. Summarize the facts of the case.
2. List all of the issues that the court is considering.
3. Identify the issues that are relevant to the reader's inquiry.
4. Locate the holding on these issues and identify whether the appellate court decision is different from the lower court decision.
5. Review the appellate court's reasoning on each issue to determine how it reached its decision.
6. Consider the final disposition—what is going to happen. Identify whether the issues that are relevant to the reader's inquiry had any bearing on the final disposition.
7. Review all concurring and dissenting opinions to determine if the issues selected are mentioned. Identify the areas of concurrence and dissent.

Cases involving health care providers can be very complicated, involving issues concerning the hospital and the physicians as well as the nurses. The ability to identify all of the issues and to isolate and analyze those that are relevant to the nurse manager's inquiry will make it easier to understand case law as it applies to nurses and the nursing profession.

SKILL 3: UNDERSTANDING THE CIVIL TRIAL PROCESS*

The civil trial process consists of a sequence of events that begins with the filing of a complaint and ends with the final decision of a state or federal appellate court (Figure 18-3). The events of the civil trial process can be classified into five stages: (1) pretrial, (2) discovery, (3) negotiation, (4) trial, and (5) appeal. Each stage has a specific purpose and process, and all of the stages are guided and governed by either the federal or the state's rules of civil procedure.

PRETRIAL

The purpose of the pretrial stage is to determine what facts are in dispute. The process consists of pretrial preparation; pleadings, which include the complaint, summons, answer, counterclaims, demurrers, and reply; pretrial procedures; and pretrial conferences.

Pretrial Preparation

Decisions that must be made prior to filing a complaint include the type of civil action (e.g., negligence, battery), the statute of limitations for the civil action, the person or persons who will be named as defendants, and the court in which the action will be filed.

Pleadings

Pleading is the term used for the process that brings the case before the court. The parties are given the opportunity to ''plead their case''—to place their version of the facts

---

*Major source used in presenting this section: William T. Schantz, *The American Legal Environment* (St. Paul, Minn.: West Publishing Co., 1976), 163–199.

PRETRIAL
PREPARATION

SUMMONS

ANSWER/COUNTER CLAIM

DISCOVERY

PRETRIAL HEARING

NEGOTIATION FOR SETTLEMENT

TRIAL
OPENING STATEMENTS

PLAINTIFF
PRESENTS CASE

DEFENDANT
PRESENTS CASE

CLOSING
STATEMENTS

JURY
INSTRUCTION

JURY
DELIBERATION

VERDICT

APPEAL

Figure 18-3 Civil Trial Process

before the court. The pleadings serve four functions: (1) to notify the court of the nature of the claim, (2) to notify the parties of the basis of the claim, (3) to identify and narrow the issues, and (4) to define the controversy by setting the boundary lines of the litigation. The following demonstrates the usual sequence of events.

1. *Plaintiff files a complaint.* The *complaint* states the name of the court and the basis for the court's jurisdiction and power, the name of the parties, the legal rights that have been violated, and the specific events that constitute a violation of those rights. The plaintiff is stating certain facts, alleging that they are true and that as a result he or she is entitled to money damages or some other type of relief.
2. *Defendant served with a summons and a copy of the complaint.* A *summons* is a legal notice issued by the court or in some jurisdictions by an attorney or public official who then files the summons with the court. It is usually served on the defendant by a sheriff or in the federal courts by a U.S. marshall. The summons informs the defendant that a lawsuit has been filed against him or her and requires an appearance before the court on a particular date. The defendant is warned that failure to appear before the court at that time could result in the suit being decided against him or her, a procedure known as a default judgment.
3. *Defendant answers the complaint.* The defendant's answer can consist of

   - A challenge to the court's authority to hear the case
   - A denial of the facts alleged in the complaint
   - An admission of some facts and a denial of some facts alleged in the complaint
   - The filing of a counterclaim in which the defendant alleges a cause of action against the plaintiff. For example, if the hospital were sued for negligence, it could counterclaim that the patient was also negligent by alleging facts to that effect.
   - The filing of a demurrer or motion to dismiss for failure to prove a cause of action. A demurrer is a legal ''so what.'' It asserts that even if the facts are true (although the defendant does not concede that they are) there is no cause for action.
4. *Plaintiff files a reply.* When the defendant's answer alleges new facts such as in a counterclaim or in a demurrer, the plaintiff must file a reply that either admits or denies the new facts.

Pretrial Procedures

The challenges to a court's jurisdiction and the demurrer are legal questions that are considered by the court through pretrial motions. When the defendant files a demurrer or motion to dismiss, the judge will make a determination of whether to grant the motion by asking, ''If all of the facts alleged by the plaintiff are true could he or she win the case.'' If the answer is ''no,'' then the judge will dismiss the action.

In some jurisdictions after the pleadings are completed either party may file a motion for a judgment on the pleadings. If the motion is made, the court will examine the entire case and determine whether to enter judgment on the merits of the case as indicated in the pleadings.

Pretrial Conferences

A pretrial conference can be ordered by the judge or requested by either of the parties. The purpose of a pretrial conference is to provide an informal discussion at which the judge and the attorneys can agree on issues, eliminate issues that are not in dispute, and settle procedural matters.

DISCOVERY

The Federal Rules of Civil Procedure were adopted by the federal courts in 1938 and have since been adopted in whole or in part by the majority of the states. The rules eliminate the element of surprise as a legitimate trial tactic and encourage full and fair disclosure of the facts prior to trial. The purpose of discovery is to determine what evidence is available to prove the facts. The process consists of depositions, interrogatories, production of documents, and physical and mental examinations (see Skill 4, Participating in Discovery). A party must comply with the discovery requests of the opposing party. Failure to do so could result in the court compelling compliance, dismissing the case, or entering a default judgment.

NEGOTIATION

The purpose of the negotiations is to determine whether the dispute can be settled without a trial. The rules of civil procedure require full discovery as an encouragement to pretrial settlements. Pretrial conferences that foster the informal discussion and exchange of information can sometimes result in a settlement. Negotiation can continue throughout the trial, and the parties can enter into a settlement at any time before the final judgment is rendered. Once a settlement is reached the plaintiff will be required to sign a release surrendering the right of action against the defendant. The plaintiff's spouse may also be required to sign a release surrendering any cause of action he or she may have against the plaintiff for loss of consortium. Court approval is generally required for the settlement of a claim involving a minor.

TRIAL

The purpose of a civil trial is to determine what the evidence shows the facts to be. Trial procedure consists of eleven steps.

Jury Selection

Prospective jury members are examined to determine their impartiality in a particular case. They are asked to swear to give true answers to all of the questions asked of them in the qualifying examination, which is called a *voir dire*. If the attorney believes the juror is not qualified to serve on the jury, he or she can challenge the juror for cause. If the judge agrees that the juror is not impartial, the juror is dismissed. The attorney can also ask that the juror be dismissed without stating a reason. Having a juror dismissed without cause is called a peremptory challenge. The number of peremptory challenges available to an attorney ranges from two to six as determined by state law. The *voir dire* continues until the full jury is impaneled.

Opening Statements

The opening statements give the jury an overall picture of the case. The attorneys outline what they intend to prove and how they intend to prove it. The plaintiff's attorney makes his or her opening statement first. The defense attorney can make his or her opening statement after the plaintiff's attorney or can elect to wait until the plaintiff completes the presentation of his or her case.

Presentation of the Plaintiff's Case

The plaintiff is the person who is asking for damages or other relief. Therefore, the plaintiff has the burden of proof. Evidence is introduced by examining witnesses and expert witnesses and by producing documents and exhibits that will support the allegations. The examination of witnesses follows a specific pattern of direct examination by the plaintiff's attorney and cross-examination by the defendant's attorney, followed by redirect examination and recross-examination until all questions have been asked (see Skill 5, Testifying As a Witness).

Motion for a Directed Verdict

After the plaintiff rests his or her case, the defendant makes a motion for a directed verdict. The defense attorney is saying that the plaintiff has not made out a sufficient case and that the case should be dismissed. If the judge determines that the plaintiff has introduced sufficient evidence, the motion is denied and the trial continues with the defense.

Presentation of the Defendant's Case

The defendant presents his or her evidence in the same manner as the plaintiff by the examining witnesses and expert witnesses and by the presenting documents and other exhibits that will support the defendant's position.

Plaintiff's Rebuttal

Following the presentation of the defendant's case, the plaintiff can introduce rebuttal evidence.

Defendant's Answer to the Plaintiff's Rebuttal

The defendant may bring evidence to counter the plaintiff's rebuttal evidence. This rebuttal/answer process continues until the evidence has been completely exhausted.

Closing Arguments

Closing arguments are made by the plaintiff's attorney and the defendant's attorney, with the plaintiff's attorney speaking last. In making their summations the attorneys must stay within "the record," that is, they must base their arguments on facts that are supported by evidence introduced at trial.

Instructions to the Jury

The trial judge instructs the jury on the law that is applicable to the case. Attorneys may request that specific instructions be given to the jury. The jury must base its verdict on the evidence presented at trial and on the law as explained by the judge.

Jury Verdict

The jury reaches its verdict in the seclusion of the jury room. If the jury cannot agree on a verdict after a reasonable period of time, a mistrial is declared and a new trial ordered. Once the verdict is reached, the jury returns to the courtroom and delivers it to the judge, who reads it to the parties. The judge may "poll the jury" by asking each member of the jury if the verdict is correct.

Post-Trial Motions

Throughout the trial the attorneys for both parties have been preserving issues for appeal by voicing their objections to the judge's rulings. Before a party files for appeal he or she may ask the judge for a new trial. The rules of civil procedure indicate the time in which a party must bring a motion for a new trial. There are a number of actions that a judge can take in response to the attorneys' post-trial motions. The judge can order a new trial (only if the judge believes the evidence could not have resulted in the verdict reached by the jury); order a partial new trial; or approve the jury verdict but grant a *remittitur*, which gives the plaintiff the option of either taking less in damages or going through a new trial.

APPEAL

The purpose of the appeal is to determine whether the trial court made an error that would require a reversal of the verdict and the granting of a new trial. The most common grounds for appeal are the admission of evidence that should not have been admitted, the exclusion of evidence that should have been admitted, and the failure to give proper jury instructions. The appeals process begins with the attorneys preserving issues for appeal by their objections to the trial judge's rulings and the filing and denial of a post-trial motion for a new trial. The appellate court receives a trial transcript and written briefs prepared by the attorneys for both parties. The court may also request that the attorneys present oral arguments during which the court will question the attorneys about the issues. After reading the briefs and listening to the oral arguments, the appellate judges take a vote of first impression and assign a judge to prepare an opinion. The opinion is then circulated among the appellate judges and if approved becomes the official opinion of the court. Judges who agree with the majority opinion but for different reasons may file concurring opinions, whereas judges who disagree with the majority opinion may file dissenting opinions. The appellate decision is sent to the trial court for enforcement. Appellate courts are bound by precedent in arriving at their decisions; however, there are times when they will decide that the attitudes and needs of society have changed and that in this case it is necessary to overturn a precedent so that their decision will reflect current social values.

SKILL 4: PARTICIPATING IN DISCOVERY

DISCOVERY

Discovery is the term used to describe the acquisition of information and evidence before trial. Informal discovery begins with the initial client interview conducted before the lawsuit is filed. The attorney listens to the client's description of the problem and determines if there are any inconsistencies and areas needing clarification. Documents and records in the client's possession are reviewed and retained by the attorney. At this time the client may also be asked to sign a form authorizing the release of his or her medical, educational, financial, or employment records to the attorney. The objective is to acquire evidence that will substantiate the client's claim.

Formal discovery begins with the filing of the complaint. Through the process of discovery each side develops its own base of evidence and probes the opposing party's fund of information. The federal and state rules of civil procedure require both parties to participate fully and fairly in the process of discovery. The liberal approach to discovery is meant to minimize surprises in court that could give one side an unfair advantage and cause a delay in the trial. The legal mechanisms that are used to discover information include depositions, interrogatories, requests to produce documents or items or permission to enter upon land or other property, requests for admission, and requests for physical or mental examinations.

DEPOSITION

A *deposition* is the statement of a witness, taken under oath in a question and answer form, prior to trial. The taking of an oral deposition requires a notice to all parties to the case so that they may be present to cross-examine the witness. The testimony of the person being deposed (deponent) is officially recorded and transcribed by a court reporter. The attorney opposed to the interests of the deponent (opposing attorney) conducts the oral examination, and the attorney for the deponent (friendly attorney) advises the client concerning questions that may be unfair, prejudicial, irrelevant, or self-incriminating. Depositions may also be obtained by submitting questions in writing to the deponent. Written depositions are sometimes obtained when the person being deposed is at a distant location and the cost of having the deponent physically present for an oral deposition would be prohibitive. Depositions are an important part of an attorney's preparation for trial because the testimony obtained in a deposition will usually be repeated or invoked in some manner during the trial. Depositions have many uses, the most common of which are to

- Preserve the testimony of a witness who may not be available for trial
- Confirm the individual's version of the story, a position he or she will not be permitted to deviate from at trial
- Obtain or verify information
- Identify possible sources of new leads or information
- Identify exactly what the deponent knows and does not know
- Evaluate the effectiveness of the deponent as a potential witness at trial

Unlike interrogatories, which can only be obtained from the parties to the suit, oral or written depositions can be directed at the plaintiff, the defendant, or witnesses for either side. The deposition of a party to the suit must be preceded by proper notice in accordance with the state or federal rules of civil procedure. The deposition of a nonparty to the suit may be obtained by notice and consent or by subpoena. The notice of a deposition may be accompanied by a demand for the production of documents or with a *subpoena duces tecum*.

MOTION TO PRODUCE DOCUMENTS

A motion to produce documents is limited to the obtaining of documents that are within the possession of one of the parties to the suit. The federal rules of civil procedure permit the inspection of a party's documents that are relevant to pending litigation. The term *document* includes writings, drawings, graphs, charts, photographs, tapes, and other data compilations from which information can be obtained. The party making the request for production must specifically identify the documents that are being sought.

For example, documents can be requested by subject matter, classification, or time periods. The party making the request for production is generally required to pay the reasonable cost of copying or reproducing the information. The party receiving the request for production is required to respond in a timely, complete, and accurate manner. Objections to the request for documents must be filed within the time period specified by the rules of civil procedure. Failure to file the objections within the required time constitutes a waiver of the objection.

In addition to the production of documents, either party may make a motion to "enter upon land for the purpose of inspection or for other purposes." This motion permits entry onto the designated land or property in the possession or control of the party on whom the request is served. The motion may permit the party making the request to inspect, measure, survey, photograph, or test the property or any designated object or operation on the property.

SUBPOENA

A *subpoena* is a court order commanding a person to appear to give testimony at a judicial proceeding. A *subpoena duces tecum* is a court order commanding the person to appear at the judicial proceeding and to bring to the proceeding certain books, documents, or tangible items that are in his or her possession or control. Unlike the motion to produce documents, which can only be directed at a party to the suit, a subpoena can be directed at nonparties, compelling their appearance and the production of documents or other items in their possession. A valid subpoena generally includes the name of the court; title and docket number of the case; names of the plaintiff and defendant; date, time, and place where the person is to appear; specific documents or items that the person is to bring with him or her to the proceeding (*subpoena duces tecum*); and witness and mileage fee.

In the federal courts, the subpoenas are issued by the clerks of the courts and served on the person by a U.S. marshall. The procedure varies from state to state; however, in some states subpoenas are issued by the clerks of the courts, justices of the peace, and notary publics. Service of the subpoena can be performed by a sheriff, by a sheriff's deputy, by the attorney of record, or by any person authorized by state rule or statute. In some jurisdictions, the service of the subpoena is accompanied by the tendering of a witness fee and mileage allotment to the person being served. A subpoena is a court order; therefore, a person who refuses to comply with a subpoena can be cited and punished for contempt of court. The proceedings to enforce a subpoena must provide the person with an adequate opportunity to object or offer reasonable justification for not complying with the subpoena.

PROTECTION FROM DISCOVERY

In order to encourage the open and candid discussion of issues affecting safe and competent patient care, many states have enacted statutes that protect the proceedings, records, and reports of quality assurance and peer review committees from discovery in a legal proceeding. Hospitals can refuse an attorney's request for this type of information; however, the statutory immunity is limited to review activities. The courts have generally drawn a distinction between review committee records and administrative personnel records and have held that the administrative records are not protected from discovery. In *Good Samaritan v. Maroney*, 365 N.W.2d 887 (Wis. 1985), the court ruled that the records and proceedings of the peer review committee were protected but that the records made by the hospital's governing body pertaining to staff appointments and retention were not protected by the privilege statute.

INTERROGATORIES

Interrogatories are written questions that must be answered under oath. They can be requested by both parties after the complaint and initial responses have been served on the parties. Interrogatories can only be directed toward parties to the lawsuit, unlike depositions on written questions, which can be served on parties and nonparties. The basic purposes of interrogatories are to

- Discover facts under oath
- Identify where facts may be discovered
- Establish dates
- Locate potential witnesses
- Determine a person's medical condition
- Determine a person's financial condition
- Inquire about the existence of documents and evidence

The party receiving the interrogatories has a duty to provide true, explicit, responsive, and candid answers to the questions within the time period specified in the court rules. Evasive or incomplete answers are treated as a failure to answer. The response to the interrogatories is generally accompanied by a sworn statement that the answers provided are true and correct to the best of the party's knowledge and belief. Interrogatories to corporations are served on any officer or agent and must speak to the composite knowledge of the corporation. Corporations must also supply information that can be obtained from sources under their control.

The court rules determine the number of interrogatories that can be requested by a party. For example, some courts limit the interrogatories to 50, which includes all subparts that constitute separate questions. The court rules generally require that each interrogatory be answered separately and fully in writing. If there is an objection to the question, the objection and the reasons for the objection are written instead of the answer. The answers are signed by the person making them, and the objections are signed by the attorney making them. The party that refuses to answer the interrogatory has the burden of convincing the court that the question is improper and need not be answered.

REQUESTS FOR ADMISSION

Requests for admission are used to establish the truth of any matter, including the genuineness of documents and the authenticity of signatures and endorsements. They speed the civil trial process by eliminating the necessity of proving routine matters. Court rules determine the number or admissions that a party is entitled to request. Each matter on which an admission is requested must be set forth separately. A written answer or objection to the request for admission must be submitted within the time specified by the court rules. If an objection is claimed, the reasons for the objection must be stated. The court determines whether the objection is justified or whether the party must answer the request for admission. A matter admitted is considered to be conclusively established unless the court permits the withdrawal or amendment of the admission.

MOTION FOR PHYSICAL OR MENTAL EXAMINATION

The court will order a party to submit to a physical or mental examination if the party's mental or physical condition (including blood groups) is in controversy and if the party requesting the examination demonstrates good cause. In any case involving serious physical injury a party is generally entitled to have the plaintiff examined and independently evaluated. Prior to the physical or mental examination a notice must be sent to the person who is to be examined and to all the parties. The notice must specify the time, place, manner, condition, and scope of examination and the person by whom it is to be made. The person against whom the order is made can request a copy of the written report of the examining physician setting out the physician's findings and including the results of all tests made and the diagnosis and conclusions.

LIMITATION ON DISCOVERY

Parties may obtain discovery regarding any matter, not privileged, that is relevant to the subject matter involved in the pending action. The parties cannot object to the requests for discovery on the basis that the information sought would not be admissible at trial if the information sought appears reasonably calculated to lead to the discovery of admissible evidence. The court rules determine the frequency and extent of the use of the discovery methods. The court may limit the discovery process when

- The discovery sought is unreasonably cumulative or duplicative
- The information is available from some other source that is more convenient, less burdensome, and less expensive
- The party seeking discovery has had ample opportunity to obtain the information sought
- The discovery requested is unduly burdensome or expensive taking into account the needs of the case, the amount in controversy, limitations on the parties' resources, and the importance of the issues at stake in the litigation

SKILL 5: TESTIFYING AS A WITNESS

A *witness* is a person whose statement under oath is received as evidence. There are two types of witnesses: fact witnesses and expert witnesses.

FACT WITNESS

A fact witness, also called a material witness, is a person who testifies about what he or she personally observed. The fact witness' testimony consists of a recounting of events that were personally heard or seen by the witness. In most cases a fact witness is not permitted to render a personal opinion as to what happened or should have happened. A fact witness is used to (1) provide the necessary facts in sufficient detail to make out a *prima facie* case, (2) corroborate other witnesses or evidence, and (3) lay a foundation for the introduction of evidence. In a case involving nursing malpractice a fact witness might be anyone who was present while the patient was receiving nursing care or anyone who came into contact with the patient before or after the act or omission that allegedly caused the injury. A fact witness can include any of the many people who visit or are employed by a hospital, including family, visitors, physicians, nurses, nursing assistants, housekeeping personnel, and laboratory personnel.

EXPERT WITNESS

An *expert* is a person who has acquired specialized knowledge and skill not possessed by the average person. A person with specialized knowledge and skill who agrees to review the circumstances of a case in order to form an opinion and testify is referred to as an *expert witness*. The credentials of a nurse expert witness should demonstrate general intelligence, ability, education, experience, and qualifications with respect to nursing, as well as accuracy and validity as a source of information. An expert witness examines the evidence; draws inferences, deductions, and conclusions; and expresses an opinion as to what should or should not have happened. The purpose of an expert witness is to assist the jury to interpret technical facts and understand technical evidence. An expert witness is permitted to use reliable and relevant published materials in establishing authority and credibility.

Qualification of an Expert Witness

In order to testify as an expert witness a person must be qualified as an expert according to the procedure required by the court rules. The qualification of a person as an expert witness is achieved by analyzing his or her particular qualifications in light of the circumstances on which an opinion is required. The usual procedure is for the expert witness to be asked questions concerning his or her background, education, and experience. The judge, after hearing the witness' credentials, determines whether the person is qualified to testify as an expert in the case. Nurse expert witnesses might be expected to answer questions related to their basic and graduate education, clinical expertise, specialty certification, continuing education, and research activities. After the person has been qualified as an expert witness he or she is permitted to render an opinion in the case. There are two methods by which the opinion of the expert witness is obtained:

1. The attorney asks the expert witness if he or she has reviewed the relevant records and heard the plaintiff's testimony. The witness is then asked to render an opinion as to the facts in the case. The attorney then questions the witness as to the basis of the opinion.
2. The attorney presents the expert witness with a hypothetical situation that is similar to the actual case, and the expert witness is asked to give an opinion.

OBTAINING THE TESTIMONY OF A WITNESS

A fact witness who refuses to testify can be subpoenaed and compelled to testify. Witnesses who persist in their refusal to testify can be cited and punished for contempt of court. Individuals who are declared to be "hostile" witnesses can be asked leading questions and are subject to cross-examination by the party that called them to testify.

The purpose of an expert witness is to assist the judge and the jury to understand the technical aspects of a case. An expert witness is hired by the attorney and paid a fee that is commensurate with his or her qualifications and based on the extent of his or her involvement in the case. An expert witness must voluntarily agree to work with the attorneys; therefore, he or she cannot be subpoenaed to testify. On the other hand, once a person has agreed to serve as an expert witness, the court rules generally indicate that the person can be made to answer questions by means of depositions and interrogatories. The rules also require that the opposing party be given advance notice of the names of persons who will be testifying as expert witnesses.

PREPARATION OF WITNESSES

The examination of witnesses introduces an unpredictable element into the trial in the form of a third person over whom the attorneys have only limited control. Attorneys will usually meet with the witnesses prior to the trial in order to familiarize them with the process of examination. Pretrial meetings and witness interviews permit the attorney to

- Discover what the witness can and cannot testify to at trial
- Evaluate the witness' general demeanor and ability to answer questions clearly and concisely
- Make the witness aware of the most critical parts of the testimony
- Introduce the witness to the types of questions that will be asked on direct examination
- Prepare the witness for cross-examination

The ethics of the legal profession do not permit an attorney to suggest the answer to a question during the pretrial interview; however, there is nothing wrong or unethical in an attorney discussing the witness' testimony before trial. The witness can be made aware of the attorney's objectives and of the critical areas of direct examination. In addition, he or she can be made to understand the purpose and process of direct examination and cross-examination at trial.

DIRECT EXAMINATION AND CROSS-EXAMINATION

The purpose of direct examination is to elicit facts that cover each element of the claim or defense of a case. The direct examination is conducted by the attorney who has called the witness to testify. The witness is placed under oath and questioned about the facts with which he or she is familiar. The rules of direct examination prohibit the attorney from asking leading questions that suggest the answer. After the attorney completes the direct examination, the attorney for the opposing side is given the opportunity to cross-examine the witness. Cross-examination can touch on anything that the witness said or referred to during the direct examination. The purpose of cross-examination is to test the witness' facts and credibility. Cross-examination is sometimes called the "truth finder." The basic technique of cross-examination is for the attorney to ask short, plain, unambiguous leading questions to which the answer will be yes or no. The leading questions may begin with statements such as "Isn't it a fair statement that" and "It's only natural that." The tactics of cross-examination are aimed at exposing inconsistencies and uncovering answers to direct examination that were evasive, erroneous, or unclear.

Expert Witness Cross-Examination

Expert witnesses are subject to cross-examination concerning their opinion and the methods they used in arriving at the opinion. Many attorneys prepare their expert witness for cross-examination by role playing the part of the cross-examiner and attempting to anticipate the types of questions that will be asked of the witness. The cross-examiner will attempt to appear in control of the expert witness by his or her attitude, manner, physical positioning, choice of language, and form of question. The expert witness must be prepared to answer questions concerning the text, journals, or standards that were used in forming the opinion. He or she must also be familiar with the current professional literature and with any recognized minority or conflicting opinions in the area in which they are testifying. The expert witness is an aid to the jury not an advocate. He or she is often advised not to get angry, not to argue with the cross-examiner, and to keep in mind that it is the attorney's responsibility to correct any errors or counteract any unfair impressions that may have been created by the cross-examination. The process of examination consists of

- Direct examination
- Cross-examination

- Redirect examination
- Recross-examination
- Reredirect examination
- Rerecross-examination

The questions that the attorneys can ask are limited to those matters raised in the preceding examination; therefore, the testimony becomes narrower and narrower until there are no more questions. The plaintiff's witnesses are presented first and the defendant's second. When all of the evidence has been presented, the attorneys make their closing arguments, in which they attempt to discredit their opponent's witnesses and evidence. Each attorney must base his or her arguments on facts that are supported by evidence that was introduced during the trial. The defense attorney presents his or her closing argument first, and the plaintiff's attorney speaks last. In most cases the plaintiff's attorney has the first and last word, in that he or she makes the opening statement first and the closing argument last.

TESTIFYING UNDER OATH

A person may be required to testify under oath in a number of legal proceedings, the most common of which are the taking of depositions, testifying before an administrative board or legislative committee, and testifying at a civil or criminal trial. The following illustrates the type of advice that many attorneys give their clients concerning what they say and how they say it. The statements defy precise classification; however, they seem to address two areas: (1) the testimony itself, including the manner of testifying and the grammar or sentence structure, and (2) the attitude of the witness.

Testimony

1. Tell the truth.
2. Think before you speak.
3. Listen to the question; pay particular attention to the introductory clause.
4. Take time to prepare your answer; the examiner must wait for your answer.
5. Answer the question but do not volunteer information or expand or elaborate on the answer.
6. Do not refer to documents that are not going to be introduced into evidence.
7. Do not guess, assume, invent, or vacillate.
8. Do not answer a question you do not understand; ask that the question be repeated, clarified, or rephrased.
9. Be as specific as your memory allows. If you know the date, state it; if not, state it as an approximate date.
10. Ask to review the documents that are in evidence before answering a question concerning information they contain.
11. If you do not remember, state that you do not remember; if a document refreshes your memory, so state; if not, indicate that you still do not remember.

12. Answer in complete sentences.
13. Indicate when you are quoting or paraphrasing.
14. Do not characterize your own testimony with statements such as "honestly," "I think," "I believe," or "I'm doing the best I can."
15. Avoid adjectives and superlatives, such as "I never" or "I always."
16. Do not let the examiner put words in your mouth; rephrase the question if necessary.
17. If you are interrupted by the attorney, stop, indicate that you were interrupted, and continue your answer.
18. If an objection is made, stop immediately and wait for the judge's decision as to whether you should answer the question.

Attitude

1. Dress appropriately.
2. Speak clearly and distinctly and in a tone of voice that will be heard by the jury.
3. Direct your answers to the jury.
4. Avoid levity.
5. Do not express anger.
6. Do not argue with the examiner.
7. Avoid obscenities, ethnic slurs, sexist comments, or derogatory references.
8. Do not attempt to educate the examiner about the technical aspects of your profession.
9. Do not become upset or panic if you make a mistake or are caught in an inconsistency. Your attorney will have the opportunity to rehabilitate (correct and clarify) your testimony on redirect examination.
10. If you are asked, "Did you talk to a lawyer and did he or she tell you what to say," indicate that you did talk to your lawyer and that he or she told you to tell the truth.

SKILL 6: RETAINING AN ATTORNEY

NEEDING AN ATTORNEY

Nurses and the nursing profession are involved in all of the major areas of law. The following illustrates the variety of situations in which a nurse may need to consult and retain an attorney. An attorney can be retained to

1. Draft, interpret, or negotiate a contract
2. Advise on policy and procedure
3. Interpret a law or court decision
4. Negotiate a settlement in a dispute
5. File charges of civil rights violations (sexual harassment or employment discrimination)
6. File a breach of contract claim against an employer for improper termination

7. File a libel or slander charge against another health care provider
8. Defend a civil suit charging professional malpractice
9. Defend a board of nursing charge of unprofessional conduct
10. Defend a criminal charge of drug diversion or murder
11. Defend charges of violation of a patient's civil rights
12. Defend a charge of violation of a reporting statute, such as the child protection statute

SELECTING AN ATTORNEY

The nature of the legal problem will determine the type of attorney that is needed. There are a number of sources that can help a nurse in selecting the appropriate attorney:

- The recommendation from someone who has had a similar problem and had it resolved to his or her satisfaction
- The recommendation of personal acquaintances
- The attorney's reputation in the community
- The state bar association's lawyer referral service, which is usually listed in the yellow pages of the telephone directory
- The *Martindale-Hubbell Directory of Attorneys,* a publication that contains a complete roster of the members of the bar of the United States and Canada. The directory gives brief biographical sketches of the lawyers and describes the areas of practice offered by the law firms. It is available at most public and law libraries.
- Legal clinics that are available in most communities to provide services in specific areas of law
- Legal aid (civil cases) and public defender (criminal cases) services are available without cost or at a nominal charge for individuals who cannot afford an attorney.

CRITERIA FOR SELECTION OF AN ATTORNEY

The four areas that should be considered in arriving at the decision to retain a specific attorney are competence, accessibility, price, and compatibility.

Competence

The state rules of professional conduct that are promulgated by some of the state supreme courts require that a lawyer provide competent representation to a client. For example, New Hampshire Rule 1.1 states that legal competence at a minimum requires (1) specific knowledge about the fields of law in which the lawyer practices; (2) performance of the techniques of practice with skill; (3) identification of areas beyond a lawyer's competence and bringing those areas to the client's attention; (4) proper preparation; and (5) attention to details and schedules necessary to ensure that the matter undertaken is completed with no avoidable harm to the client's interest.

Accessibility

Accessibility refers to the lawyer's willingness to discuss the client's concerns and to keep the client fully informed of the progress of the client's case. Accessibility is determined by evaluating the frequency and manner in which the lawyer communicates with the client. For example, how many meetings are planned, does the lawyer return the client's phone calls promptly, does the lawyer respond to the client's correspondence promptly and completely, and how often is the client provided with a report concerning the status of the case.

Price

The cost of legal services varies according to the expertise of the lawyer or firm and the nature of the legal problem. The fee should be discussed during the initial interview and confirmed when the client decides to retain the attorney. There are four types of fee arrangements:

1. *Fee for service*: A set fee is charged for a particular service regardless of the amount of time involved. The client should be advised if there are any add-ons, such as serving court papers or property settlement costs.
2. *Hourly rate*: The rate is the dollar amount for each hour that the attorney works on the client's case. The attorney usually charges a higher hourly rate for the time spent representing the client in court. The client should also be billed at a lower rate for work performed by nonattorneys such as paralegals. In addition to the hourly rate the client will usually be billed for services such as filing papers with the court and for the attorney's out-of-pocket expenses, including telephone and travel expenses.
3. *Retainer*: Compensation is paid in advance for services to be performed in a specific case. The retainer may represent the total amount that is due; however, it is often considered as a sort of first payment with the attorney rendering a statement for additional sums owed at the conclusion of the case.
4. *Contingency fee*: An agreement to represent the client is exchanged for a percentage of the amount of money recovered for the client at the end of the litigation. A contingency fee can only be used in civil litigation. The client should know whether the fee will be assessed off the gross amount of the award or on the net amount of the award after expenses. The usual contingency fee is 33⅓ percent; however, in malpractice cases the percentage may be limited by state law.

There are legal clinics in most communities that will handle routine legal matters such as uncontested divorces and simple wills at a reasonably low cost. In addition, people who cannot afford a lawyer can seek the services of legal aid agencies in areas such as small money claims, client and lender disputes, landlord–tenant disputes, and domestic relations. The public defender's office handles criminal cases in which the defendant is unable to pay for an attorney.

Compatibility

The relationship between an attorney and a client is similar to that of a nurse and patient in that there must be a sense of trust and a willingness to work together to accomplish a specific objective. The behaviors and expectations that characterize a professional and productive attorney–client relationship include sincerity, accord, credibility, and confidentiality.

INITIAL INTERVIEW

The attorney–client relationship is not established unless, and until, both parties wish it to be. During the initial interview the client evaluates the attorney's professional demeanor and the attorney evaluates the client's legal problem in relation to his or her area of interest and expertise. The client should

- Discuss the problem chronologically
- Provide all of the facts, allowing the attorney to decide which are important and which are unimportant
- Supply any documents or records that are relevant to the problem
- Ask the attorney whether he or she has handled this type of case before

The attorney should

- Listen attentively to the client
- Explain the legal issues involved in the case
- Determine whether any preliminary research is needed
- Determine whether there might be a need to call in another lawyer
- Estimate the amount of time it will take to handle the client's case
- Advise the client of what actions can be taken and of the results that can be reasonably anticipated
- Indicate the fee and the methods of payment available to the client

CLIENT OBLIGATIONS

Once an attorney–client relationship has been established both parties have obligations that must be met. Client obligations include the following:

- Complete and absolute honesty
- Prompt and complete responses to questions
- Prompt response to requests for documents and requests for information
- Cooperation in keeping appointments
- Prompt payment of fees and charges

ATTORNEY OBLIGATIONS

The obligations of an attorney in performing client services are prescribed by the state's rules of professional conduct. For example, New Hampshire Rule 1.1 (c) states that in the performance of client services a lawyer shall at a minimum:

1. Gather sufficient facts regarding the client's problem from the client and from other relevant sources
2. Formulate the material issues raised, determine applicable law, and identify alternative legal responses
3. Develop a strategy, in collaboration with the client, for solving the legal problems of the client
4. Undertake actions on the client's behalf in a timely and effective manner, including, where appropriate, associating with another lawyer who possesses the skill and knowledge required to ensure competent representation.

The American Bar Association's Model Code of Professional Responsibility, which has been adopted in some version by most jurisdictions, lists nine canons of professional conduct that express in general terms the standards of professional conduct expected of lawyers in their relationship with the public, with the legal system, and with the legal profession.

Canon 1	A lawyer should assist in maintaining the integrity and competence of the legal profession.
Canon 2	A lawyer should assist the legal profession in fulfilling its duty to make legal counsel available.
Canon 3	A lawyer should assist in preventing the unauthorized practice of law.
Canon 4	A lawyer should preserve the confidences and secrets of a client.
Canon 5	A lawyer should exercise independent professional judgment on behalf of a client.
Canon 6	A lawyer should represent a client competently.
Canon 7	A lawyer should represent a client zealously within the bounds of the law.
Canon 8	A lawyer should assist in improving the legal system.
Canon 9	A lawyer should avoid even the appearance of professional impropriety.

The concepts expressed in the canons also serve as the basis of the ethical considerations and the disciplinary rules of the legal profession.

SKILL 7: UNDERSTANDING THE LEGISLATIVE PROCESS

CONGRESS

The U.S. Congress is made up of two houses: the Senate and the House of Representatives. Each state is represented by two senators, who are elected to serve in the Senate for six years. The six-year terms are staggered so that the two senators do not run for office at the same time.

Congress has limited the number of U.S. representatives to 435. The Supreme Court has established the principle of one person one vote; therefore, the number of people that each representative represents must be as equal as possible. The average congressional district encompasses approximately 50,000 people. The number of representatives per state ranges from 1 in Vermont to 45 in California. An increase or decrease in population changes the number of representatives that a state is entitled to, and requires the readjustment of congressional districts. U.S. representatives are elected for two-year terms. Elections are held for the entire House of Representatives in even-numbered years.

STATE LEGISLATURES

The U.S. Constitution mandates that all states have a legislative body. The state constitution prescribes the organization of the state government, the state legislature, and the state courts. Each state determines the nature of its political districts and the number of senators and representatives in their legislature. State legislatures have significant differences and similarities. For example

- Forty-nine states are bicameral, having a senate and a house of representatives. Nebraska is unicameral, having only one legislative body, which is called the legislature.
- The legislature is called the general court in 2 states, the legislative assembly in 2 states, the general assembly in 17 states, and the legislature in 29 states.
- Forty-two state legislatures convene annually, and eight state legislatures convene biannually. Annual and biannual sessions are both referred to as regular sessions. Special sessions are sometimes convened between regular sessions to handle urgent problems. In 1981, the New Hampshire Legislature failed to renew the state's nurse practice act during its regular session and reestablished it during a special session.
- All legislative bodies have four major functions: (1) lawmaking; (2) representation; (3) administrative oversight; and (4) specific electoral, judicial, and constitutional responsibilities.

FORMS OF LEGISLATION

The ideas for legislative proposals arise from a number of sources, including the chief executive, the department heads, standing committees of the legislature, constituents, trade associations, professional groups, consumer groups, and individual legislators. There are five forms of legislative proposals, each with a different purpose and a different designation:

1. *Bill*: This is the most common type of proposal because it has the widest application. Designated as "H.R." in the House of Representatives and "S." in the Senate, each abbreviation is followed by a number. If a bill passes both houses of Congress and is signed by the President, it is assigned a public law number, which indicates the Congress that passed it and the order of signing (e.g., P.L. 98-5).

2. *Joint resolution*: This proposal is similar to and has the same legal effect as a bill. It originates in either house but has sponsors from both the House and the Senate. It is designated as "H.J. Res." or "S.J. Res." followed by a number.
3. *Resolution*: This proposal is generally used for the internal business of one house and is designated as "H.R. Res." or "S. Res." followed by a number.
4. *Concurrent resolution*: This proposal affects the internal business of both houses or expresses the "sense of Congress" on an issue that affects both bodies. It is designated as "H.R. Con. Res." or "S. Con. Res." depending on where it was originated, and the abbreviation is followed by a number.
5. *Amendment*: A rider can be attached to a bill, joint resolution, resolution, or concurrent resolution for the purpose of getting it incorporated and passed along with the original proposal. House amendments must be germane to the original proposal, whereas Senate amendments must only be germane if the original proposal is an appropriations bill.

SPONSORS

All bills, resolutions, and amendments must have a sponsor in the legislature. In general, requests for legislation from executive, departmental, and legislative committees are automatically forwarded to the appropriate standing committee. Requests from constituents, professional or trade associations, or other groups must seek the support of one or more individual legislators. Ideally, the legislator sponsoring the legislation will be committed to the legislation and have the power and ability to promote the bill through the committee process. Sponsors will have to include members of the majority party because members of the minority party often have difficulty moving pieces of legislation through the legislative process.

DRAFTING A BILL

A bill can be drafted before or after a sponsor is obtained. At the federal level the proposal goes to the bill-drafting service of the legislature under the sponsor's name. On the state level, drafting the bill is the responsibility of the primary sponsor of the legislation. Organizations and individuals can assist the sponsors of state legislation by providing information concerning the intent and specific objectives of the bill and the areas of potential discord and compromise. Examples of similar bills in other states are especially useful as a starting point.

Proposed legislation contains five basic items of information: (1) name, (2) date of introduction, (3) sponsors' names, (4) establishment clause, and (5) enactment clause. In addition, the need for cost containment has prompted most legislatures to require that all bills be accompanied by a fiscal impact statement estimating the costs or savings of the legislation.

LEGISLATIVE PROCESS OF A BILL

The process of moving a bill through the legislature is similar for Congress and the state legislatures.

- A bill may originate in either house except for bills that raise revenue or general appropriations bills, which must originate in the House of Representatives.
- In Congress, a bill may be introduced any time that the Congress is in session. State constitutions generally limit the introduction of bills to the first 30 days of the session.
- A Senator or Representative introduces the bill. The presiding officer refers the bill to one of the standing committees. Congress has 22 standing committees in the House of Representatives and 15 standing committees in the Senate.
- The standing committee may consider the bill; however, the committee chairperson usually refers it to a subcommittee that has jurisdiction over the subject matter.
- The subcommittee holds public hearings at which interested parties can present their views on the bill. Witnesses are usually required to submit copies of their testimony in advance and to limit their oral presentations to summaries. The subcommittee can report the bill favorably with or without amendments to the full committee, or it can table the bill, which is an action that usually kills it.
- The full committee may amend the bill further, redraft it, or vote on it. If the bill is approved, it is submitted to the full house of the Senate or House of Representatives. The committee report to the full House or Senate contains (1) a statement on the origin and purpose of the bill, (2) a summary of the hearings held, (3) a description of adopted amendments, (4) a section-by-section analysis, and (4) occasionally individual and/or minority views.
- A reported bill is ready for floor action, which means that it will be debated, amended, or voted on. The House or Senate approval of a bill requires a majority vote of the members that are present when the vote is taken.
- A bill that has been passed by a majority vote is sent to the other house where the entire committee, subcommittee, and floor action process is repeated.
- When both houses pass a different version of a bill, one house may accept the other's version without a conference. If neither house will accept the other's version of the bill, a conference committee is convened.
- Conference committee members are selected by the speaker of the House and the full Senate. The conferees generally consist of members of the House or Senate committees that reported the bill. Their discussion is limited to the areas of disagreement between the two versions of the bill. The conference committee negotiates the areas of disagreement in the bill and attempts to obtain compromises and language that is acceptable to both houses.
- The agreement that is reached by the conference committee is presented as a conference report to both houses for approval. If the conference report is ratified by

both houses the bill goes to the President for his signature. If the conference committee fails to reach an agreement, the bill "dies in conference."

- The President has ten days in which to act on a bill. If he signs it, or fails to sign it, within the ten-day period while the Congress is in session, the bill becomes law. If he vetoes the bill, it is returned to Congress where it will become law if a two-thirds majority of each house votes to override the President's veto. If Congress has adjourned during the ten-day period and the President does not sign or veto a bill, it dies. This strategy is commonly referred to as a "pocket veto."

- A signed bill is assigned a public law number, which indicates the Congress that passed it and the order of signing. For example, P.L. 97-5 means public law, 97th Congress, 5th bill.

- All bills in Congress become law on the date of the President's signature or on the date that Congress overrides the President's veto unless the bill provides for an effective date. State constitutions determine the procedures by which a governor signs or vetoes a bill. State legislation that is signed by the governor usually becomes effective 90 days after the adjournment of the legislature unless the bill specifies a different effective date. A bill will become law without the governor's signature if no action occurs during the next five to ten days after adjournment. The legislature may override the governor's veto by a two-thirds vote, and the bill will become law 90 days after adjournment. The legislation may contain an emergency clause that allows it to become law immediately. These bills usually require the approval of two thirds of both the senate and house and the signature of the governor. If the governor vetoes the bill three fourths of both the senate and the house must vote approval to override the governor's veto.

OBTAINING A COPY OF A BILL

After a bill has been printed anyone can obtain a copy. Congress will send free one copy of each bill requested. The request should contain the number and title of the bill or, if this information is unknown, a description of the subject matter and approximate date of its introduction.

House Bills and Public Laws: House Document Room
U.S. Capitol H 226
Washington, DC 20515

Senate Bills and Public Laws: Senate Document Room
U.S. Capitol 5321
Washington, DC 20515

State Bills: Information on how to obtain state bills is available from the secretary of state's office. Your state senator or representative or the sponsor of the bill may also be able to provide you with a copy.

SKILL 8: LOBBYING

Nurses need power to achieve the passage, amendment, or defeat of legislation that affects nursing practice and the nursing profession. Nurses have sought to influence state and federal legislation in a number of ways, the most effective of which have been the forming of political action committees, the hiring of professional lobbyists, and personally expressing their views on legislation by testifying before legislative committees.

POLITICAL ACTION COMMITTEES

There are two types of political action committees (PACs): the nonconnected PACs and the separate segregated fund (SSF). The nonconnected PAC is neither connected to nor sponsored by a corporation, association, or labor organization. Nonconnected PACs pay all of their costs of administration and solicitation. Any support that is received from a sponsor is considered subject to the yearly limits on contributions. PACs of health care associations such as the American Nurses' Association's N-PAC are considered SSFs under the classification of labor organizations. The SSFs are connected to a corporation or labor organization and function as the political arm of these organizations. The organization pays the operational expenses of the SSFs, including their administrative and solicitation costs. These contributions are not subject to the yearly limits on contributions. Another important distinction is the people who may be solicited by the two types of PACs. Nonconnected PACs may solicit any individual, group, or committee for funds. SSFs, such as N-PAC, can only solicit the members of the organization and their families. The major purpose of a PAC such as the American Nurses' Association's N-PAC is to develop political power by electing candidates who are likely to support the issues that are endorsed by N-PAC and the nursing organization that it represents. The major functions of PACs are to

- Endorse and actively campaign for candidates
- Contribute to the campaigns of candidates who have supported the organization's views
- Contribute to the campaigns of challengers who have a good chance of unseating incumbents who have been indifferent or opposed to the organization's concerns
- Raise funds
- Educate their membership in the political process
- Interview candidates to ascertain their views on the issues that are of importance to the profession
- Communicate directly with legislators by telephone or in person to urge them to support the organization's stance
- Examine and expose the voting records of the legislators
- Review every election in their jurisdiction

PACs have been extremely effective in gathering support for the issues and interests of their organizations. The success and rapid proliferation of PACs have engendered criticism from people and organizations who are concerned with the amount of money that is coming into the political system from the PACs.

PROFESSIONAL LOBBYIST

A professional lobbyist is a person who is paid to represent an organization before the legislature. The three major sources of lobbyists are law firms, public relations firms, and independent lobbyists. A lobbyist can be hired for the entire legislative session or for the support of a particular piece of legislation. The lobbyist is the spokesperson for the organization. The lobbyist's skill and expertise lies in knowing how to get the organization's position and views acknowledged and supported by the legislators. The organization must supply the information and resources to support its position. The lobbyist must understand the organization's objective in seeking to pass or defeat specific bills. On professional practice issues it is often useful to know how other states, especially neighboring states, have handled the issues. The organization must also support the lobbyist's efforts by mounting telephone and letter-writing campaigns. They will also need to provide members of the organization who are willing and able to testify before the legislature.

TESTIFYING BEFORE A LEGISLATIVE COMMITTEE

The effectiveness of witnesses who choose or are selected to testify before a legislative committee depends to a large extent on what they have to say and how they say it. A belief in one's position, careful preparation of the testimony, and an adequate number of people who are in attendance to support the position without disrupting the proceedings will set the stage for a successful presentation. Witnesses who make a good impression are generally those who are knowledgeable, able to speak clearly, able to control their nervousness, and able to answer the committee's questions concisely and completely. The following suggestions address both the manner and the matter of the testimony:

1. Dress conservatively.
2. Arrive on time and report to the appropriate person.
3. Begin your testimony by identifying yourself and the organization that you represent.
4. Deliver a clear, concise summary of your position in the time allotted by the committee.
5. Listen attentively to the committee's questions and take the time to formulate an organized answer.
6. Answer the committee's questions as concisely, clearly, and completely as your knowledge allows.
7. Maintain your composure even if you are confronted with a hostile question or attitude by a legislator. Do not argue with or threaten committee members.
8. After you have completed your presentation, express your appreciation to the committee and its staff for their time and attention.

9. Submit your written testimony to the appropriate legislative staff members. Make sure that you have a copy for each committee member. (Giving it to them prior to your testimony may result in their reading it rather than listening to your presentation.)
10. After leaving the hearing room, assess their reaction to your presentation. Identify which legislators appeared to support or oppose your position and which seemed uncommitted.
11. If you remain in the hearing room after your presentation, pay particular attention to the testimony of people who oppose your position. Identify the nature and validity of their opposition.

Nurses are independent professional women and men who do not adjust easily to the conditions of negotiation and compromise demanded by the legislative process. Reinhold Niebuhr described the dilemma by stating, "Politics will, to the end of history, be an area where conscience and power meet, where the ethical and coercive factors of human life will interpenetrate and work out their tentative and uneasy compromises." It is to their credit that nurses remain uneasy and alert to the potential uses and abuses of power.

BIBLIOGRAPHY

Books

A Uniform System of Citation. 12th ed. Cambridge Mass.: Harvard Law Review Association, 1976.

Bagwell, Marilyn and Clements, Sallee. *A Political Handbook for Health Professionals*. Boston: Little, Brown, and Co., 1985.

Cohen, Morris L. *Legal Research in a Nutshell*. St. Paul, Minn.: West Publishing Co., 1978.

Eimermann, Thomas E. *Fundamentals of Paralegalism*. Boston: Little, Brown and Co., 1980, pp. 141–165; 279–311.

Hasse, Paul. *Using a Law Library*. 2nd ed. Washington, D.C.: HALT, 1985.

Llewellyn, Karl. *The Common Law Tradition*. Boston: Little, Brown and Co., 1980.

Niebuhr, Reinhold. *Moral Man and Immoral Society: A Study in Ethics and Politics*. New York: Charles Scribner's and Sons, 1953, pp. 3–4.

Schantz, William T. *The American Legal Environment*. St. Paul, Minn.: West Publishing Co., 1976, pp. 163–175.

"The American Lawyer: How to Choose and Use One." American Bar Association, 1978, pp. 18–23.

Wehringer, Cameron K. "When and How to Choose an Attorney," *Legal Almanac Series #63*. New York: Oceana Publications Inc., 1979, pp. 82–90.

Weinerman, Chester S. *Practical Law, A Layperson's Handbook*. Englewood Cliffs, N.J.: Prentice-Hall, Inc., 1978, pp. 236–248.

West's Law Finder, A Legal Research Manual. St. Paul, Minn.: West Publishing Co., 1985.

Journal Articles

Baurer, Theodore. "Deposition: A Voyage of Discovery, or Just a Fishing Expedition." *Journal of Hospital Supply, Processing and Distribution*, 1985, pp. 66–70.

Eble, Timothy E. "Case Preparation in Federal Court: Formal Discovery." *Case & Comment* 92 (1987):30–35.

Hart, Thomas H. III. "Case Preparation in Federal Court: Informal Discovery." *Case & Comment* 92(1987):22–26.

Josberger, Marie and Ries, Darryl T. "Nurse Experts: Selecting and Preparing Them for Litigation." *Trial* 21(1985):68–71.

Purver, Jonathan M.; Young, Douglas R.; and Davis, James J. III. "Winning the Trial Through Direct Examination." *Case & Comment* 93(1988):10–17.

Rench, Stephen C. "Trade Secrets of a Trial Lawyer: Preparation of Defense Witnesses." *NLADA Washington Memo*, April 1978, pp. 5–6.

Sanbar, S.S. and Pataki, Leonard I. "The Expert Witness in Medical Liability Cases." *MEDICOLEGAL NEWS* 6(1978):7–10.

Wells, Robert. "Lawyer Credibility." *Trial* 21(1985):69–71.

Index

A

Avery v. St. Francis Hospital, 144

B

Barber v. Superior Court, 72, 197
Bartling v. Superior Court, 70, 197
Blum v. Yaretsky, 56
Boyd v. United States, 62
Breithaupt v. Abram, 65
Brenner v. Diagnostic Center Hospital, 59
Buckley v. Corp. of America, 76
Buschi v. Kirven, 61

C

Campbell v. Glenwood Hills Hospital, Inc., 54
Canterbury v. Spence, 188
Cantwell v. Connecticut, 57
Carey v. Piphus, 49
Carey v. Population Services International, 70
Colorado State Board of Nursing v. Hohu, 116
Craig v. Boren, 50

D

Darling v. Charleston Community Memorial Hospital, 131

Delatti v. Genovese, 54
Doe v. Bolton, 69
Doe v. Charleston Area Medical Center Inc., 56

E

Eisenstadt v. Baird, 69
Erickson v. Dilgard, 57
Everson v. Board of Education, 57

F

Fries v. Barnes, 64

G

Gitlow v. New York, 60
Greene v. St. Elizabeth's Hospital, 55
Griswold v. Connecticut, 68

H

Hitt v. North Broward Hosp. Dist., 61
Holmes v. Silver Cross Hospital, 56

I

In re Brooks Estate, 57
In re Osborne, 58

K

Katzenbach v. Morgan, 53
Katz v. United States, 64
Kramer v. Heckler, 56

L

Laidlow v. Lion Gate Hospital, 145
Leggett v. State Board of Nursing, 115
Lombard v. Eunice Kennedy Shriver Center, 56
Luker v. Nelson, 64
Lunsford v. Board of Nurse Examiners, 116

M

McDonald v. Massachusetts General Hospital, 131
McPherson v. Rankin, 61
Marbury v. Madison, 39
Matter of Karen Quinlan, 70
Meredith v. Allen County War Memorial Hospital Commission, 54
Michigan Dept. of Civil Rights, ex rel. Cornell v. Edward A. Sparrow Hospital, 93
Miranda v. Arizona, 277
Morrell v. Department of Social Services, 54

N

New York Times v. Sullivan, 215
Norfolk Protestant Hospital v. Plunkett, 125

O

Oklahoma City v. Tuttle, 55
O'Neill v. Grayson County War Memorial Hospital, 56

P

People v. Film Recovery Systems, 296
Phillips v. Singletary, 54
Pisel v. Stanford Hospital, 137

R

Reynolds v. United States, 57
Richardson v. Brunelle, 116

Robinson v. Jordan, 54
Rochin v. California, 65
Roe v. Wade, 43, 69
Rozier v. St. Mary's Hospital, 61

S

Schloendorff v. Society of New York Hospital, 131, 187
Schmerber v. California, 65
Schor v. Francis Hospital, 75
Sermchief v. Gonzales, 118, 126, 301
Smith v. United States, 60
State v. Allen, 65
State v. Gans, 62
Stevens v. Blake, Alabama Board of Nursing, 117
St. Mary's Hospital v. Ramsey, 58, 72
Superintendent of Belchertown State School v. Saikewicz, 70

T

Tinker v. Des Moines Independent Com. Sch. Dist., 60
Tuma v. Board of Nursing, 117

U

United States v. Borchardt, 63
United States v. Crowder, 65
United States v. Jane Doe, 280
United States v. Miranda, 287
United States v. Newton, 64
Utter v. United Hospital Center, 125

W

Wallace v. Jaffree, 57
Ward v. Oregon State Board of Nursing, 117
Wildman v. Axelrod, 116
Williamson v. Lee Optical Company, 46
Winters v. Miller, 57
Wrighten v. Metropolitan Hospitals, Inc., 61, 78

Index

A

Abandonment of patient, litigation
  related to, 163-164
Abortion
  federal funding issue, 71
  privacy, 69-70
Accreditation
  Joint Commission Standards, 97
  regulation of hospitals, 97-98
  voluntary, 97
Accreditation Manual for Hospitals, 97
Actus rea, 280-281
"Additional acts" clause, nursing
  practice, 109-110
Adjudicatory hearings, administrative
  agencies, 92
Administrative agencies
  as commissions, 88
  as departments, 88
  federal agencies
    Equal Employment Opportunity
     Commission, 101-102
    National Labor Relations Board,
     102, 104-106
  hearings, 91-92
  adjudicatory hearings, 92
  due process rights, 92
  rule-making, 91-92

investigations, 91
judicial review, 93-94
power of, 99
process/procedure of, 99-101
purposes of, 99
rules
  interpretive rules, 89-90
  procedural rules, 89
  rule-making, 90
  substantive rules, 90
types of, 87
Administrative law
  federal administrative law, 88
  source for, 87
  state administrative law, 88, 89
Administrative Procedures Acts, 89 112
Administrative rules/decisions, as source
  of law, 16-17
Admission
  antidiscrimination statutes, 152-153
  common law right to, 152
  contractual right to, 152
  right to emergency care, 153-154
  right to refuse admission, hospital, 154
  statutory right to, 152
  transfer, 154-155
Age, discrimination prohibition, 75-76
Age Discrimination Act of 1975, 75

Agency/ostensible agency doctrine,
    liability, 134-135
Alcohol intoxication, as criminal
    defense, 283
Alibi, as criminal defense, 284
Altering/replacing records, 181-182
American Nurses' Association
    Publications, 34, 83, 123
Antiestablishment clause, 56
Antitrust law, 260-264
    Clayton Act, 261, 262
    Federal Trade Commission Act, 261
    and health care industry, 260, 262-263
    legal interpretation
        per se doctrine, 261-262
        rule of reason, 262
    litigation, examples of, 262-263
    nonphysician staff privileges, 263-264
    penalties for violation of, 262
    Sherman Antitrust Act, 261, 262
Appeal. See Criminal procedure
Appellate courts, 24
    federal, 26
    state, 28, 30
Arraignment, process of, 289-290
Arrest, process of, 286
Assault and battery
    civil assault and battery, 202-203
    criminal assault and battery, 203
    defenses to, 203
    as felony, 303
    legal definitions, 201-202
    litigation, examples of, 203-204
Assessment, nursing, litigation
    related to, 161-163
Assumption of the risk, negligence
    defense, 150-151
Attorney
    attorney obligations, 356
    client obligations, 355
    initial interview, 355
    retaining attorney, reasons for,
        352-353
    selection of, 353-355
        accessibility, 354
        compatibility, 355
        competence factors, 353-354
    price factors, 354
    sources of information, 353

B

Bail, process of, 288
Battery form, consent, 191
Battery. See Assault and battery
Benefits and burdens approach, right to
    refuse treatment, 197
Best interests of patient approach, right to
    refuse treatment, 197
Bill
    drafting of, 358
    obtaining copy of, 360
    process of, 359-360
Bill of Rights, 40
Blanket form, consent, 191
Board of nursing
    appointment to, 111
    challenges to
        board investigation, 116
        constitutionality of law, 116
        expansion of nursing practice,
            118
        hearing procedure, 116
        jurisdiction, 115-116
        regulation interpretation, 116-117
        unprofessional conduct
            interpretation, 117-118
    composition of, 110
    hearings, 113-115
        due process rights, 114
        grounds for discipline, 113-114
        judicial review, 114-115
    licensure, 111-112
        endorsement, 112
        foreign educated nurses, 112
        methods of, 111-112
        reciprocity, 112
    powers of, 111
    rule-making, 112-113
Booking, process of, 286-287
"Borrowed servant" doctrine, 133
Breach of contract, 240
Burden of proof, 22
    trial, 292

C

"Captain of the ship" doctrine, 133
Cases
  abbreviations used, 334-336
  format for, 336
  locating cases, 333
  reading of, 336-337
Causation (legal), 145-146
  res ipsa loquitut, 146
  two-pronged inquiry, 145-146
Certification
  nurses, 98
  physicians, 98
  regulation of hospitals, 98
Chain of custody, maintaining, evidence,
  318-319
Charitable immunity, 131
Chief executive officer (CEO), role of,
  128
Child abuse, reporting requirements,
  310-311
Christian Scientists, 57
Circuit courts, 26
Civil law, 127
Civil Rights Act of 1871, 53, 64, 73
Civil Rights Act of 1964, Title VII,
  58-59, 61, 73, 74, 76
Civil Rights Act of 1967, Title VI, 153
Civil rights legislation
  color of law, 54
  private conduct, 55-56
  Section 1983 action, 54, 55, 64
  state action, 54-55, 56
Clayton Act, 261, 262
Code of Federal Regulations, 17, 20
Code of Federal Regulations, 90
Collective bargaining agreements,
  240-248
  appropriate bargaining units, 241-244
    groups of, 241
    professionals, definition of, 241
    RN only, 242
  bargain in good faith duty, 244
  contract in, 240-241
  contract provisions, listing of, 245-246
  grievance procedures, 246-247

"just cause" termination, 247-248
subjects
  illegal subjects, 244
  mandatory subjects, 244
  voluntary subjects, 245
supervisors, exclusion of, 242-244
Color of law, 54
Commissions, administrative agencies
  as, 88
Common law
  and development of law, 13
  precedent, 17, 18
  revisions to, 18
  stare decisis, 17-18
Communicable diseases, reporting
  requirements, 309-310
Comparative negligence, negligence
  defense, 150
Compensatory damages, 146, 147
Competency, and consent, 189-190
Computer records, medical records, 221
Confidentiality
  defamation, 213-218
  medical records, 219-231
  nurse manager, responsibility of,
    231-232
  privacy, 208-213
  See also individual topics.
Congress, 356-357
  U.S., 20
Conscience clause, and employment, 59
Consent
  exceptions to
    emergency, 195
    patient waiver, 196
    prior patient knowledge, 196
    therapeutic privilege, 195-196
  express consent, 191
  forms
    battery form, 191
    blanket form, 191
    detailed consent form, 191
    inaccurate/misleading forms, 193
    invalid patient signature, 193
    period of validity for, 191-192
    unintelligible forms, 192-193
  implied consent, 190

informed consent, standards, 188
liability sources, 187
refusal/withdrawal of consent
    assault/battery litigation, 201-204
    discharge against medical advice,
        200-201
    do not resuscitate orders, 198-199
    false imprisonment litigation,
        204-206
    natural death acts, 199-200
    right to refuse treatment,
        196-198
requirements for
    competency, 189-190
    knowledge, 189
    voluntariness, 189
responsibility for
    hospitals, 194
    nurse managers, 195
    nurses, 194-195
    physicians, 193
right to consent, 187
Constitution of United States, 19
    Bill of Rights, 40
    interpretations of, 37
    as law/as document, 37
Constitutional rights
    and health care, 41-42
    human rights, 38
    institutional rights, 39
    interpretation of, 39
    legal rights, 39
    moral rights, 38
    origin of, 38
    patients' rights, 38
    sources of, 39-42
        Bill of Rights, 40
        procedural rights, 40-41
        substantive rights, 40
    See also Fourteenth Amendment.
Constitutions, as source of law, 16
Contract law, 22, 127
    versus tort law, 235
Contracts
    antitrust law, 260-264
    breach of contract, 240
        legal remedies, 240

collective bargaining agreements,
    240-248
elements of
    capacity to contract, 237
    consideration, 237
    lawful agreement, 238
    mutual assent, 236-237
employee at will doctrine, 248-254
express contract, 238, 258-260
    negotiation of, 258-259
implied contract, 238, 251-253
insurance contracts, 264-269
nursing, need for, 260
oral contract, 238
parol evidence rule, 239
refusal to provide care, 254-257
    moral/medical/philosophical basis,
        255
    and nurse manager, 257
    unsafe work assignments, 255
statute of frauds, 238-239
termination of, 239
written contract, 238
See also specific topics.
Contributory negligence, negligence
    defense, 149-150
Corporate liability, 130-132
    charitable immunity, 131
    corporate negligence, 131-132
Corporate negligence, 131-132
Corporations, as legal persons, 53-54
Court of Chancery, 19
Court of Claims, 26
Court system
    appellate courts, 24
    federal system
        appellate courts, 26
        courts of limited jurisdiction, 26
        district courts, 24, 26
        Supreme Court, 26, 28
    state system
        appellate courts, 28, 30
        courts of limited jurisdiction, 28
        trial courts, 28
    trial courts, 23-24
Crime
    defenses, 282-284

alcohol intoxication, 283
alibi, 284
duress, 283-284
entrapment, 283
insanity, 282-283
mistake of fact, 283
mistake of law, 283
definition of, 280
types of crime, 282
See also Health-care related crimes.
Criminal law
penalties, types of, 279
scope of, 279
Criminal procedure
appeal, 294-295
habeas corpus, writ of, 295
refusal of, 295
pretrial procedure, 284-291
arraignment, 289-290
arrest, 286
bail, 288
booking, 286-287
discovery, 291
grand jury indictment, 289
investigation, 287-288
plea bargaining, 290-291
preliminary hearing, 289
prosecutor information, 289
trial, 292-294
burden of proof, 292
jury in, 293
jury selection, 292-293
major events of, 293-294
postconviction procedures, 294
rights of the accused, 293
Criminal process
criminal act, 280-281
criminal intent, 281
prosecution, 280
Cross-examination, 350
expert witness, 350-351
Customs Court, 26

D

Damages
compensatory damages, 146, 147

nominal damages, 146
punitive damages, 146-147
Deceased patients, access to medical
records, 225
Decision-making, of nurse manager, 8-9
Declaration of Independence, and
development of law, 14
Defamation, 213-218
defense to, 214-216
privilege, 214-215
qualified privilege, 215-216, 217-218
truth, 214
litigation, examples of, 216-218
scope of, 213-214
libel, 213
slander, 213
Defenses. *See* Crime defenses;
Negligence, defenses/counterclaims
De novo review, 93
Deposition, 344
Detailed consent form, consent, 191
Diagnostic related groups (DRGs)
basic premise of, 155
and liability, 155-156
Direct examination, 350
Discharge
against medical advice, requirements
for, 200-201
liability, 155
Discipline
grounds, nursing practice, 113-114
unprofessional conduct
definitional difficulty, 114, 117
interpretation of, 117-118
Disclosure, common law duty to
disclose, 228-229
Discovery, 343-347
access to medical records, 226-227
beginning of process, 343
deposition, 344
documents, motion to produce,
344-345
interrogatories, 346
limitation on, 347
physician/mental examination, motion
for, 347
process of, 291

protection from discovery, 345-346
request for admission, 347
subpoena, 345
Discrimination
age, 75-76
constitutional protection, 73
employment discrimination, 76-77
    disproving discrimination, 77
    proving discrimination, 77
equal pay, 76
handicapped persons, 74-75
patient advocacy, 78
public accommodations, 74
race/color/national origin, 74
sexual harassment, 78
District courts, 24, 26
Documentary evidence, standard of
care, 143
Documents, nursing, litigation related
to, 182-183
Domesday Survey, 12-13
Domestic violence, reporting
requirements, 311-312
Do not resuscitate orders, 198-199
Driving while intoxicated (DWI),
evidence, 317-318
Due process, 45-47
Fifth Amendment, 45, 46, 47
substantive due process, 45-46
Due process rights, administrative
agencies, 92
Duress, as criminal defense, 283-284
Duty, and negligence, 141-142

E

Elderly abuse, reporting requirements,
311
Emergency care
exception to consent, 195
right to, 153-154
Employee at will doctrine, 248-254
and employee handbook, 252-253
implied contract in, 251-253
limitation of
    promises of good faith/fair dealing,
    253-254

public policy, 248-251
and risk of patient advocacy, 250-251
Employees
privacy, 210-211
    abuses of privacy, 210
    false information, 210-211
rights under NLRA, 103
unreasonable searches, 65-66
Employment discrimination, 76-77
disproving discrimination, 77
proving discrimination, 77
Endorsement, nursing licensure, 112
Entrapment, as criminal defense, 283
Equal Employment Opportunity
Commission, 76
judicial proceedings, 102
powers of, 101
process/procedure for complaints, 102
Equal pay, discrimination prohibition, 76
Equal Pay Act of 1963, 76
Equal protection, 47-48
fundamental right, 47-48
suspect class, 47
Equipment, nursing, litigation related to,
167-168
Equity, as source of law, 18
Euthanasia, 296
Evidence
chain of custody, maintaining, 318-319
definition of, 316-317
disposal of, 316
driving while intoxicated (DWI), 317-318
police/hospital relations, 313-315
preservation of, 317
searches/seizures, lawful, 315-316
Exculpatory agreement, 147-148
Executive branch, of government, 20-21
Expert witness testimony, 143-144,
348-349
cross-examination, 350-351
no requirement for, 144
qualification of, 348-349
Express consent, 191
Express contract, 238, 258-260
negotiation of, 258-259
External requests, access to medical
records, 226

F

Fact witness, 348
Fair Labor Standards Act, 76
Fairness, concept in, due process, 46-47
False imprisonment
  defenses to, 204-205
  legal definitions, 204
  litigation, examples of, 205-206
Family requests, nursing, litigation related to, 164-165
Federal administrative law, 88
Federal agencies
  Equal Employment Opportunity Commission, 101-102
  National Labor Relations Board, 102, 104-106
  regulation of hospitals, 96
Federal Mediation and Conciliation Services (FMCS), 103
Federal Register, 17, 20, 90
Federal Torts Claim Act, 26
Federal Trade Commission Act, 261
Fees, attorney, 354
Fifth Amendment, 40
  due process, 45, 46, 47
First Amendment
  freedom of religion, 56-59
  freedom of speech, 60-62
Foreign educated nurses, nursing licensure, 112
Forms, consent
  battery form, 191
  blanket form, 191
  detailed consent form, 191
  inaccurate/misleading forms, 193
  invalid patient signature, 193
  period of validity for, 191-192
  unintelligible forms, 192-193
Fourteenth Amendment, 41-42
  due process 45-47
    fairness, concept in, 46-47
    procedural due process, 46
    substantive due process, 45-46

equal protection 47-48
  fundamental right, 47-48
  suspect class, 47
judicial review 48-51
  procedural due process review, 48-49
  quasi-suspect classification, 50
  rational basis standard, 50-51
  strict scrutiny, 49-50
  substantive due process review, 49
liberty interpretation of, 44
"person" in, 43
property concept of, 45
state action in, 44-45
Fourth Amendment, unreasonable searches, 62-66
Fraud
  definition of, 302
  Medicare fraud, 302-303
  records, falsifying, 302
Freedom of Information Act, 227-228
Free exercise clause, 56-57

G

Good Samaritan statutes, 151
Government of United States
  Constitution, 19
  separation of powers, 19-21
    executive branch, 20-21
    judicial branch, 21
    legislative branch, 20
Grand jury indictment, process of, 289
Grievance procedures, 246-247
Gunshot wound laws, 313

H

Habeas corpus, writ of, 295
Handicap, scope of term, 153
Handicapped persons, discrimination prohibition, 74-75
Health care, and constitutional rights, 41-42
Health Care Amendments of 1974, 103
Health care related crimes, 295-304
  assault and battery, 303

drugs
  diversion by nurses, 305-306
  incidence of diversion, 305
  nurse drug abusers, 306-308
  fraud, 302-303
  manslaughter
    conviction/reversal, example of, 300
    scope of, 296
  murder, 296-300
    corporate murder, 296
    life-support treatments and, 300-301
    nurses convicted for, 298-300
    nurses prosecuted for, 297-298
  practice of medicine without license,
    301-302
  theft, 303-304
  See also Evidence; Reporting/
    recording statutes.
Health care services, stages of
  development, 3
Health and Human Services (HHS),
  discrimination and, 74-75
Hearings
  administrative agencies, 91-92
    adjudicatory hearings, 92
    due process rights, 92
    rule-making, 91-92
  board of nursing, 113-115
    due process rights, 114
    grounds for discipline, 113-114
    judicial review, 114-115
  National Labor Relations Board
    (NLRB), 105-106
Hospital governance
  administrator/chief executive
    officer, 128
  governing board, 128
  organized medical staff, 128-129
  organized nursing service, 129-130
  and ultra vires acts, 127-128
Hospital organization, methods of, 127
Hospitals, and consent, 194
Hospital staff, access to medical
  records, 226
Hospital Survey and Construction Act
  of 1944, 153
Hot pursuit, arrest, 286
Human rights, 38

I

Illegal subjects, collective bargaining,
  244
Immunity statutes, negligence defense,
  151
Implied consent, 190
Implied contract, 238, 251-253
  and employer's rights, 251-253
Incompetent patients
  access to medical records, 225
  right to refuse treatment, 197-198
Indemnification
  and insurance contracts, 265
  nurse manager, 137
Independent contractors, liability, 134
Informed consent
  standards, 188
  See also Consent.
Injury, damages awarded, 146-147
Insanity, as criminal defense, 282-283
Institutional rights, 39
Insurance contracts, 264-269
  hospitals
    indemnification in, 265
    nurses, noncoverage by hospital,
      264-265
    respondeat superior and, 265
    subrogation in, 265
  malpractice insurance litigation,
    examples of, 268-269
  National Nurse Claims Data Base, 269
  professional liability insurance,
    265-268
    sections of, 266-268
Intentional tort liability, 136
Interpretive rules, administrative
  agencies, 89-90
Interrogatories, 346
Interstate Commerce Commission, 87
Investigations
  administrative agencies, 91
  process of, 287-288

J

Jehovah's Witnesses, 57

Joint Commission on Accreditation of
Healthcare Organizations, 97
Joint liability, 133-135
  independent contractors, 134
  respondeat superior, 134
Judges
  Supreme Court, 26
  trial courts, 23
Judicial branch, of government, 21
Judicial review, 39, 48-51
  administrative agencies, 93-94
  board of nursing, hearings, 114-115
  private conduct issues, 55
  procedural due process review, 48-49
  quasi-suspect classification, 50
  rational basis standard, 50-51
  strict scrutiny, 49-50
  substantive due process review, 49
Jury 23
  selection of, 292-293
"Just cause" termination, 247-248

K

Knowledge, and consent, 189

L

Law
  burden of proof, 22
  definition of, 14-15
  knowledge of, for nurse managers,
    32-34
  language of, 30
  nursing law, 8
  origins of
    common law, 13
    Declaration of Independence, 14
    Magna Carta, 13-14
    Norman conquest, 12-13
  private law, 22
  public law, 21-22
  sources of
    administrative rules/decisions, 16-17
    constitutions, 16
    equity, 18
    precedent, 17, 18

revision of common law, 18
    stare decisis, 17-18
    statutes, 16
    values supporting precedent, 18
  See also Constitutional law;
    Court system.
Legal information
  guide for integration of, 9-11
  needs for, 7-8
Legal rights, 39
Legislative branch, of government, 20
Legislative process
  bill
    drafting of, 358
    obtaining copy of, 360
    process of, 359-360
  Congress, 356-357
  legislative proposals, types of,
    357-358
  sponsors, 358
  state legislatures, 357
Liability
  corporate liability, 130-132
    charitable immunity, 131
    corporate negligence, 131-132
  joint liability, 133-135
    agency/ostensible agency doctrine,
      134-135
    independent contractors, 134
    respondeat superior, 134
  nurse manager, 136-137
    indemnification, 137
  and right to refuse treatment, 72
  tort liability, 135-136
    intentional tort liability, 136
    strict liability, 135
    unintentional tort liability, 136
  vicarious liability, 132-133, 137
    "borrowed servant" doctrine, 133
    "captain of the ship" doctrine, 133
    respondeat superior, 132-133
    scope of employment, 133
Liability insurance
  hospitals, 264-265
  nurses, 265-269
    malpractice litigation, examples of,
      268-269

National Nurse Claims Data Base, 269
sections of contract, 266-268
Libel, 213
See also Defamation.
Liberty, interpretation of, Fourteenth
Amendment, 44
License, practicing medicine without,
criminal liability, 301-302
Licensure
nursing, 111-112
advanced practice, 109-110
endorsement, 112
foreign educated nurses, 112
methods of, 111-112
reciprocity, 112
regulation of hospitals, 97
by state agencies, 97
Life-support systems
removal of, 70, 71
interests of the state, 71
withholding/withdrawing, criminal
liability, 300-301
Lobbying
political action committees (PACs),
361-362
professional lobbyist, 362
testimony, before legislative
committee, 362-363
Locality rule, standard of care, 145

M

Magna Carta, and development of law,
13-14
Malpractice, 136
meaning of, 140
versus negligence, 140
See also Nursing malpractice
litigation; Negligence.
Malpractice insurance
National Nurse Claims Data Base, 269
nurses, 265-269
malpractice litigation, examples of,
268-269
sections of contract, 266-268
Management, nursing, administrative
levels, 159-160

Mandatory subjects, collective
bargaining, 244
Manslaughter
conviction/reversal, example of, 300
scope of, 296
Marriage, and privacy, 68-69
*Martindale-Hubbell Directory of
Attorneys*, 353
Medical records, 219-231
access without patient authorization,
224-226
deceased patients, 225
external requests, 226
hospital staff, 226
incompetent persons, 225
minors, 224-225
access with patient authorization,
223-224
alcohol/drug abuse cases, 224
common uses of, 219-220
information contained in, 220
legal access, 226-229
common law duty to disclose,
228-229
by discovery, 226-227
by reporting statutes, 227-228
limitations on access, 229-231
peer review activities, 230
privileged communications,
230-231
statutory limitations, 229-230
nurse manager, responsibility of,
231-232
patient access, 222-223
denial of access, 223
security, 220-221
computer records, 221
policies/procedures, 220-221
Medical staff, organized, and hospital
governance, 128-129
Medicare/Medicaid
antidiscrimination, 152-153
"Conditions for Participation," 128
diagnostic related groups (DRGs),
155-156
discrimination prohibition, 74-75
fraud, 302-303

Mens rea, 281
Minors
access to medical records, 224-225
right to privacy, 70-71
right to refuse treatment, 197-198
Miranda warning, 63
Mistake of fact, as criminal defense, 283
Mistake of law, as criminal defense, 283
Moral rights, 38
Murder, 296-300
corporate murder, 296
life-support treatments and, 300-301
nurses convicted for, 298-300
nurses prosecuted for, 297-298

N

National Labor Relations Act (NLRA)
federal laws of, 103
Federal Mediation and Conciliation
Services (FMCS), 103
Health Care Amendments of 1974, 103
religious exemption, 59
rights of employees, 103
unfair labor practices, 104
National Labor Relations Board (NLRB)
collective bargaining, appropriate
bargaining units, 241-244
composition of, 104
election process, 104
hearings, 105-106
petition process, 105
process for charges, 105
Natural death acts, 199-200
Negligence
admission, 152-155
causation, 145-146
res ipsa loquitur, 146
comparative, 150
contributory, 149-150
defenses/counterclaims, 142
assumption of the risk, 150-151
comparative negligence, 150
contributory negligence, 149-150
failure to prove negligence, 149
immunity statutes, 151
release, 147-148

statutes of limitations, 148-149
unavoidable accident, 151
discharge, 155-156
duty, 141-142
injury, 146-147
versus malpractice, 140
meaning of, 140
standard of care, 143-144
types of, 141
Newborn diseases, reporting
requirements, 309
Nominal damages, 146
Non obstante veredicto (NOV), 149
Norman conquest, and development of
law, 12-13
Nurse managers
assuming management position, 5-6
decision-making and, 8-9
first-time managers, common errors,
5-6
information needs, 6-8
knowledge of, for nurse managers,
32-34
legal information
guide for integration, 9-11
needs for nursing manager, 7-8
liability, 136-137
indemnification, 137
model for, 4-5
role of, 4-5
working environment, 6
Nurse/physician relationship
litigation related to, 170-171
failure to follow physician's orders,
171-172
failure to report significant
information, 172-173
legal liability, 170-171
nurse's duty for positive action,
173-174
telephone communication, 174-176
Nurses' notes
content, observations/assessments,
178-179
forms used, 177-178
litigation related to, 177-182
absence of entries, 179-180

altered/replaced records,
181-182
illegible/conflicting notes, 180
inadequate notes, 180-181
purposes of, 177
requirements for, 178
Nursing malpractice litigation
equipment related cases, 167-168
family involvement/requests, 164-165
and nurse managers, 163
nurse/physician relationship, 170-171
failure to follow physician's orders,
171-172
failure to report significant
information, 172-173
legal liability, 170-171
patient abandonment, 163-164
procedure related cases, 168-170
verdict for hospital, examples,
165-166, 169-170
Nursing practice
administrative levels, 159-160
advanced practice, 109-110
board of nursing, 110-118
definition of, 108-109
licensure, 111-112
nursing practice acts, 108
See also Board of nursing.
Nursing practice litigation
assessment related, 161-163
hospital documents, examples of,
182-183
nurse/physician relationship
nurses duty for positive action,
173-174
telephone communication, 174-176
nurses' notes, 177-182
absence of entries, 179-180
altered/replaced records,
181-182
illegible/conflicting notes,
180
inadequate notes, 180-181
refusal to provide care 254-257
Nursing process, steps in, 161-162
Nursing staff, organized, and hospital
governance, 129-130

O

Occupational Safety and Health Act
(OSHA), 296
Office of Civil Rights, compliance wi
Rehabilitation Act section 504, 74-
Oral contract, 238
Ostensible agency doctrine, liability,
134-135

P

Parol evidence rule, contracts, 239
Paternalism, 37-38
Patient abandonment, litigation relate
to, 163-164
Patient advocacy, discrimination
prohibition, 78
Patients
Patient's Bill of Rights, 209
patients' rights, 38
unreasonable searches, 62-64
waiver, exception to consent, 196
Peer review activities, qualified
privilege, 230
Per se doctrine, antitrust law, 261-262
Per se negligence, 144
Physicians, and consent, 193
See also Nurse/physician relationsh
Plea bargaining, process of, 290-291
Police power, 108
Police searches, 64-65
Policy and procedure manuals, as
implied contract, 252-253
Political action committees (PACs),
361-362
Precedent
appellate courts, 24
as source of law, 17, 18
Preliminary hearing, process of, 289
Prenatal injuries, 147
Pretrial procedure. *See* Criminal
procedure
Prima facie, 147
Privacy, 208-213
abortion, 69-70
definition of, 208
employees, 210-211

abuses of privacy, 210
  false information, 210-211
invasion of privacy, 211-213
  defenses to, 212-213
  litigation, examples of, 212
  types of invasion, 211
life-support systems, removal of,
  70, 71
limitation of right, 71-72
marital privacy, 68-69
minors, 70-71
and physician/hospital liability, 72
right of privacy, 209-210
  list of rights, 209-210
  meaning of, 68
self-determination, 70
unmarried persons, 69
Privacy Act of 1974, 210, 227, 229
Private agencies, regulation of
  hospitals, 97
Private conduct, 55-56
Private employment, freedom of
  speech, 61
Private law, 22
Privilege, defamation, defense to,
  214-215
Privileged communications, 230-231
Procedural due process, 46
  judicial review, 48-49
Procedural rights, 40-41
Procedural rules, administrative
  agencies, 89
Procedures, nursing, litigation
  related to, 168-170
Professionalism, meaning of, 140-141
Professional organizations, regulation of
  hospitals, 98
Professionals, definition of, 241
Property, concept of, Fourteenth
  Amendment, 45
Prosecutor information, process of,
  289
Public accommodations, discrimination
  prohibition, 74
Public employment, freedom of speech,
  60-61
Public figures, invasion of privacy, 216

Public law, 21-22
Punitive damages, 146-147

Q

Qualified privilege, defamation,
  defense to, 215-216, 217-218
Quasi-suspect classification, judicial
  review, 50
Quinlan case, 42, 70

R

Race/color/national origin,
  discrimination prohibition, 74
Rational basis standard, judicial review,
  50-51
Reasonable force, arrest, 286
Reciprocity, nursing licensure, 112
Refusal to provide care
  contracts, 254-257
    moral/medical/philosophical basis,
      255
    and nurse manager, 257
    unsafe work assignments, 255
Regulation of hospitals
  accreditation, 97-98
  certification, 98
  federal agencies, 96
  licensure, 97
  private agencies, 97
  professional organizations, 98
  state agencies, 96-97
Rehabilitation Act of 1973, 74 153
Release, negligence defense, 147-148
Religion (freedom of), 56-59
  and employment, 58-59
    conscience clause, 59
    religious exemption, 59
  free exercise clause, 56-57
  right to refuse treatment, 57-58
    overturned, 58
    upheld, 57-58
Religious exemption, and employment, 59
Reporting/recording statutes
  access to medical records, 227-228
  child abuse, 310-311

communicable diseases, 309-310
domestic violence, 311-312
elderly abuse, 311
newborn diseases, 309
suspicious deaths/injuries, 312-313
vital statistics, 308
Res ipsa loquitur, 146
Respected minority rule, 145
Respondeat superior
and insurance contracts, 265
joint liability, 134
Rights. *See* Constitutional rights
Right to admission, 152
Right to refuse treatment, 57-58,
196-206
assault/battery litigation, 201-204
decision-making and
benefits and burdens approach, 197
best interests of patient approach,
197
substitute judgment approach, 197
discharge against medical advice,
200-201
do not resuscitate orders, 198-199
false imprisonment litigation, 204-206
incompetent patients, 197-198
minors, 197-198
natural death acts, 199-200
overturned, 58
and physician/hospital liability, 72
upheld, 57-58
Rule of reason, antitrust law, 262
Rules/rule-making
administrative agencies
interpretive rules, 89-90
procedural rules, 89
rule-making, 90
substantive rules, 90
board of nursing, 112-113

S

"Scene of an emergency," 151
Searches/seizures, lawful, 315-316
Section 1983 action, 54-55, 64
Security, medical records, 220-221
Self-determination, 70

Separation of powers, 19-21
executive branch, 20-21
judicial branch, 21
legislative branch, 20
Sexual harassment, 78
Sherman Antitrust Act, 261, 262
Slander, 213
See also Defamation.
Social Security Act of 1935, 87
Speech (freedom of), 60-62
and private employment, 61
and public employment, 60-61
symbolic speech, 60
Sponsors, legislative process, 358
Standard of care
documentary evidence, 143
expert witness testimony, 143-144
no requirement for, 144
locality rule, 145
and nurses, 143
respected minority rule, 145
Standards, nursing services, 129-130
*Standards for Organized Nursing
Services,* 129
Stare decisis, as source of law, 17-18
State action, 54-55, 56
State administrative law, 88, 89
State agencies, regulation of hospitals,
96-97
State legislation, Tenth Amendment, 108
State legislatures, 357
Statute of frauds, contracts, 238-239
Statutes, 331-333
abbreviations used, 331-332
construction of, 333
judicial interpretation of, 333
locating statutes, 331
reading of, 332
as source of law, 16
Statutes of limitation
and discovery rule, 148
multiple statutes, 148-149
negligence defense, 148-149
"starts to run," 148
Strict liability, 135
Strict scrutiny, judicial review, 49-50
Subpoena, 345

Subrogation, and insurance contracts, 265
Substantive due process, 45-46
  judicial review, 49
Substantive rights, 40
Substantive rules, administrative agencies, 90
Substitute judgment approach right to refuse treatment, 197
Supervisors
  definition/scope of role, 243
  exclusion of, collective bargaining agreements, 242-244
  liability, and staff nurses, 163
Supreme Court, 26, 28
  judicial review, 39
Suspicious deaths/injuries, reporting requirements, 312-313
Symbolic speech, 60

T

Telephone communication
  hospital policies, 175
  litigation related to, 175-176
  requirements of nurses/physicians, 175
  risk in, 174
Tenth Amendment, state legislation, 108
Termination
  "just cause" termination, 247-248
  See also Employee at will doctrine.
Testimony
  before legislative committee, 362-363
  witness, 351-352
    attitude for, 352
    guidelines for, 351-352
  See also Witnesses.
Theft
  criminal liability, 303-304
  employees, detention/search of, 304
Therapeutic privilege, exception to consent, 195-196
Tort feasor, 135
Tortious conduct, 135
Tort law, 22, 127
  versus contract law, 235
Transfer, procedure for, 154-155

Trial courts, 23-24
  state, 28
Trial. *See* Criminal procedure
Truth, defamation, defense to, 214

U

Ultra vires acts, 127-128
Unavoidable accident, negligence defense, 151
Understaffing
  legal implications, 255-257
  and nurse manager, 257
Unfair labor practices
  listing of, 104
  See also National Labor Relations Board (NLRB).
Unintentional tort liability, 136
United States Code (U.S.C.), 16
Unmarried persons, privacy, 69
Unprofessional conduct
  definitional difficulty, 114, 117
  interpretation of, 117-118
Unreasonable searches, 62-66
  by administrative agencies, 91
  hospital employees, 65-66
  hospital patients, 62-64
  police searches, 64-65

V

Vicarious liability, 132-133, 137
  "borrowed servant" doctrine, 133
  "captain of the ship" doctrine, 133
  respondeat superior, 132-133
  scope of employment, 133
Vital statistics, reporting requirements, 308
Voluntariness, and consent, 189
Voluntary subjects, collective bargaining, 245

W

Waivers
  of consent, 196
  of privilege, 231

Warrants, arrest, 286
William II, King of England, 12-13
Witnesses
  cross-examination, 350
  direct examination, 350
  expert witness, 348-349
    cross-examination, 350-351
    qualification of, 348-349
fact witness, 348
obtaining testimony of, 349
preparation of, 349-350
testimony, 351-352
  attitude for, 352
  guidelines for, 351-352
Writ of certiorari, 26
Written contract, 238

About the Author

Carmelle Pellerin Cournoyer received a Diploma in Nursing from the Notre Dame de Lourdes Hospital School of Nursing in 1959, a Bachelor of Science in nursing from Saint Anselm College in 1962, a Master of Arts in Social Science from Rivier College in 1976, and a Juris Doctor from Franklin Pierce Law Center in 1980. She is licensed as a registered nurse in New Hampshire and was admitted to the New Hampshire Bar in 1981. She is a member of the New Hampshire Nurses' Association, the American Nurses' Association, Sigma Theta Tau, Epsilon Tau Chapter, National Honor Society for Nursing, and Phi Alpha Delta Law Fraternity.

Mrs. Cournoyer's nursing experience includes the practice of maternal and child health nursing, head nurse of a pediatric unit, and a variety of hospital supervisory positions. She has experience in nursing education as an Instructor of Maternal and Child Health Nursing and as Director of a continuing education program. She has served as both Director of Nursing Practice and Director of Nursing Education for the New Hampshire State Board of Nursing. She also served as Director of the Health Care Management and Administration Program at Rivier College and taught the Law, Policy and Ethics course in the Graduate Nursing Program at the University of New Hampshire. She has developed and presented legal seminars in all areas of nursing practice for universities, colleges, hospitals, nursing homes, community health agencies, and health maintenance organizations throughout New England. She is the President of CRC Associates, a Health Law Education and Consultation Service.

Mrs. Cournoyer resides in Manchester, New Hampshire, with her husband Roland, who is the Industrial Arts/Technology Education Consultant for the New Hampshire Department of Education. They have a son Eric and three daughters Ann, Karen, and Dawn-Ellen.